Yagi the Bookshop Goat

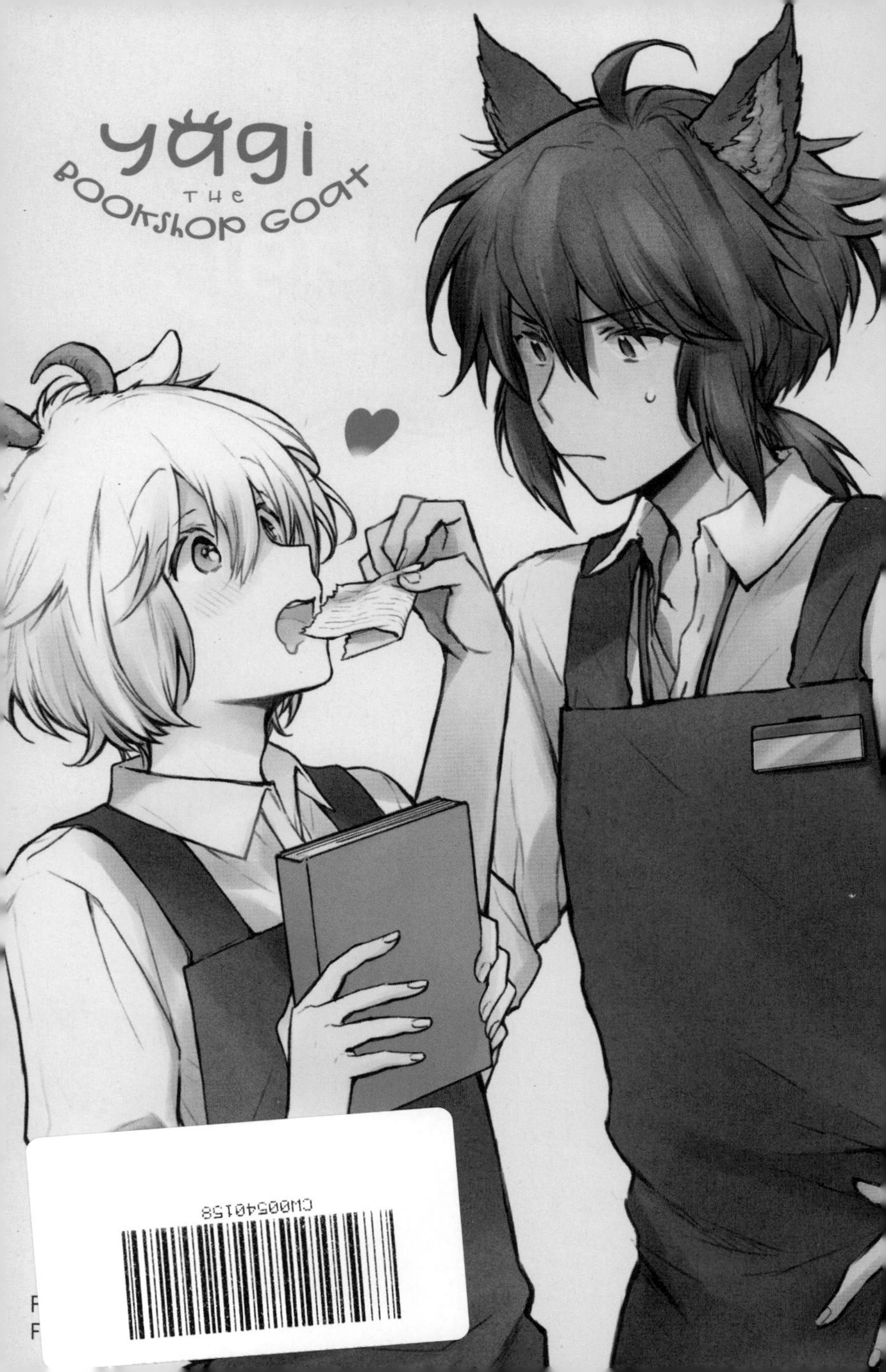

yagi
THE
bookshop goat

CONTENTS

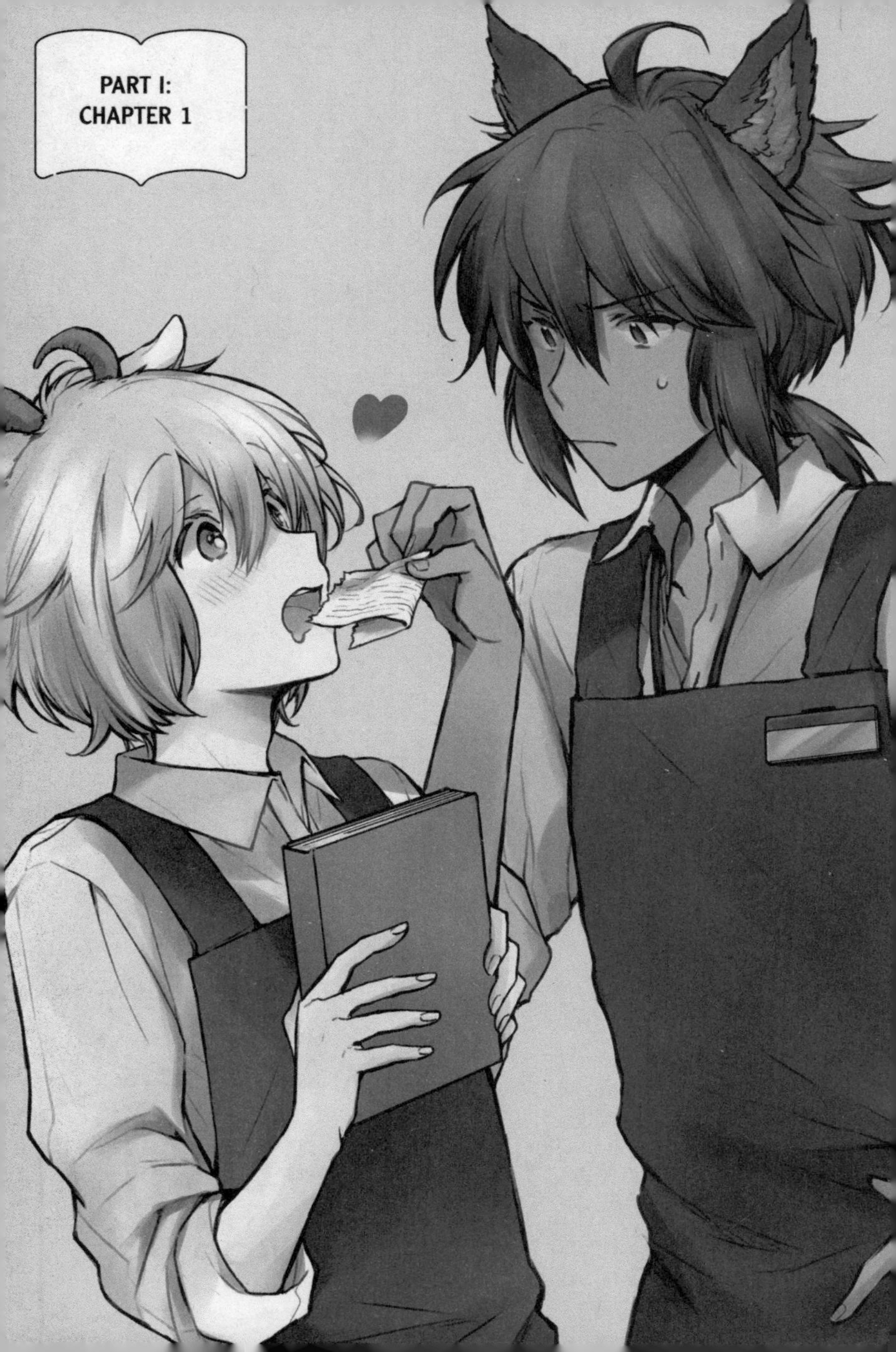
PART I:
CHAPTER 1

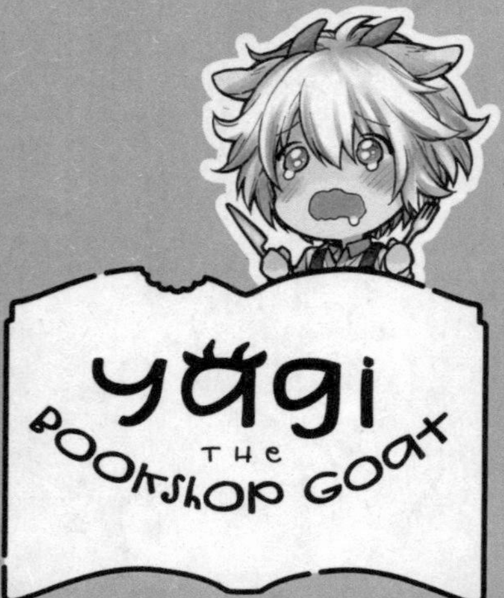
Yagi
THE
BOOKShOP GOAT

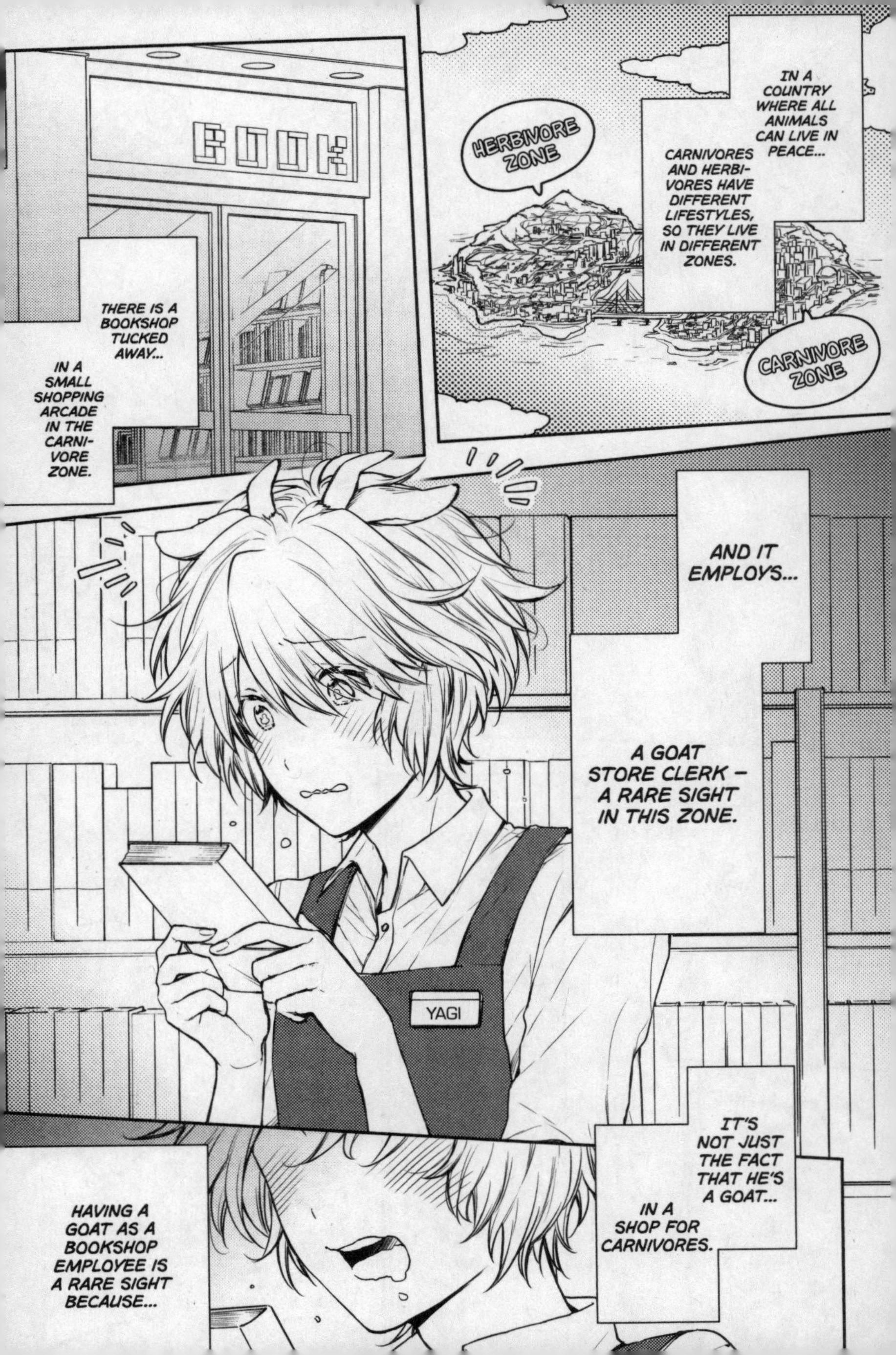

IN A COUNTRY WHERE ALL ANIMALS CAN LIVE IN PEACE...
CARNIVORES AND HERBIVORES HAVE DIFFERENT LIFESTYLES, SO THEY LIVE IN DIFFERENT ZONES.
HERBIVORE ZONE
CARNIVORE ZONE
BOOK
THERE IS A BOOKSHOP TUCKED AWAY...
IN A SMALL SHOPPING ARCADE IN THE CARNIVORE ZONE.
AND IT EMPLOYS...
A GOAT STORE CLERK – A RARE SIGHT IN THIS ZONE.
YAGI
IT'S NOT JUST THE FACT THAT HE'S A GOAT...
IN A SHOP FOR CARNIVORES.
HAVING A GOAT AS A BOOKSHOP EMPLOYEE IS A RARE SIGHT BECAUSE...

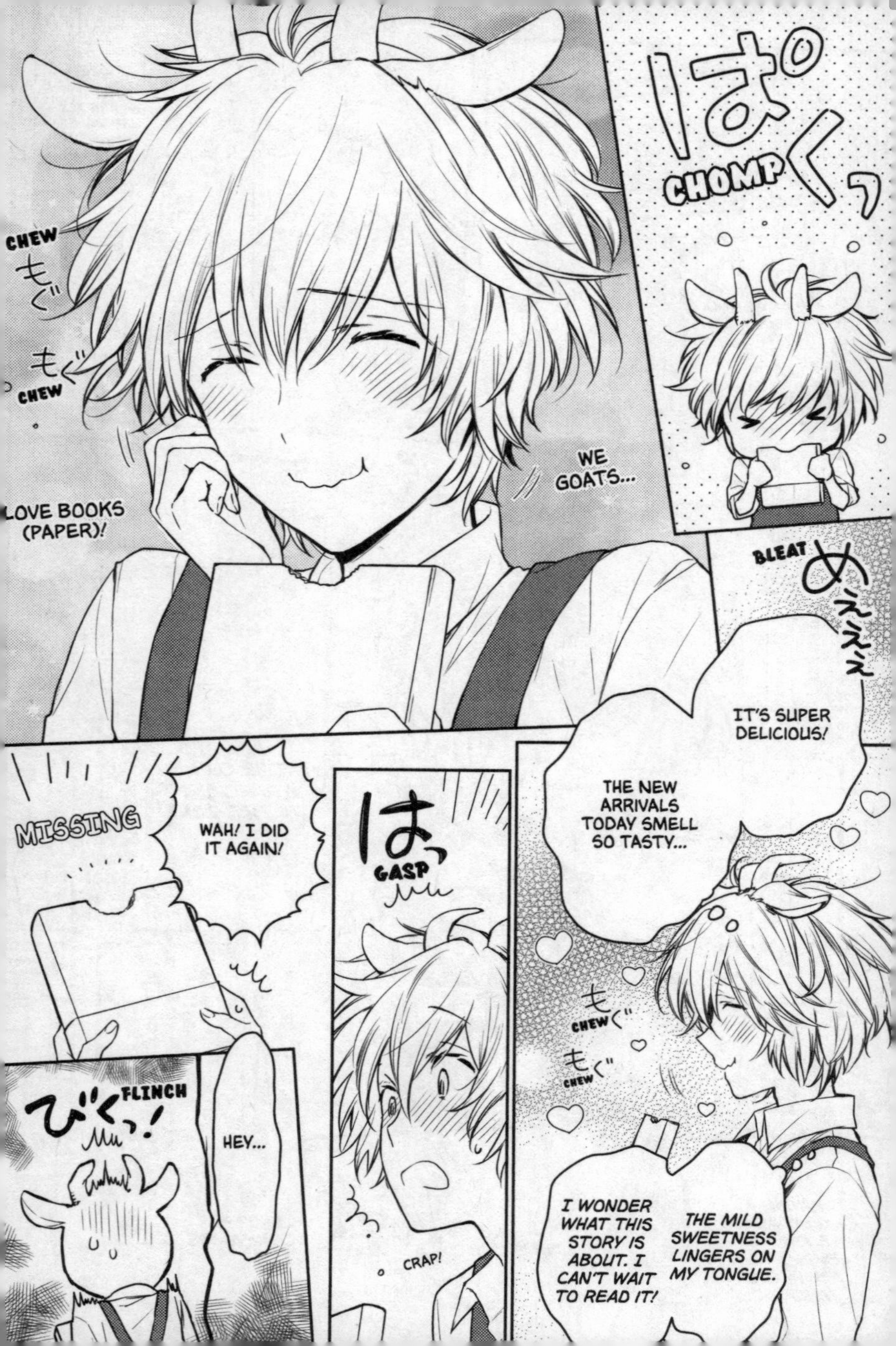
ぱくっ
CHOMP
WE GOATS...
CHEW
もぐ
もぐ
CHEW
LOVE BOOKS (PAPER)!
BLEAT
めえええ
IT'S SUPER DELICIOUS!
THE NEW ARRIVALS TODAY SMELL SO TASTY...
もぐ
CHEW
もぐ
CHEW
THE MILD SWEETNESS LINGERS ON MY TONGUE.
I WONDER WHAT THIS STORY IS ABOUT. I CAN'T WAIT TO READ IT!
はっ
GASP
CRAP!
WAH! I DID IT AGAIN!
MISSING
HEY...
びくっ!
FLINCH

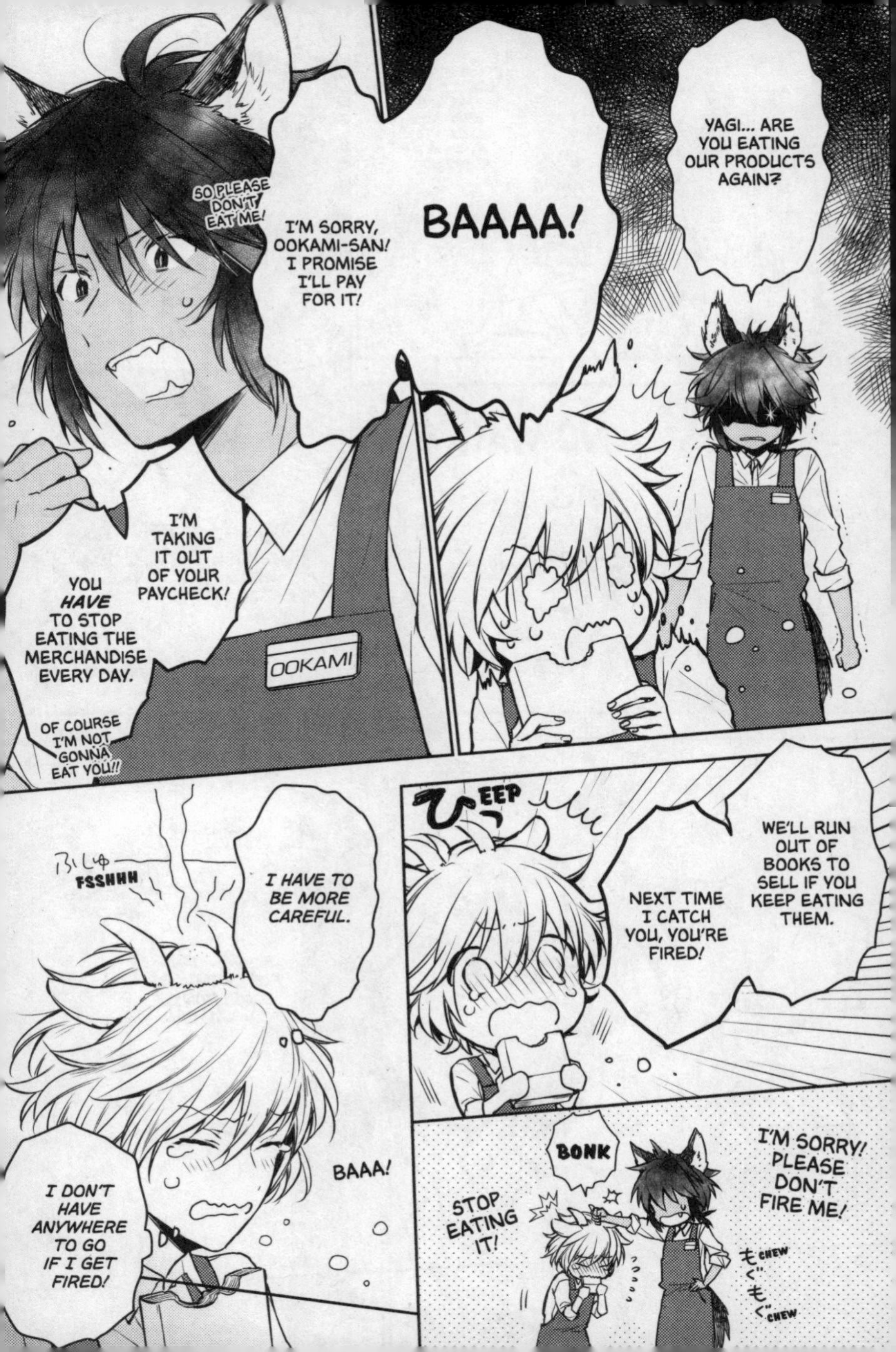
YAGI... ARE YOU EATING OUR PRODUCTS AGAIN?
BAAAA!
I'M SORRY, OOKAMI-SAN! I PROMISE I'LL PAY FOR IT!
SO PLEASE DON'T EAT ME!
I'M TAKING IT OUT OF YOUR PAYCHECK!
YOU *HAVE* TO STOP EATING THE MERCHANDISE EVERY DAY.
OOKAMI
OF COURSE I'M NOT GONNA EAT YOU!!
ひっ EEP
WE'LL RUN OUT OF BOOKS TO SELL IF YOU KEEP EATING THEM.
NEXT TIME I CATCH YOU, YOU'RE FIRED!
I'M SORRY! PLEASE DON'T FIRE ME!
BONK
もぐもぐ CHEW CHEW
STOP EATING IT!
ふしゅー FSSHHH
I HAVE TO BE MORE CAREFUL.
BAAA!
I DON'T HAVE ANYWHERE TO GO IF I GET FIRED!

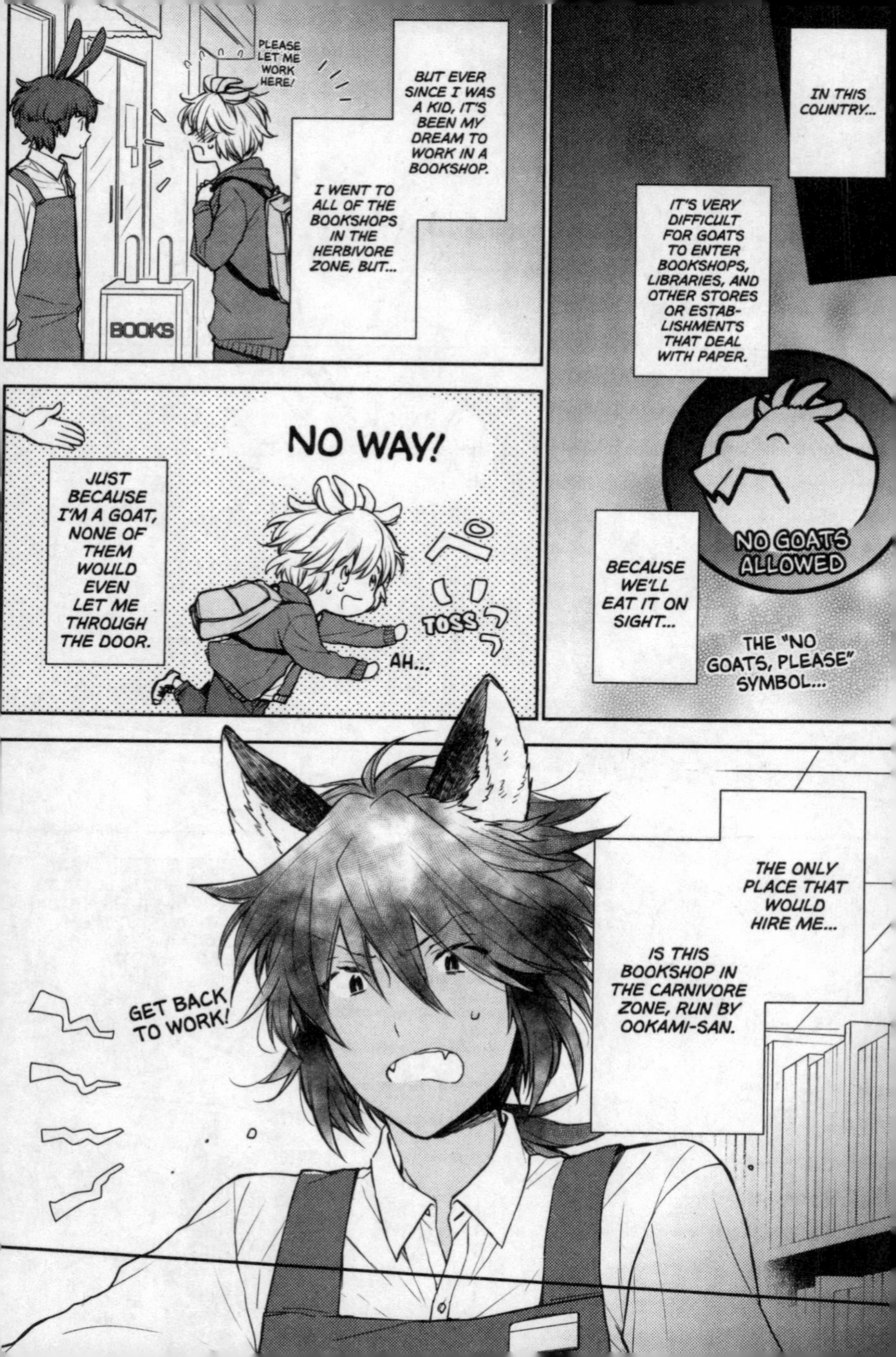
IN THIS COUNTRY...
IT'S VERY DIFFICULT FOR GOATS TO ENTER BOOKSHOPS, LIBRARIES, AND OTHER STORES OR ESTAB-LISHMENTS THAT DEAL WITH PAPER.
NO GOATS ALLOWED
BECAUSE WE'LL EAT IT ON SIGHT...
THE "NO GOATS, PLEASE" SYMBOL...
BUT EVER SINCE I WAS A KID, IT'S BEEN MY DREAM TO WORK IN A BOOKSHOP.
I WENT TO ALL OF THE BOOKSHOPS IN THE HERBIVORE ZONE, BUT...
PLEASE LET ME WORK HERE!
BOOKS
NO WAY!
JUST BECAUSE I'M A GOAT, NONE OF THEM WOULD EVEN LET ME THROUGH THE DOOR.
TOSS
AH...
THE ONLY PLACE THAT WOULD HIRE ME...
IS THIS BOOKSHOP IN THE CARNIVORE ZONE, RUN BY OOKAMI-SAN.
GET BACK TO WORK!

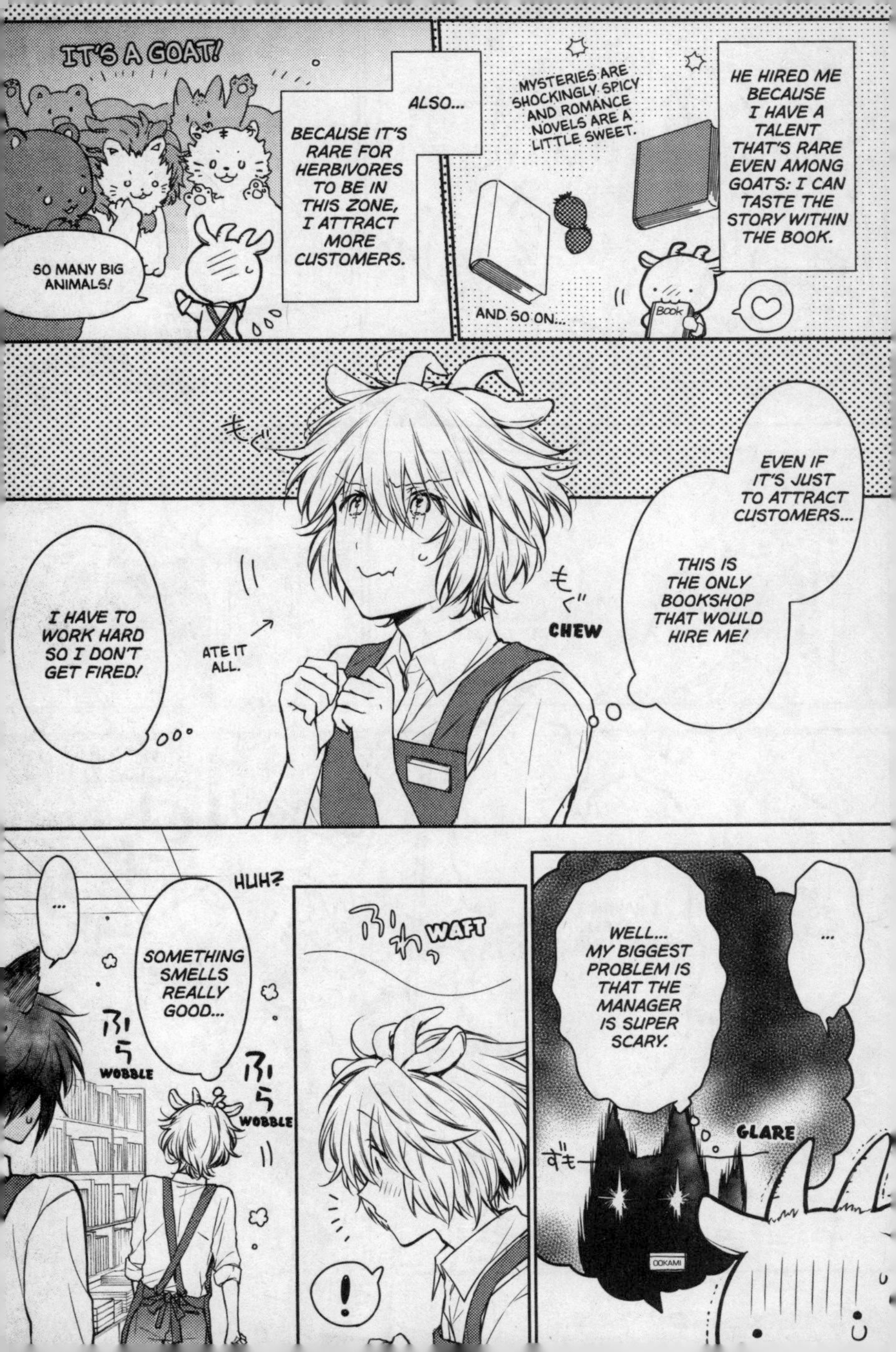
HE HIRED ME BECAUSE I HAVE A TALENT THAT'S RARE EVEN AMONG GOATS: I CAN TASTE THE STORY WITHIN THE BOOK.
MYSTERIES ARE SHOCKINGLY SPICY AND ROMANCE NOVELS ARE A LITTLE SWEET.
Book
AND SO ON...
ALSO...
BECAUSE IT'S RARE FOR HERBIVORES TO BE IN THIS ZONE, I ATTRACT MORE CUSTOMERS.
IT'S A GOAT!
SO MANY BIG ANIMALS!
EVEN IF IT'S JUST TO ATTRACT CUSTOMERS...
THIS IS THE ONLY BOOKSHOP THAT WOULD HIRE ME!
もぐ
もぐ
CHEW
ATE IT ALL.
I HAVE TO WORK HARD SO I DON'T GET FIRED!
...
WELL... MY BIGGEST PROBLEM IS THAT THE MANAGER IS SUPER SCARY.
ずもー
GLARE
OOKAMI
ふわっ
WAFT
!
HUH?
SOMETHING SMELLS REALLY GOOD...
ふら
WOBBLE
ふら
WOBBLE
...

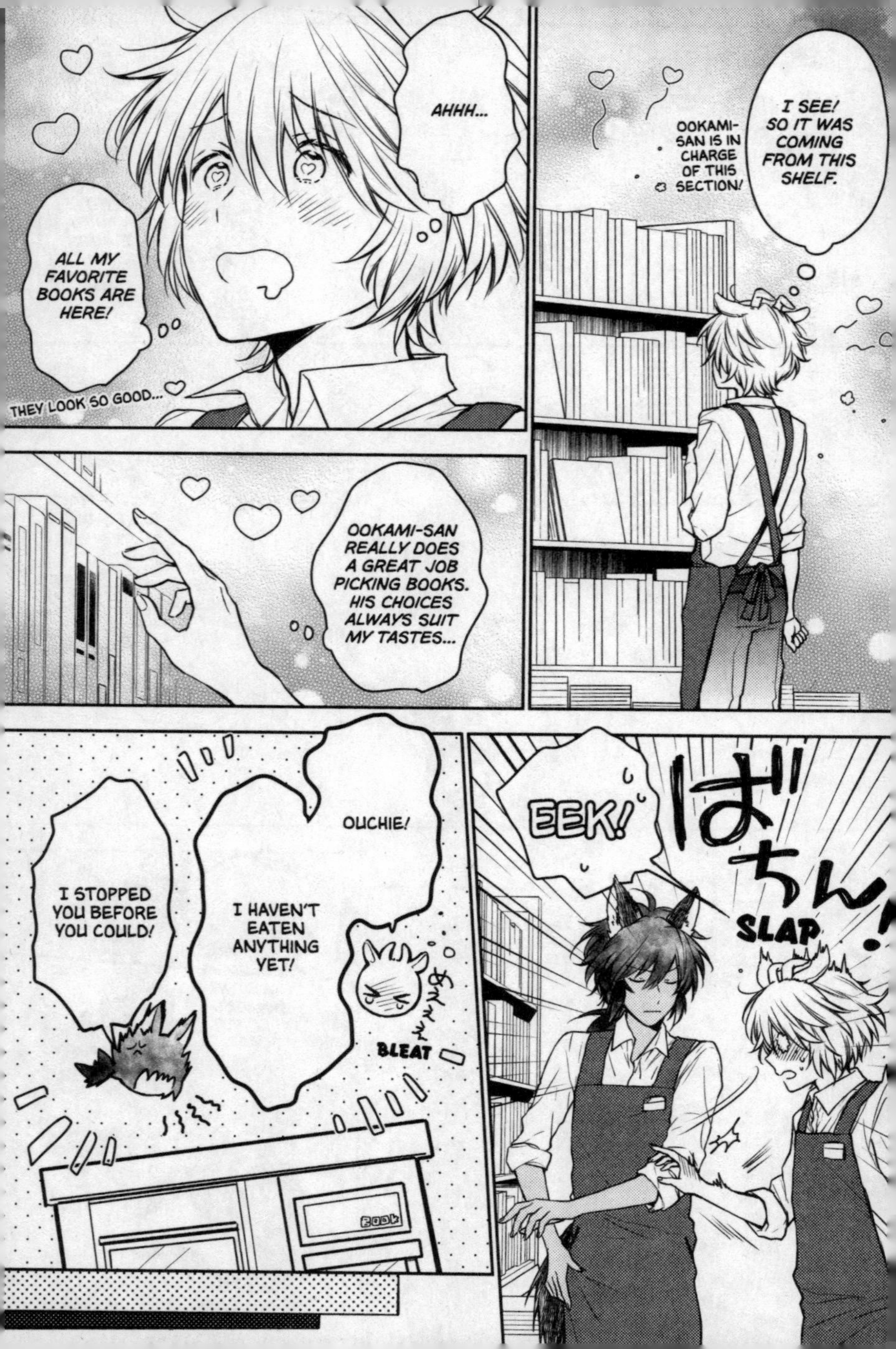
I SEE! SO IT WAS COMING FROM THIS SHELF.
OOKAMI-SAN IS IN CHARGE OF THIS SECTION!
AHHH...
ALL MY FAVORITE BOOKS ARE HERE!
THEY LOOK SO GOOD...
OOKAMI-SAN REALLY DOES A GREAT JOB PICKING BOOKS. HIS CHOICES ALWAYS SUIT MY TASTES...
EEK!
ばちん!
SLAP
OUCHIE!
I HAVEN'T EATEN ANYTHING YET!
BLEAT
I STOPPED YOU BEFORE YOU COULD!

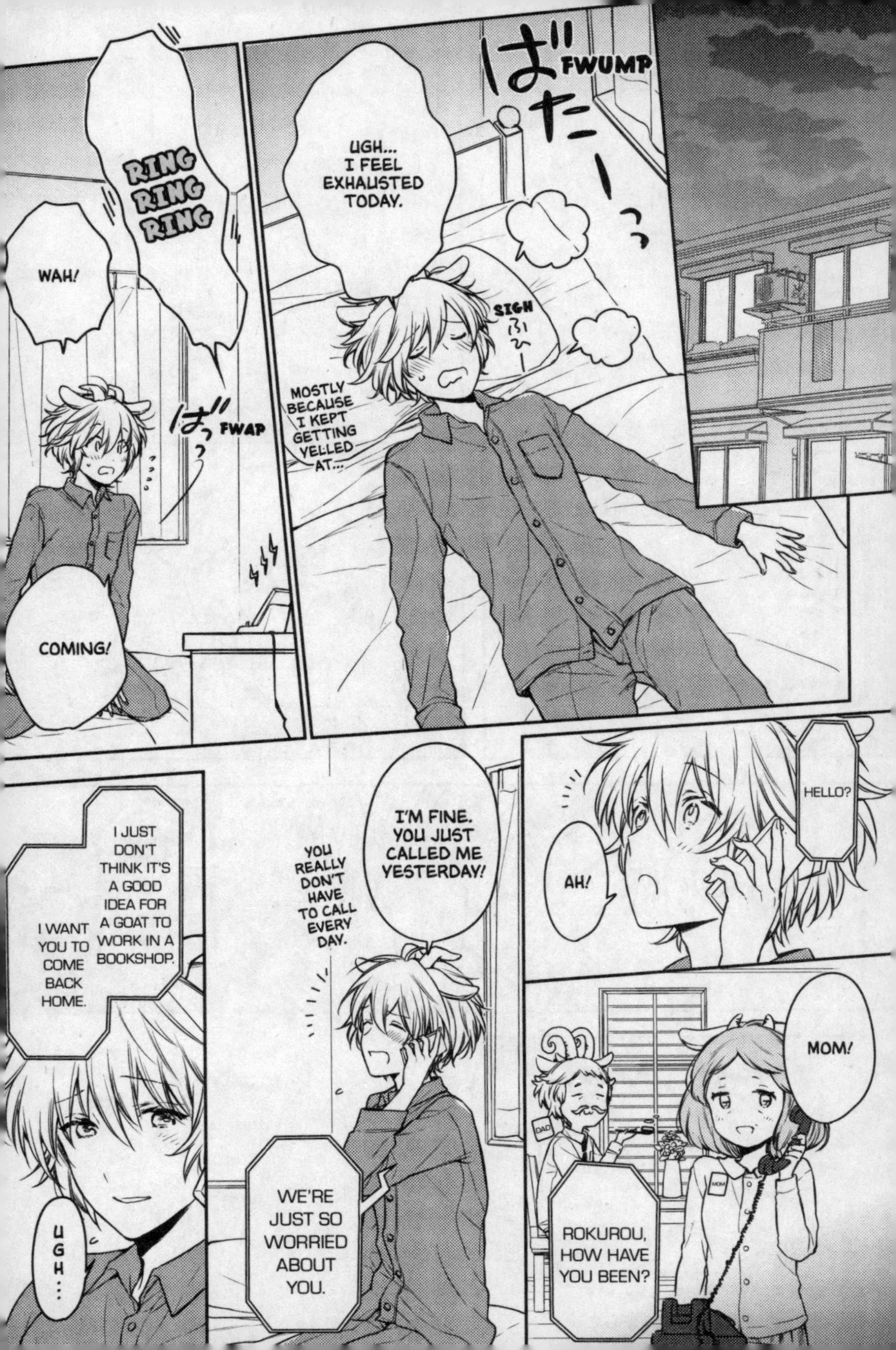
ばたーっ
FWUMP
UGH... I FEEL EXHAUSTED TODAY.
SIGH
ふひー
MOSTLY BECAUSE I KEPT GETTING YELLED AT...
RING RING RING
WAH!
ばっ
FWAP
COMING!
HELLO?
AH!
MOM!
DAD
MOM
ROKUROU, HOW HAVE YOU BEEN?
I'M FINE. YOU JUST CALLED ME YESTERDAY!
YOU REALLY DON'T HAVE TO CALL EVERY DAY.
WE'RE JUST SO WORRIED ABOUT YOU.
I JUST DON'T THINK IT'S A GOOD IDEA FOR A GOAT TO WORK IN A BOOKSHOP.
I WANT YOU TO COME BACK HOME.
UGH...

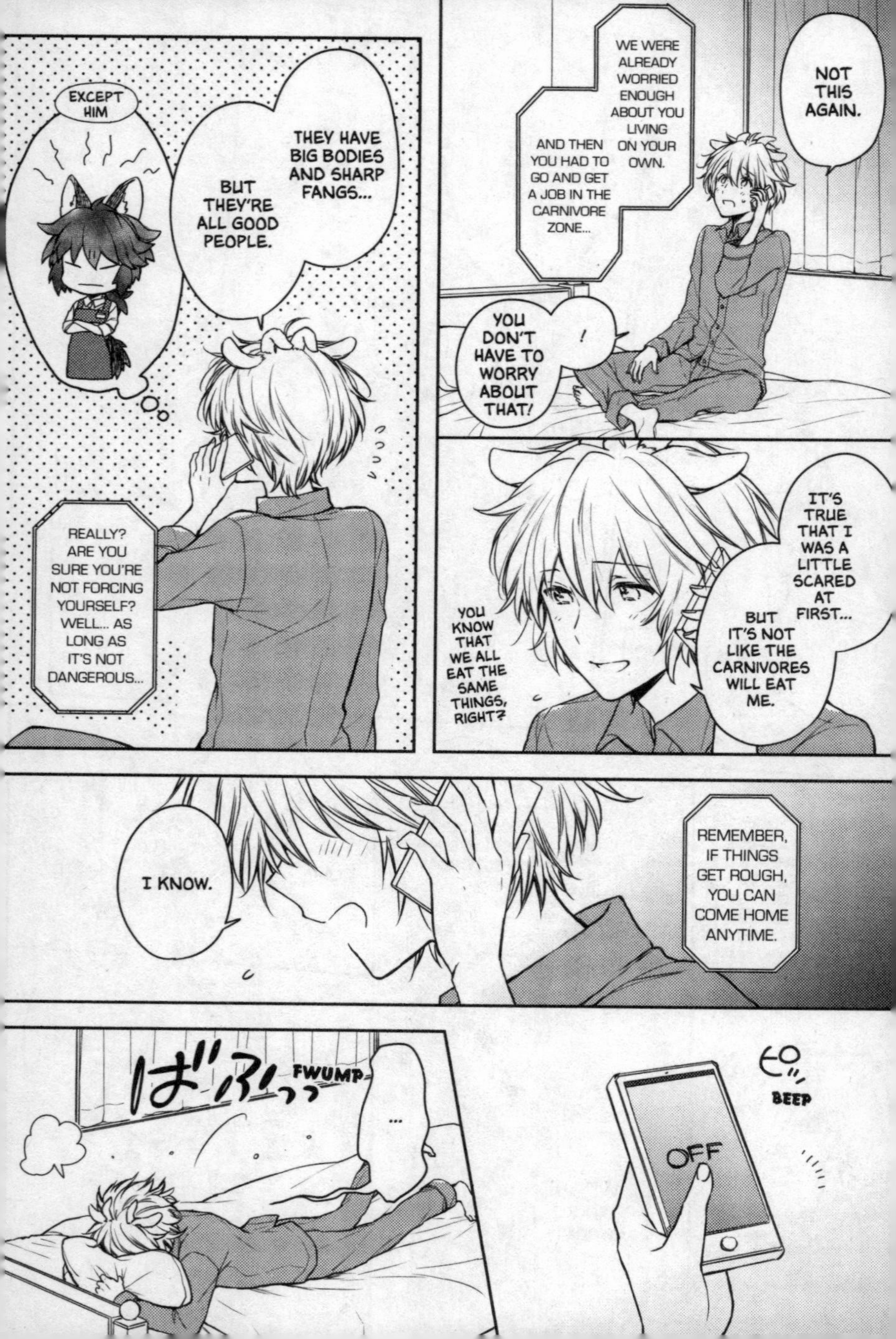
NOT THIS AGAIN.
WE WERE ALREADY WORRIED ENOUGH ABOUT YOU LIVING ON YOUR OWN.
AND THEN YOU HAD TO GO AND GET A JOB IN THE CARNIVORE ZONE...
!
YOU DON'T HAVE TO WORRY ABOUT THAT!
IT'S TRUE THAT I WAS A LITTLE SCARED AT FIRST...
BUT IT'S NOT LIKE THE CARNIVORES WILL EAT ME.
YOU KNOW THAT WE ALL EAT THE SAME THINGS, RIGHT?
THEY HAVE BIG BODIES AND SHARP FANGS...
BUT THEY'RE ALL GOOD PEOPLE.
EXCEPT HIM
REALLY? ARE YOU SURE YOU'RE NOT FORCING YOURSELF? WELL... AS LONG AS IT'S NOT DANGEROUS...
REMEMBER, IF THINGS GET ROUGH, YOU CAN COME HOME ANYTIME.
I KNOW.
ピッ
BEEP
OFF
ばふっ
FWUMP
...

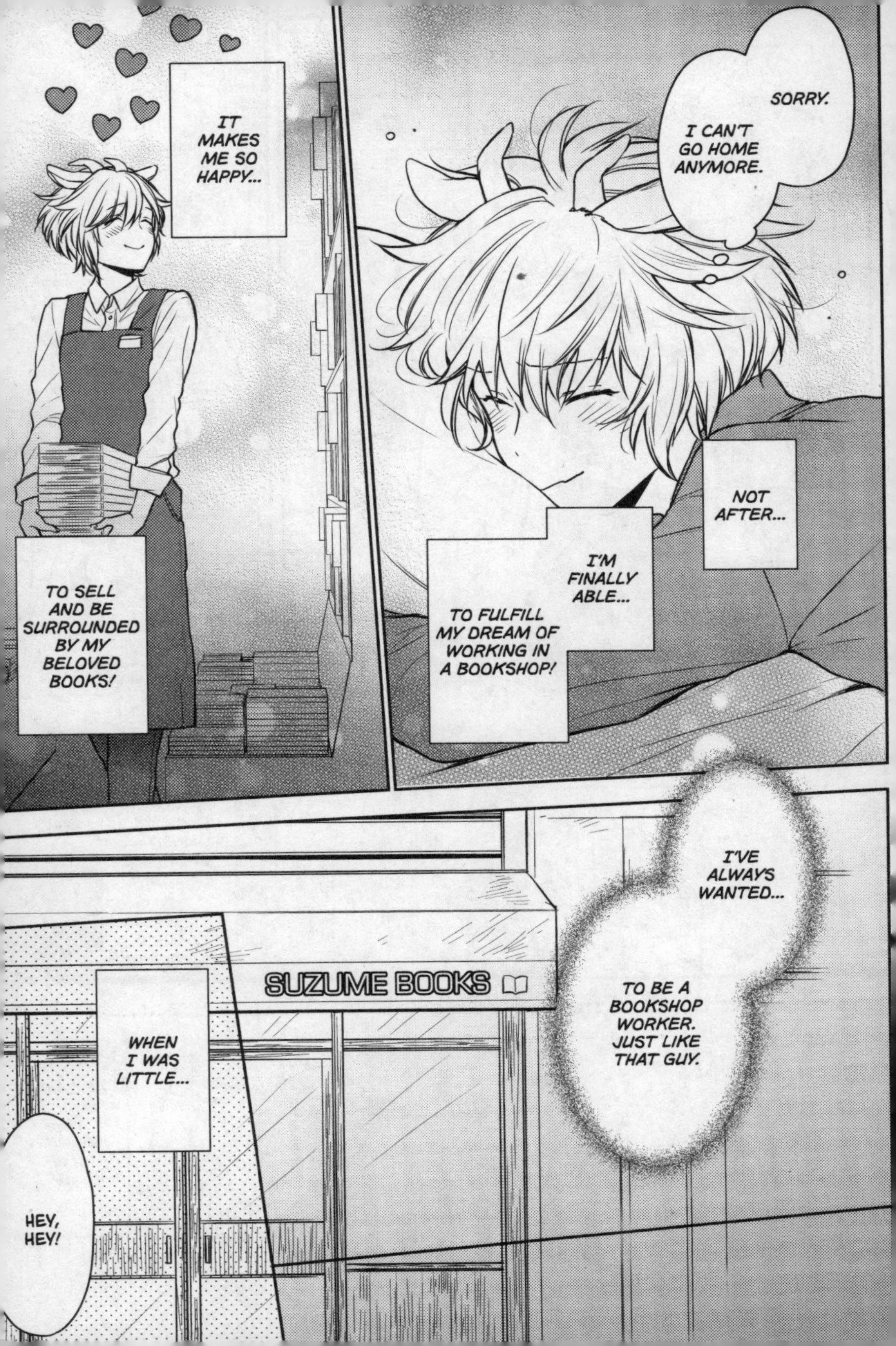
SORRY. I CAN'T GO HOME ANYMORE.
NOT AFTER...
I'M FINALLY ABLE...
TO FULFILL MY DREAM OF WORKING IN A BOOKSHOP!
IT MAKES ME SO HAPPY...
TO SELL AND BE SURROUNDED BY MY BELOVED BOOKS!
I'VE ALWAYS WANTED...
TO BE A BOOKSHOP WORKER. JUST LIKE THAT GUY.
SUZUME BOOKS
WHEN I WAS LITTLE...
HEY, HEY!

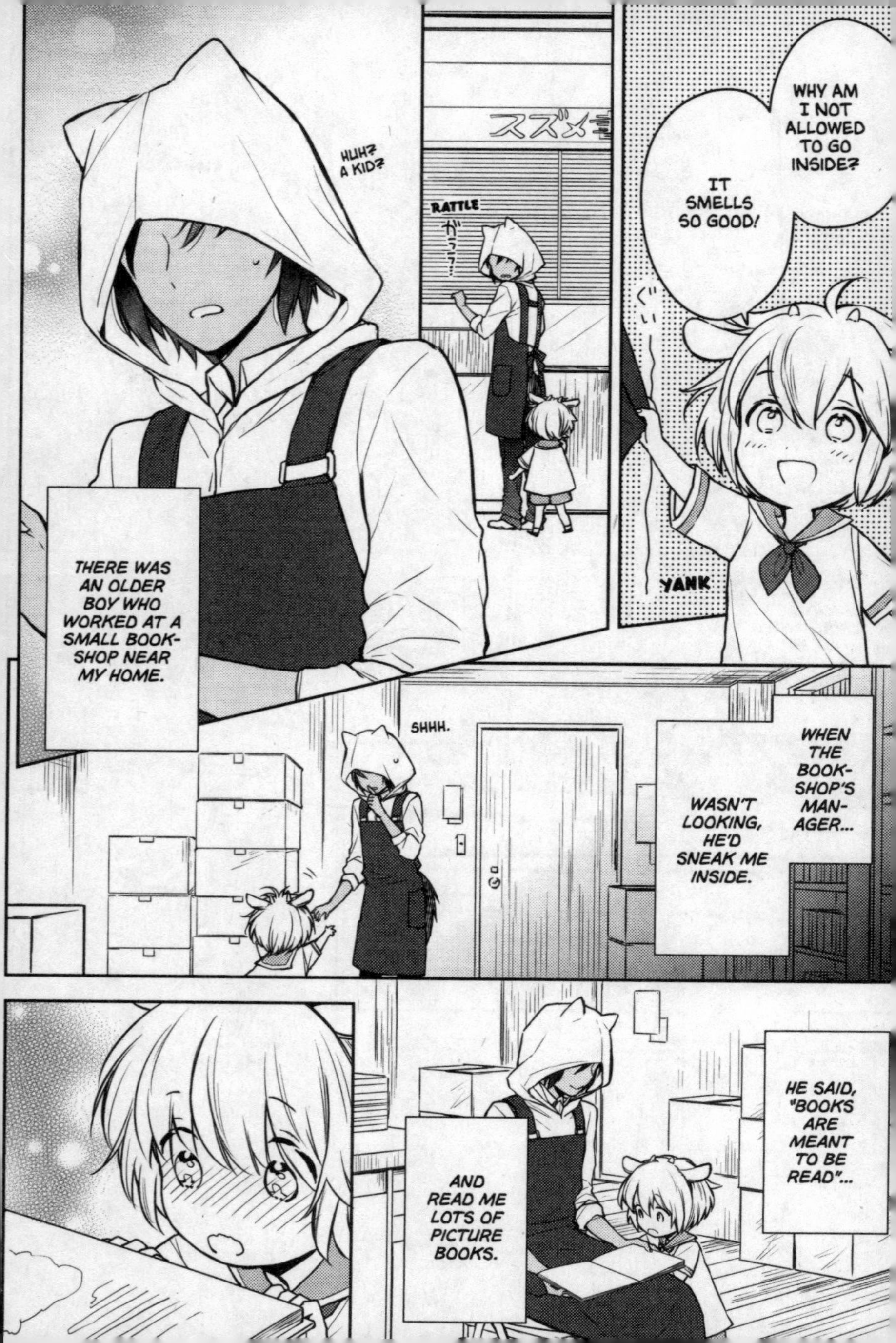
WHY AM I NOT ALLOWED TO GO INSIDE?
IT SMELLS SO GOOD!
ぐい
YANK
RATTLE
ガラララ
HUH? A KID?
THERE WAS AN OLDER BOY WHO WORKED AT A SMALL BOOK-SHOP NEAR MY HOME.
WHEN THE BOOK-SHOP'S MAN-AGER...
WASN'T LOOKING, HE'D SNEAK ME INSIDE.
SHHH.
HE SAID, "BOOKS ARE MEANT TO BE READ"...
AND READ ME LOTS OF PICTURE BOOKS.

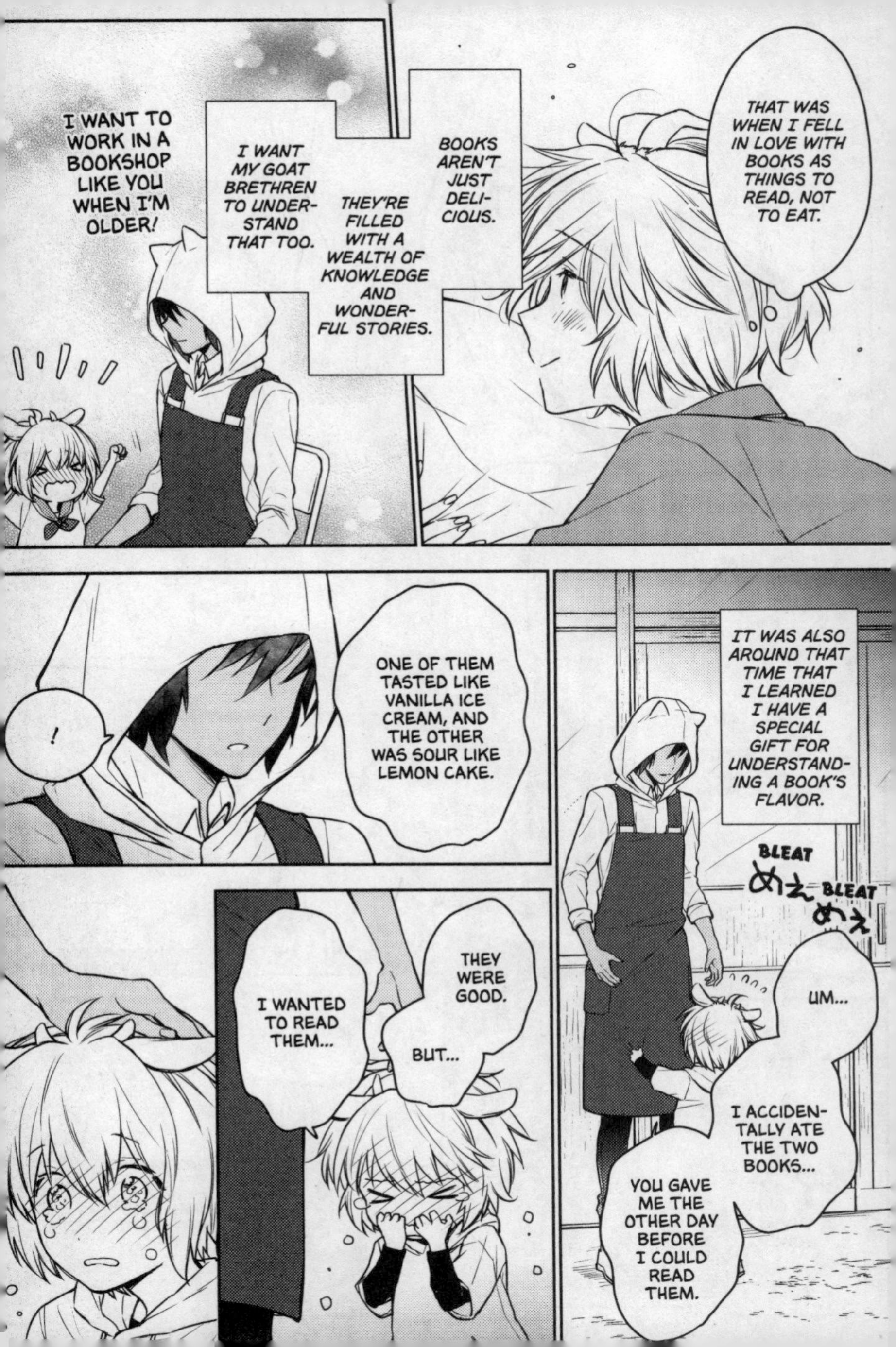
THAT WAS WHEN I FELL IN LOVE WITH BOOKS AS THINGS TO READ, NOT TO EAT.
BOOKS AREN'T JUST DELICIOUS.
THEY'RE FILLED WITH A WEALTH OF KNOWLEDGE AND WONDERFUL STORIES.
I WANT MY GOAT BRETHREN TO UNDERSTAND THAT TOO.
I WANT TO WORK IN A BOOKSHOP LIKE YOU WHEN I'M OLDER!
IT WAS ALSO AROUND THAT TIME THAT I LEARNED I HAVE A SPECIAL GIFT FOR UNDERSTANDING A BOOK'S FLAVOR.
BLEAT めえ
BLEAT めえ
UM...
I ACCIDENTALLY ATE THE TWO BOOKS...
YOU GAVE ME THE OTHER DAY BEFORE I COULD READ THEM.
ONE OF THEM TASTED LIKE VANILLA ICE CREAM, AND THE OTHER WAS SOUR LIKE LEMON CAKE.
!
THEY WERE GOOD.
BUT...
I WANTED TO READ THEM...

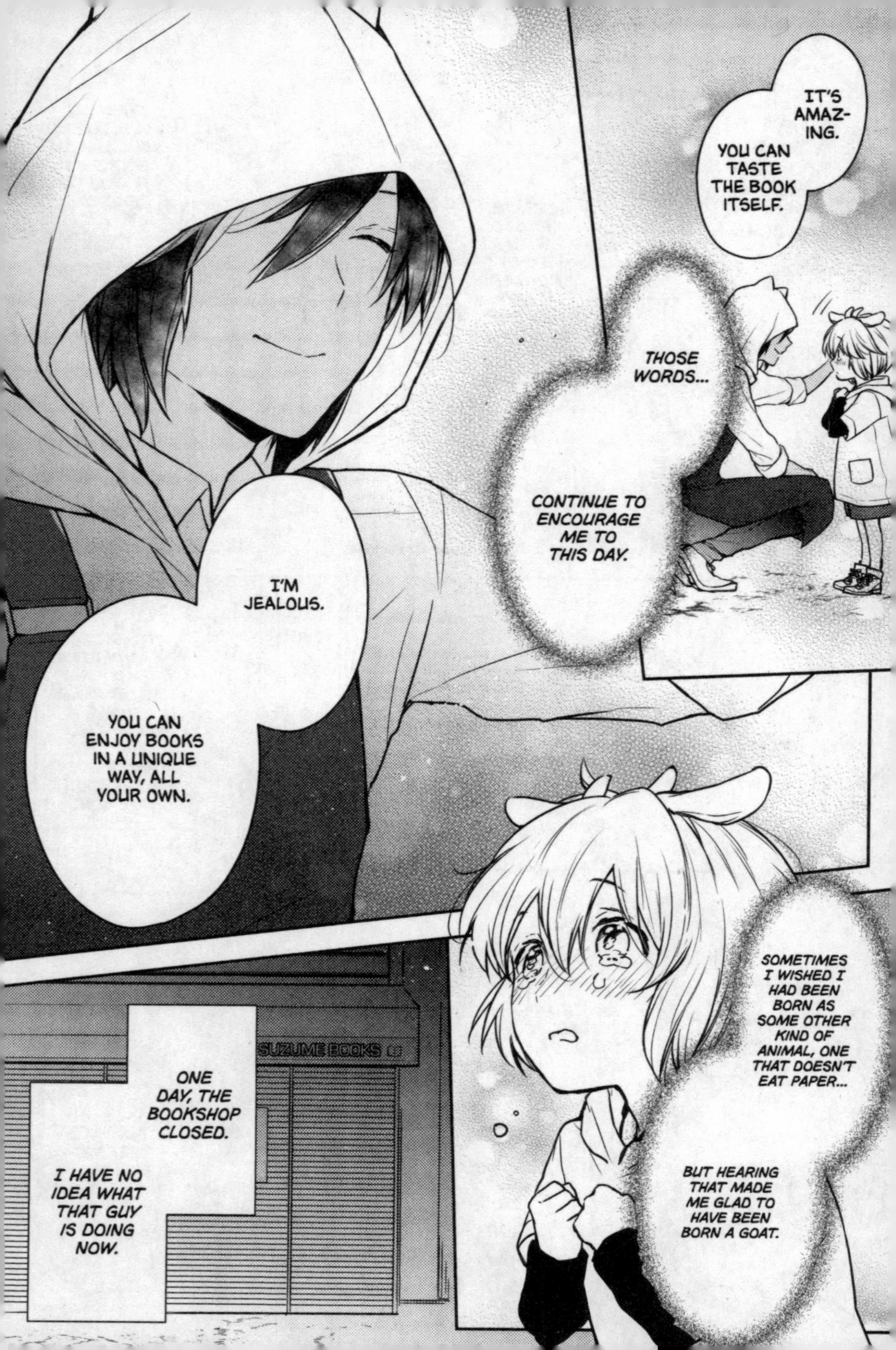
IT'S AMAZ-ING.
YOU CAN TASTE THE BOOK ITSELF.
THOSE WORDS...
CONTINUE TO ENCOURAGE ME TO THIS DAY.
I'M JEALOUS.
YOU CAN ENJOY BOOKS IN A UNIQUE WAY, ALL YOUR OWN.
SOMETIMES I WISHED I HAD BEEN BORN AS SOME OTHER KIND OF ANIMAL, ONE THAT DOESN'T EAT PAPER...
BUT HEARING THAT MADE ME GLAD TO HAVE BEEN BORN A GOAT.
SUZUME BOOKS
ONE DAY, THE BOOKSHOP CLOSED.
I HAVE NO IDEA WHAT THAT GUY IS DOING NOW.

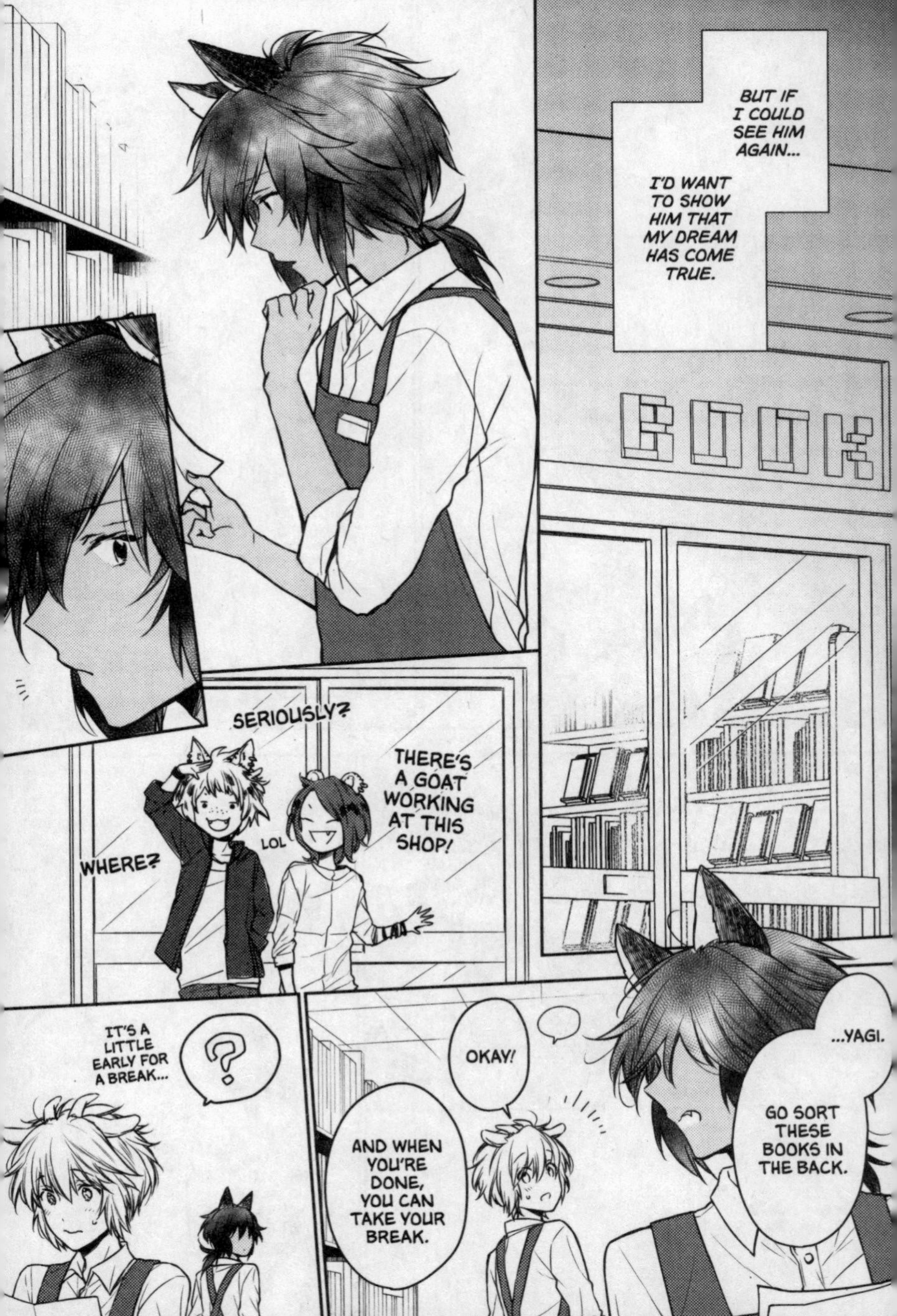
BUT IF I COULD SEE HIM AGAIN...
I'D WANT TO SHOW HIM THAT MY DREAM HAS COME TRUE.
THERE'S A GOAT WORKING AT THIS SHOP!
SERIOUSLY?
LOL
WHERE?
...YAGI.
GO SORT THESE BOOKS IN THE BACK.
OKAY!
AND WHEN YOU'RE DONE, YOU CAN TAKE YOUR BREAK.
IT'S A LITTLE EARLY FOR A BREAK...
?

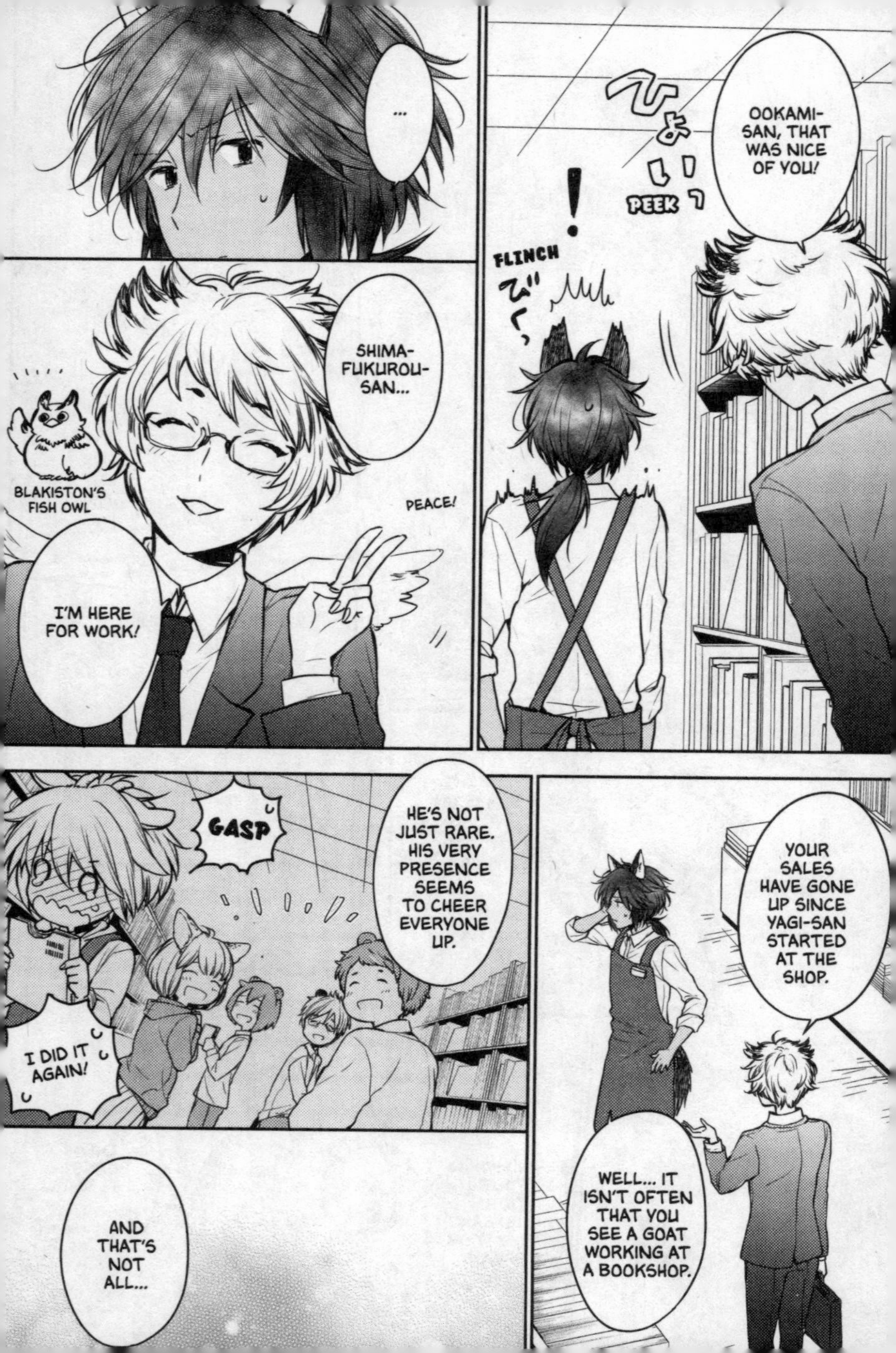
OOKAMI-SAN, THAT WAS NICE OF YOU!
PEEK
!
FLINCH
...
SHIMA-FUKUROU-SAN...
BLAKISTON'S FISH OWL
PEACE!
I'M HERE FOR WORK!
YOUR SALES HAVE GONE UP SINCE YAGI-SAN STARTED AT THE SHOP.
WELL... IT ISN'T OFTEN THAT YOU SEE A GOAT WORKING AT A BOOKSHOP.
HE'S NOT JUST RARE. HIS VERY PRESENCE SEEMS TO CHEER EVERYONE UP.
GASP
I DID IT AGAIN!
AND THAT'S NOT ALL...

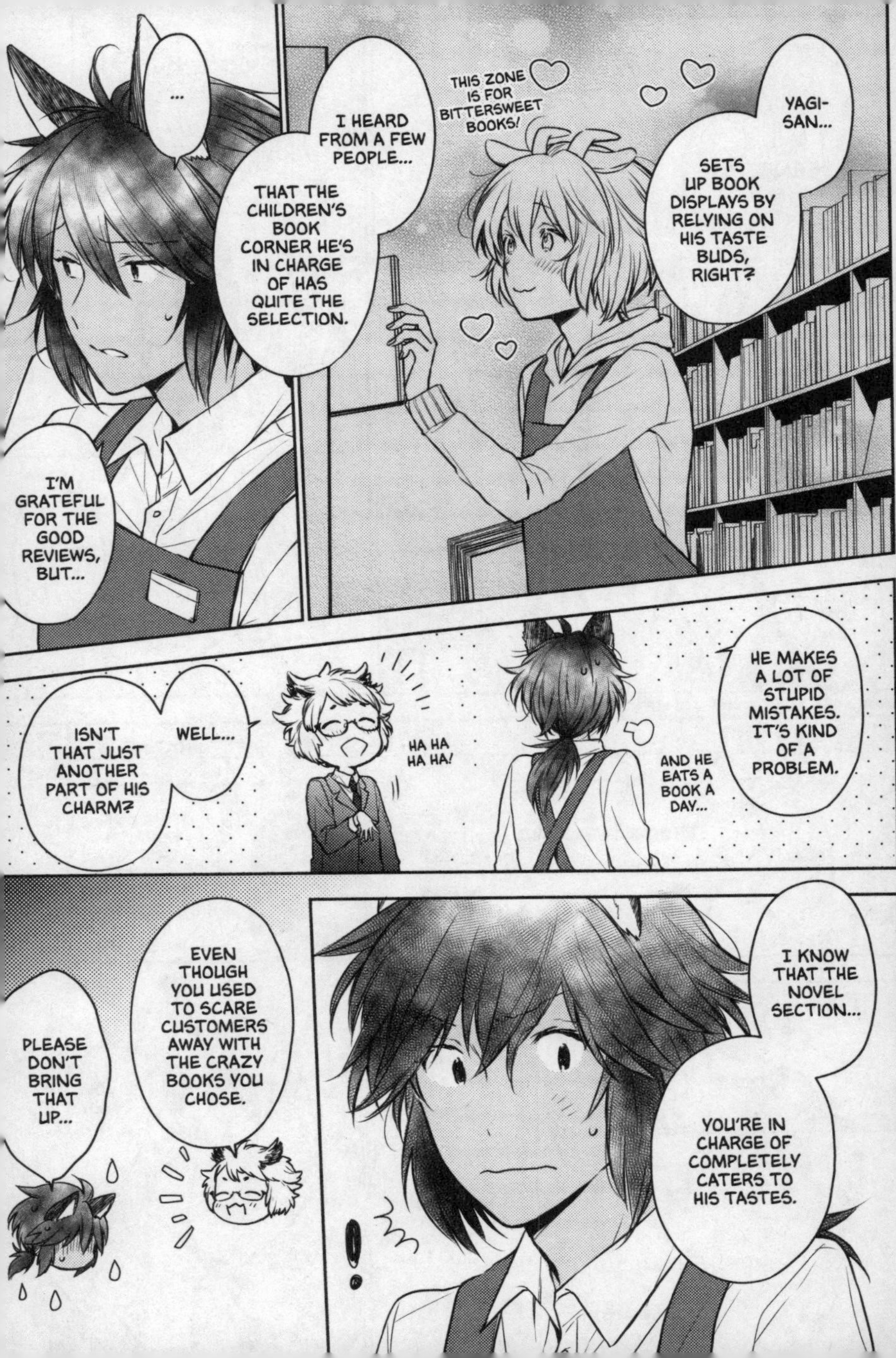
YAGI-SAN...
SETS UP BOOK DISPLAYS BY RELYING ON HIS TASTE BUDS, RIGHT?
THIS ZONE IS FOR BITTERSWEET BOOKS!
I HEARD FROM A FEW PEOPLE...
THAT THE CHILDREN'S BOOK CORNER HE'S IN CHARGE OF HAS QUITE THE SELECTION.
...
I'M GRATEFUL FOR THE GOOD REVIEWS, BUT...
HE MAKES A LOT OF STUPID MISTAKES. IT'S KIND OF A PROBLEM.
AND HE EATS A BOOK A DAY...
HA HA HA HA!
WELL...
ISN'T THAT JUST ANOTHER PART OF HIS CHARM?
I KNOW THAT THE NOVEL SECTION...
YOU'RE IN CHARGE OF COMPLETELY CATERS TO HIS TASTES.
!
EVEN THOUGH YOU USED TO SCARE CUSTOMERS AWAY WITH THE CRAZY BOOKS YOU CHOSE.
PLEASE DON'T BRING THAT UP...

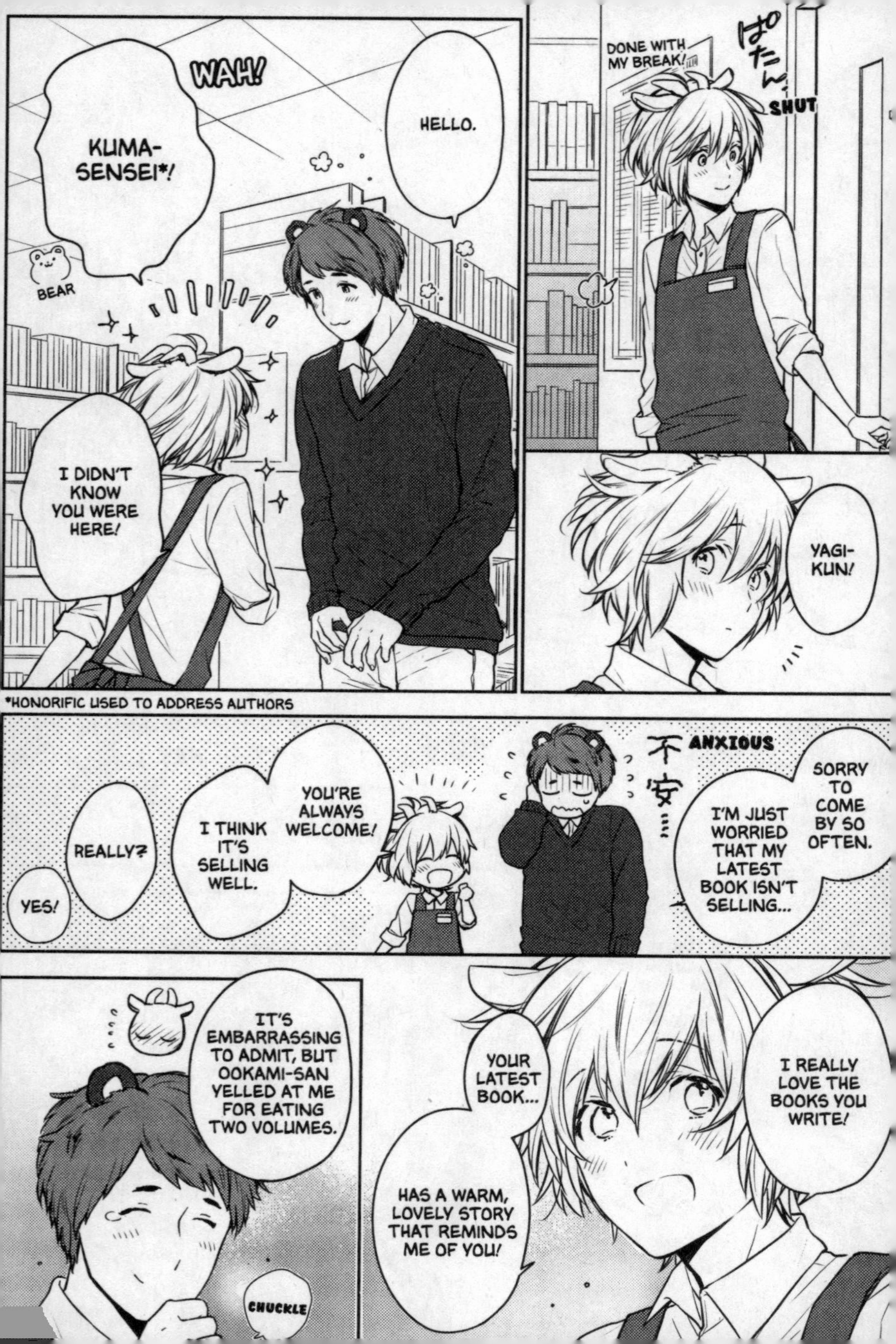
DONE WITH MY BREAK!
ぱたん
SHUT
YAGI-KUN!
HELLO.
WAH!
KUMA-SENSEI*!
BEAR
I DIDN'T KNOW YOU WERE HERE!
SORRY TO COME BY SO OFTEN.
I'M JUST WORRIED THAT MY LATEST BOOK ISN'T SELLING...
不安…
ANXIOUS
YOU'RE ALWAYS WELCOME!
I THINK IT'S SELLING WELL.
REALLY?
YES!
I REALLY LOVE THE BOOKS YOU WRITE!
YOUR LATEST BOOK...
HAS A WARM, LOVELY STORY THAT REMINDS ME OF YOU!
IT'S EMBARRASSING TO ADMIT, BUT OOKAMI-SAN YELLED AT ME FOR EATING TWO VOLUMES.
CHUCKLE

*HONORIFIC USED TO ADDRESS AUTHORS

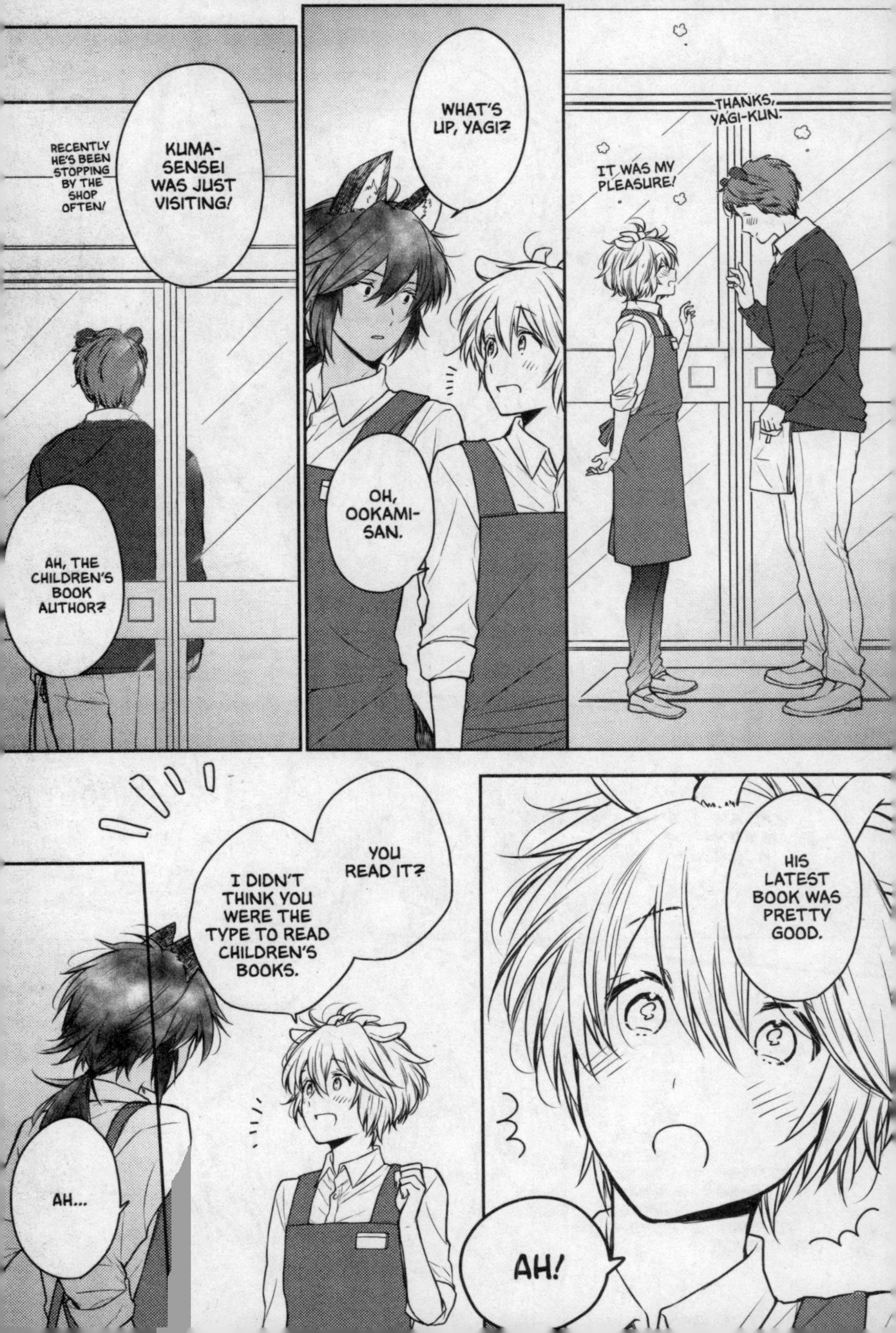
THANKS, YAGI-KUN.
IT WAS MY PLEASURE!
WHAT'S UP, YAGI?
OH, OOKAMI-SAN.
KUMA-SENSEI WAS JUST VISITING!
RECENTLY HE'S BEEN STOPPING BY THE SHOP OFTEN!
AH, THE CHILDREN'S BOOK AUTHOR?
HIS LATEST BOOK WAS PRETTY GOOD.
AH!
YOU READ IT?
I DIDN'T THINK YOU WERE THE TYPE TO READ CHILDREN'S BOOKS.
AH...

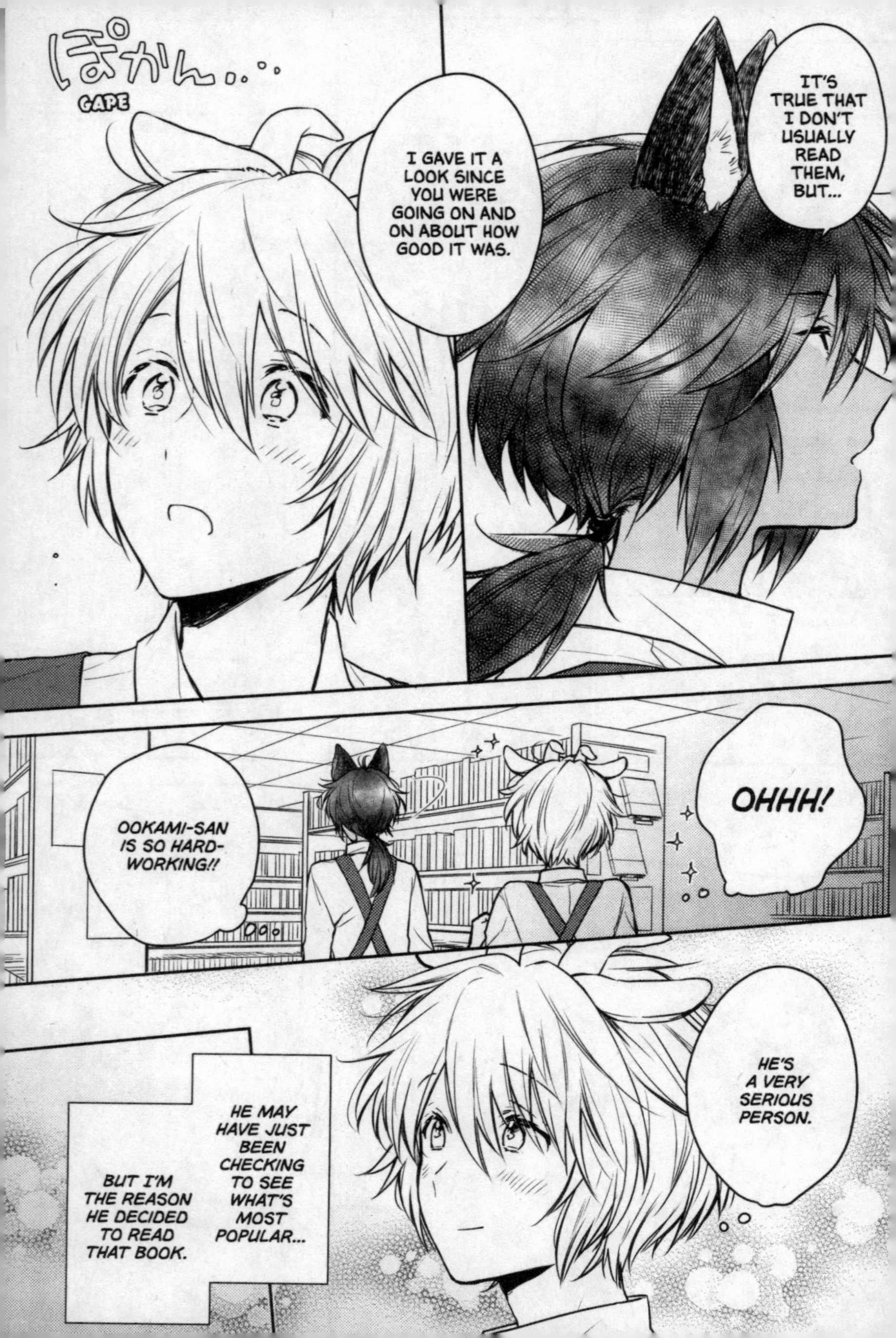
IT'S TRUE THAT I DON'T USUALLY READ THEM, BUT...
I GAVE IT A LOOK SINCE YOU WERE GOING ON AND ON ABOUT HOW GOOD IT WAS.
ぽかん…
GAPE
OHHH!
OOKAMI-SAN IS SO HARD-WORKING!!
HE'S A VERY SERIOUS PERSON.
HE MAY HAVE JUST BEEN CHECKING TO SEE WHAT'S MOST POPULAR...
BUT I'M THE REASON HE DECIDED TO READ THAT BOOK.

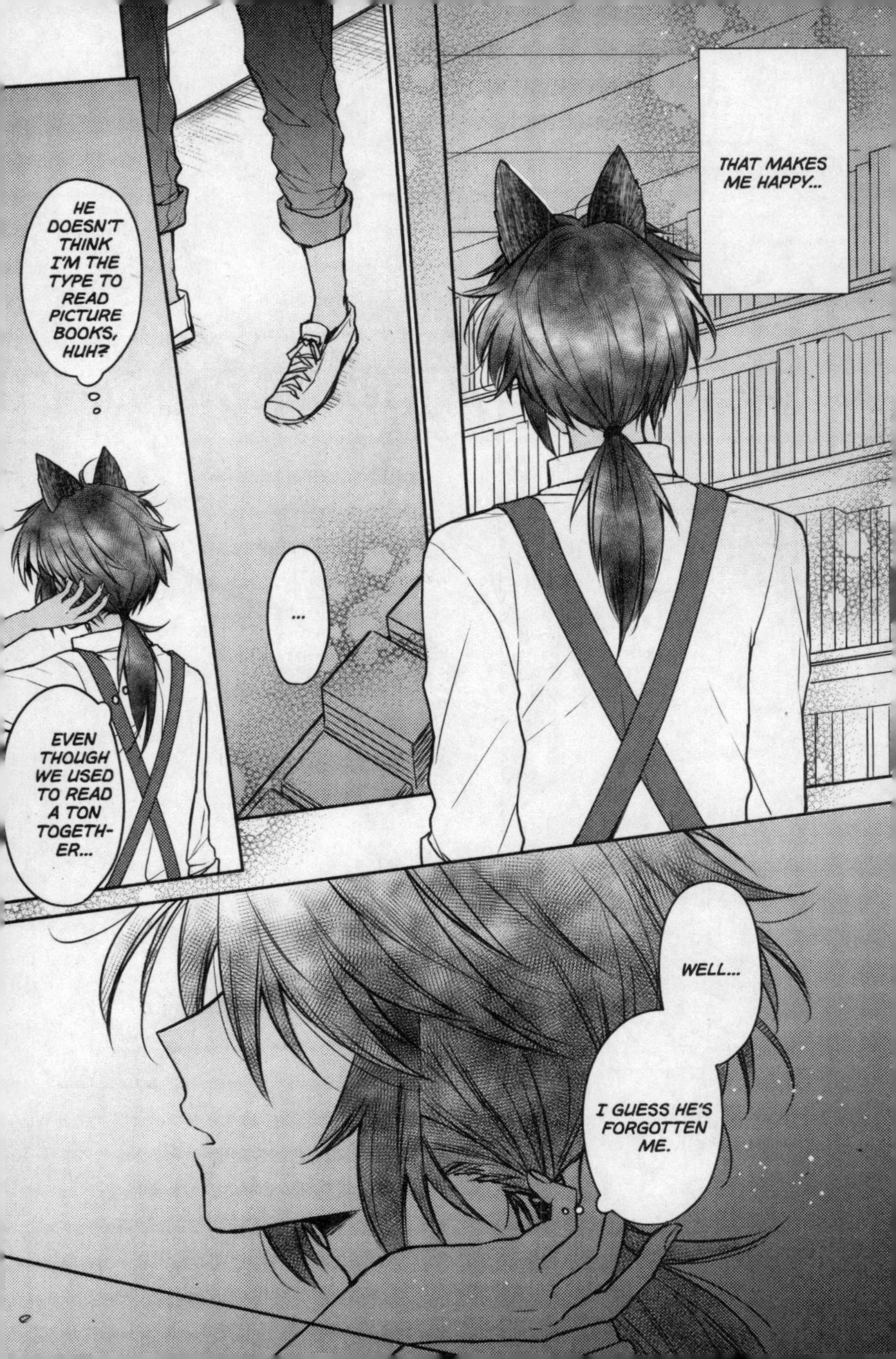
THAT MAKES ME HAPPY...
...
HE DOESN'T THINK I'M THE TYPE TO READ PICTURE BOOKS, HUH?
EVEN THOUGH WE USED TO READ A TON TOGETH-ER...
WELL...
I GUESS HE'S FORGOTTEN ME.

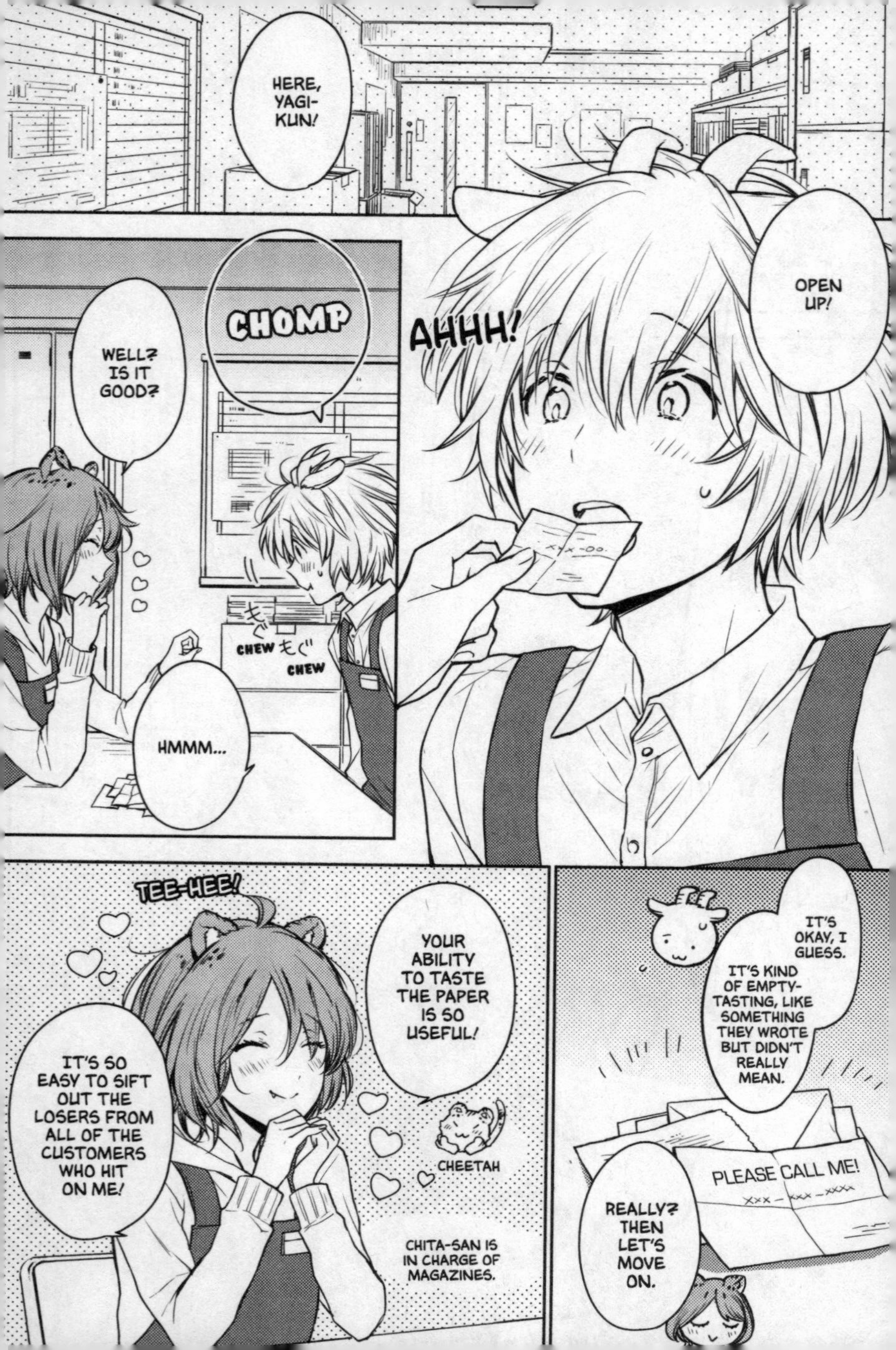
HERE, YAGI-KUN!
OPEN UP!
AHHH!
CHOMP
WELL? IS IT GOOD?
もぐ CHEW もぐ CHEW
HMMM...
IT'S OKAY, I GUESS.
IT'S KIND OF EMPTY-TASTING, LIKE SOMETHING THEY WROTE BUT DIDN'T REALLY MEAN.
PLEASE CALL ME!
REALLY? THEN LET'S MOVE ON.
TEE-HEE!
YOUR ABILITY TO TASTE THE PAPER IS SO USEFUL!
IT'S SO EASY TO SIFT OUT THE LOSERS FROM ALL OF THE CUSTOMERS WHO HIT ON ME!
CHEETAH
CHITA-SAN IS IN CHARGE OF MAGAZINES.

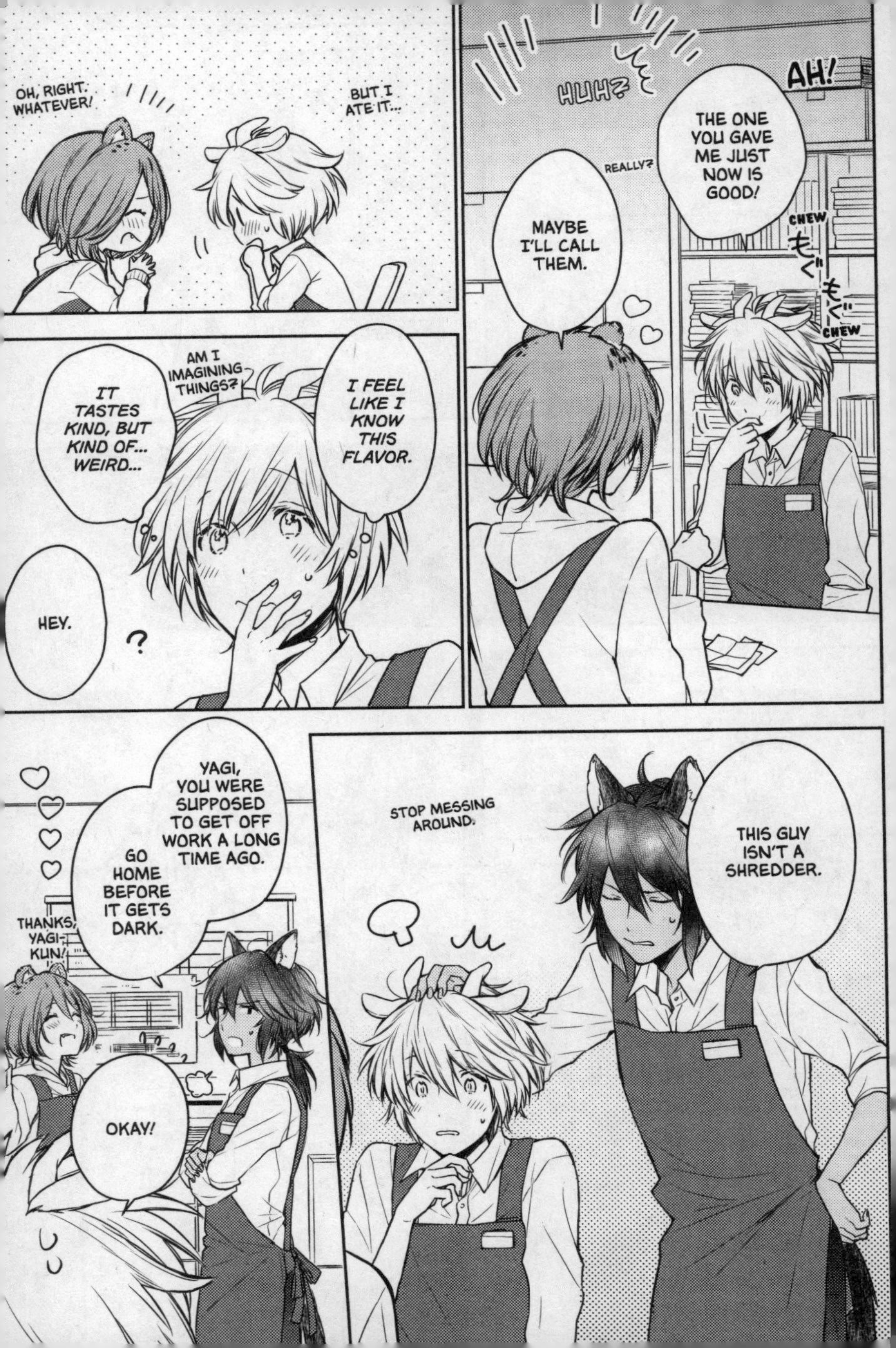
AH!
THE ONE YOU GAVE ME JUST NOW IS GOOD!
HUH?
REALLY?
MAYBE I'LL CALL THEM.
CHEW
もぐ
もぐ
CHEW
BUT I ATE IT...
OH, RIGHT. WHATEVER!
I FEEL LIKE I KNOW THIS FLAVOR.
AM I IMAGINING THINGS?
IT TASTES KIND, BUT KIND OF... WEIRD...
HEY.
THIS GUY ISN'T A SHREDDER.
STOP MESSING AROUND.
YAGI, YOU WERE SUPPOSED TO GET OFF WORK A LONG TIME AGO.
GO HOME BEFORE IT GETS DARK.
THANKS, YAGI-KUN!
OKAY!

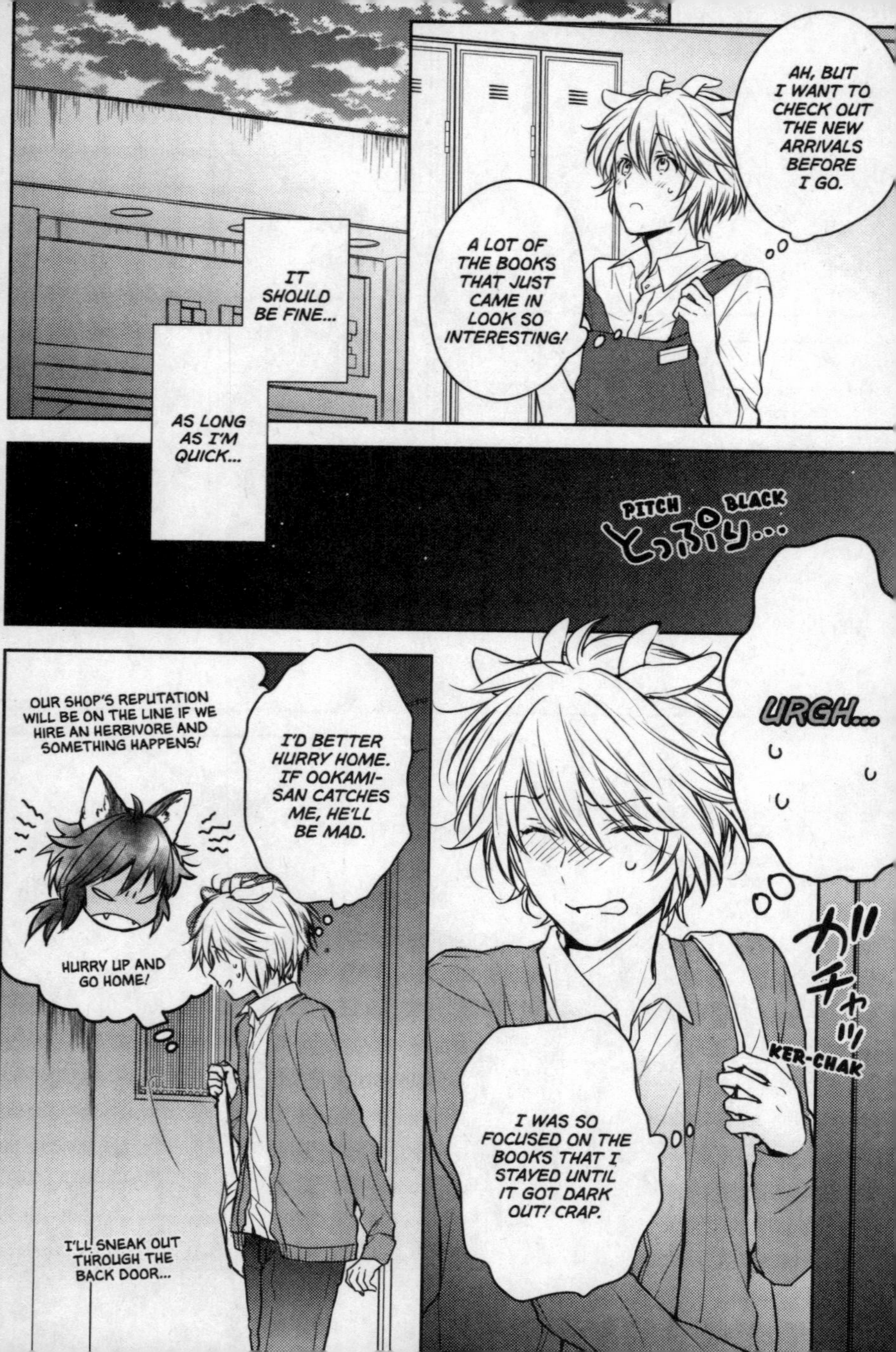
AH, BUT I WANT TO CHECK OUT THE NEW ARRIVALS BEFORE I GO.
A LOT OF THE BOOKS THAT JUST CAME IN LOOK SO INTERESTING!
IT SHOULD BE FINE...
AS LONG AS I'M QUICK...
とっぷり...
PITCH BLACK
URGH...
ガチャッ
KER-CHAK
I WAS SO FOCUSED ON THE BOOKS THAT I STAYED UNTIL IT GOT DARK OUT! CRAP.
I'D BETTER HURRY HOME. IF OOKAMI-SAN CATCHES ME, HE'LL BE MAD.
OUR SHOP'S REPUTATION WILL BE ON THE LINE IF WE HIRE AN HERBIVORE AND SOMETHING HAPPENS!
HURRY UP AND GO HOME!
I'LL SNEAK OUT THROUGH THE BACK DOOR...

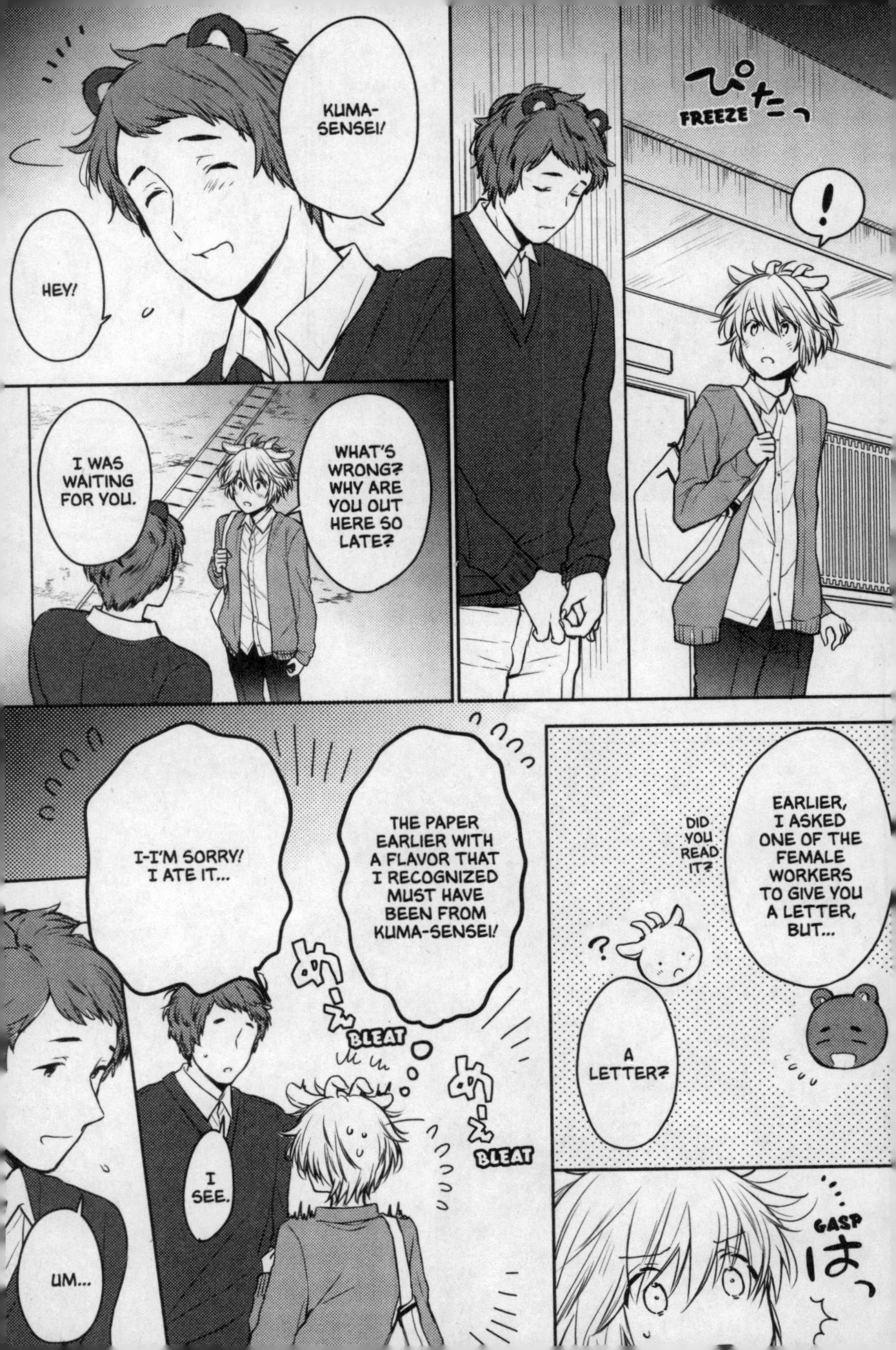
ぴたっ
FREEZE
!
KUMA-SENSEI!
HEY!
WHAT'S WRONG? WHY ARE YOU OUT HERE SO LATE?
I WAS WAITING FOR YOU.
EARLIER, I ASKED ONE OF THE FEMALE WORKERS TO GIVE YOU A LETTER, BUT...
DID YOU READ IT?
A LETTER?
GASP
はっ
THE PAPER EARLIER WITH A FLAVOR THAT I RECOGNIZED MUST HAVE BEEN FROM KUMA-SENSEI!
めえ
BLEAT
めえ
BLEAT
I-I'M SORRY! I ATE IT...
I SEE.
UM...

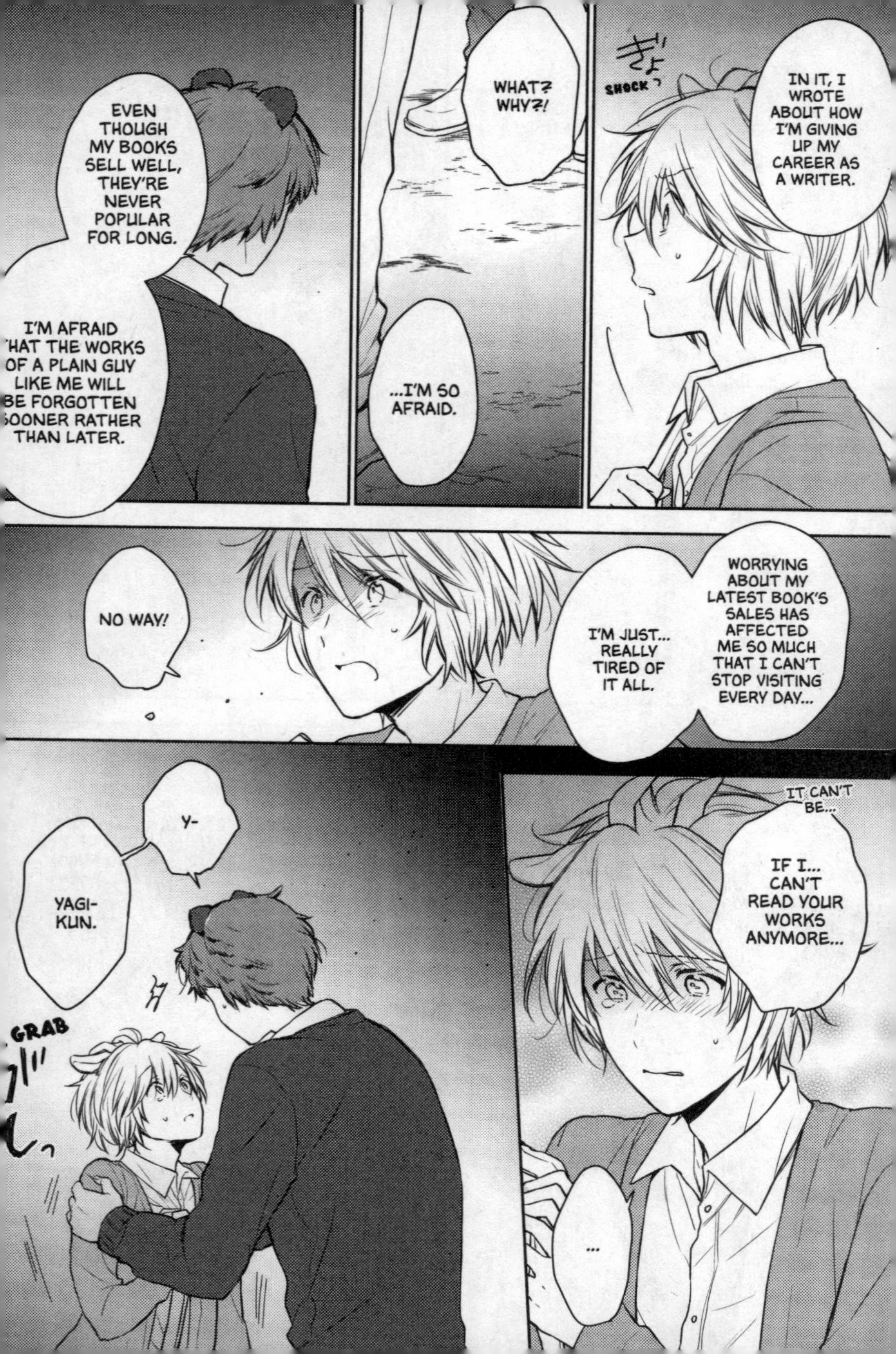

ぎょっ
SHOCK
IN IT, I WROTE ABOUT HOW I'M GIVING UP MY CAREER AS A WRITER.
WHAT? WHY?!
...I'M SO AFRAID.
EVEN THOUGH MY BOOKS SELL WELL, THEY'RE NEVER POPULAR FOR LONG.
I'M AFRAID THAT THE WORKS OF A PLAIN GUY LIKE ME WILL BE FORGOTTEN SOONER RATHER THAN LATER.
WORRYING ABOUT MY LATEST BOOK'S SALES HAS AFFECTED ME SO MUCH THAT I CAN'T STOP VISITING EVERY DAY...
I'M JUST... REALLY TIRED OF IT ALL.
NO WAY!
IT CAN'T BE...
IF I... CAN'T READ YOUR WORKS ANYMORE...
...
Y-
YAGI-KUN.
GRAB

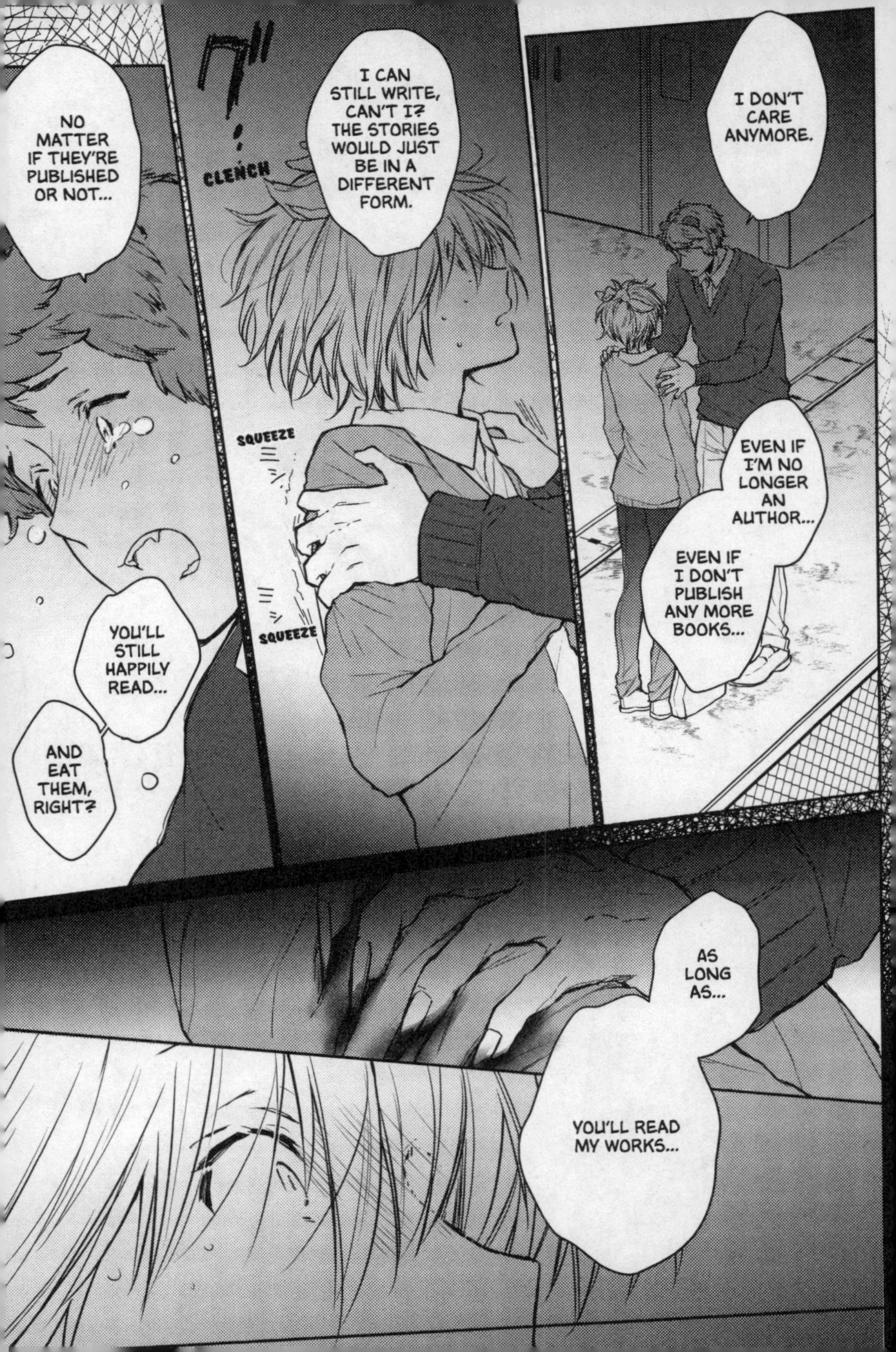

I DON'T CARE ANYMORE.
EVEN IF I'M NO LONGER AN AUTHOR...
EVEN IF I DON'T PUBLISH ANY MORE BOOKS...
CLENCH
I CAN STILL WRITE, CAN'T I? THE STORIES WOULD JUST BE IN A DIFFERENT FORM.
SQUEEZE
SQUEEZE
NO MATTER IF THEY'RE PUBLISHED OR NOT...
YOU'LL STILL HAPPILY READ...
AND EAT THEM, RIGHT?
AS LONG AS...
YOU'LL READ MY WORKS...

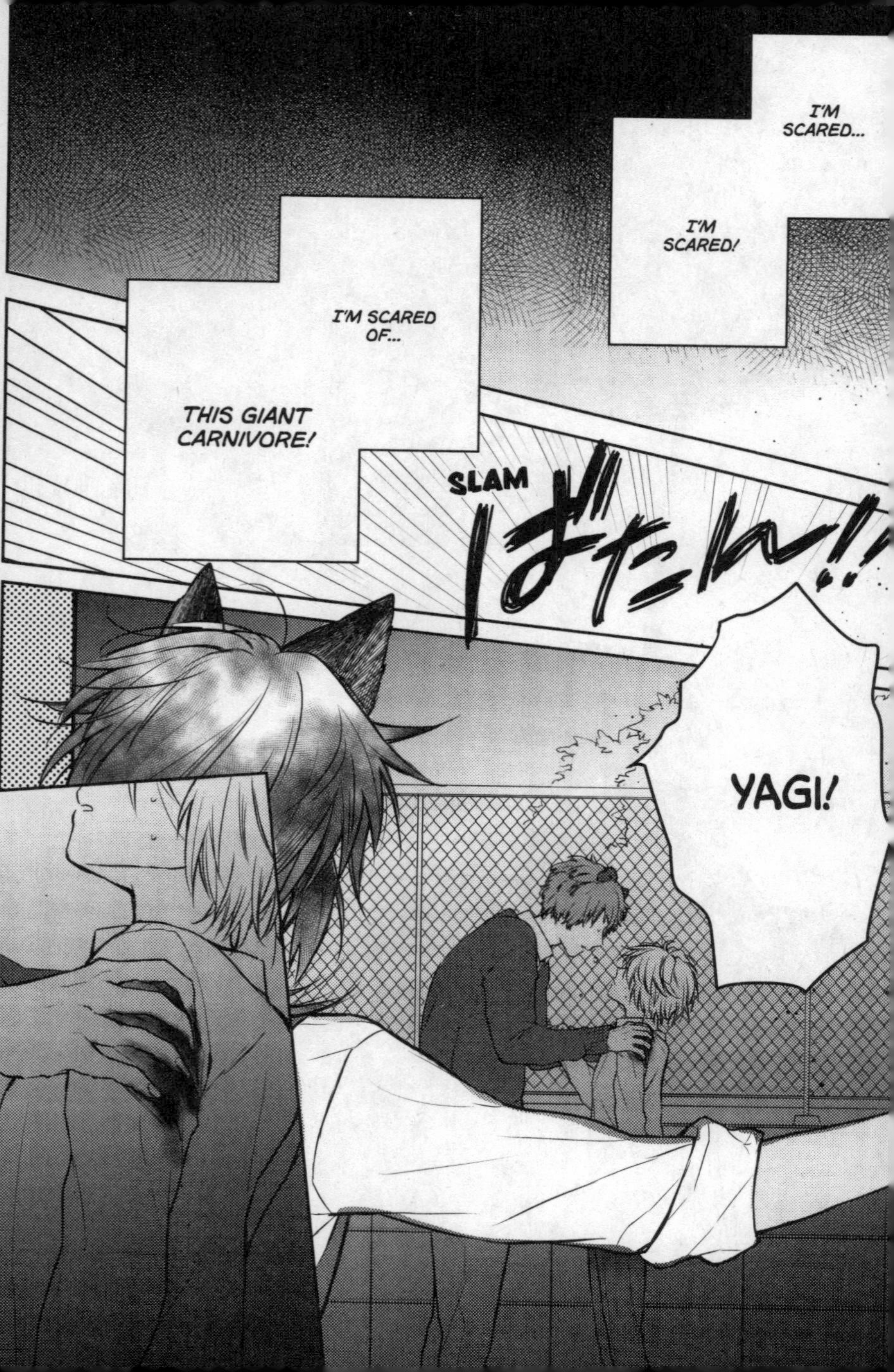
I'M SCARED...
I'M SCARED!
I'M SCARED OF...
THIS GIANT CARNIVORE!
SLAM
ばたん!!
YAGI!

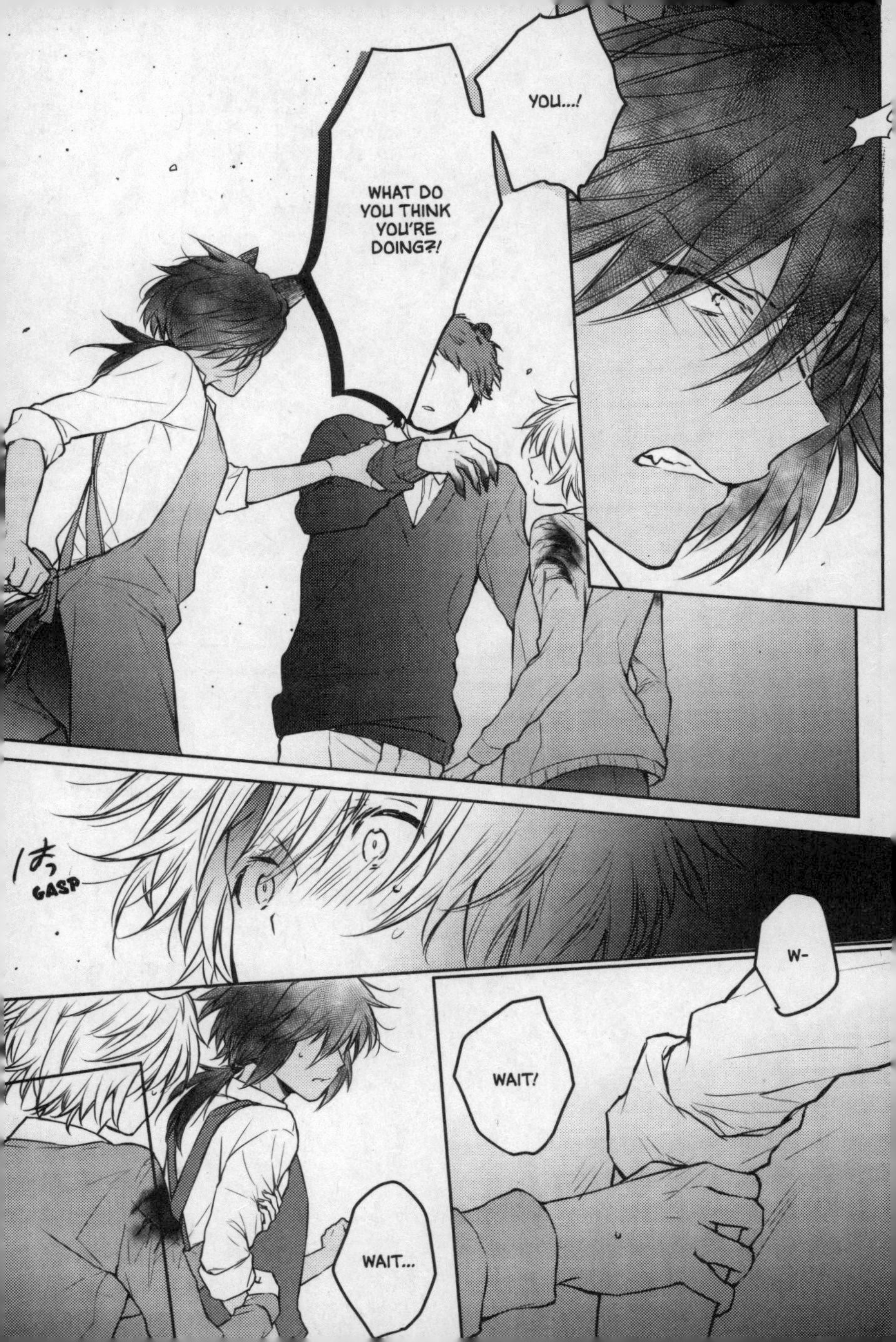
YOU...!
WHAT DO YOU THINK YOU'RE DOING?!
はっ
GASP
W-
WAIT!
WAIT...

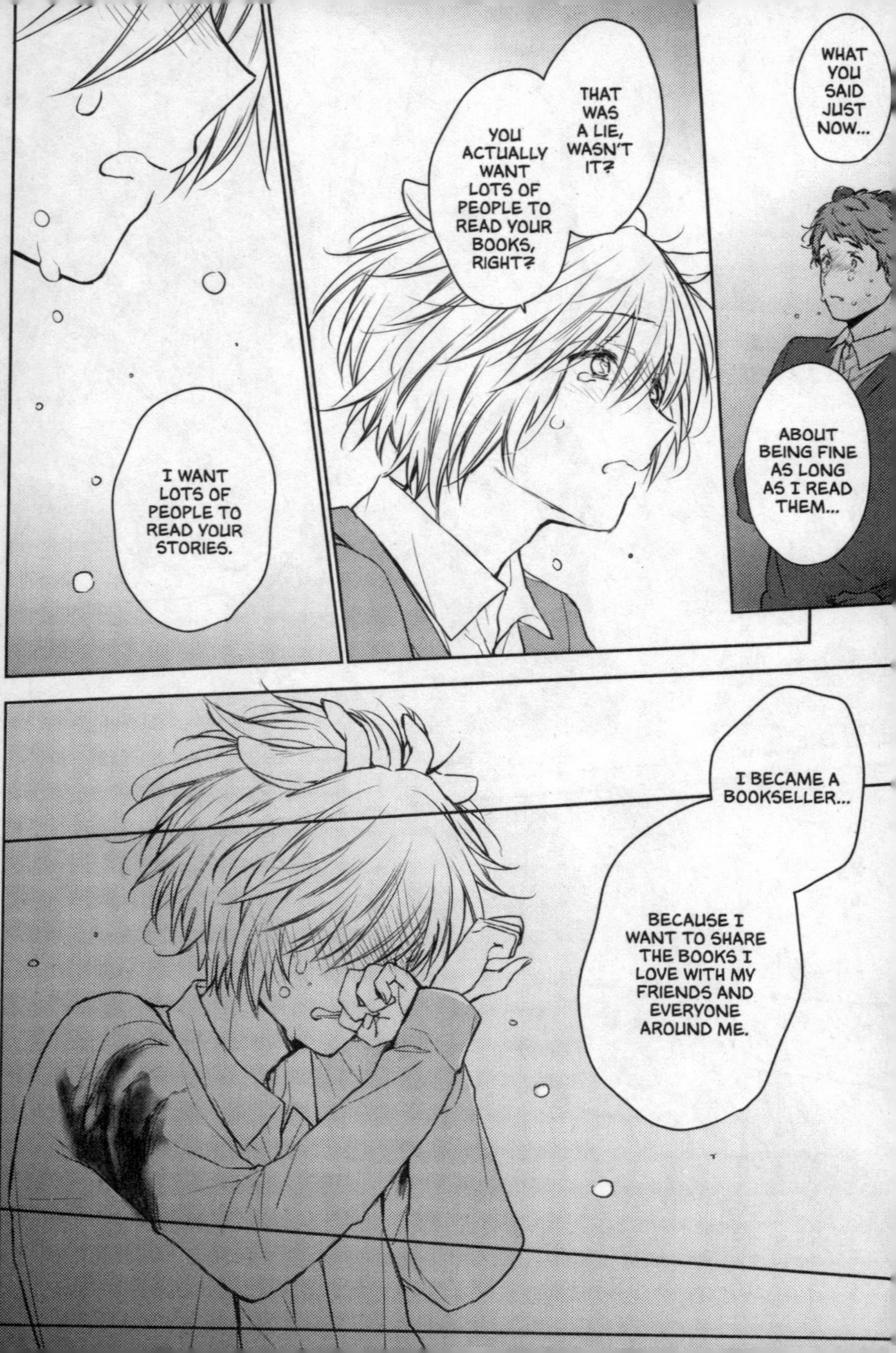
WHAT YOU SAID JUST NOW...
ABOUT BEING FINE AS LONG AS I READ THEM...
THAT WAS A LIE, WASN'T IT?
YOU ACTUALLY WANT LOTS OF PEOPLE TO READ YOUR BOOKS, RIGHT?
I WANT LOTS OF PEOPLE TO READ YOUR STORIES.
I BECAME A BOOKSELLER...
BECAUSE I WANT TO SHARE THE BOOKS I LOVE WITH MY FRIENDS AND EVERYONE AROUND ME.

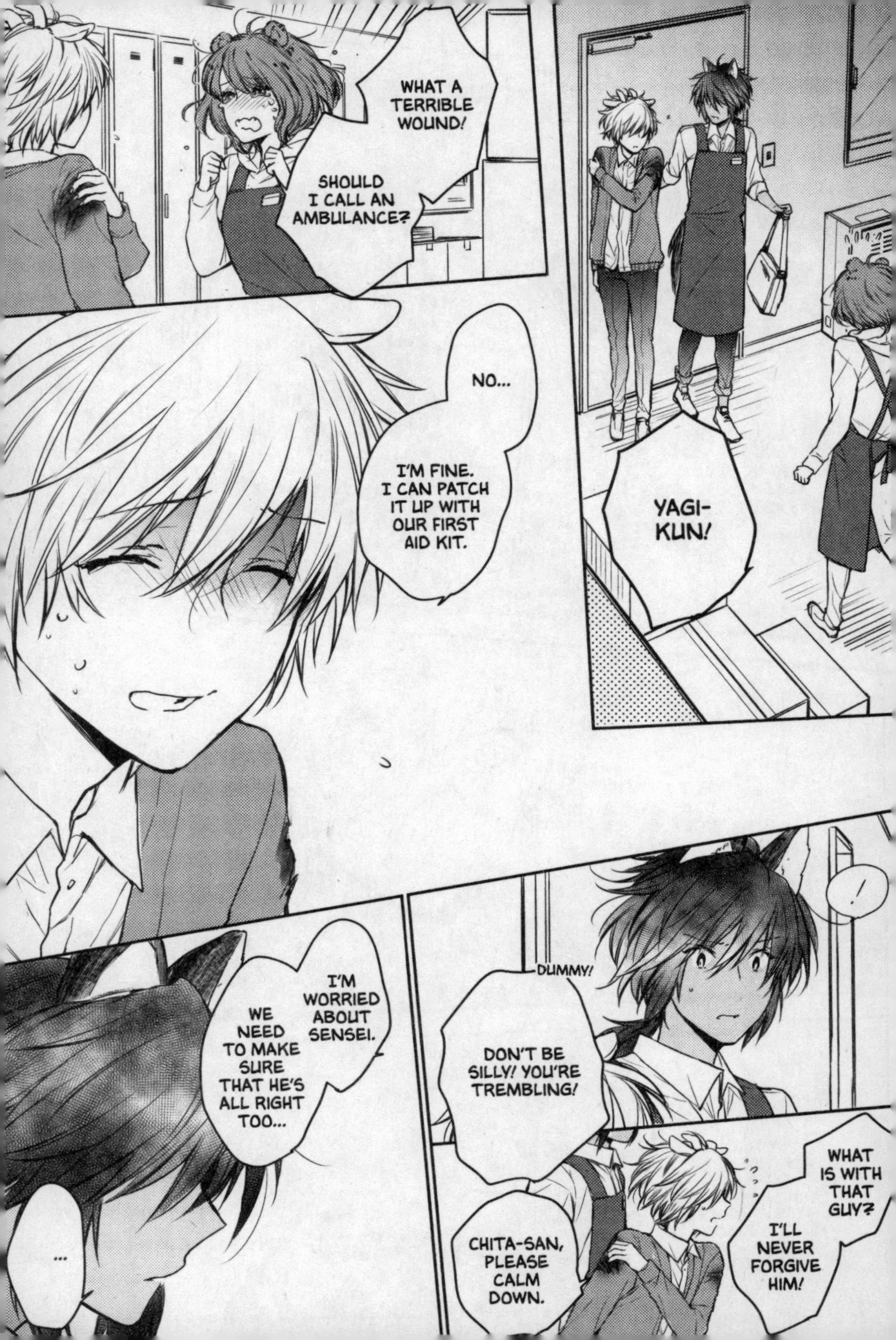
YAGI-KUN!
WHAT A TERRIBLE WOUND!
SHOULD I CALL AN AMBULANCE?
NO...
I'M FINE. I CAN PATCH IT UP WITH OUR FIRST AID KIT.
!
DUMMY!
DON'T BE SILLY! YOU'RE TREMBLING!
WHAT IS WITH THAT GUY?
I'LL NEVER FORGIVE HIM!
CHITA-SAN, PLEASE CALM DOWN.
I'M WORRIED ABOUT SENSEI.
WE NEED TO MAKE SURE THAT HE'S ALL RIGHT TOO...
...

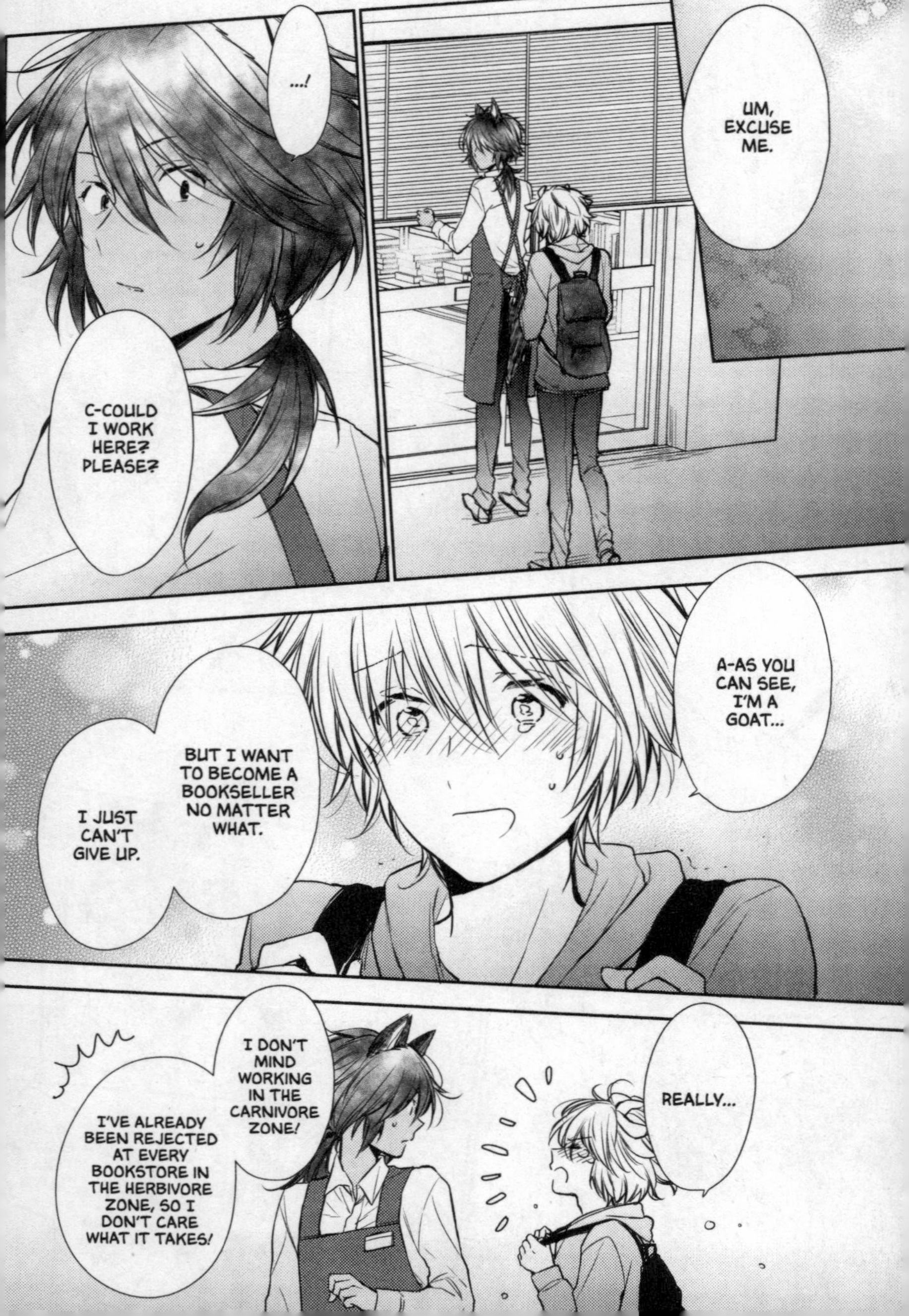
UM, EXCUSE ME.
...!
C-COULD I WORK HERE? PLEASE?
A-AS YOU CAN SEE, I'M A GOAT...
BUT I WANT TO BECOME A BOOKSELLER NO MATTER WHAT.
I JUST CAN'T GIVE UP.
REALLY...
I DON'T MIND WORKING IN THE CARNIVORE ZONE!
I'VE ALREADY BEEN REJECTED AT EVERY BOOKSTORE IN THE HERBIVORE ZONE, SO I DON'T CARE WHAT IT TAKES!

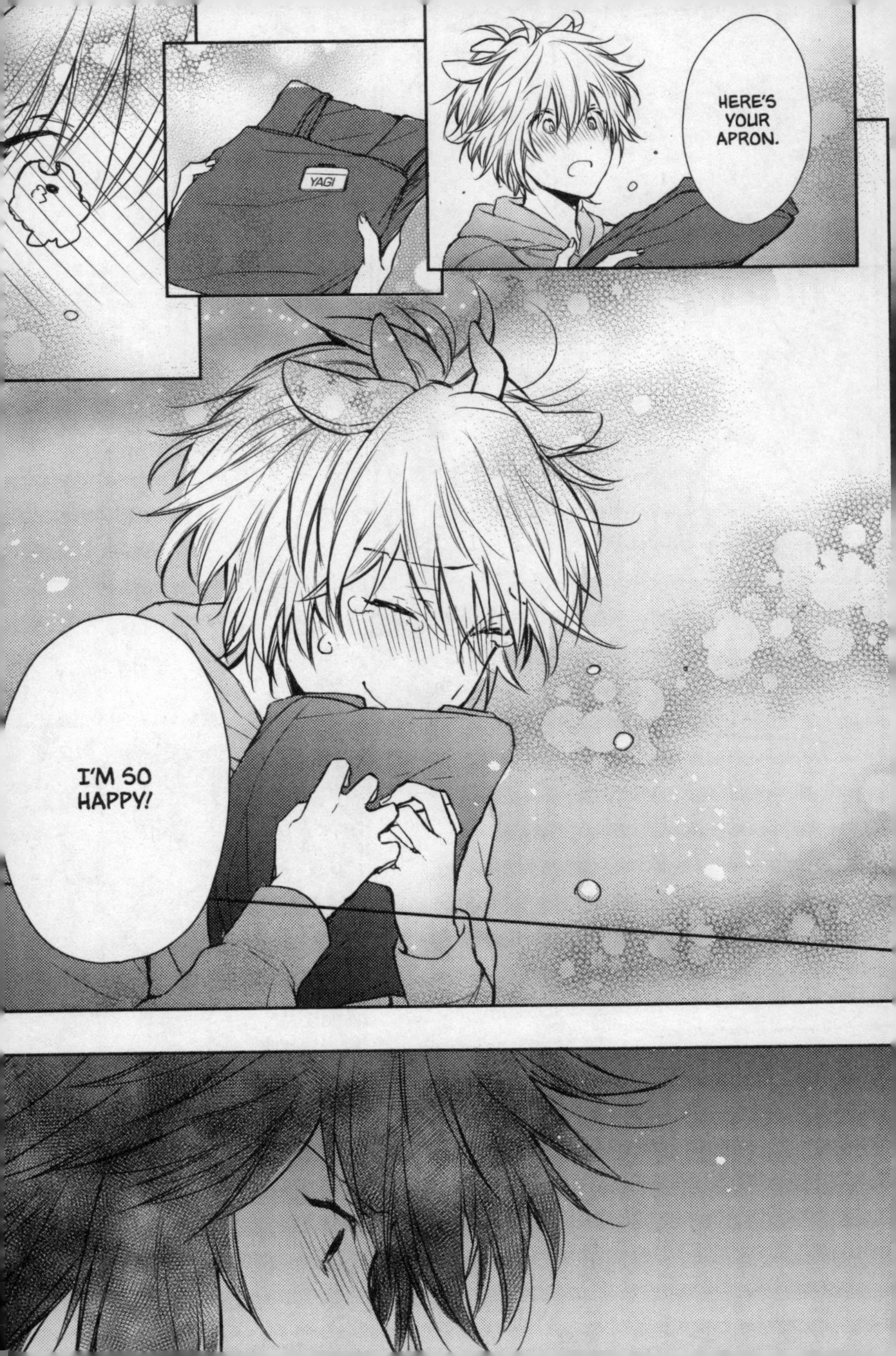
YAGI
HERE'S YOUR APRON.
I'M SO HAPPY!

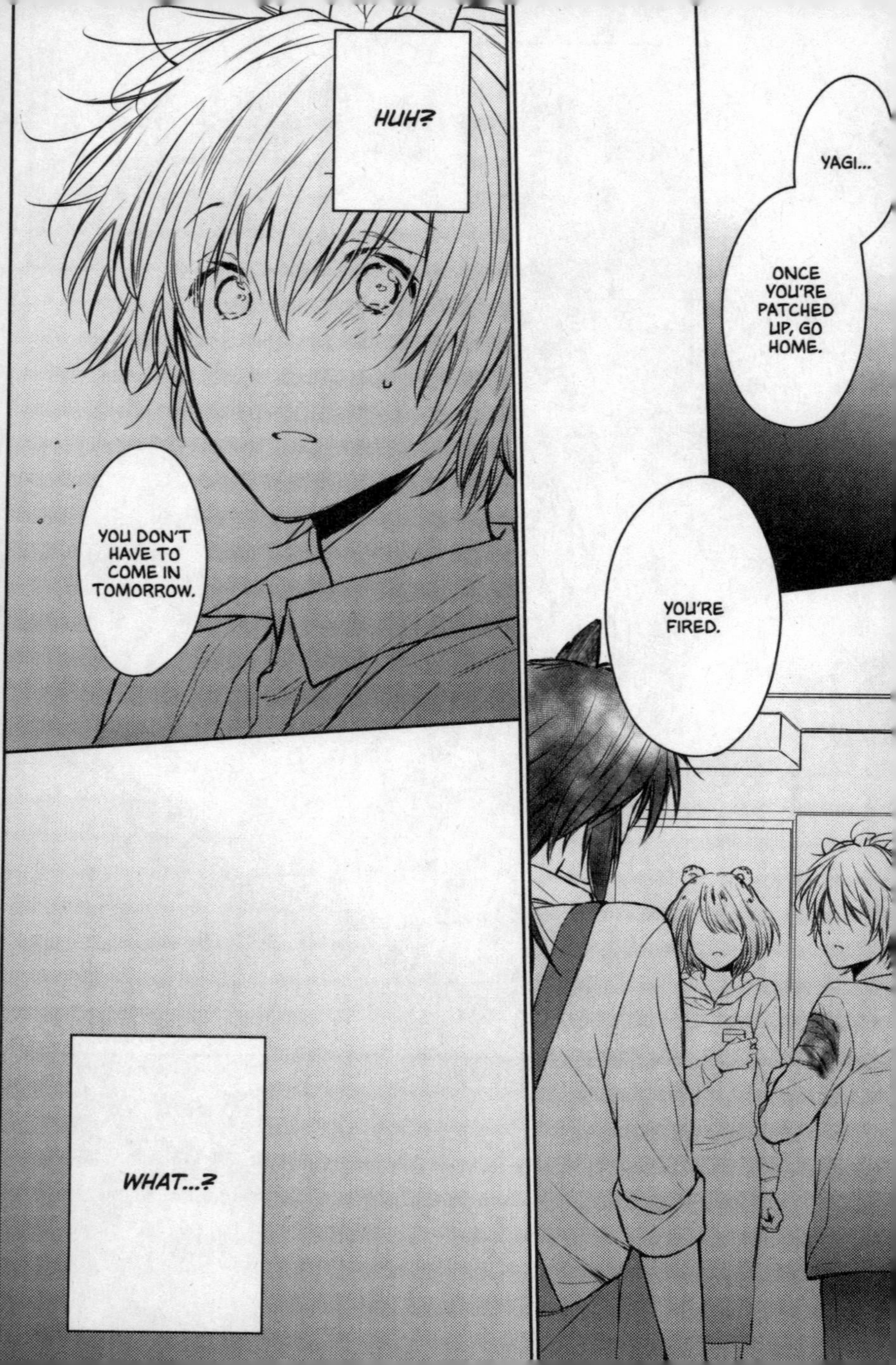
YAGI...
ONCE YOU'RE PATCHED UP, GO HOME.
YOU'RE FIRED.
HUH?
YOU DON'T HAVE TO COME IN TOMORROW.
WHAT...?

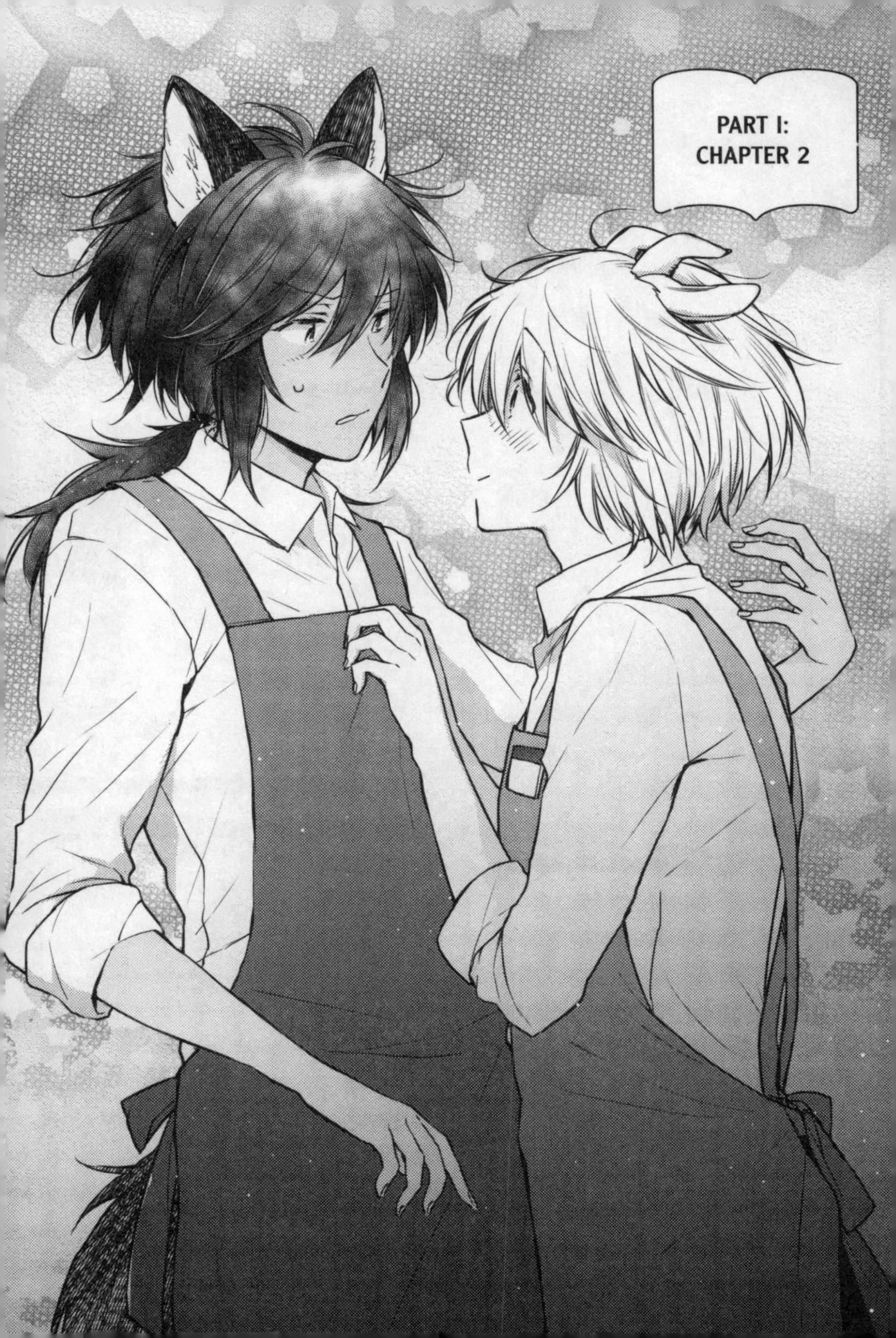
PART I:
CHAPTER 2

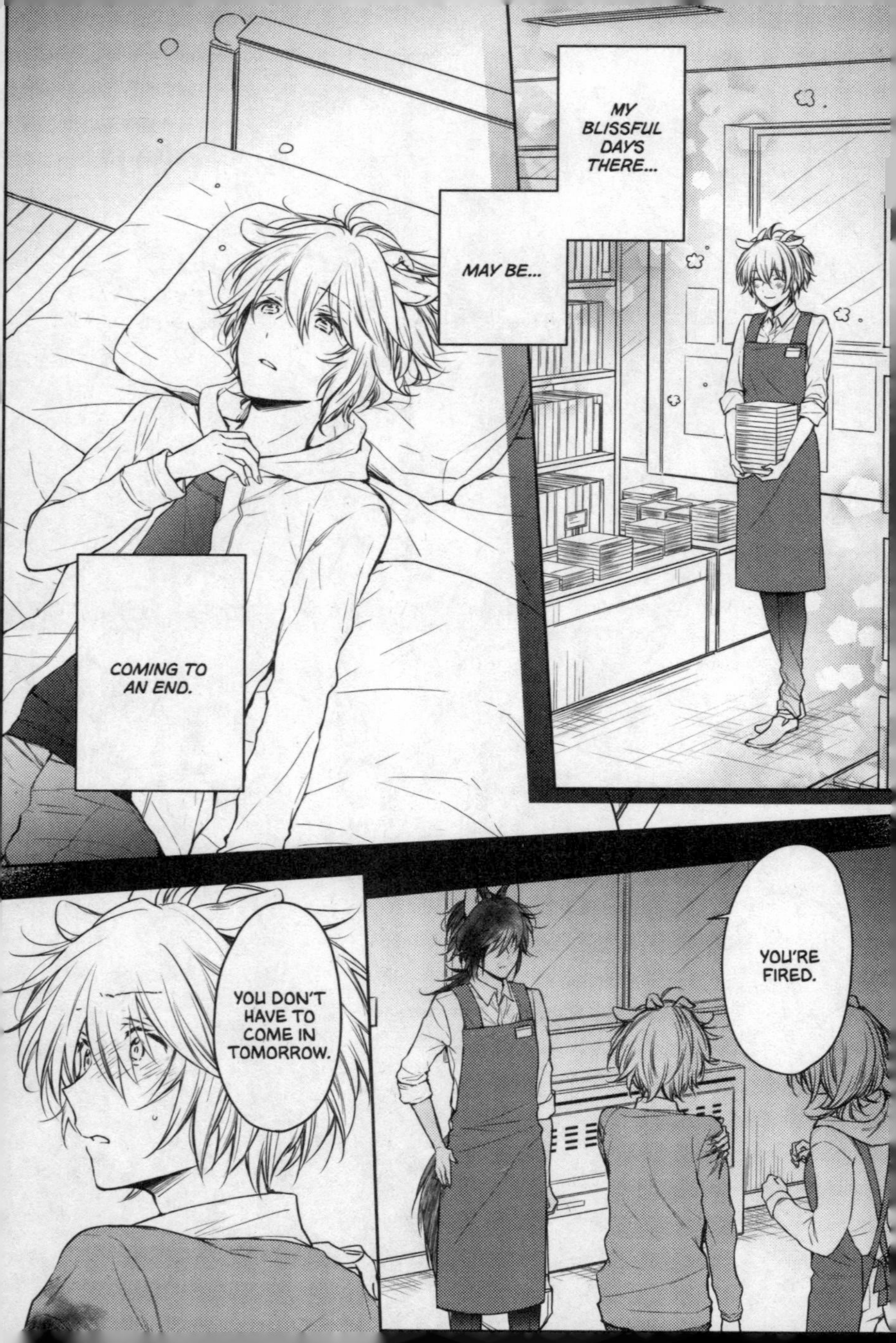
MY BLISSFUL DAYS THERE...
MAY BE...
COMING TO AN END.
YOU'RE FIRED.
YOU DON'T HAVE TO COME IN TOMORROW.

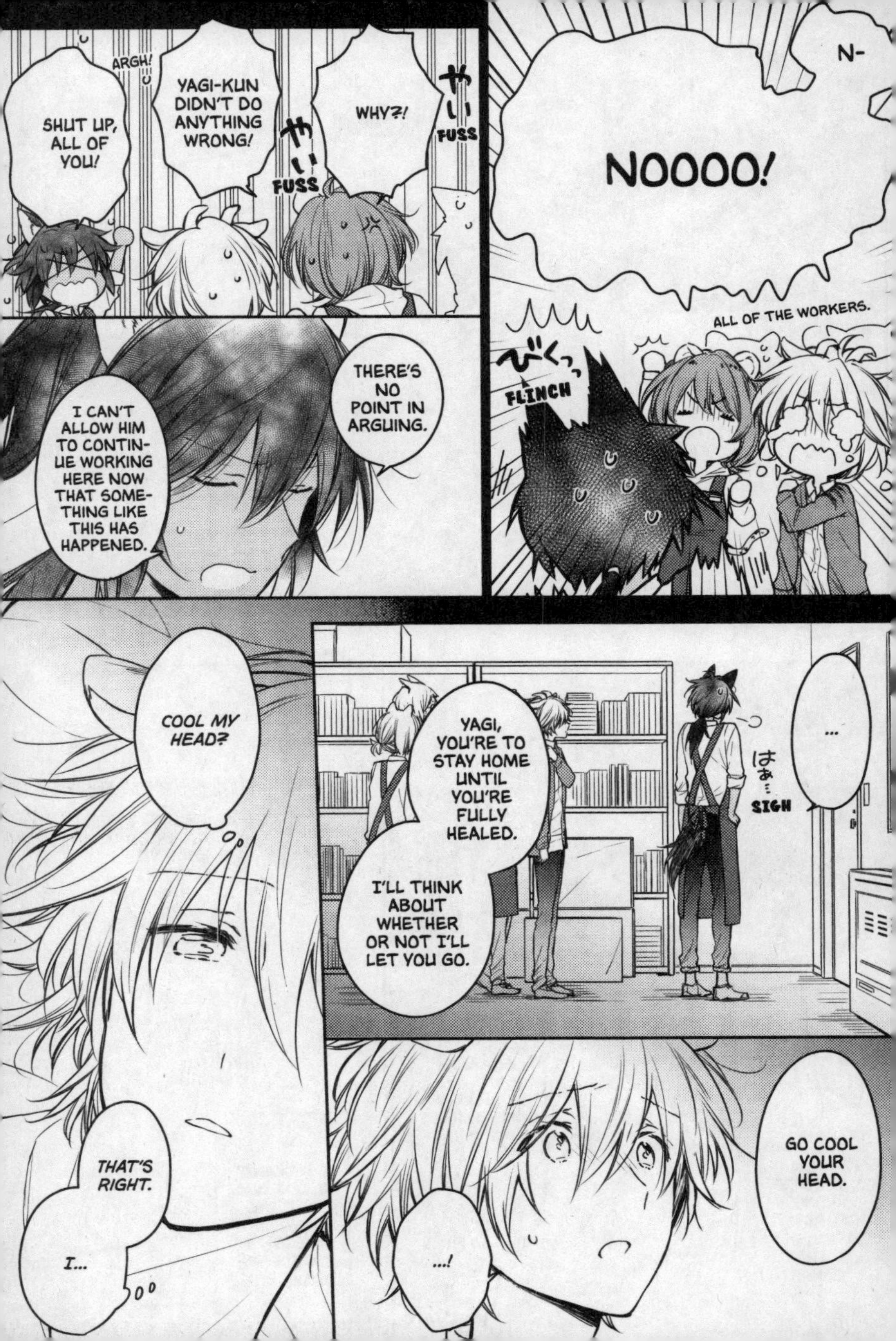
N-
NOOOO!
ALL OF THE WORKERS.
びくっ
FLINCH
WHY?!
やい FUSS
やい FUSS
YAGI-KUN DIDN'T DO ANYTHING WRONG!
ARGH!
SHUT UP, ALL OF YOU!
THERE'S NO POINT IN ARGUING.
I CAN'T ALLOW HIM TO CONTINUE WORKING HERE NOW THAT SOMETHING LIKE THIS HAS HAPPENED.
...
はぁ… SIGH
YAGI, YOU'RE TO STAY HOME UNTIL YOU'RE FULLY HEALED.
I'LL THINK ABOUT WHETHER OR NOT I'LL LET YOU GO.
GO COOL YOUR HEAD.
...!
COOL MY HEAD?
THAT'S RIGHT.
I...

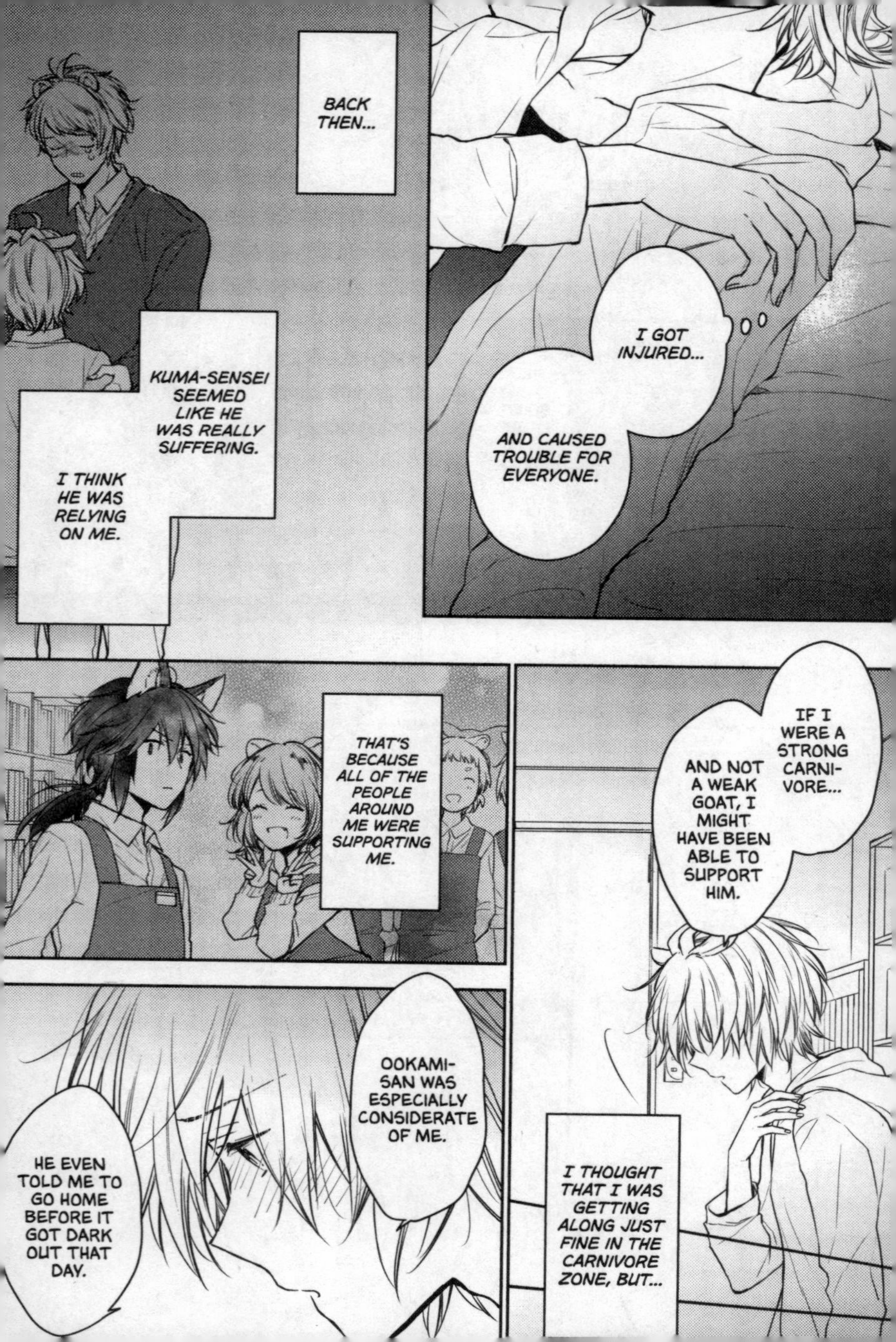
I GOT INJURED...
AND CAUSED TROUBLE FOR EVERYONE.
BACK THEN...
KUMA-SENSEI SEEMED LIKE HE WAS REALLY SUFFERING.
I THINK HE WAS RELYING ON ME.
IF I WERE A STRONG CARNIVORE...
AND NOT A WEAK GOAT, I MIGHT HAVE BEEN ABLE TO SUPPORT HIM.
I THOUGHT THAT I WAS GETTING ALONG JUST FINE IN THE CARNIVORE ZONE, BUT...
THAT'S BECAUSE ALL OF THE PEOPLE AROUND ME WERE SUPPORTING ME.
OOKAMI-SAN WAS ESPECIALLY CONSIDERATE OF ME.
HE EVEN TOLD ME TO GO HOME BEFORE IT GOT DARK OUT THAT DAY.

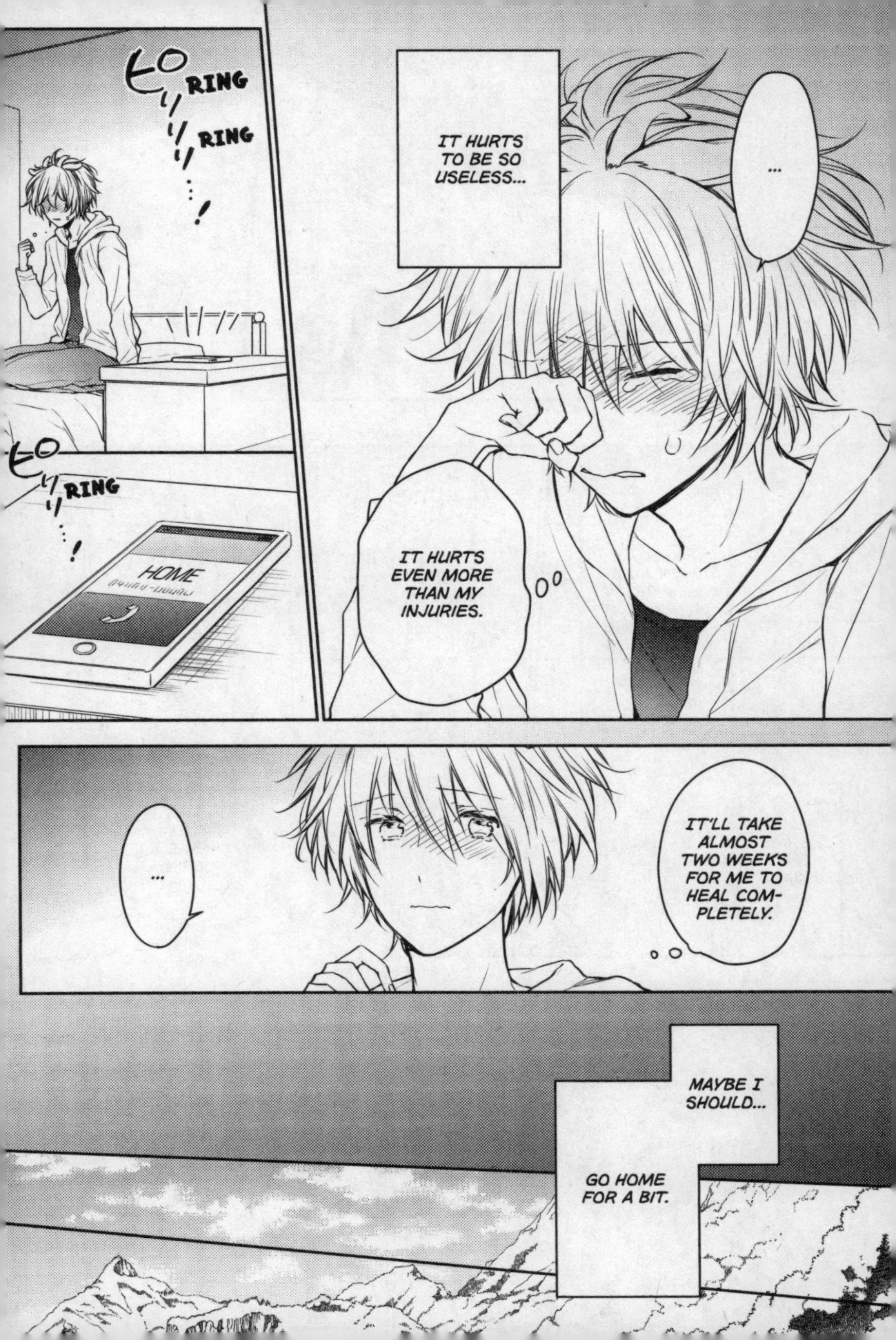
...
IT HURTS TO BE SO USELESS...
IT HURTS EVEN MORE THAN MY INJURIES.
RING
RING
...!
RING
...!
HOME
IT'LL TAKE ALMOST TWO WEEKS FOR ME TO HEAL COM-PLETELY.
...
MAYBE I SHOULD...
GO HOME FOR A BIT.

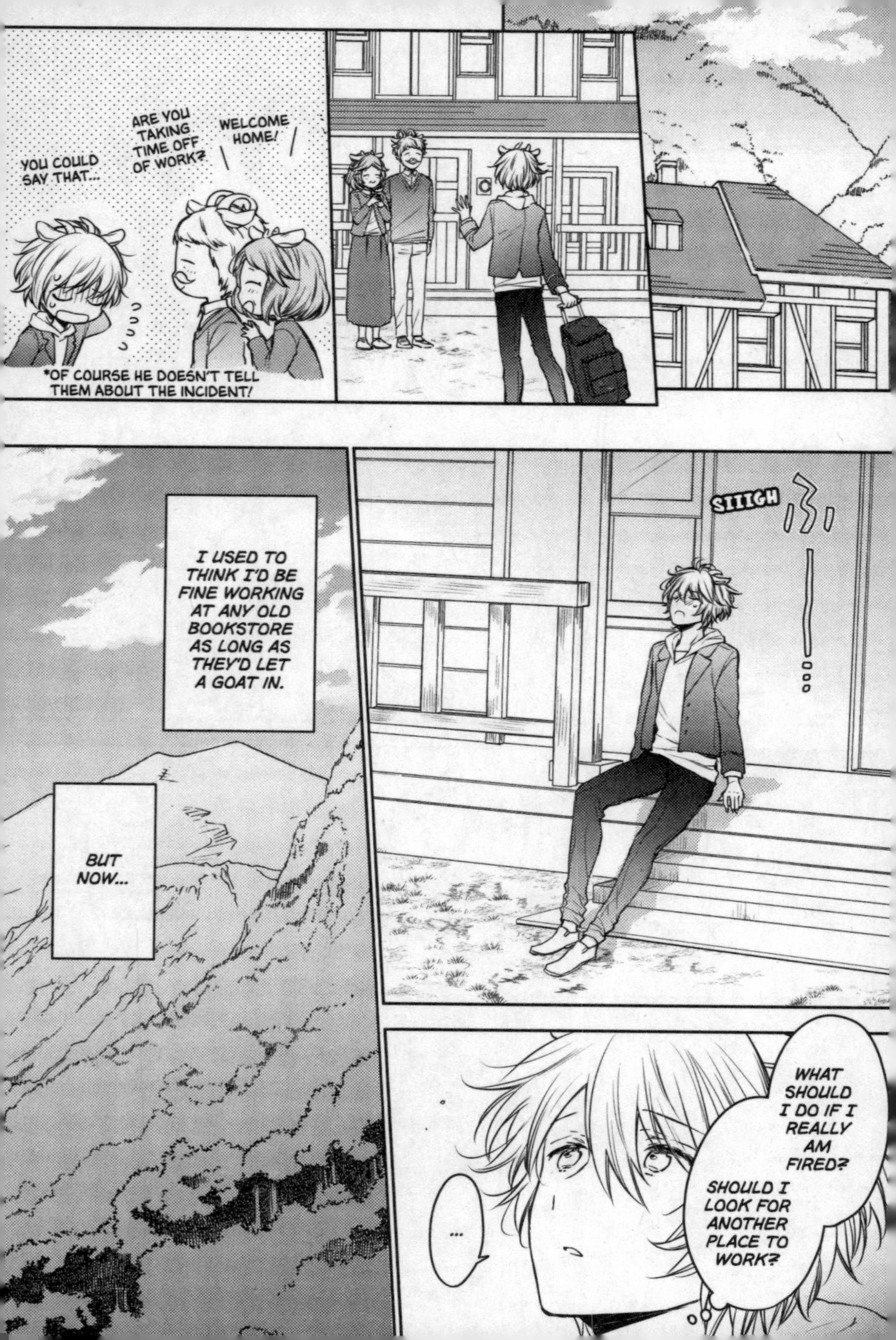

WELCOME HOME!
ARE YOU TAKING TIME OFF OF WORK?
YOU COULD SAY THAT...
*OF COURSE HE DOESN'T TELL THEM ABOUT THE INCIDENT!
SIIIGH
ふー…
WHAT SHOULD I DO IF I REALLY AM FIRED?
SHOULD I LOOK FOR ANOTHER PLACE TO WORK?
...
I USED TO THINK I'D BE FINE WORKING AT ANY OLD BOOKSTORE AS LONG AS THEY'D LET A GOAT IN.
BUT NOW...

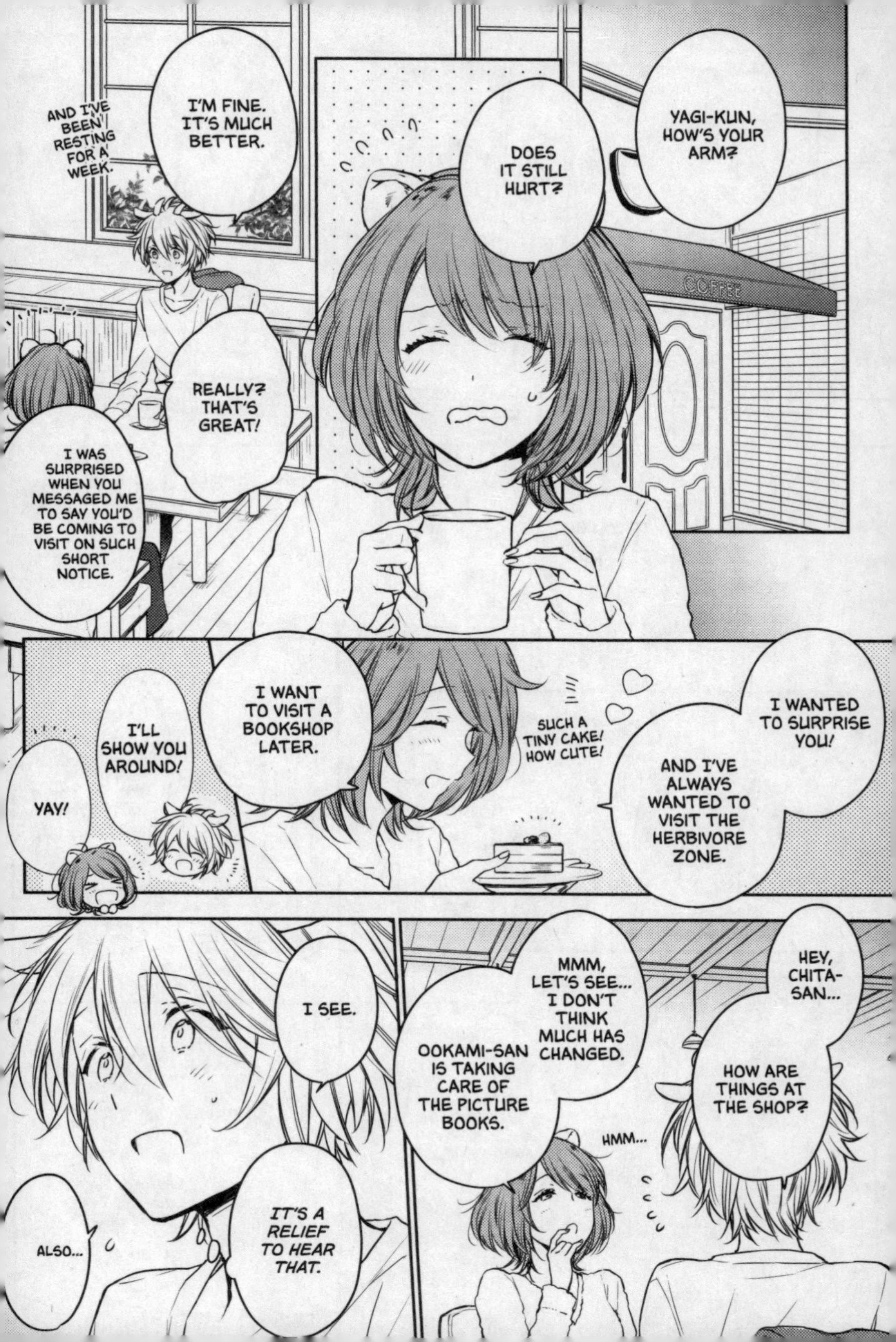
YAGI-KUN, HOW'S YOUR ARM?
DOES IT STILL HURT?
I'M FINE. IT'S MUCH BETTER.
AND I'VE BEEN RESTING FOR A WEEK.
COFFEE
REALLY? THAT'S GREAT!
I WAS SURPRISED WHEN YOU MESSAGED ME TO SAY YOU'D BE COMING TO VISIT ON SUCH SHORT NOTICE.
I WANTED TO SURPRISE YOU!
AND I'VE ALWAYS WANTED TO VISIT THE HERBIVORE ZONE.
SUCH A TINY CAKE! HOW CUTE!
I WANT TO VISIT A BOOKSHOP LATER.
I'LL SHOW YOU AROUND!
YAY!
HEY, CHITA-SAN...
HOW ARE THINGS AT THE SHOP?
HMM...
MMM, LET'S SEE... I DON'T THINK MUCH HAS CHANGED.
OOKAMI-SAN IS TAKING CARE OF THE PICTURE BOOKS.
I SEE.
IT'S A RELIEF TO HEAR THAT.
ALSO...

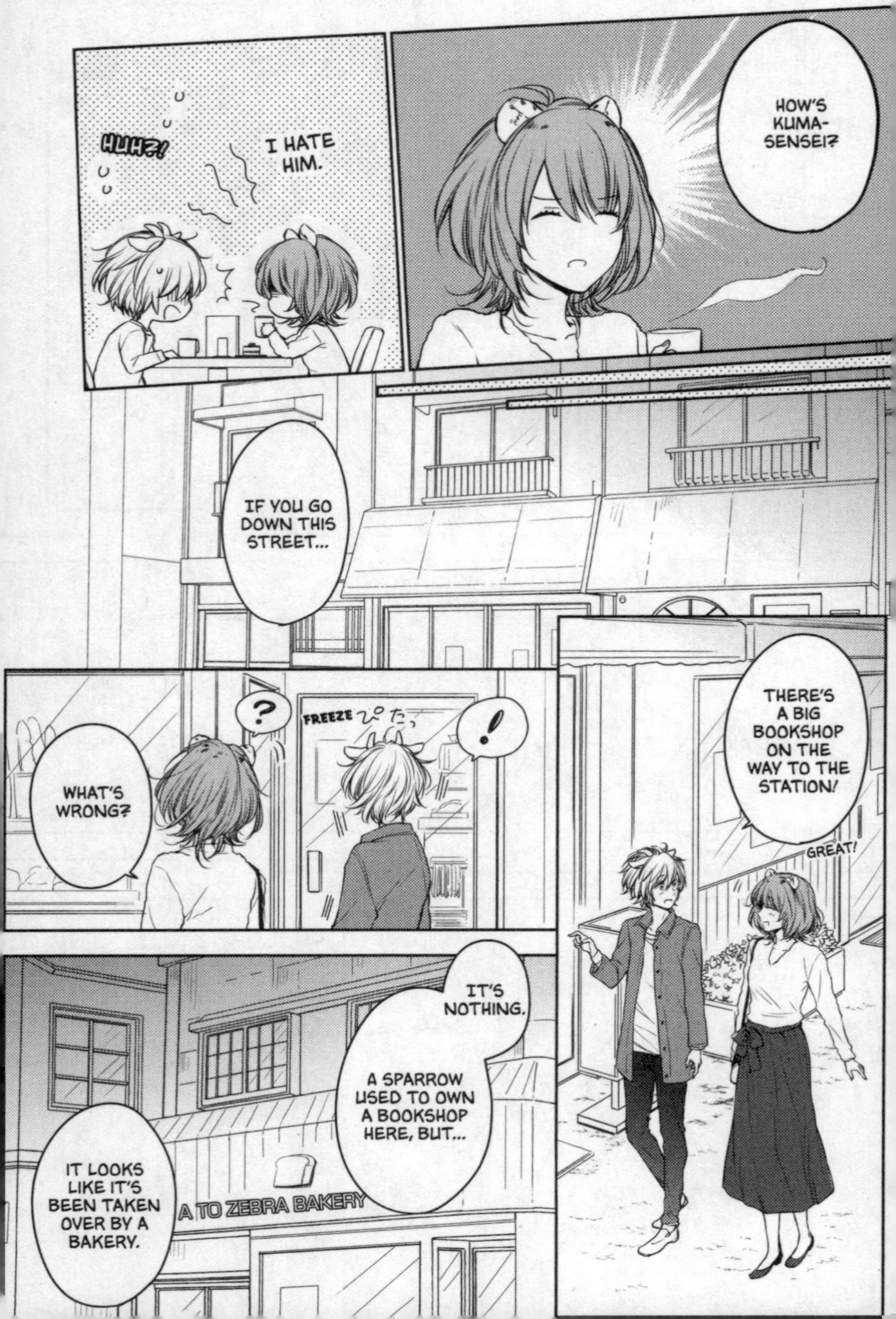
HOW'S KUMA-SENSEI?
I HATE HIM.
HUH?!
IF YOU GO DOWN THIS STREET...
THERE'S A BIG BOOKSHOP ON THE WAY TO THE STATION!
GREAT!
!
FREEZE ぴたっ
?
WHAT'S WRONG?
IT'S NOTHING.
A SPARROW USED TO OWN A BOOKSHOP HERE, BUT...
IT LOOKS LIKE IT'S BEEN TAKEN OVER BY A BAKERY.
A TO ZEBRA BAKERY

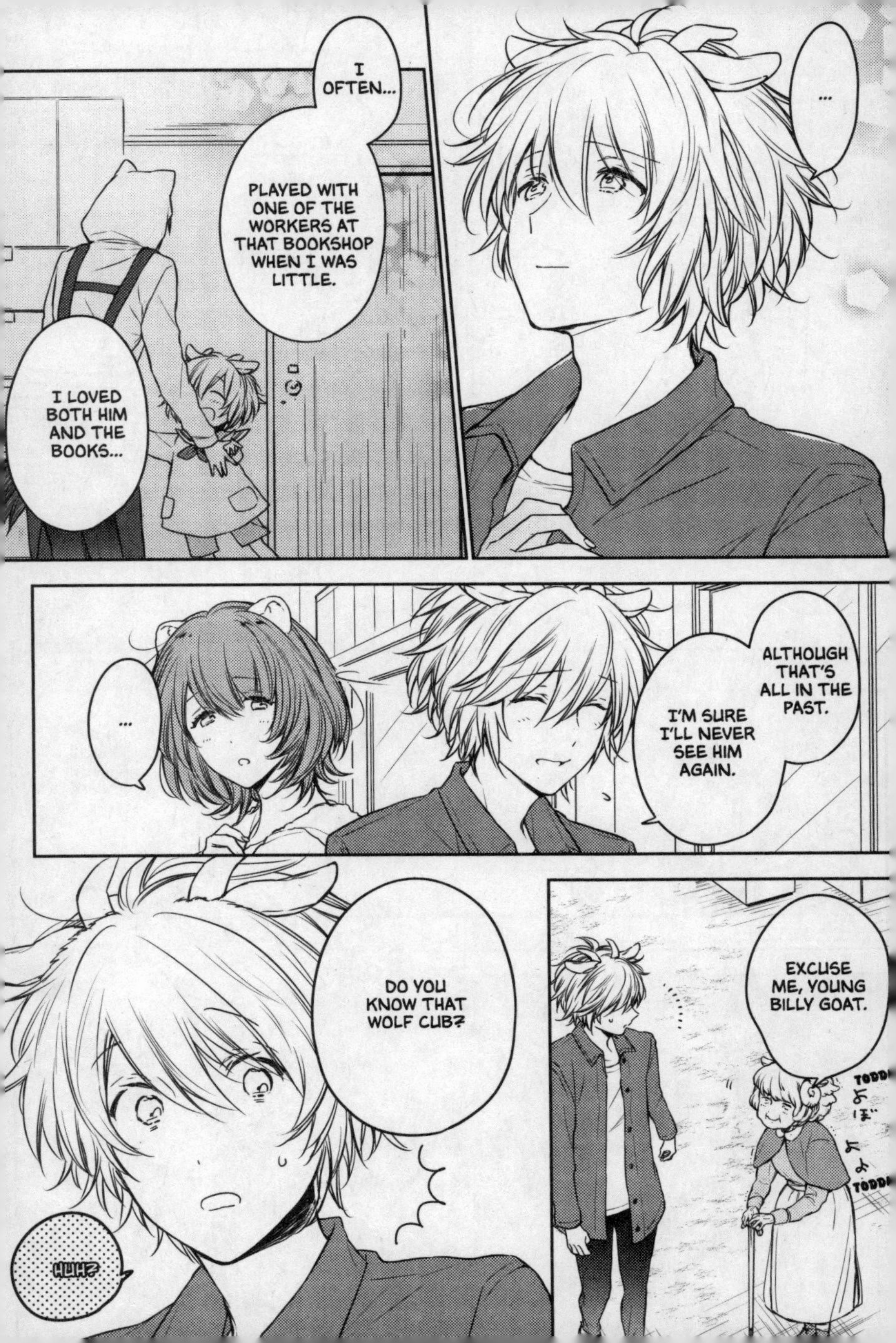
...
I OFTEN...
PLAYED WITH ONE OF THE WORKERS AT THAT BOOKSHOP WHEN I WAS LITTLE.
I LOVED BOTH HIM AND THE BOOKS...
ALTHOUGH THAT'S ALL IN THE PAST.
I'M SURE I'LL NEVER SEE HIM AGAIN.
...
EXCUSE ME, YOUNG BILLY GOAT.
DO YOU KNOW THAT WOLF CUB?
HUH?

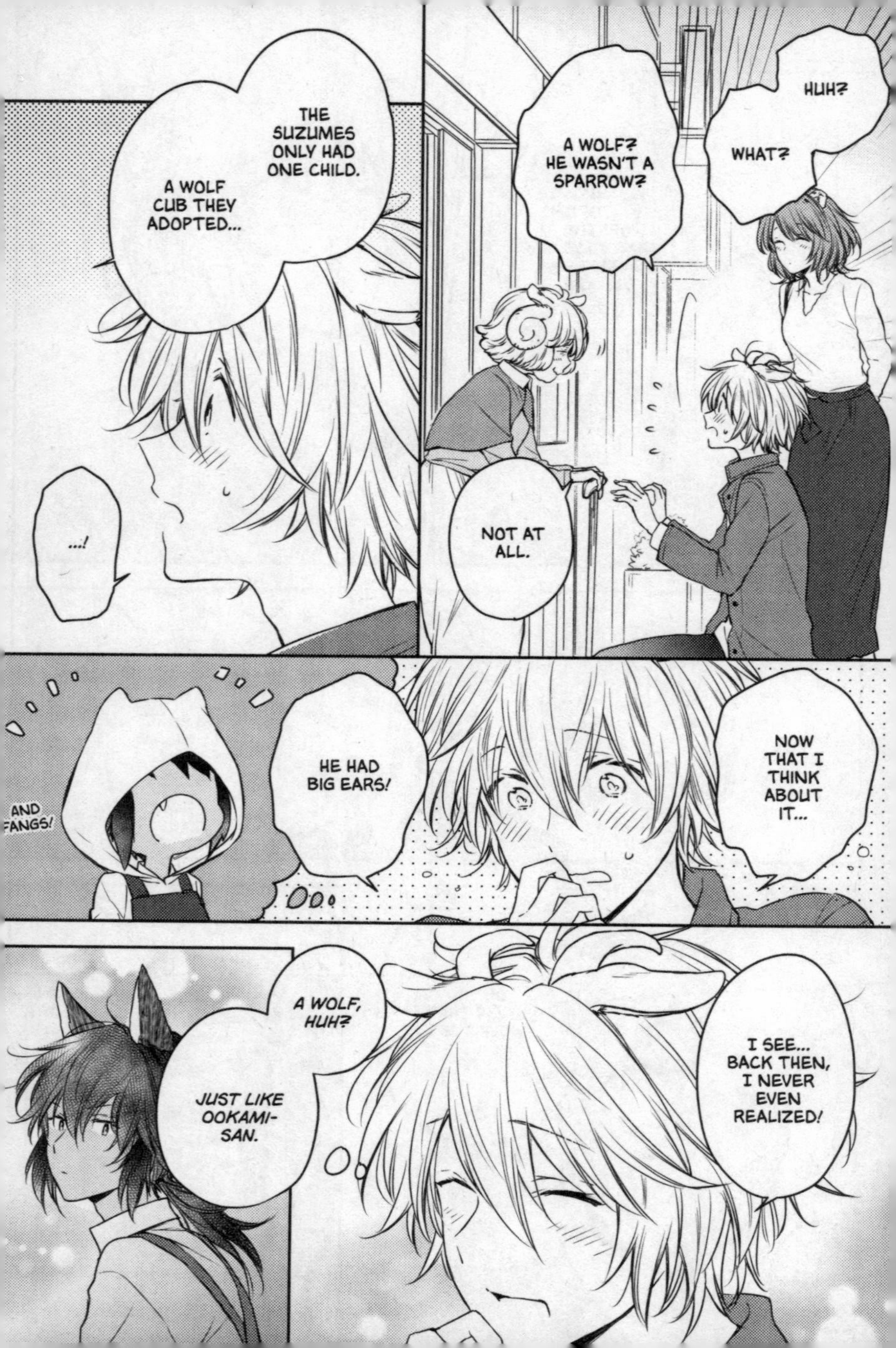
HUH?
WHAT?
A WOLF? HE WASN'T A SPARROW?
NOT AT ALL.
THE SUZUMES ONLY HAD ONE CHILD.
A WOLF CUB THEY ADOPTED...
...!
NOW THAT I THINK ABOUT IT...
HE HAD BIG EARS!
AND FANGS!
I SEE... BACK THEN, I NEVER EVEN REALIZED!
A WOLF, HUH?
JUST LIKE OOKAMI-SAN.

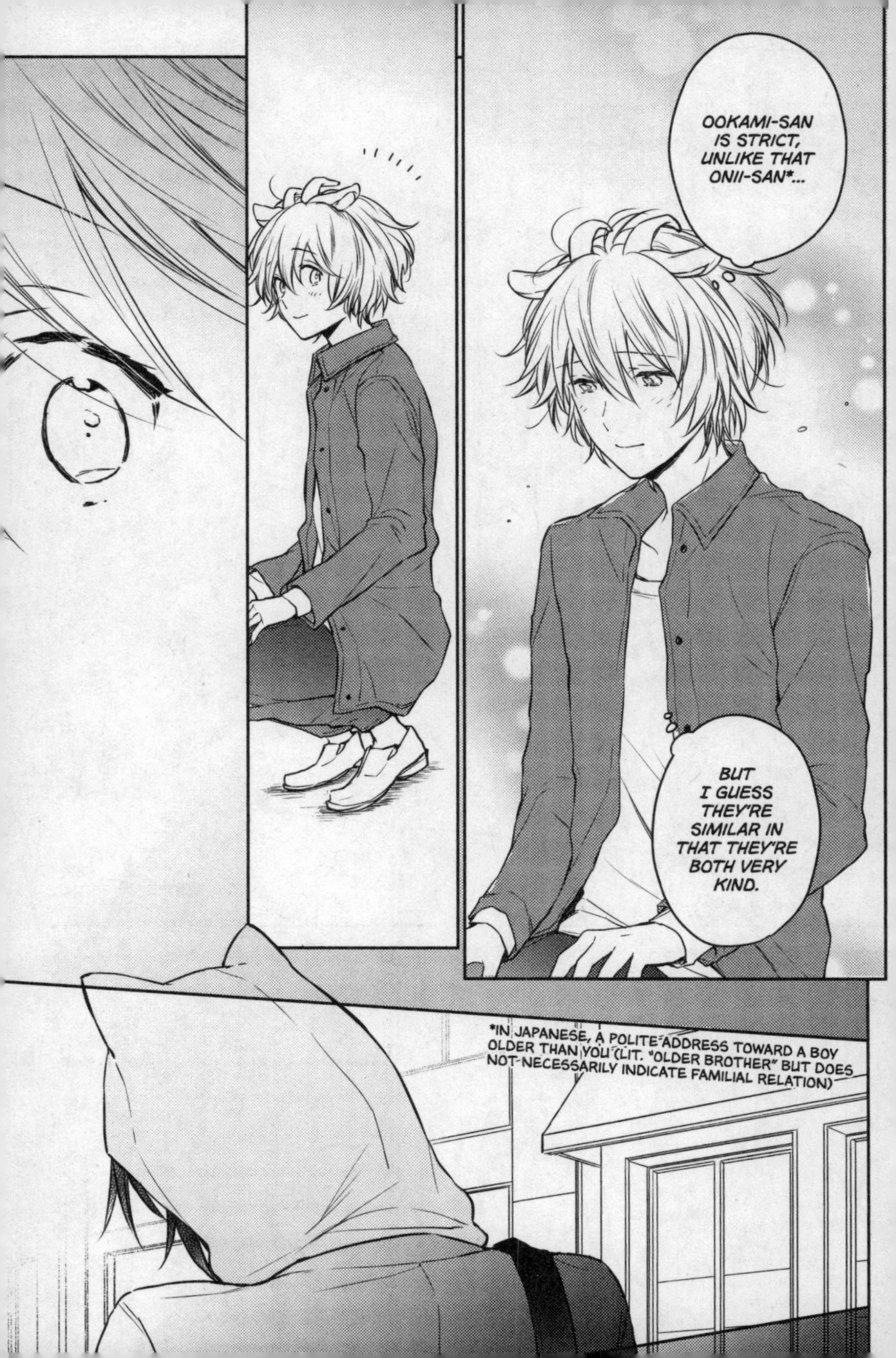
OOKAMI-SAN IS STRICT, UNLIKE THAT ONII-SAN*...
BUT I GUESS THEY'RE SIMILAR IN THAT THEY'RE BOTH VERY KIND.
*IN JAPANESE, A POLITE ADDRESS TOWARD A BOY OLDER THAN YOU (LIT. "OLDER BROTHER" BUT DOES NOT NECESSARILY INDICATE FAMILIAL RELATION)

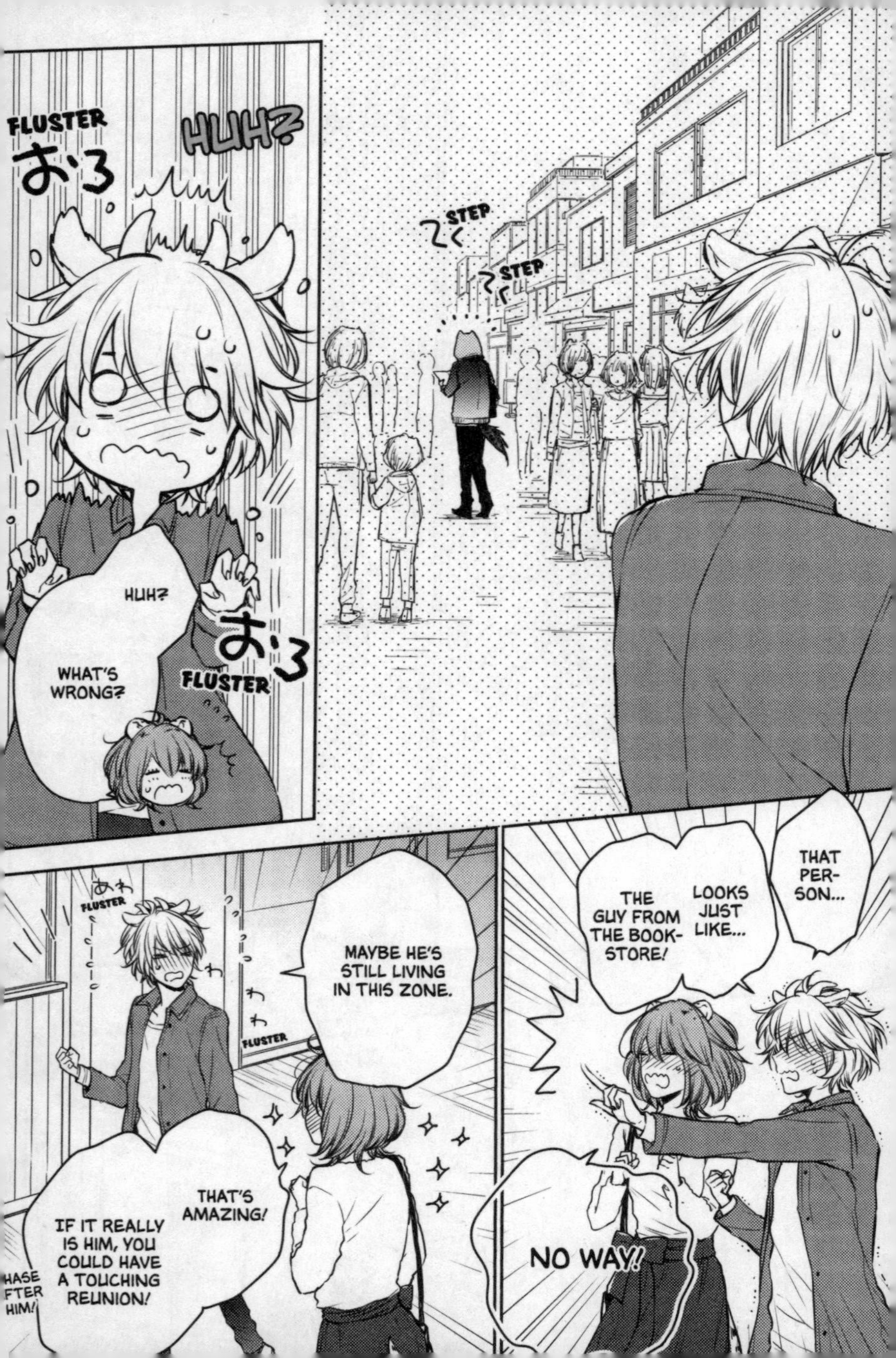
STEP
てく
STEP
てく
FLUSTER
おろ
HUH?
HUH?
WHAT'S WRONG?
おろ
FLUSTER
THAT PERSON...
LOOKS JUST LIKE...
THE GUY FROM THE BOOKSTORE!
NO WAY!
あわ
FLUSTER
わ
わ
FLUSTER
MAYBE HE'S STILL LIVING IN THIS ZONE.
THAT'S AMAZING!
IF IT REALLY IS HIM, YOU COULD HAVE A TOUCHING REUNION!
HASE FTER HIM!

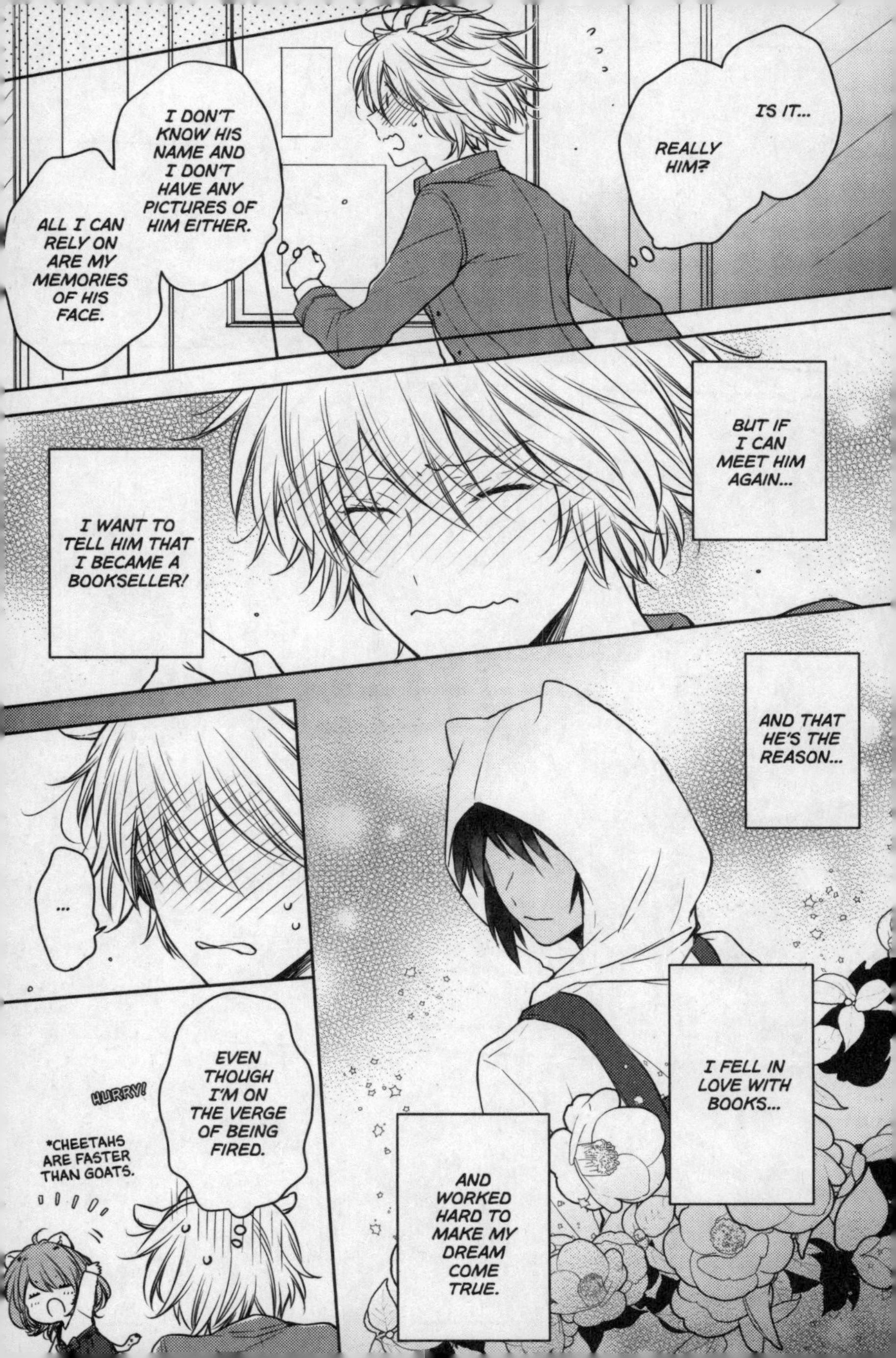
IS IT... REALLY HIM?
I DON'T KNOW HIS NAME AND I DON'T HAVE ANY PICTURES OF HIM EITHER.
ALL I CAN RELY ON ARE MY MEMORIES OF HIS FACE.
BUT IF I CAN MEET HIM AGAIN...
I WANT TO TELL HIM THAT I BECAME A BOOKSELLER!
AND THAT HE'S THE REASON...
I FELL IN LOVE WITH BOOKS...
AND WORKED HARD TO MAKE MY DREAM COME TRUE.
...
EVEN THOUGH I'M ON THE VERGE OF BEING FIRED.
HURRY!
*CHEETAHS ARE FASTER THAN GOATS.

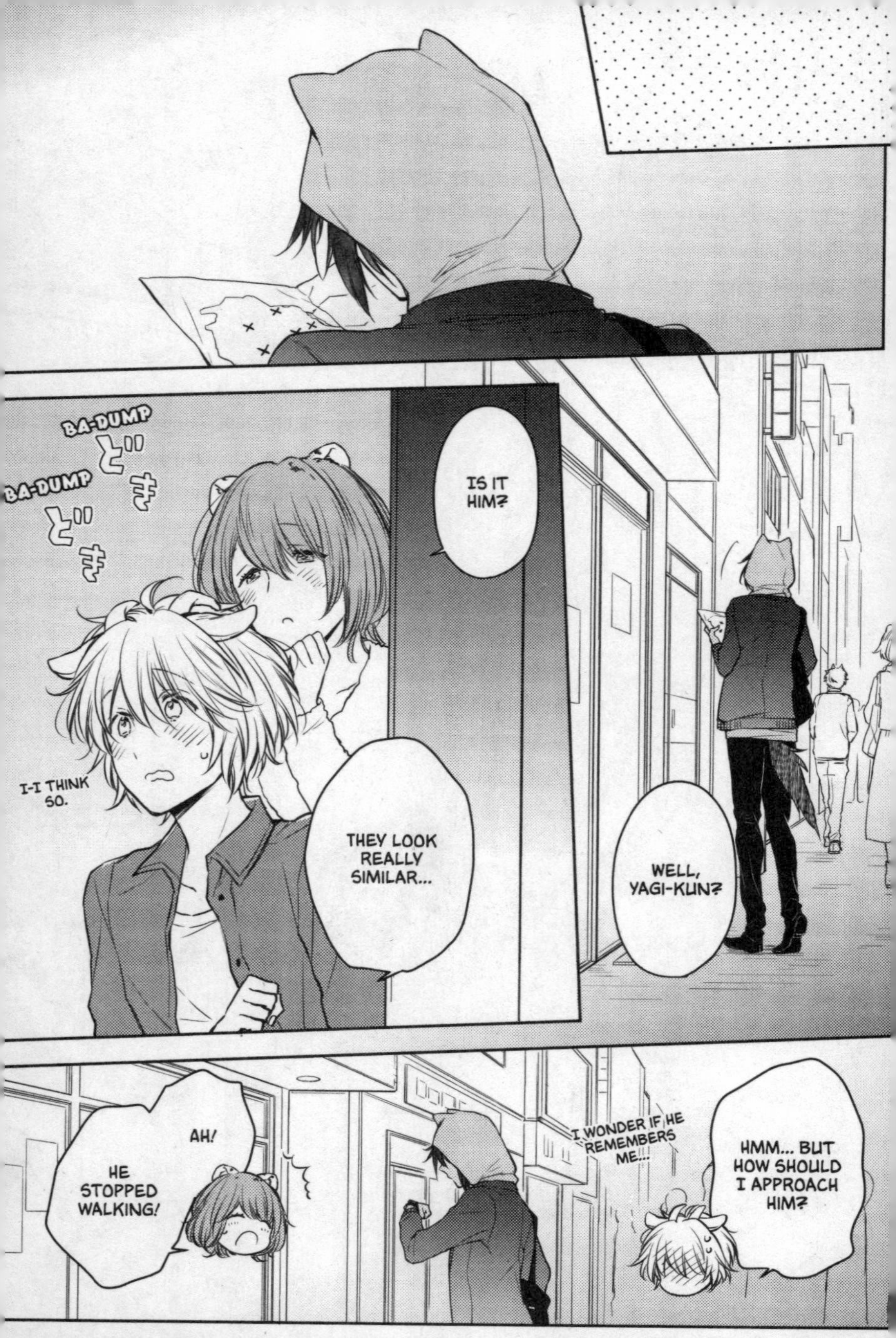
WELL, YAGI-KUN?
IS IT HIM?
THEY LOOK REALLY SIMILAR...
I-I THINK SO.
BA-DUMP どき
BA-DUMP どき
HMM... BUT HOW SHOULD I APPROACH HIM?
I WONDER IF HE REMEMBERS ME!!
AH!
HE STOPPED WALKING!

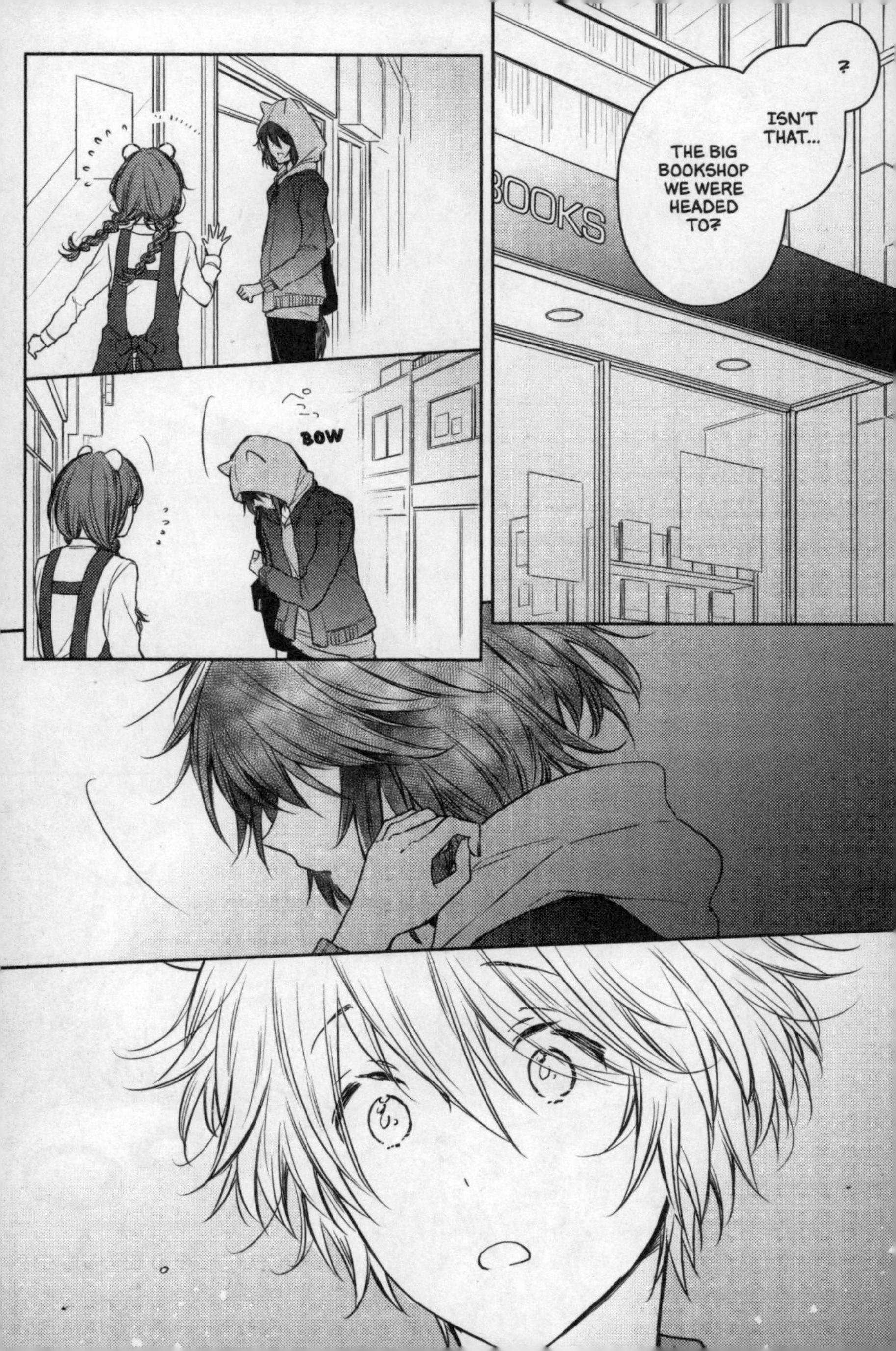
?
ISN'T THAT...
THE BIG BOOKSHOP WE WERE HEADED TO?
BOOKS
BOW

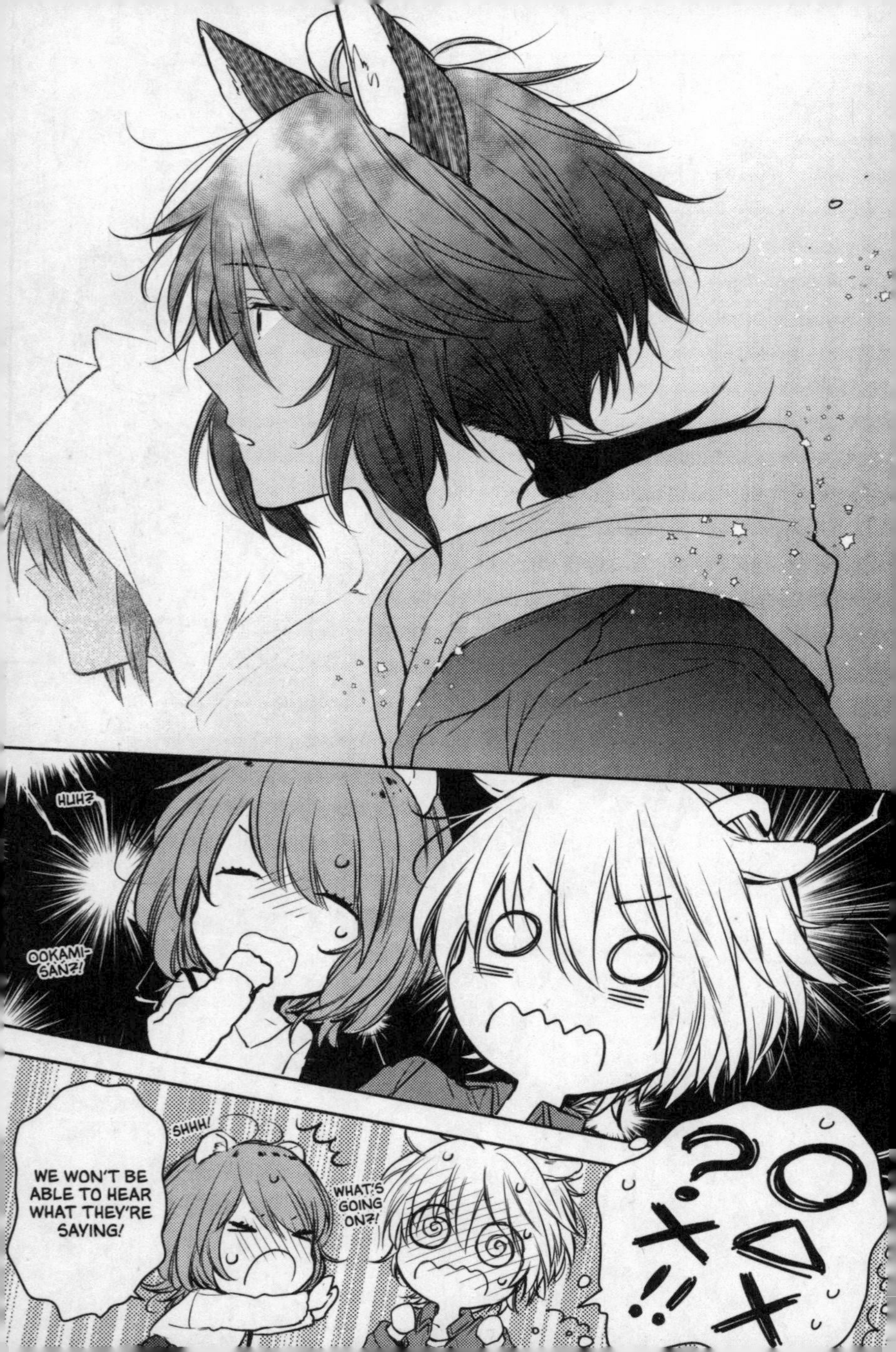
HUH?
OOKAMI-SAN?!
?○×△×!!
WHAT'S GOING ON?!
SHHH!
WE WON'T BE ABLE TO HEAR WHAT THEY'RE SAYING!

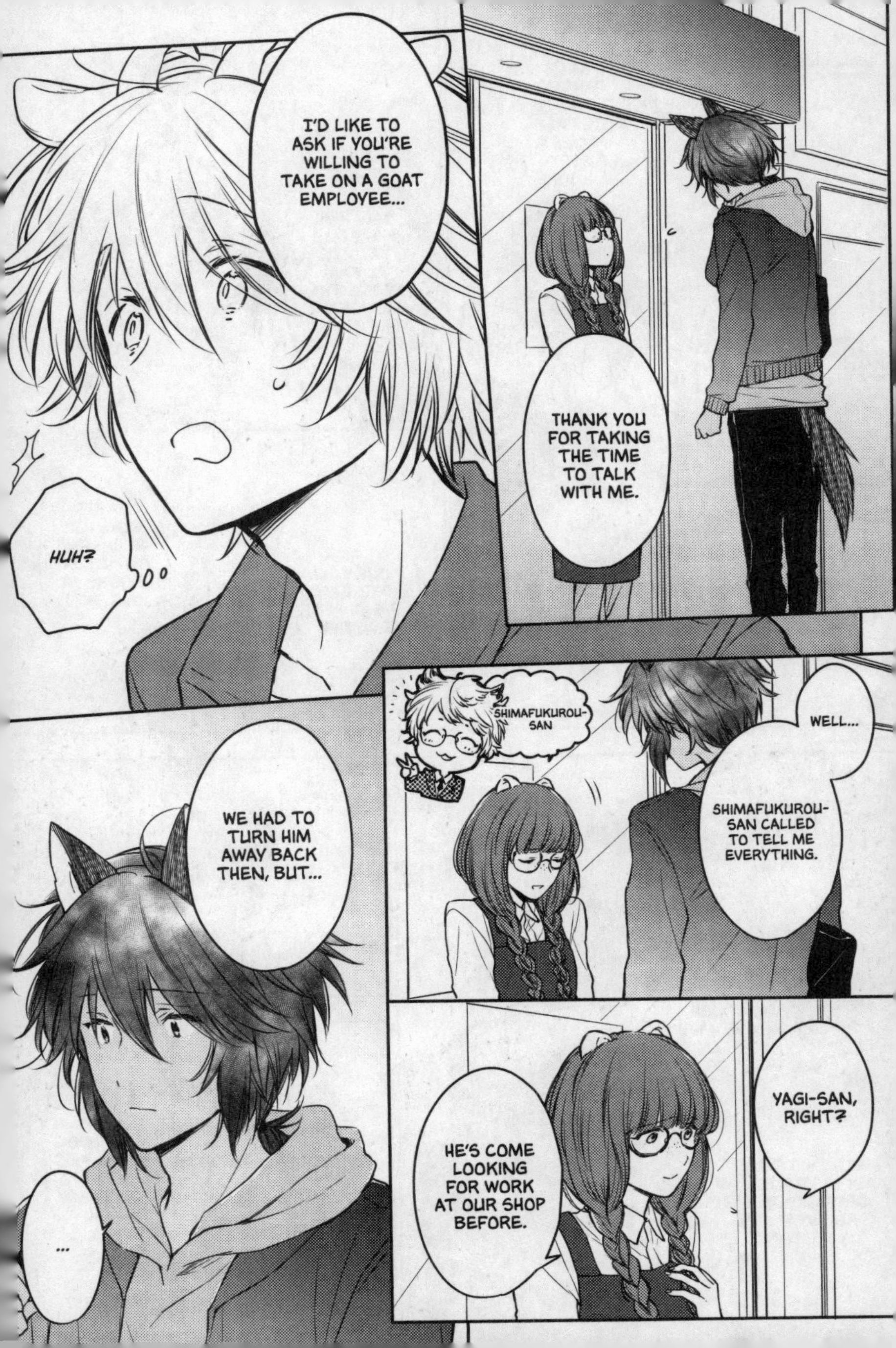
THANK YOU FOR TAKING THE TIME TO TALK WITH ME.
I'D LIKE TO ASK IF YOU'RE WILLING TO TAKE ON A GOAT EMPLOYEE...
HUH?
WELL...
SHIMAFUKUROU-SAN CALLED TO TELL ME EVERYTHING.
SHIMAFUKUROU-SAN
YAGI-SAN, RIGHT?
HE'S COME LOOKING FOR WORK AT OUR SHOP BEFORE.
WE HAD TO TURN HIM AWAY BACK THEN, BUT...
...

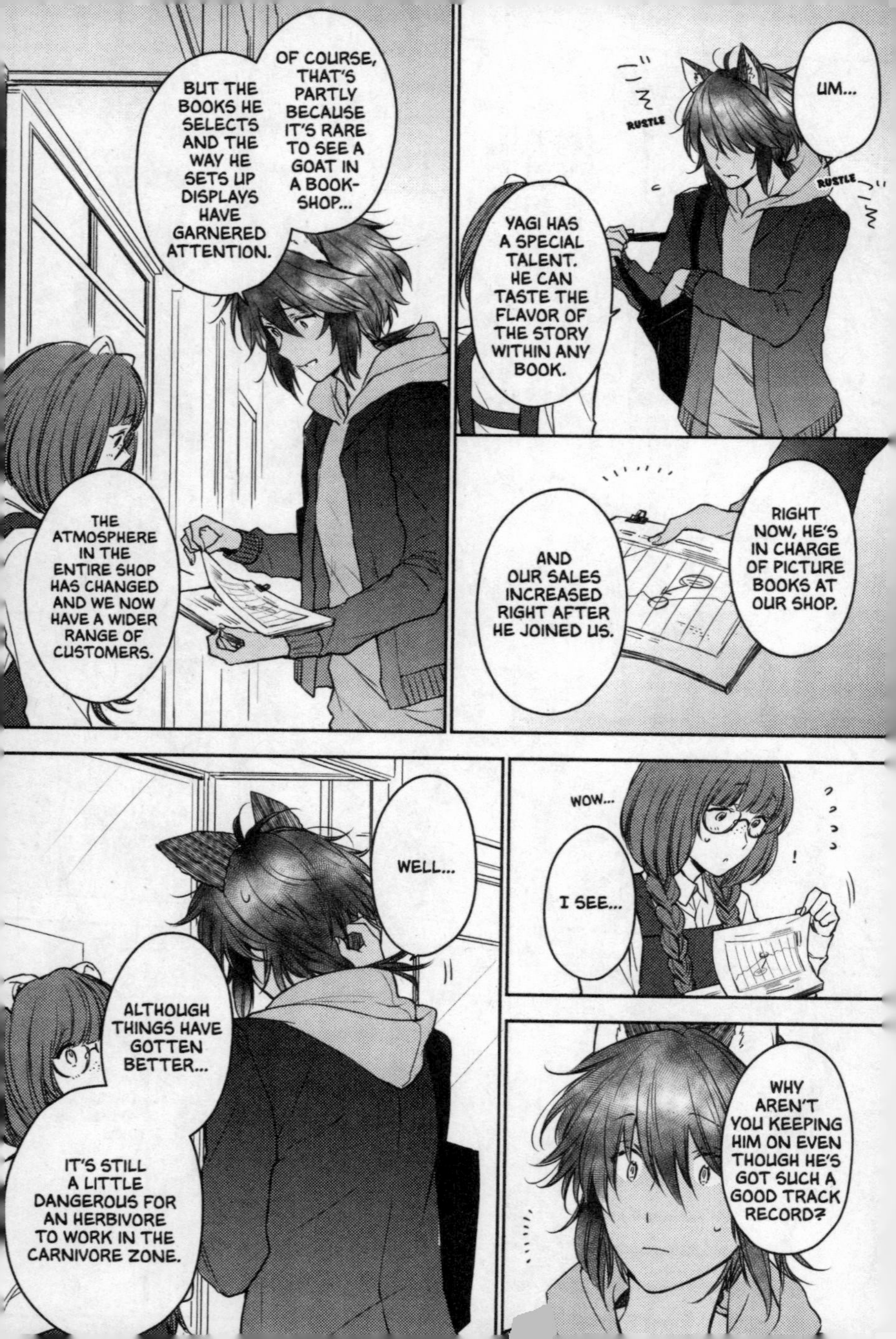
UM...
RUSTLE
RUSTLE
YAGI HAS A SPECIAL TALENT. HE CAN TASTE THE FLAVOR OF THE STORY WITHIN ANY BOOK.
RIGHT NOW, HE'S IN CHARGE OF PICTURE BOOKS AT OUR SHOP.
AND OUR SALES INCREASED RIGHT AFTER HE JOINED US.
OF COURSE, THAT'S PARTLY BECAUSE IT'S RARE TO SEE A GOAT IN A BOOK-SHOP...
BUT THE BOOKS HE SELECTS AND THE WAY HE SETS UP DISPLAYS HAVE GARNERED ATTENTION.
THE ATMOSPHERE IN THE ENTIRE SHOP HAS CHANGED AND WE NOW HAVE A WIDER RANGE OF CUSTOMERS.
WOW...
I SEE...
WHY AREN'T YOU KEEPING HIM ON EVEN THOUGH HE'S GOT SUCH A GOOD TRACK RECORD?
WELL...
ALTHOUGH THINGS HAVE GOTTEN BETTER...
IT'S STILL A LITTLE DANGEROUS FOR AN HERBIVORE TO WORK IN THE CARNIVORE ZONE.

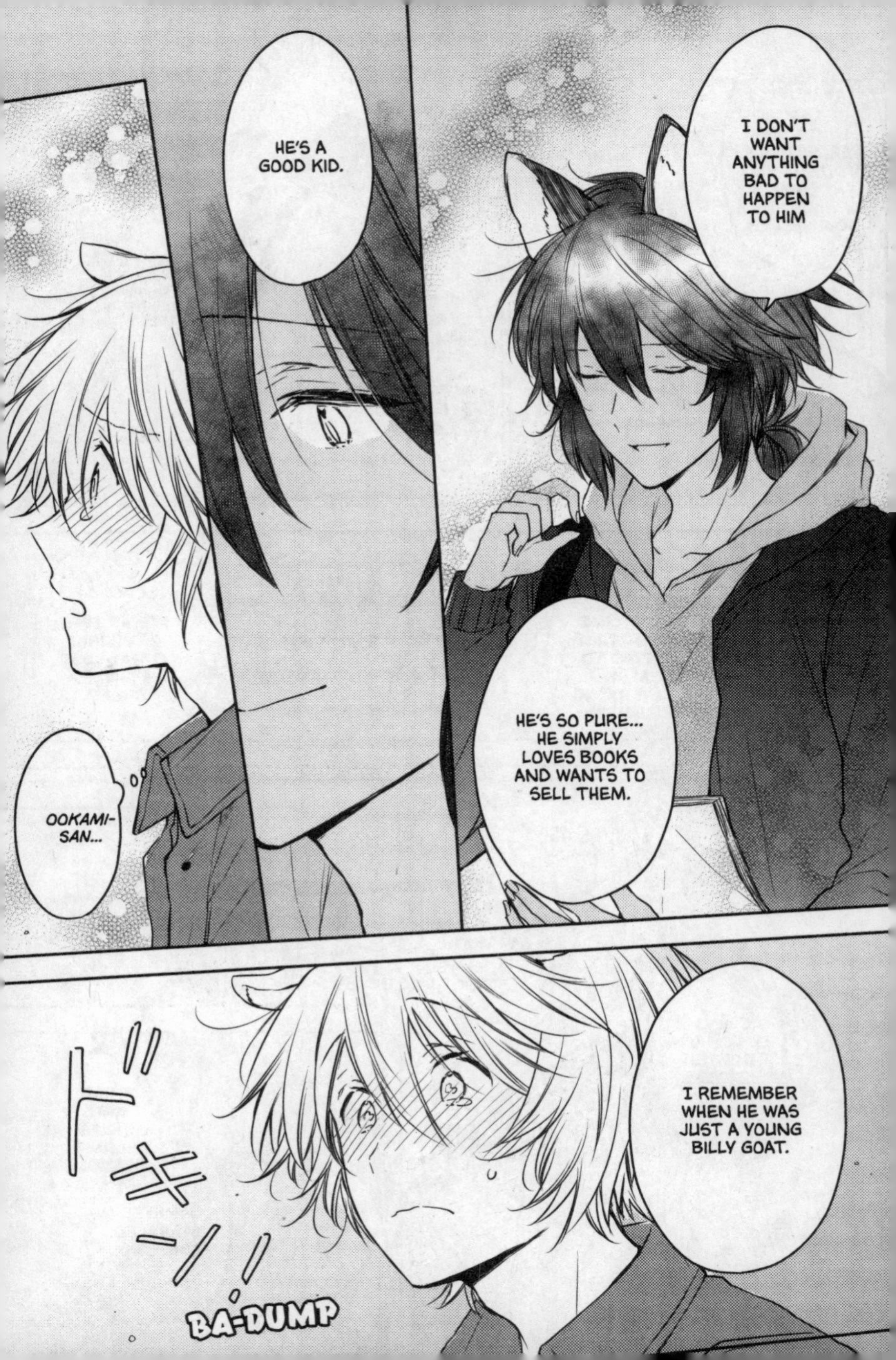
I DON'T WANT ANYTHING BAD TO HAPPEN TO HIM
HE'S SO PURE... HE SIMPLY LOVES BOOKS AND WANTS TO SELL THEM.
HE'S A GOOD KID.
OOKAMI-SAN...
I REMEMBER WHEN HE WAS JUST A YOUNG BILLY GOAT.
ドキーン!!
BA-DUMP

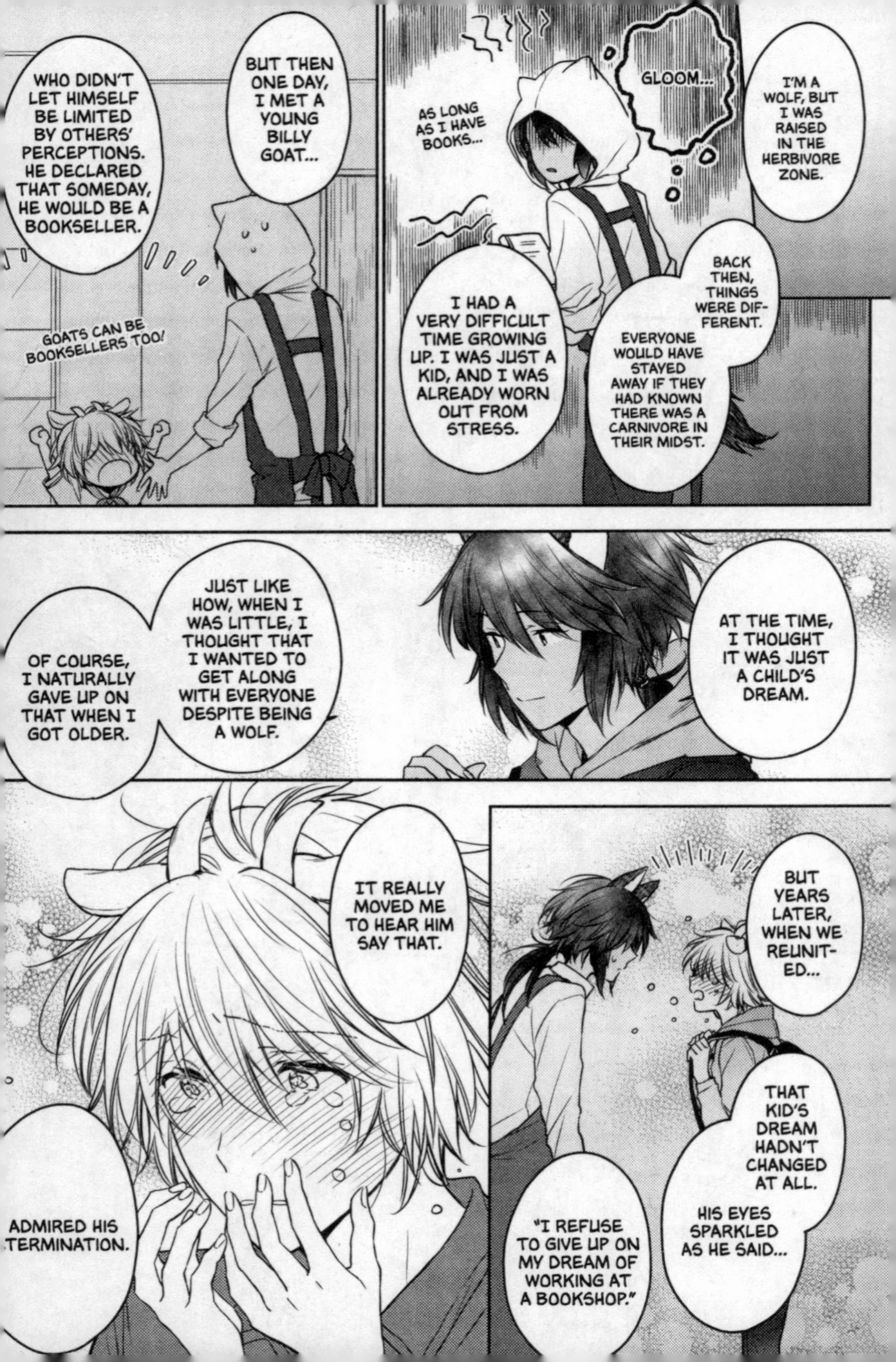
I'M A WOLF, BUT I WAS RAISED IN THE HERBIVORE ZONE.
GLOOM...
AS LONG AS I HAVE BOOKS...
BACK THEN, THINGS WERE DIF-FERENT.
EVERYONE WOULD HAVE STAYED AWAY IF THEY HAD KNOWN THERE WAS A CARNIVORE IN THEIR MIDST.
I HAD A VERY DIFFICULT TIME GROWING UP. I WAS JUST A KID, AND I WAS ALREADY WORN OUT FROM STRESS.
BUT THEN ONE DAY, I MET A YOUNG BILLY GOAT...
WHO DIDN'T LET HIMSELF BE LIMITED BY OTHERS' PERCEPTIONS. HE DECLARED THAT SOMEDAY, HE WOULD BE A BOOKSELLER.
GOATS CAN BE BOOKSELLERS TOO!
AT THE TIME, I THOUGHT IT WAS JUST A CHILD'S DREAM.
JUST LIKE HOW, WHEN I WAS LITTLE, I THOUGHT THAT I WANTED TO GET ALONG WITH EVERYONE DESPITE BEING A WOLF.
OF COURSE, I NATURALLY GAVE UP ON THAT WHEN I GOT OLDER.
BUT YEARS LATER, WHEN WE REUNIT-ED...
THAT KID'S DREAM HADN'T CHANGED AT ALL.
HIS EYES SPARKLED AS HE SAID...
"I REFUSE TO GIVE UP ON MY DREAM OF WORKING AT A BOOKSHOP."
IT REALLY MOVED ME TO HEAR HIM SAY THAT.
ADMIRED HIS TERMINATION.

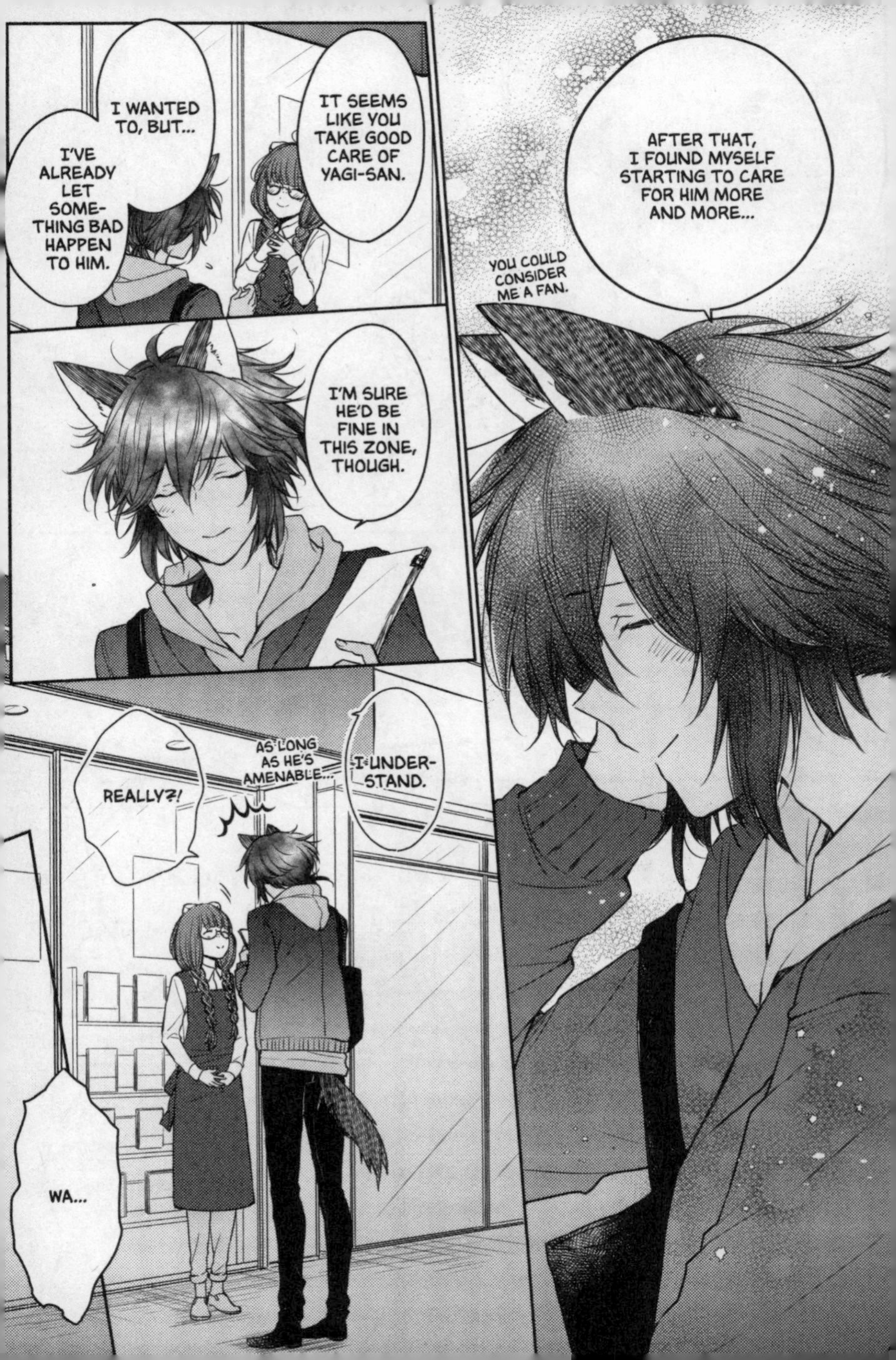
AFTER THAT, I FOUND MYSELF STARTING TO CARE FOR HIM MORE AND MORE...
YOU COULD CONSIDER ME A FAN.
IT SEEMS LIKE YOU TAKE GOOD CARE OF YAGI-SAN.
I WANTED TO, BUT...
I'VE ALREADY LET SOME-THING BAD HAPPEN TO HIM.
I'M SURE HE'D BE FINE IN THIS ZONE, THOUGH.
I UNDER-STAND.
AS LONG AS HE'S AMENABLE...
REALLY?!
WA...

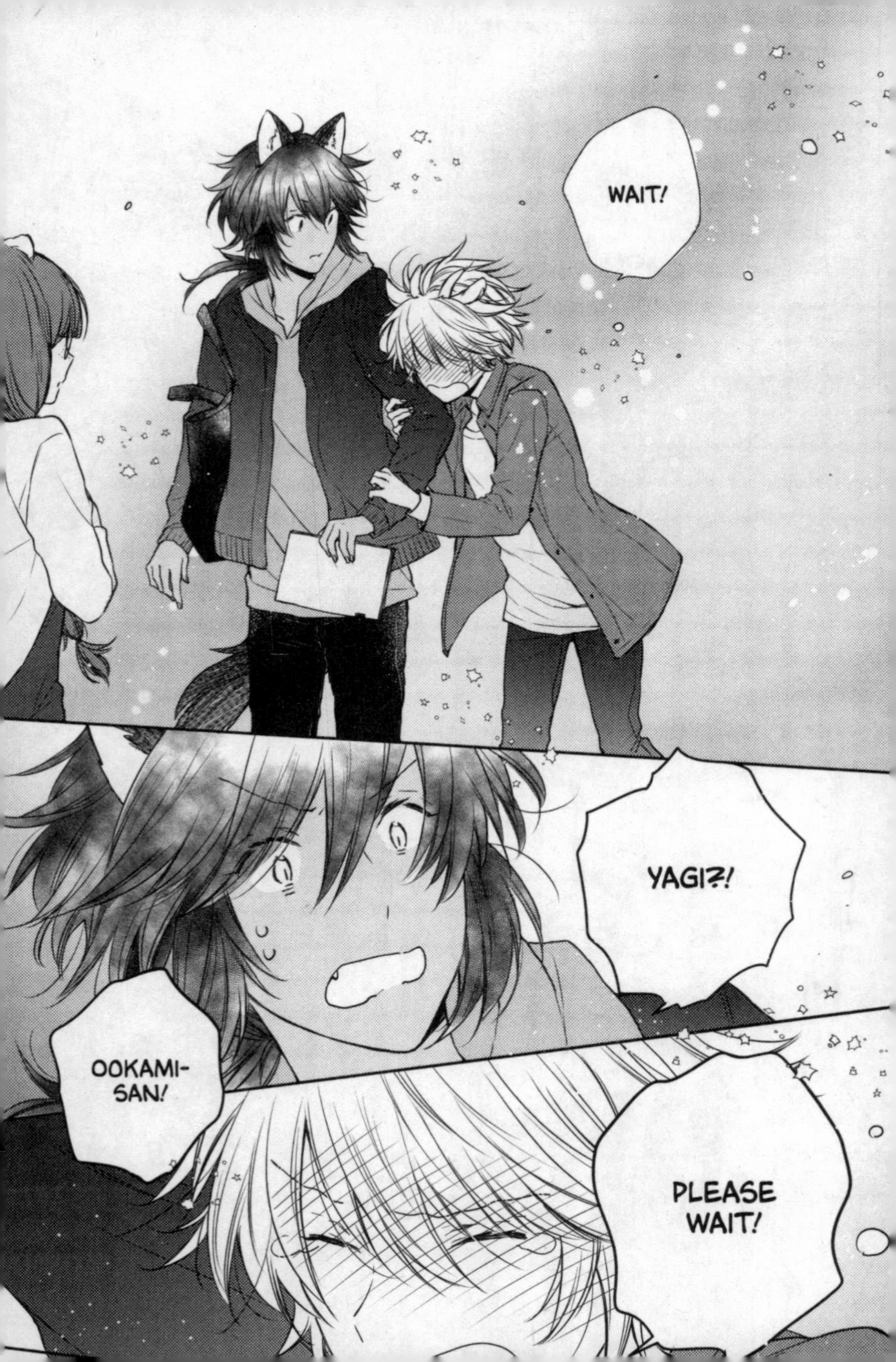
WAIT!
YAGI?!
OOKAMI-SAN!
PLEASE WAIT!

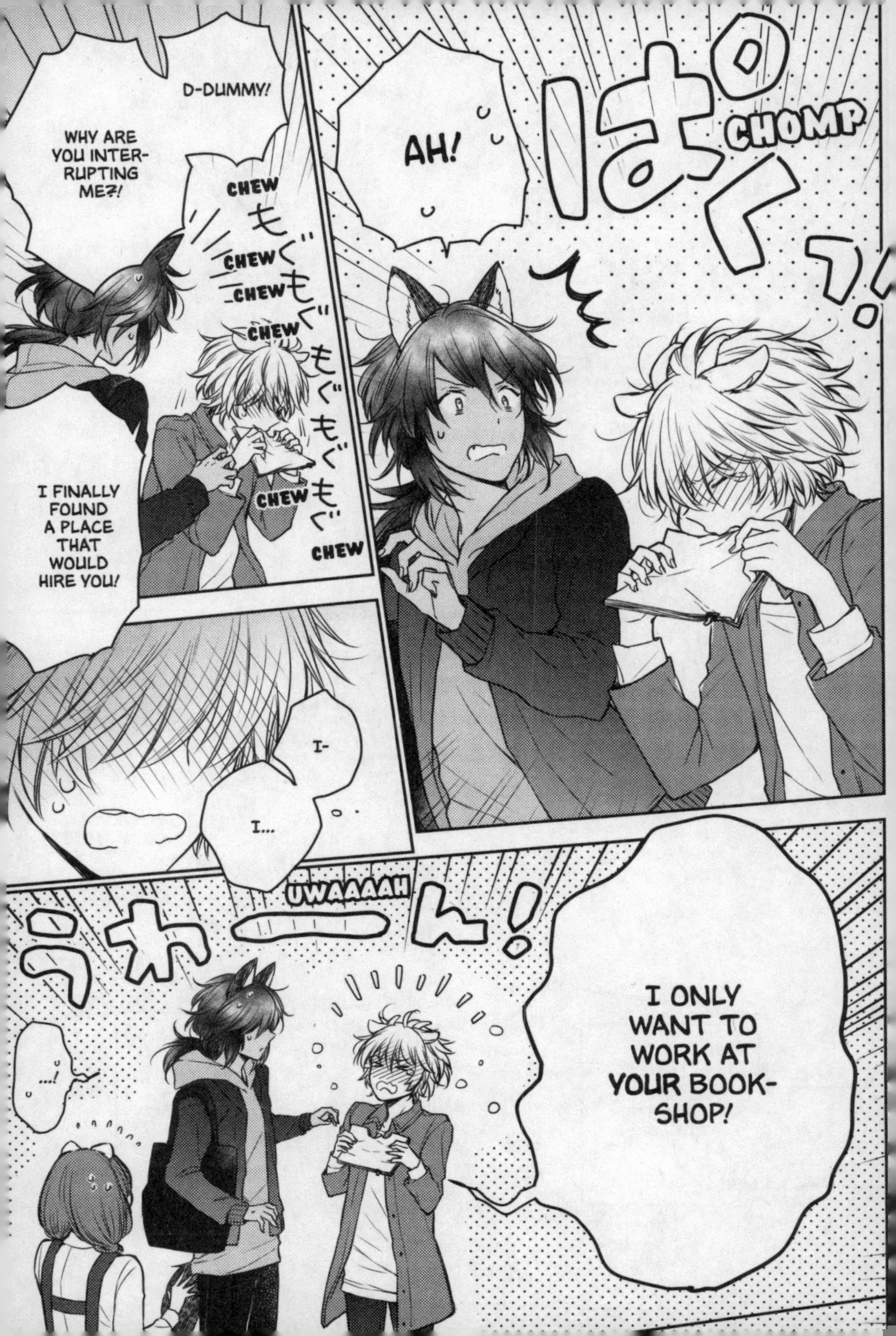
AH!
はぐっ!
CHOMP
D-DUMMY!
WHY ARE YOU INTER-RUPTING ME?!
CHEW もぐ CHEW CHEW もぐ CHEW もぐもぐもぐもぐ CHEW CHEW
I FINALLY FOUND A PLACE THAT WOULD HIRE YOU!
I-
I...
うわーーん!
UWAAAAH
I ONLY WANT TO WORK AT YOUR BOOK-SHOP!
...!

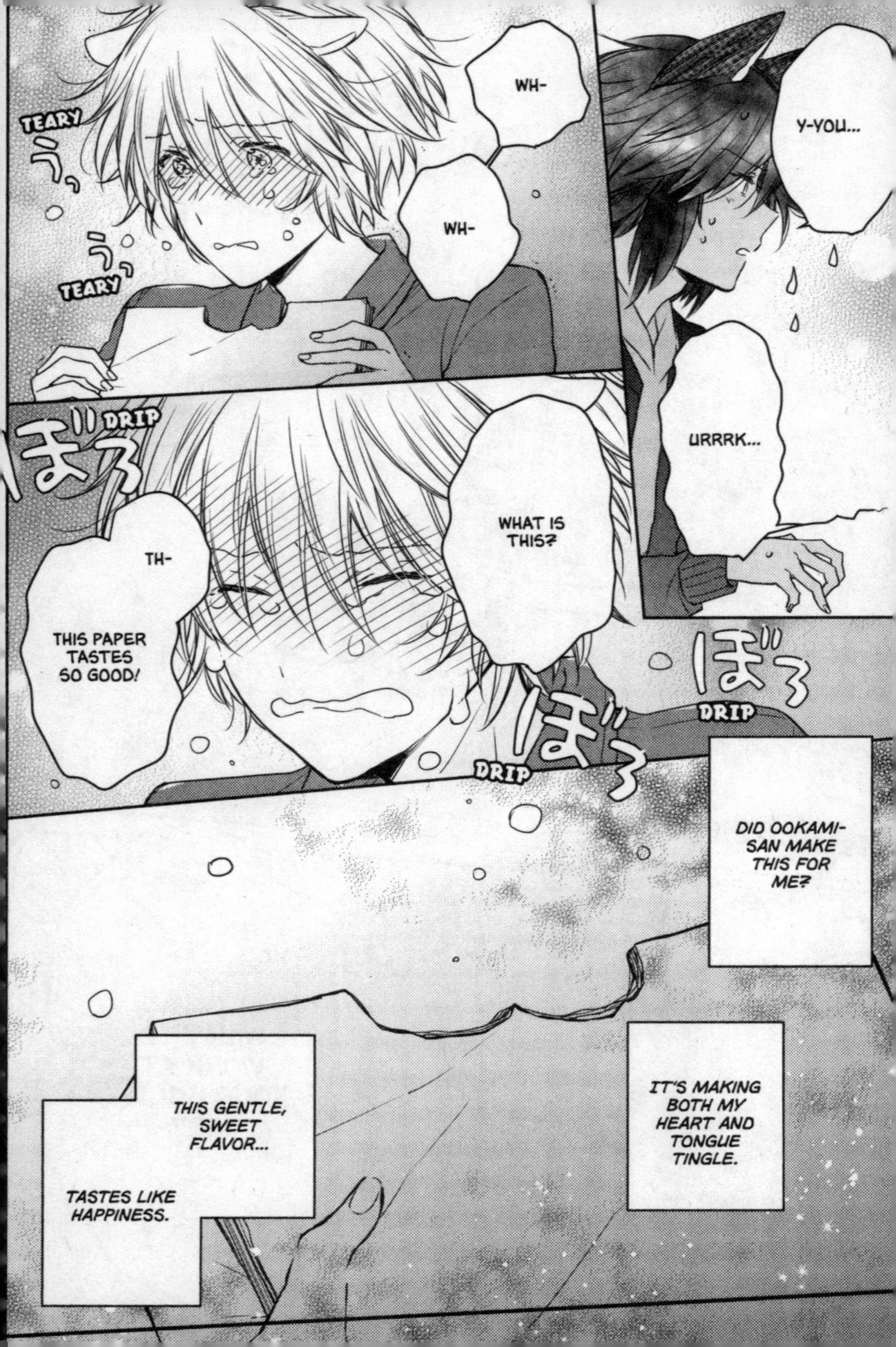
Y-YOU...
URRRK...
WH-
WH-
TEARY
う
TEARY
う
WHAT IS THIS?
ぽろ
DRIP
TH-
THIS PAPER TASTES SO GOOD!
ぽろ
DRIP
ぽろ
DRIP
DID OOKAMI-SAN MAKE THIS FOR ME?
IT'S MAKING BOTH MY HEART AND TONGUE TINGLE.
THIS GENTLE, SWEET FLAVOR...
TASTES LIKE HAPPINESS.

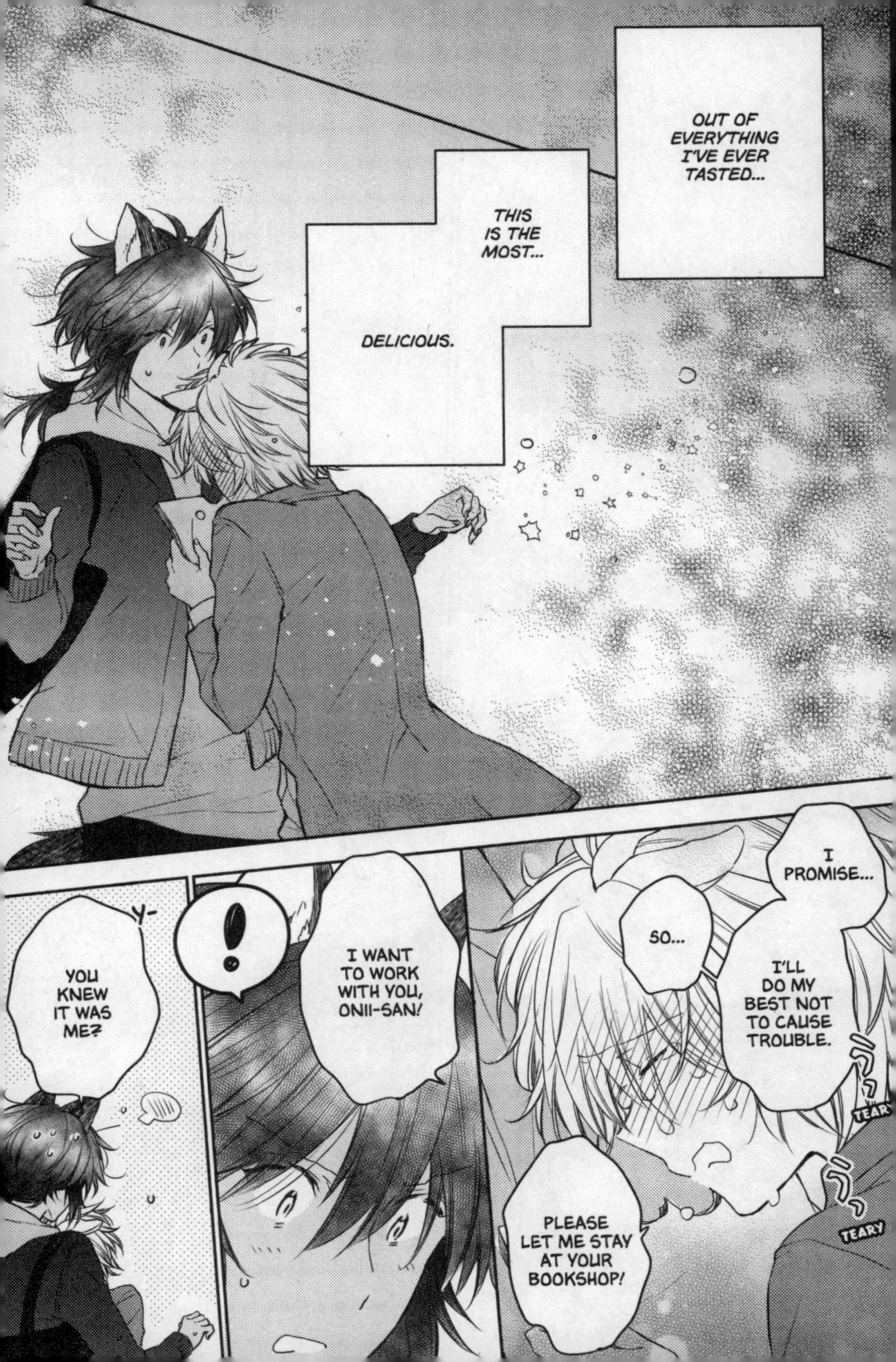
OUT OF EVERYTHING I'VE EVER TASTED...
THIS IS THE MOST...
DELICIOUS.
I PROMISE...
SO...
I'LL DO MY BEST NOT TO CAUSE TROUBLE.
TEAR
PLEASE LET ME STAY AT YOUR BOOKSHOP!
TEARY
!
I WANT TO WORK WITH YOU, ONII-SAN!
Y-
YOU KNEW IT WAS ME?

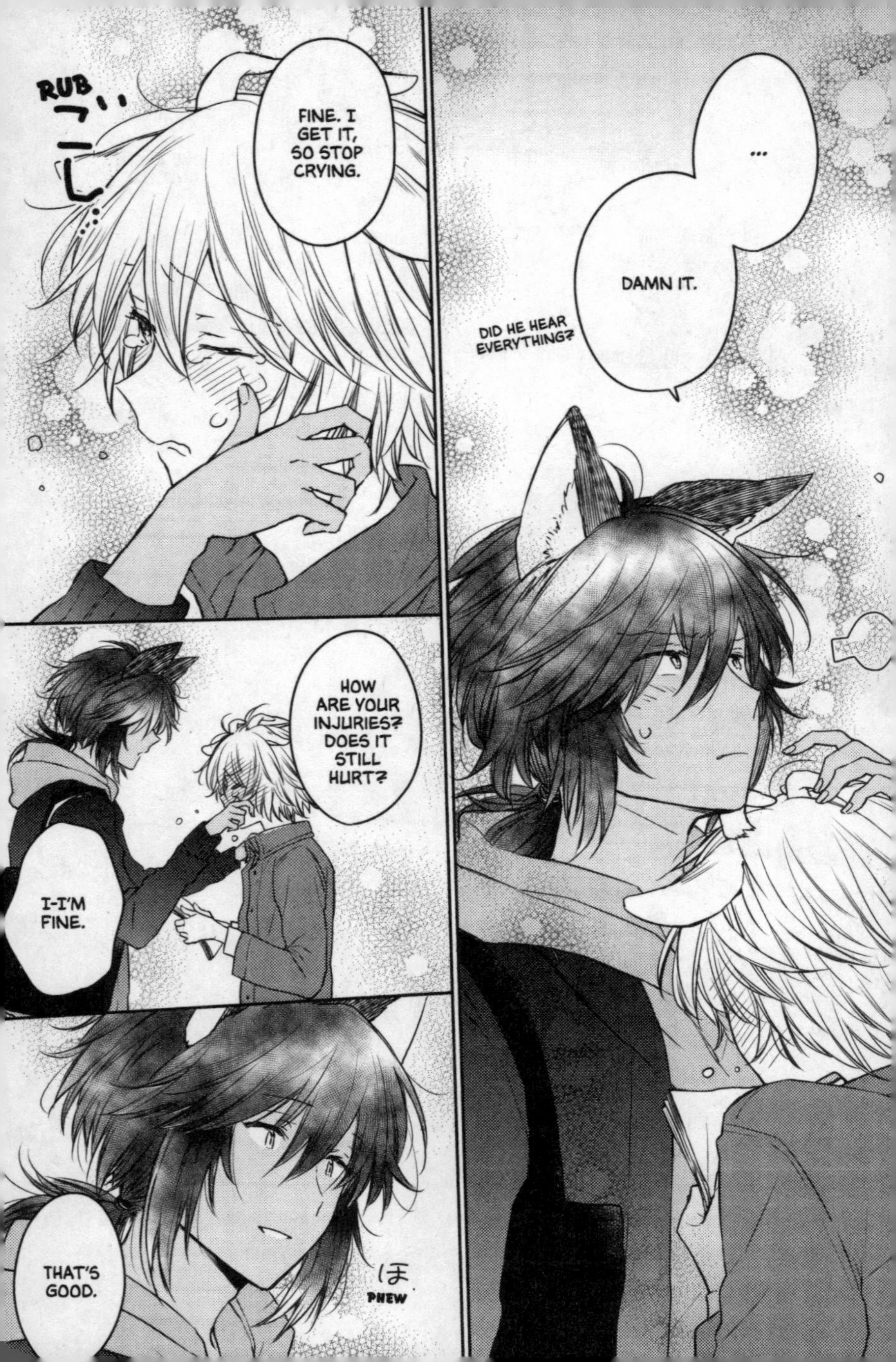
...
DAMN IT.
DID HE HEAR EVERYTHING?
RUB
FINE. I GET IT, SO STOP CRYING.
HOW ARE YOUR INJURIES? DOES IT STILL HURT?
I-I'M FINE.
ほ
PHEW
THAT'S GOOD.

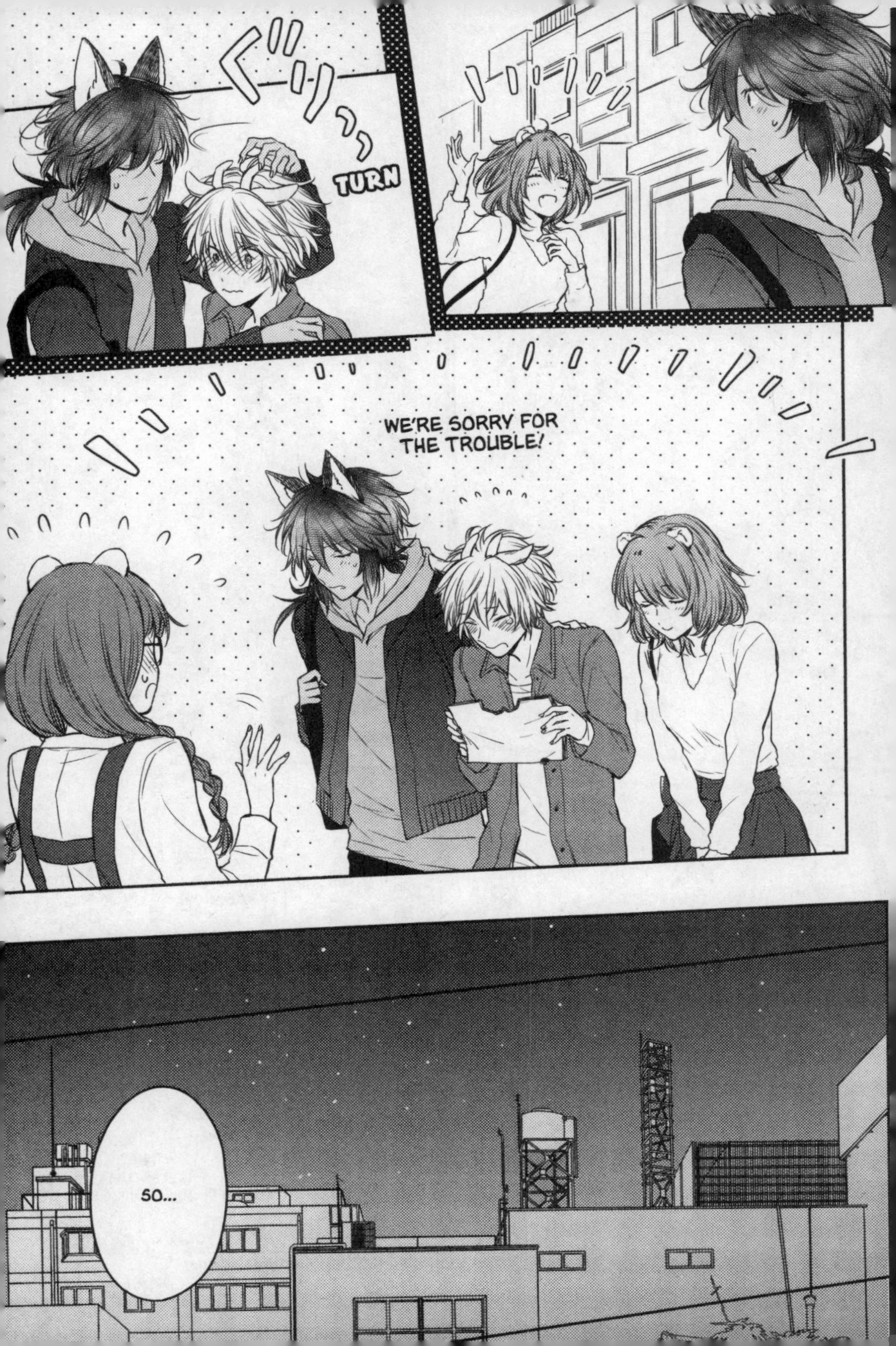
TURN
WE'RE SORRY FOR THE TROUBLE!
SO...

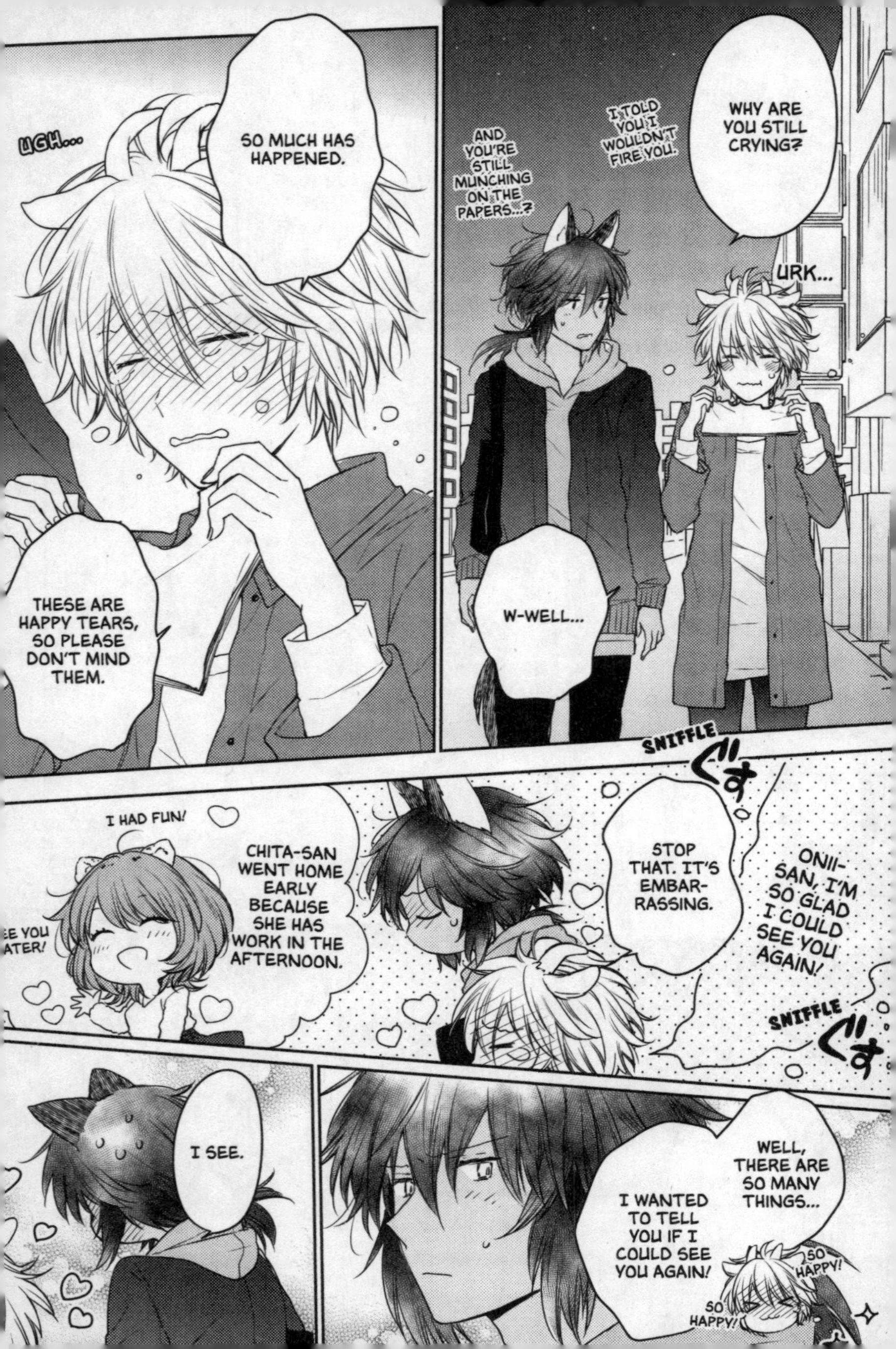
WHY ARE YOU STILL CRYING?
I TOLD YOU I WOULDN'T FIRE YOU.
AND YOU'RE STILL MUNCHING ON THE PAPERS...?
URK...
W-WELL...
SO MUCH HAS HAPPENED.
UGH...
THESE ARE HAPPY TEARS, SO PLEASE DON'T MIND THEM.
SNIFFLE
ぐす
ONII-SAN, I'M SO GLAD I COULD SEE YOU AGAIN!
STOP THAT. IT'S EMBAR-RASSING.
SNIFFLE
ぐす
CHITA-SAN WENT HOME EARLY BECAUSE SHE HAS WORK IN THE AFTERNOON.
I HAD FUN!
EE YOU ATER!
WELL, THERE ARE SO MANY THINGS...
I WANTED TO TELL YOU IF I COULD SEE YOU AGAIN!
SO HAPPY!
SO HAPPY!
I SEE.

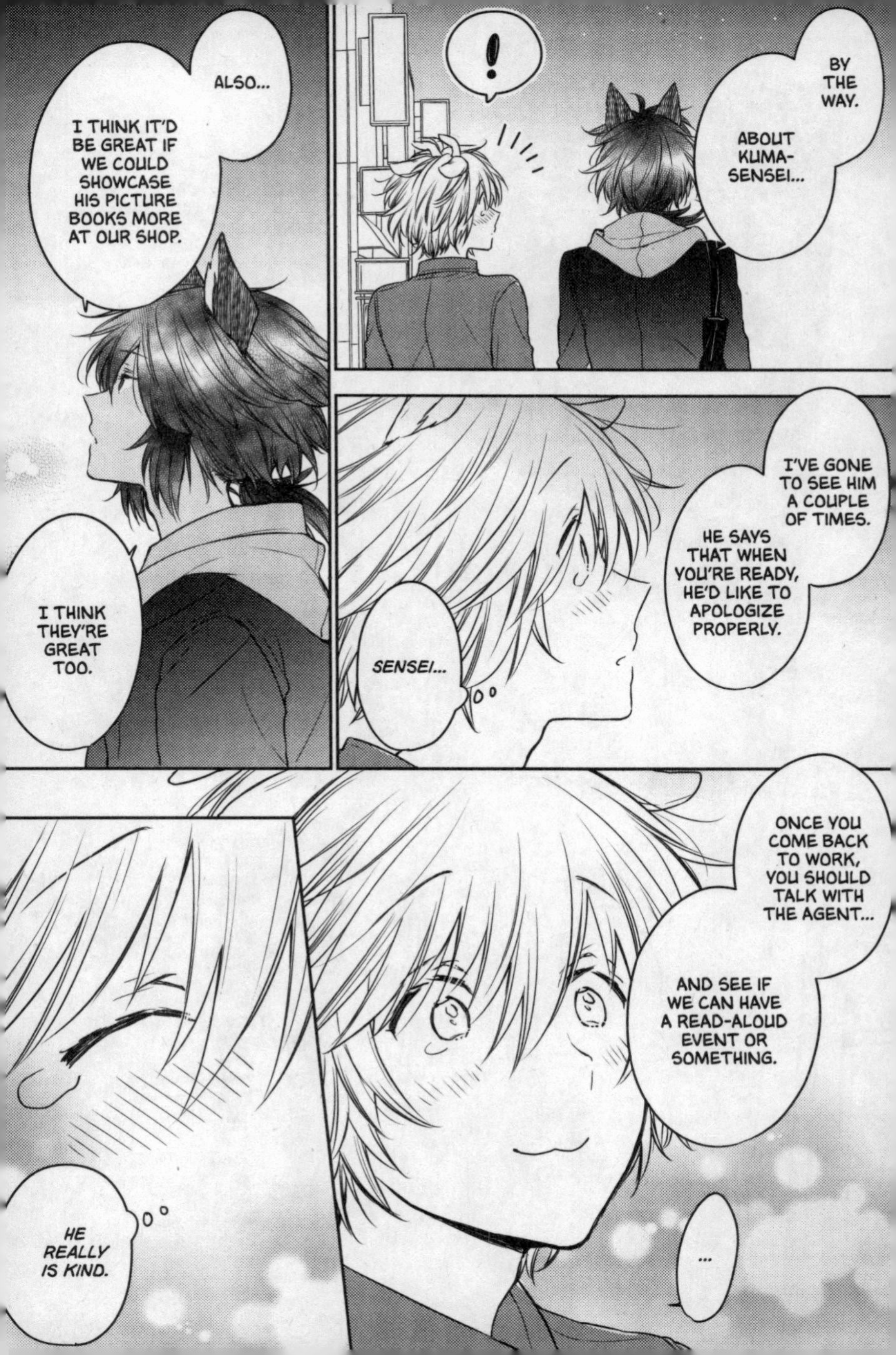
BY THE WAY.
ABOUT KUMA-SENSEI...
!
I'VE GONE TO SEE HIM A COUPLE OF TIMES.
HE SAYS THAT WHEN YOU'RE READY, HE'D LIKE TO APOLOGIZE PROPERLY.
SENSEI...
ALSO...
I THINK IT'D BE GREAT IF WE COULD SHOWCASE HIS PICTURE BOOKS MORE AT OUR SHOP.
I THINK THEY'RE GREAT TOO.
ONCE YOU COME BACK TO WORK, YOU SHOULD TALK WITH THE AGENT...
AND SEE IF WE CAN HAVE A READ-ALOUD EVENT OR SOMETHING.
...
HE REALLY IS KIND.

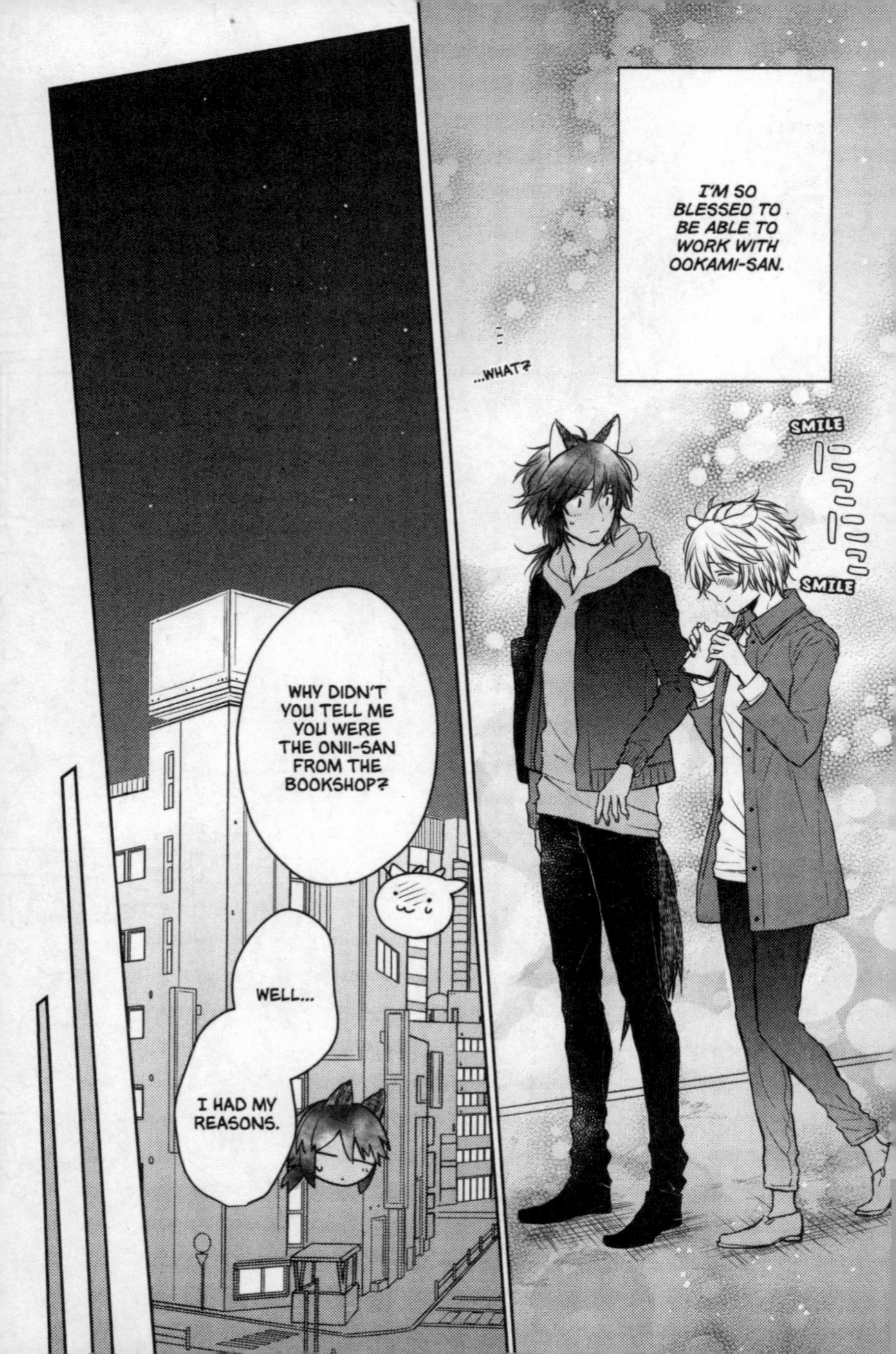
I'M SO BLESSED TO BE ABLE TO WORK WITH OOKAMI-SAN.
...WHAT?
SMILE
SMILE
WHY DIDN'T YOU TELL ME YOU WERE THE ONII-SAN FROM THE BOOKSHOP?
WELL...
I HAD MY REASONS.

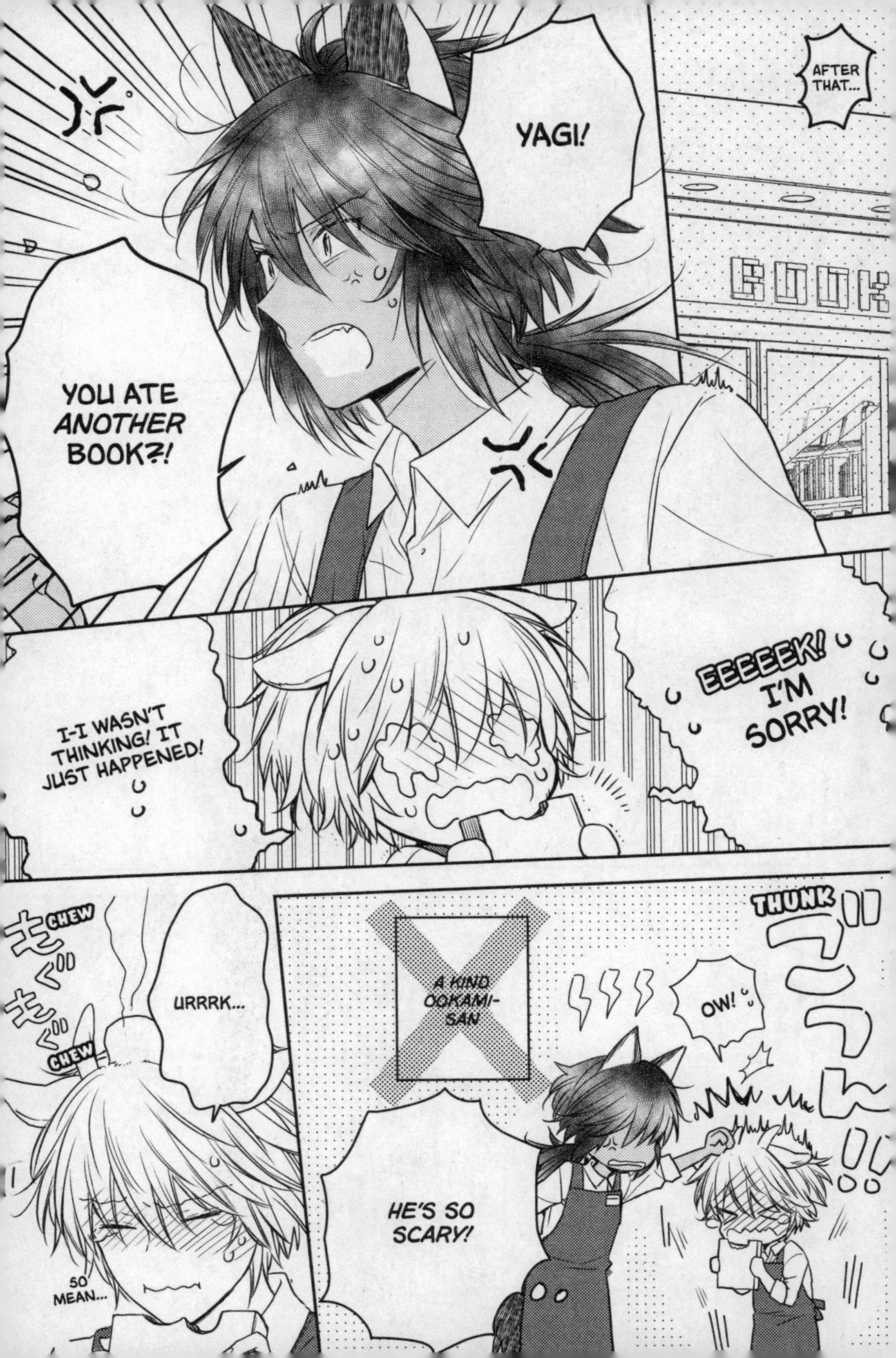
AFTER THAT...
BOOK
YAGI!
YOU ATE ANOTHER BOOK?!
EEEEEK! I'M SORRY!
I-I WASN'T THINKING! IT JUST HAPPENED!
THUNK
OW!
A KIND OOKAMI-SAN
HE'S SO SCARY!
CHEW
CHEW
URRRK...
SO MEAN...

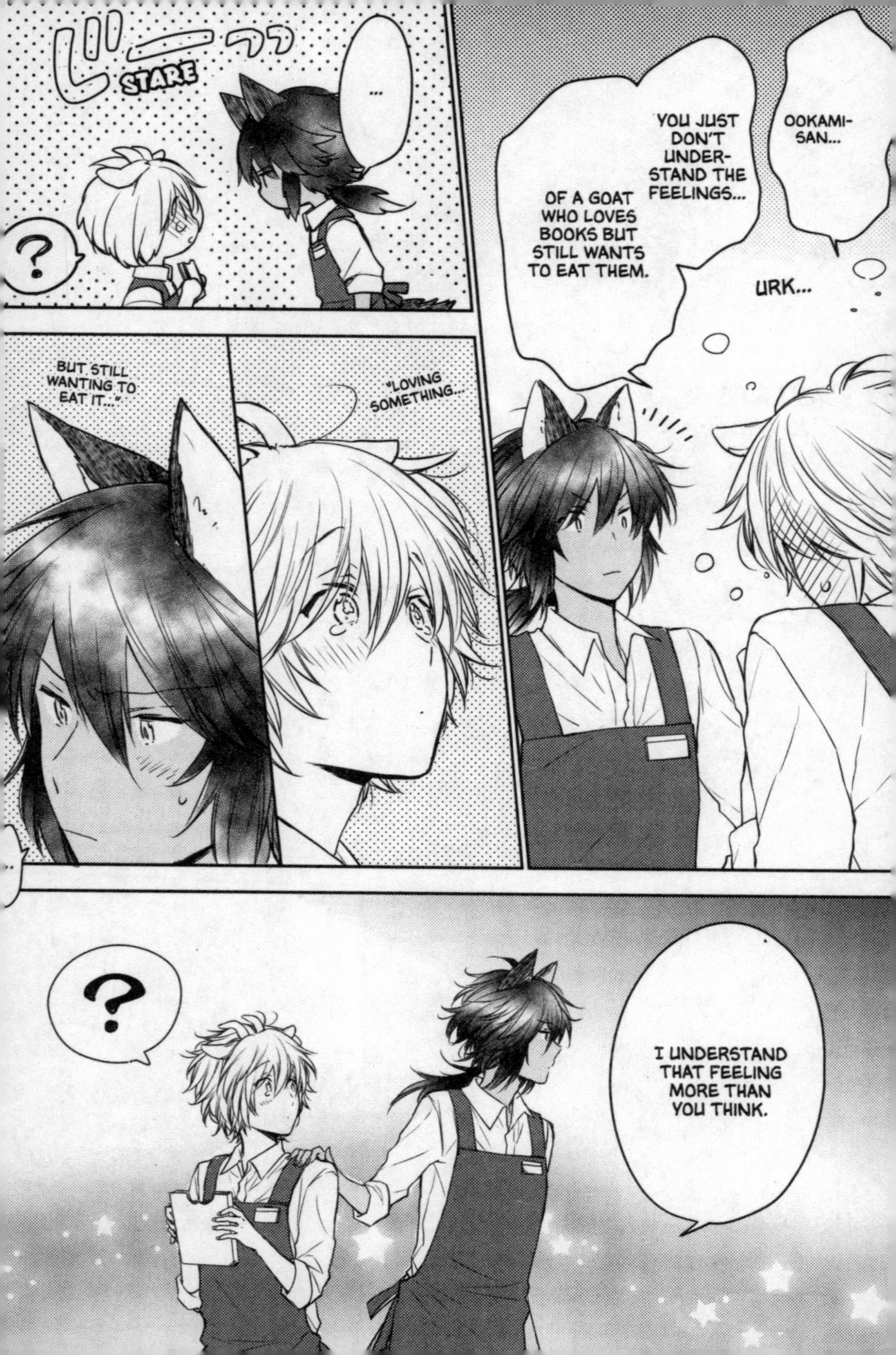
OOKAMI-SAN...
YOU JUST DON'T UNDERSTAND THE FEELINGS...
OF A GOAT WHO LOVES BOOKS BUT STILL WANTS TO EAT THEM.
URK...
じーーっっ
STARE
...
?
"LOVING SOMETHING...
BUT STILL WANTING TO EAT IT..."
I UNDERSTAND THAT FEELING MORE THAN YOU THINK.
?

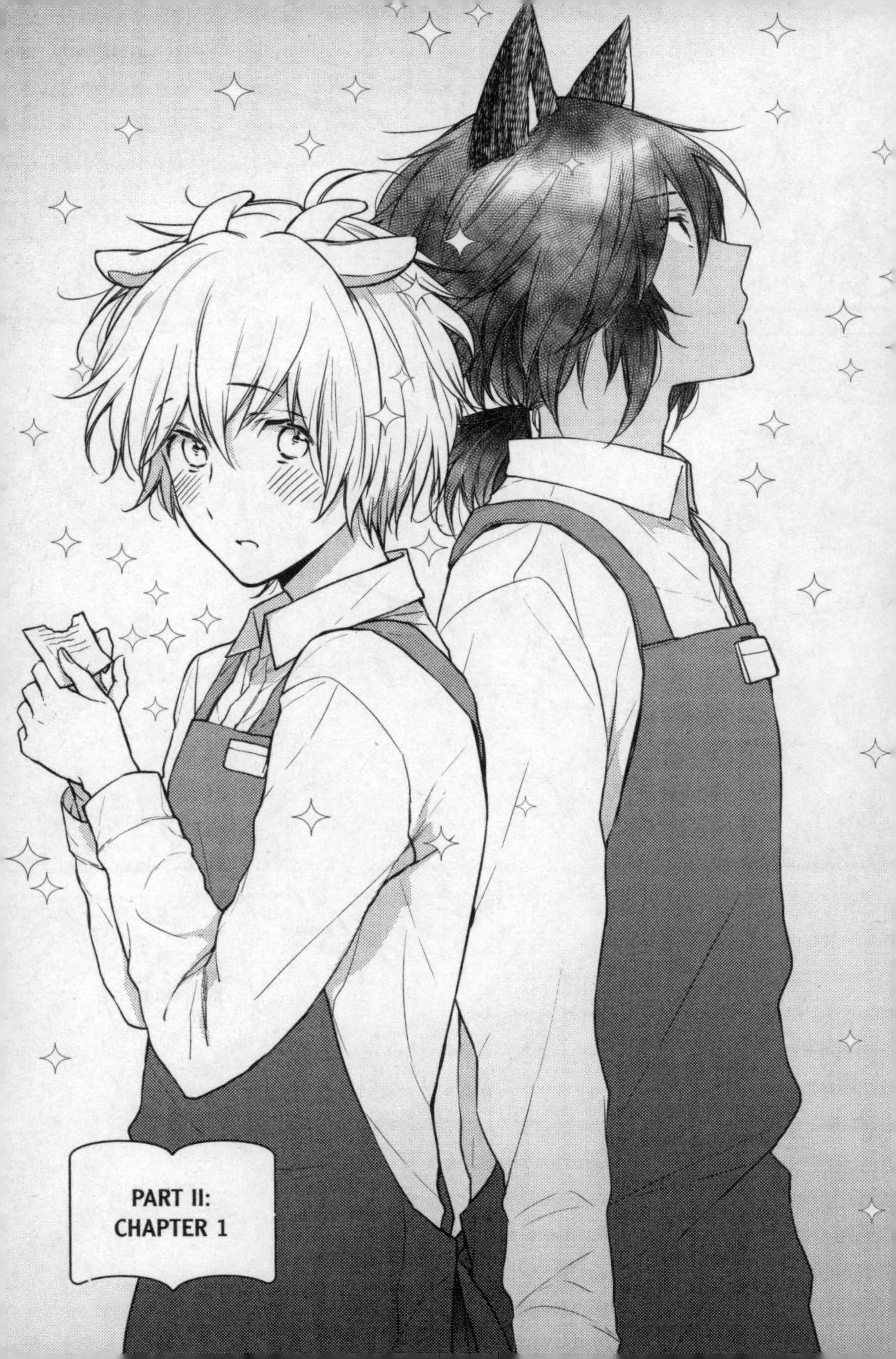
PART II:
CHAPTER 1

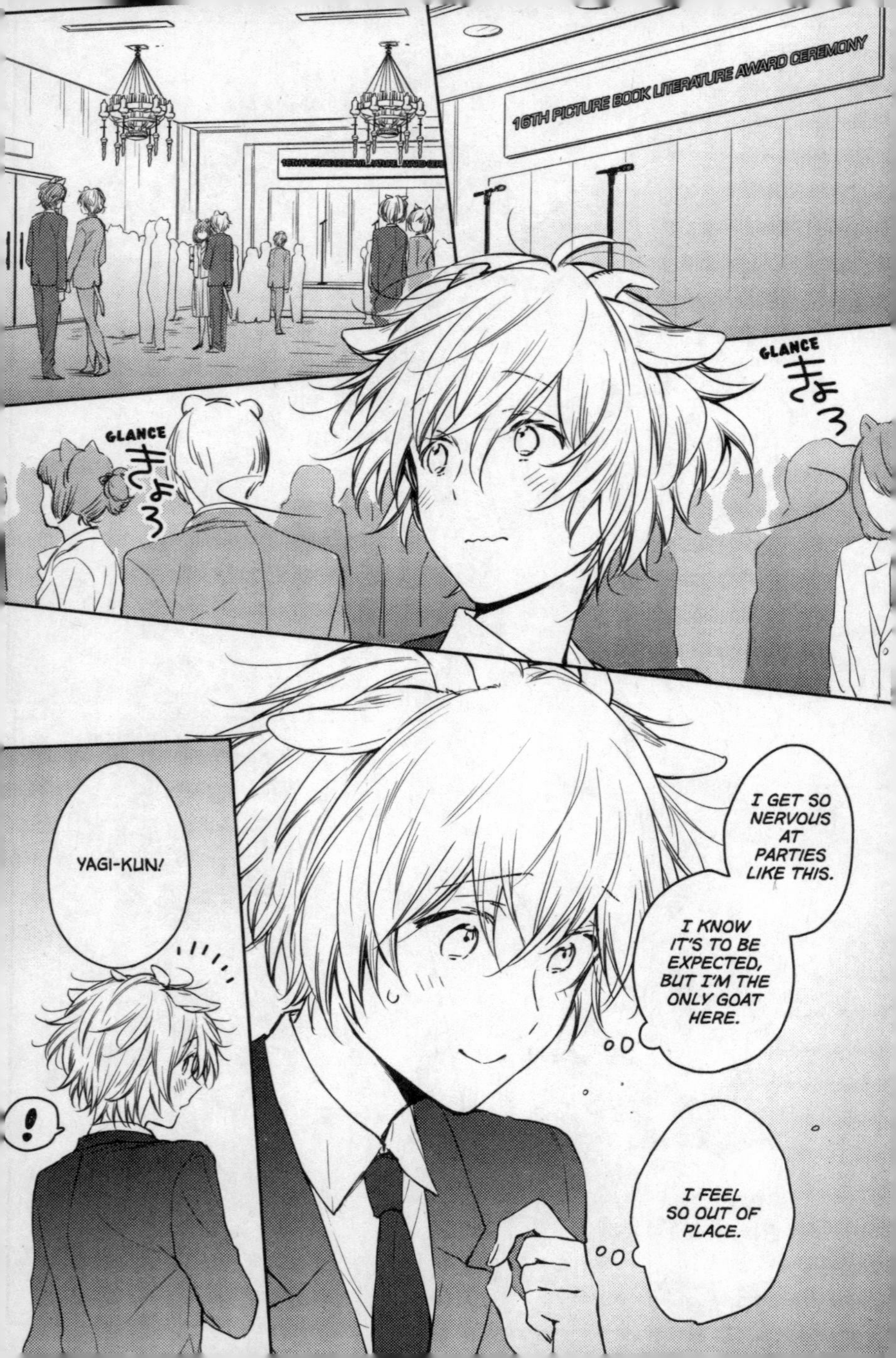
16TH PICTURE BOOK LITERATURE AWARD CEREMONY
GLANCE
きょろ
GLANCE
きょろ
I GET SO NERVOUS AT PARTIES LIKE THIS.
I KNOW IT'S TO BE EXPECTED, BUT I'M THE ONLY GOAT HERE.
I FEEL SO OUT OF PLACE.
YAGI-KUN!
!

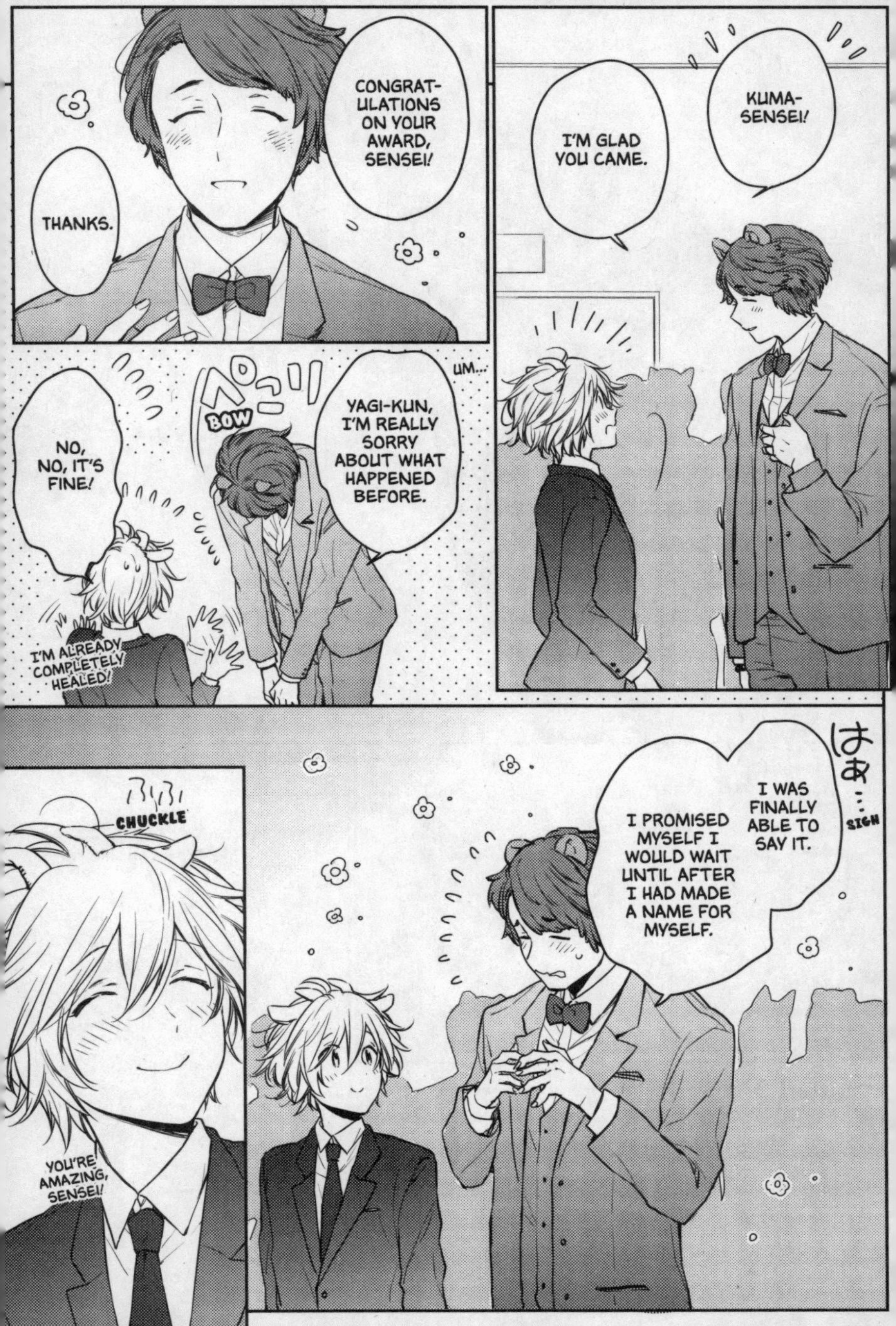
KUMA-SENSEI!
I'M GLAD YOU CAME.
CONGRATULATIONS ON YOUR AWARD, SENSEI!
THANKS.
UM...
ペコッ
BOW
YAGI-KUN, I'M REALLY SORRY ABOUT WHAT HAPPENED BEFORE.
NO, NO, IT'S FINE!
I'M ALREADY COMPLETELY HEALED!
はぁ…
SIGH
I WAS FINALLY ABLE TO SAY IT.
I PROMISED MYSELF I WOULD WAIT UNTIL AFTER I HAD MADE A NAME FOR MYSELF.
ふふ
CHUCKLE
YOU'RE AMAZING, SENSEI!

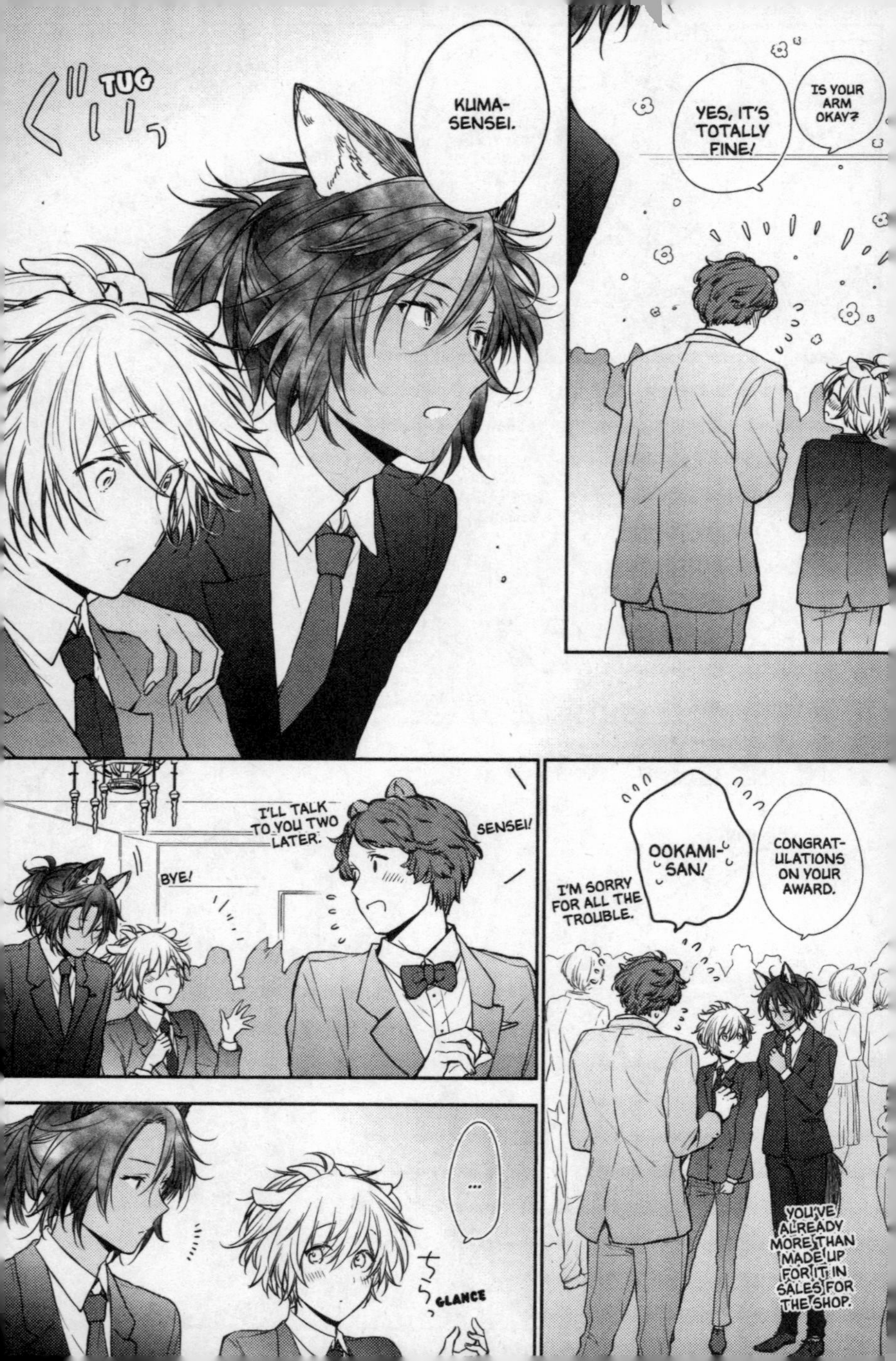

IS YOUR ARM OKAY?
YES, IT'S TOTALLY FINE!
ぐいっ
TUG
KUMA-SENSEI.
CONGRATULATIONS ON YOUR AWARD.
OOKAMI-SAN!
I'M SORRY FOR ALL THE TROUBLE.
YOU'VE ALREADY MORE THAN MADE UP FOR IT IN SALES FOR THE SHOP.
SENSEI!
I'LL TALK TO YOU TWO LATER.
BYE!
...
ちらっ
GLANCE

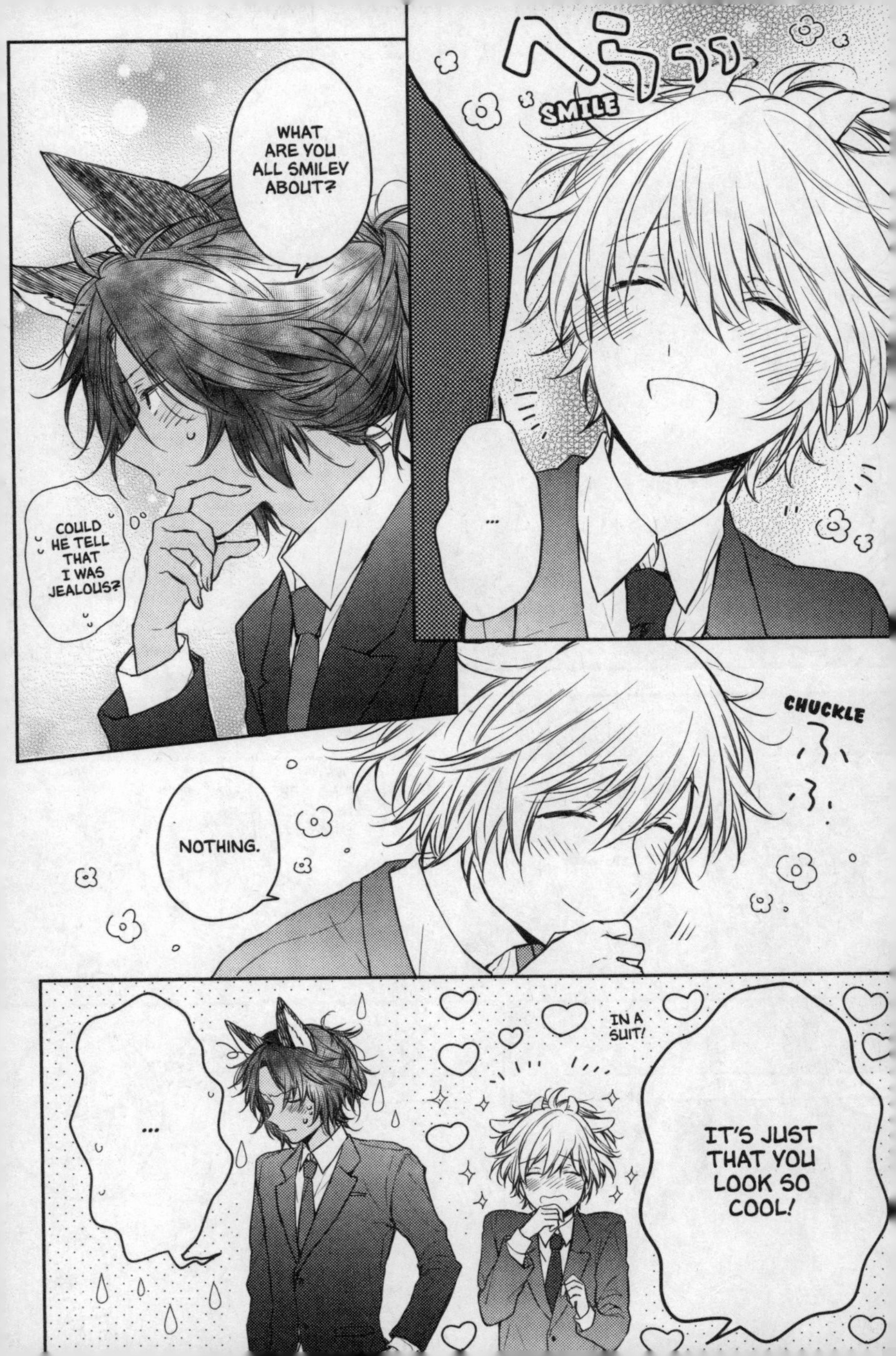

へら
SMILE
...
WHAT ARE YOU ALL SMILEY ABOUT?
COULD HE TELL THAT I WAS JEALOUS?
CHUCKLE
ふふ
NOTHING.
IT'S JUST THAT YOU LOOK SO COOL!
IN A SUIT!
...

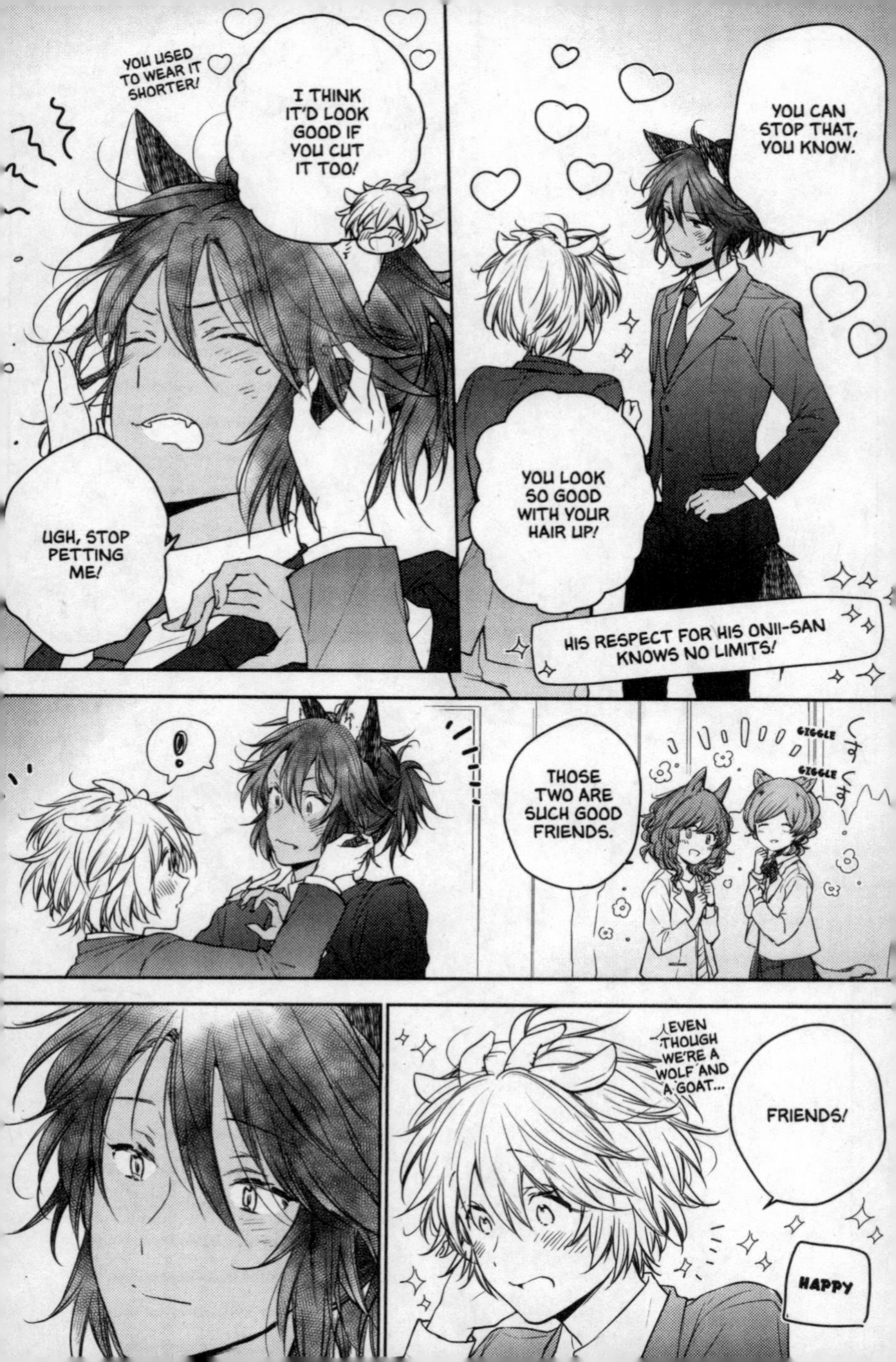
YOU CAN STOP THAT, YOU KNOW.
YOU LOOK SO GOOD WITH YOUR HAIR UP!
HIS RESPECT FOR HIS ONII-SAN KNOWS NO LIMITS!
I THINK IT'D LOOK GOOD IF YOU CUT IT TOO!
YOU USED TO WEAR IT SHORTER!
UGH, STOP PETTING ME!
GIGGLE
GIGGLE
くすくす
THOSE TWO ARE SUCH GOOD FRIENDS.
!
EVEN THOUGH WE'RE A WOLF AND A GOAT...
FRIENDS!
HAPPY

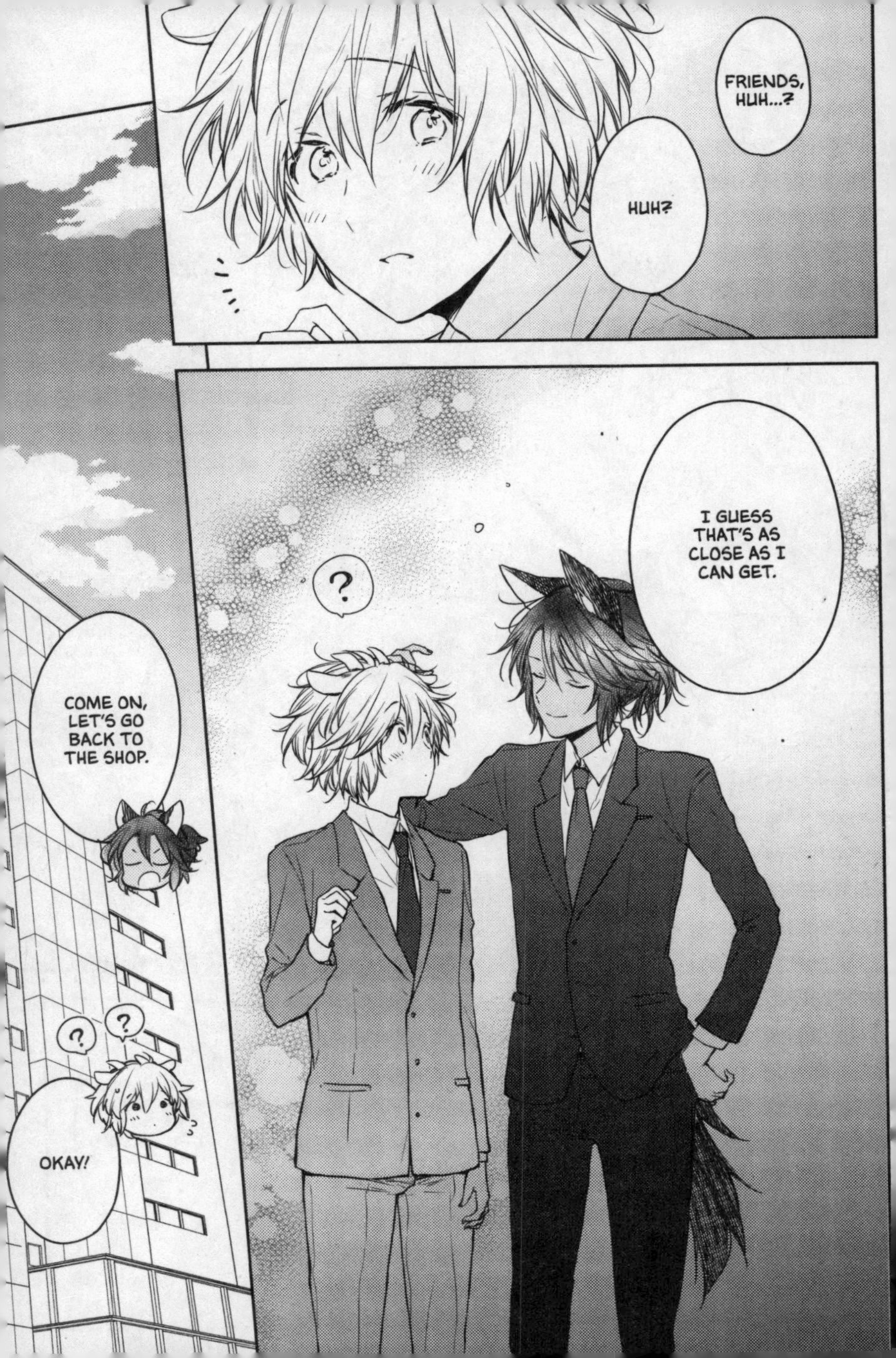
FRIENDS, HUH...?
HUH?
I GUESS THAT'S AS CLOSE AS I CAN GET.
?
COME ON, LET'S GO BACK TO THE SHOP.
?
?
OKAY!

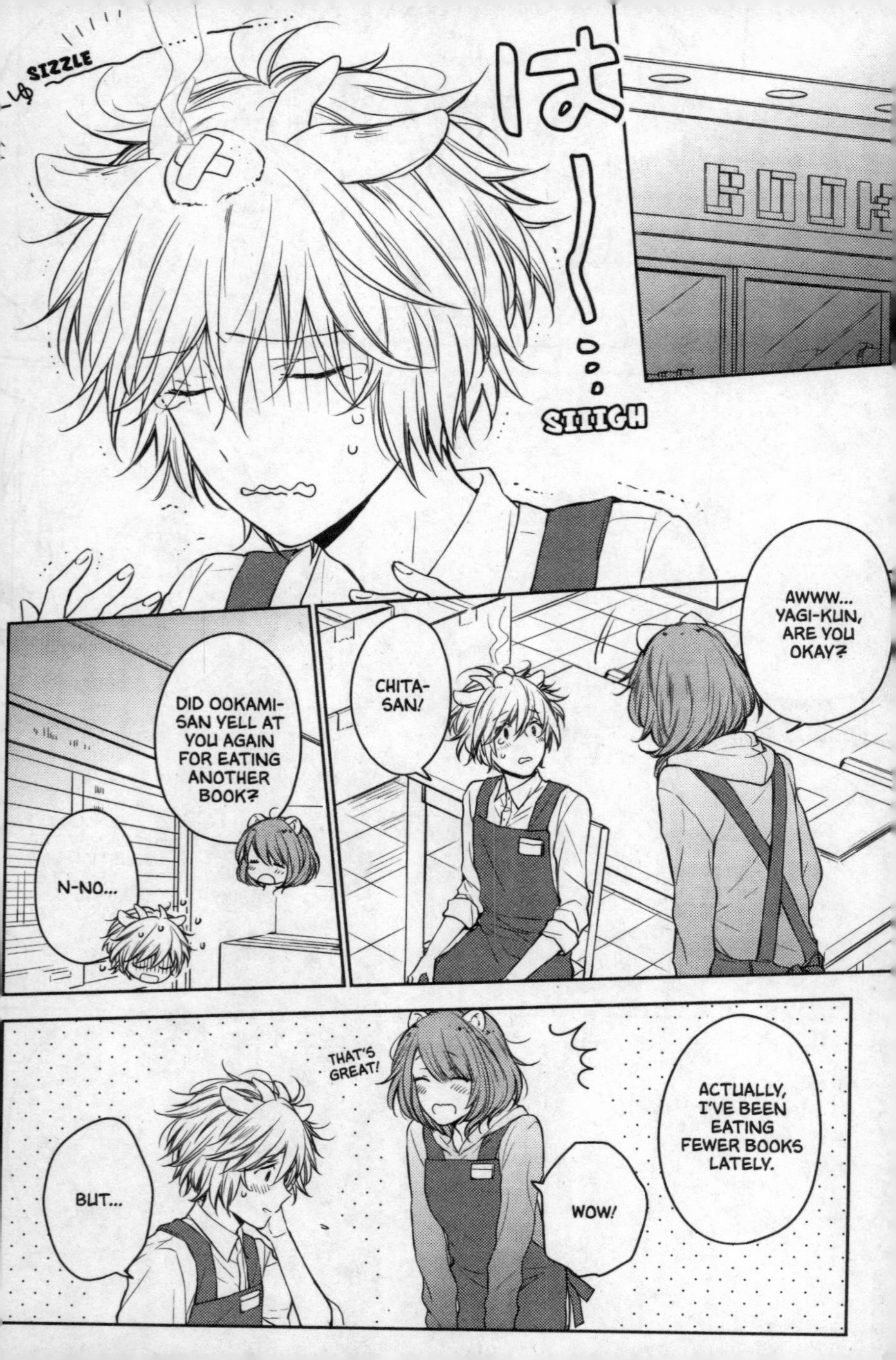

はー…
SIIIGH
SIZZLE
AWWW... YAGI-KUN, ARE YOU OKAY?
CHITA-SAN!
DID OOKAMI-SAN YELL AT YOU AGAIN FOR EATING ANOTHER BOOK?
N-NO...
ACTUALLY, I'VE BEEN EATING FEWER BOOKS LATELY.
THAT'S GREAT!
WOW!
BUT...

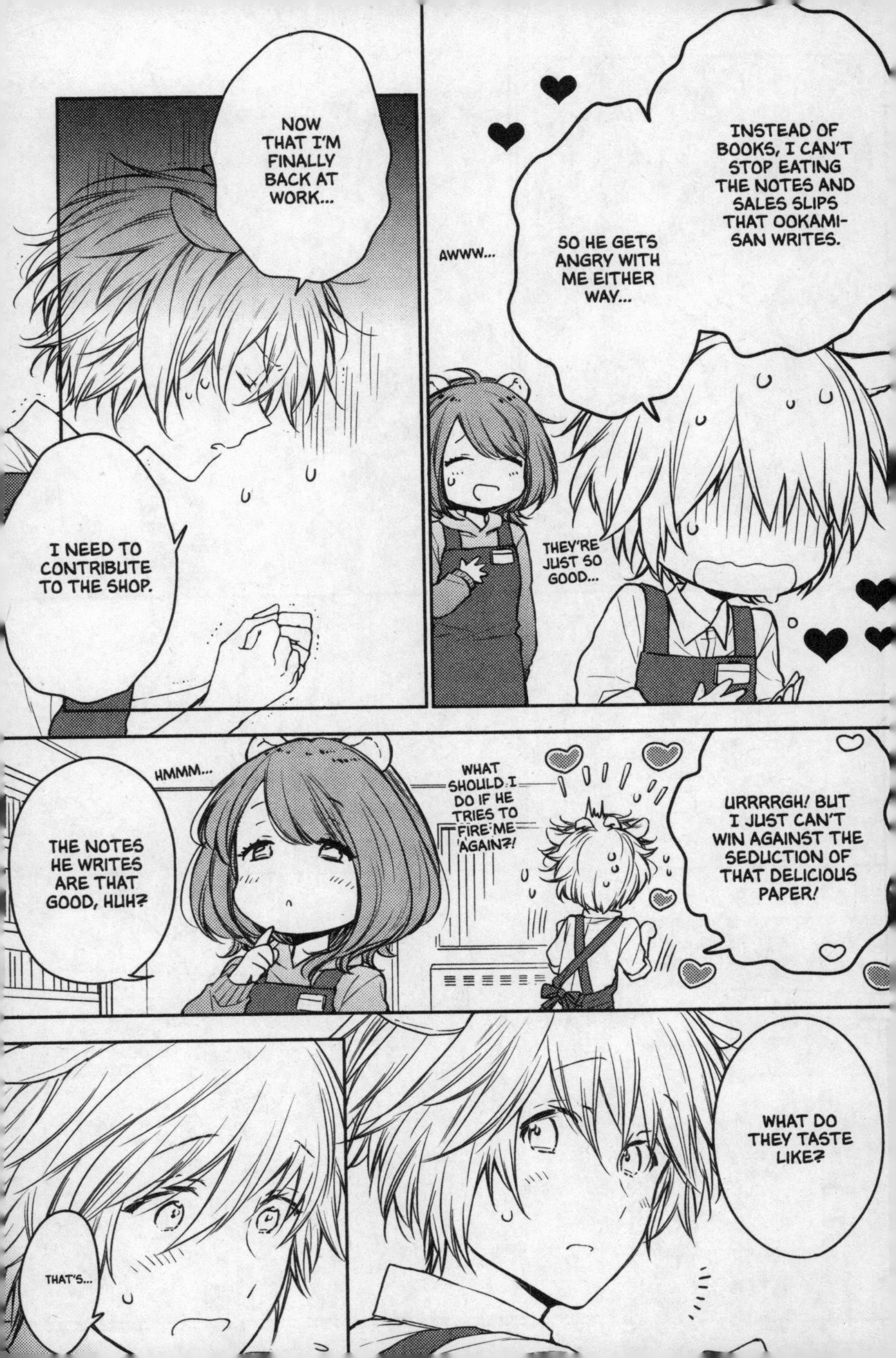
INSTEAD OF BOOKS, I CAN'T STOP EATING THE NOTES AND SALES SLIPS THAT OOKAMI-SAN WRITES.
SO HE GETS ANGRY WITH ME EITHER WAY...
AWWW...
THEY'RE JUST SO GOOD...
NOW THAT I'M FINALLY BACK AT WORK...
I NEED TO CONTRIBUTE TO THE SHOP.
URRRRGH! BUT I JUST CAN'T WIN AGAINST THE SEDUCTION OF THAT DELICIOUS PAPER!
WHAT SHOULD I DO IF HE TRIES TO FIRE ME AGAIN?!
HMMM...
THE NOTES HE WRITES ARE THAT GOOD, HUH?
WHAT DO THEY TASTE LIKE?
THAT'S...

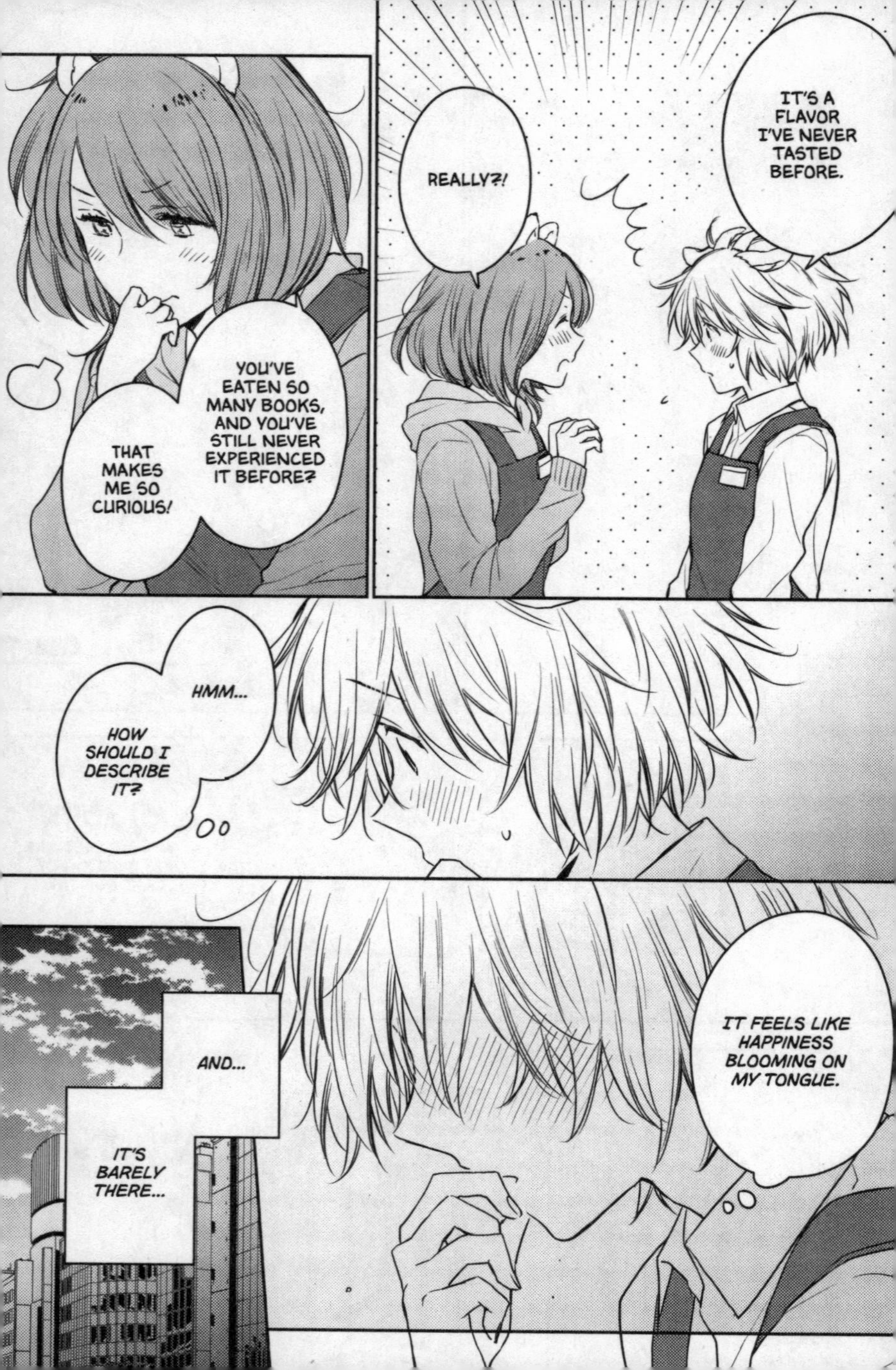
IT'S A FLAVOR I'VE NEVER TASTED BEFORE.
REALLY?!
YOU'VE EATEN SO MANY BOOKS, AND YOU'VE STILL NEVER EXPERIENCED IT BEFORE?
THAT MAKES ME SO CURIOUS!
HMM...
HOW SHOULD I DESCRIBE IT?
IT FEELS LIKE HAPPINESS BLOOMING ON MY TONGUE.
AND...
IT'S BARELY THERE...

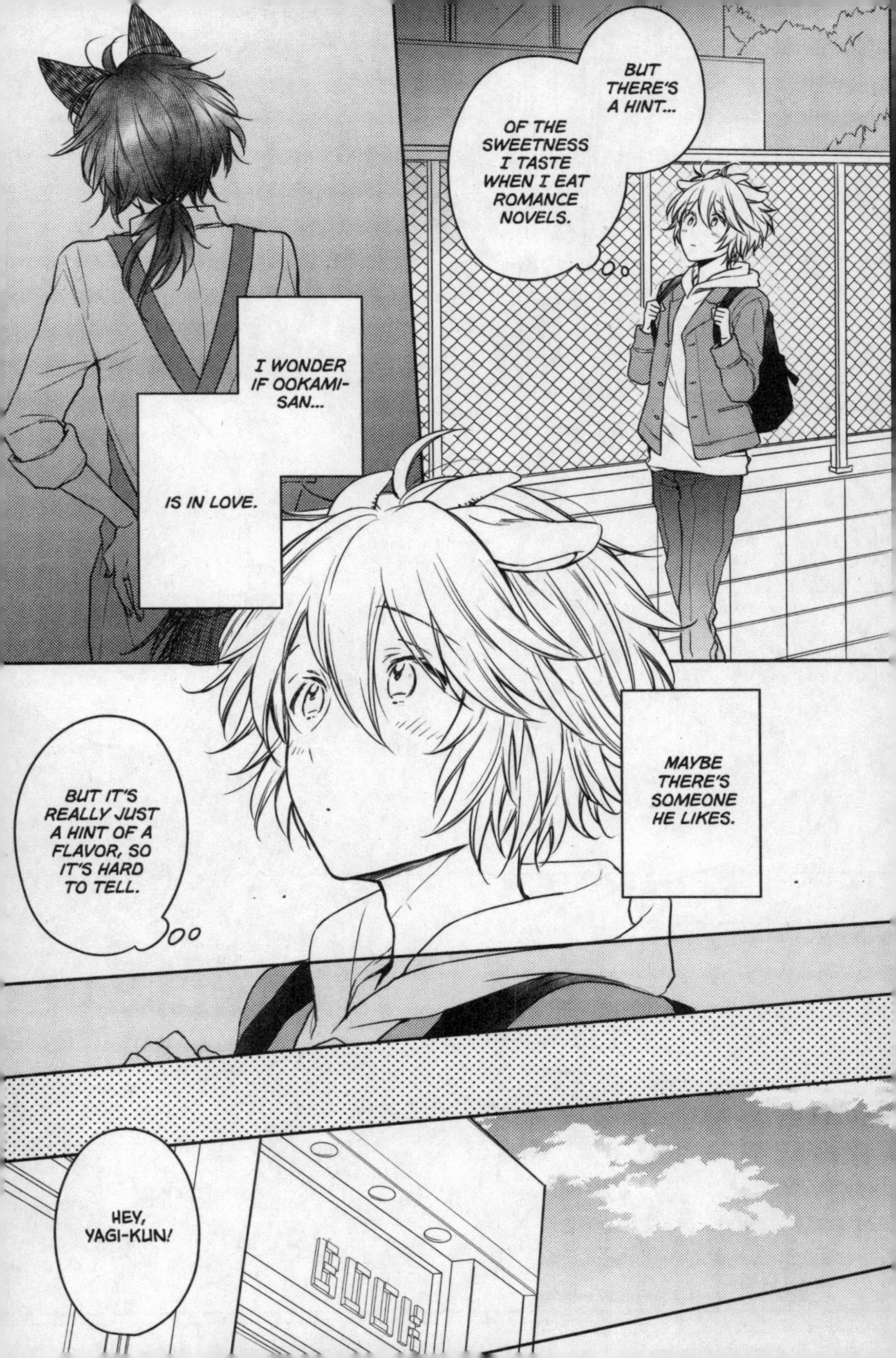
BUT THERE'S A HINT...
OF THE SWEETNESS I TASTE WHEN I EAT ROMANCE NOVELS.
I WONDER IF OOKAMI-SAN...
IS IN LOVE.
MAYBE THERE'S SOMEONE HE LIKES.
BUT IT'S REALLY JUST A HINT OF A FLAVOR, SO IT'S HARD TO TELL.
HEY, YAGI-KUN!

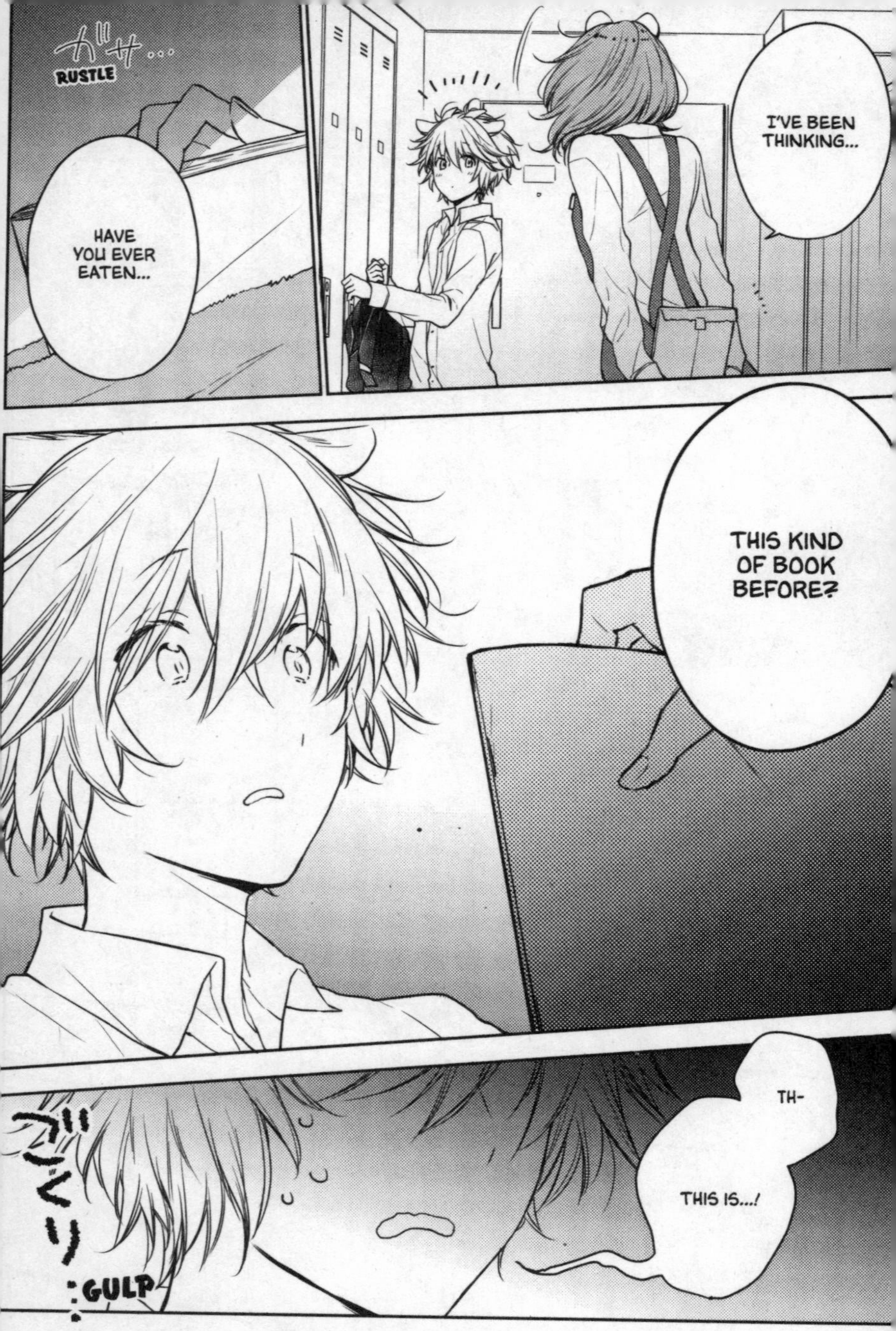
I'VE BEEN THINKING...
ガサ...
RUSTLE
HAVE YOU EVER EATEN...
THIS KIND OF BOOK BEFORE?
TH-
THIS IS...!
GULP

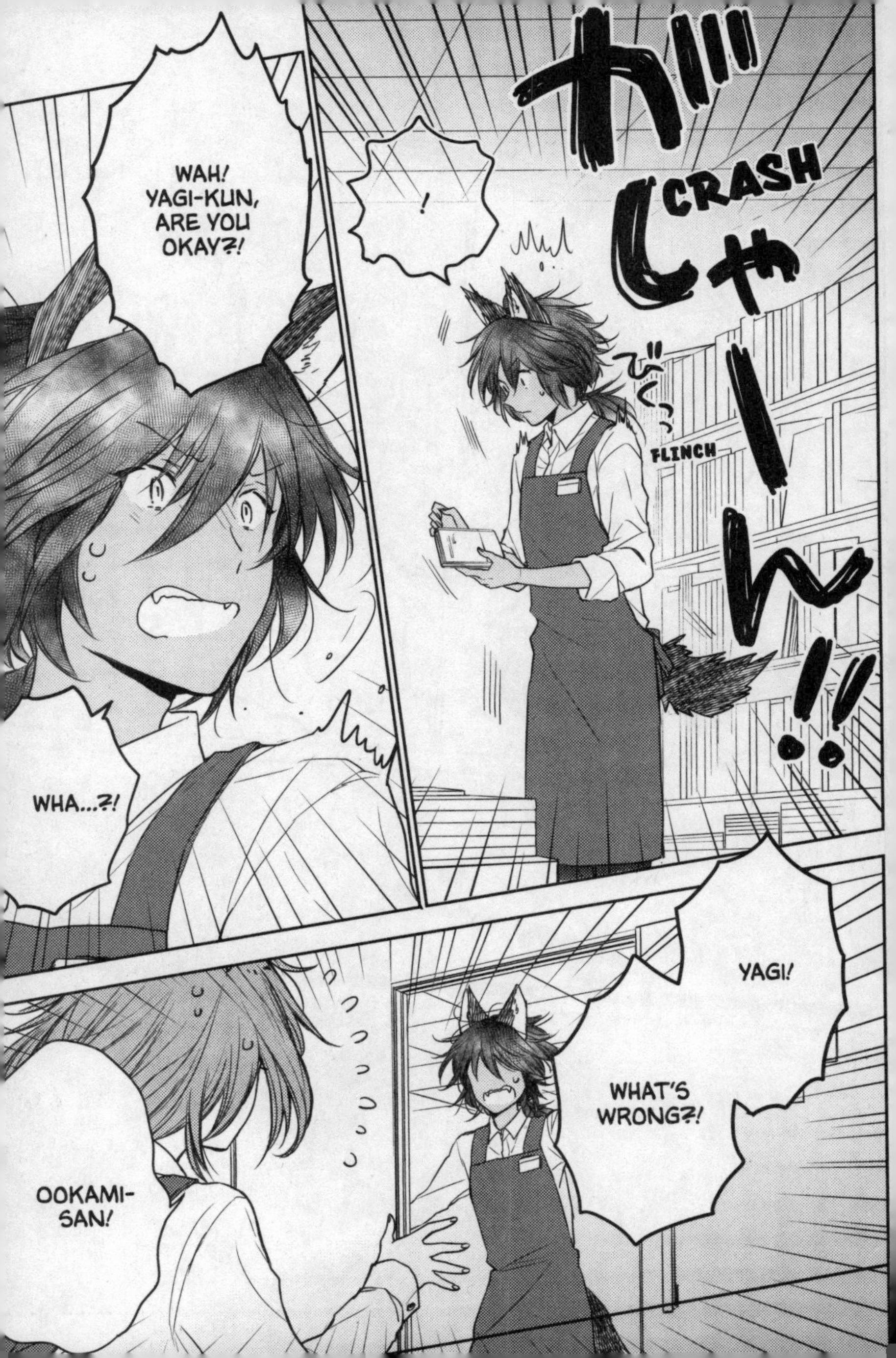
がしゃーん!!
CRASH
!
びくっ
FLINCH
WAH! YAGI-KUN, ARE YOU OKAY?!
WHA...?!
YAGI! WHAT'S WRONG?!
OOKAMI-SAN!

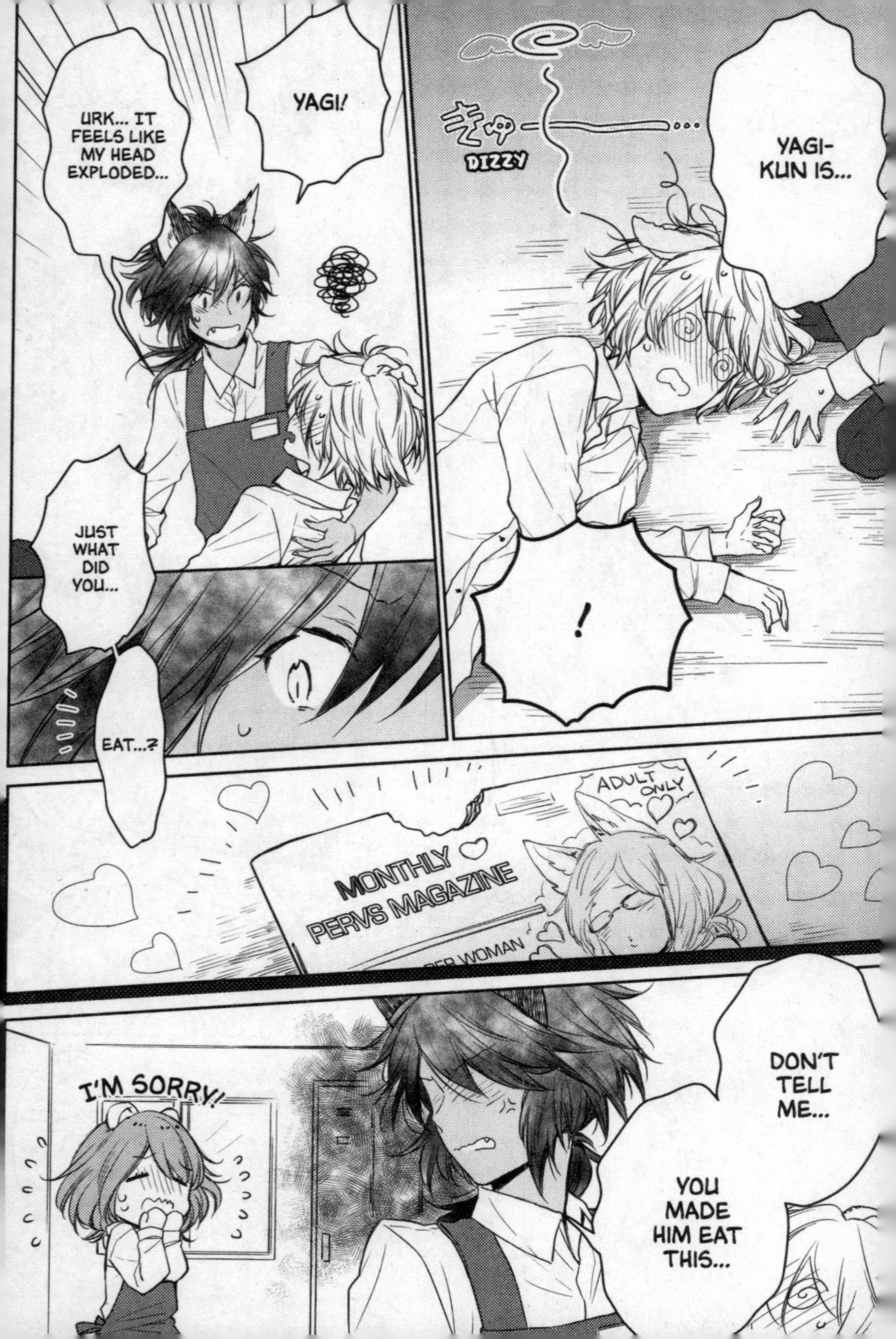
YAGI-KUN IS...
きゅ———…
DIZZY
!
YAGI!
URK... IT FEELS LIKE MY HEAD EXPLODED...
JUST WHAT DID YOU...
EAT...?
ADULT ONLY
MONTHLY PERVS MAGAZINE
DON'T TELL ME...
YOU MADE HIM EAT THIS...
I'M SORRY!

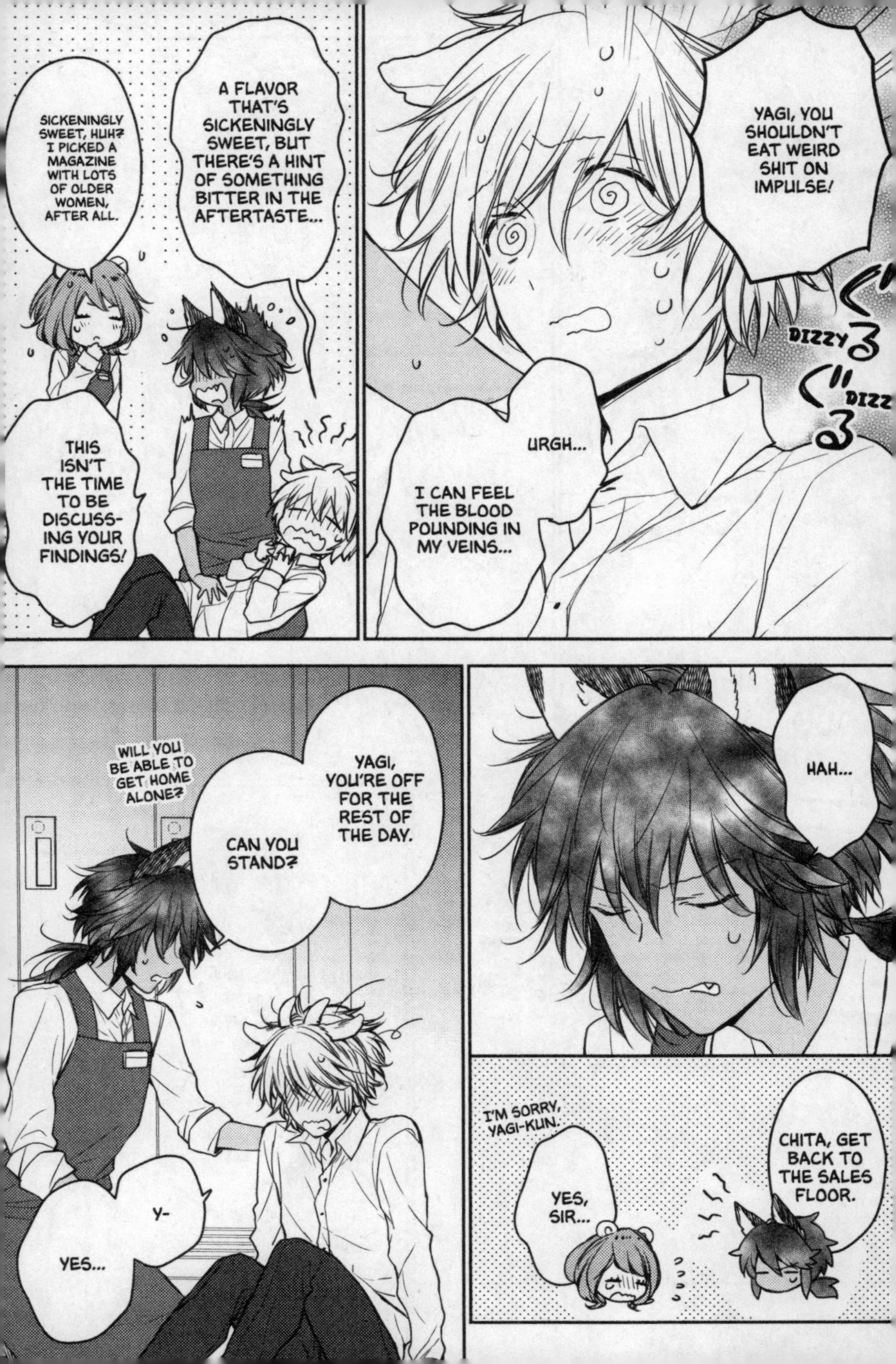
YAGI, YOU SHOULDN'T EAT WEIRD SHIT ON IMPULSE!
ぐる DIZZY
ぐる DIZZ
URGH...
I CAN FEEL THE BLOOD POUNDING IN MY VEINS...
A FLAVOR THAT'S SICKENINGLY SWEET, BUT THERE'S A HINT OF SOMETHING BITTER IN THE AFTERTASTE...
SICKENINGLY SWEET, HUH? I PICKED A MAGAZINE WITH LOTS OF OLDER WOMEN, AFTER ALL.
THIS ISN'T THE TIME TO BE DISCUSSING YOUR FINDINGS!
HAH...
CHITA, GET BACK TO THE SALES FLOOR.
I'M SORRY, YAGI-KUN.
YES, SIR...
YAGI, YOU'RE OFF FOR THE REST OF THE DAY.
CAN YOU STAND?
WILL YOU BE ABLE TO GET HOME ALONE?
Y-
YES...

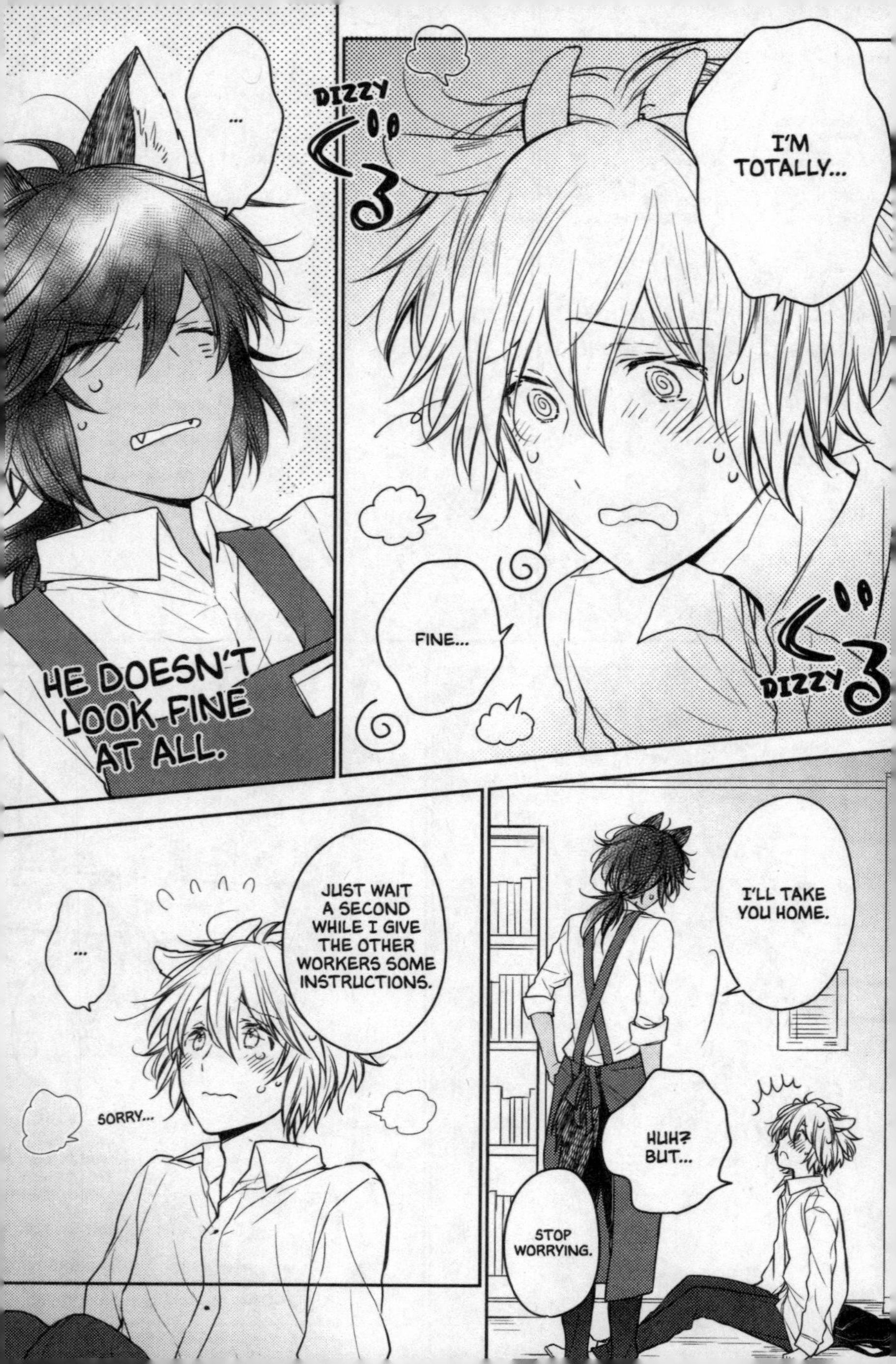

I'M TOTALLY...
DIZZY
FINE...
DIZZY
...
HE DOESN'T LOOK FINE AT ALL.
I'LL TAKE YOU HOME.
HUH? BUT...
STOP WORRYING.
JUST WAIT A SECOND WHILE I GIVE THE OTHER WORKERS SOME INSTRUCTIONS.
...
SORRY...

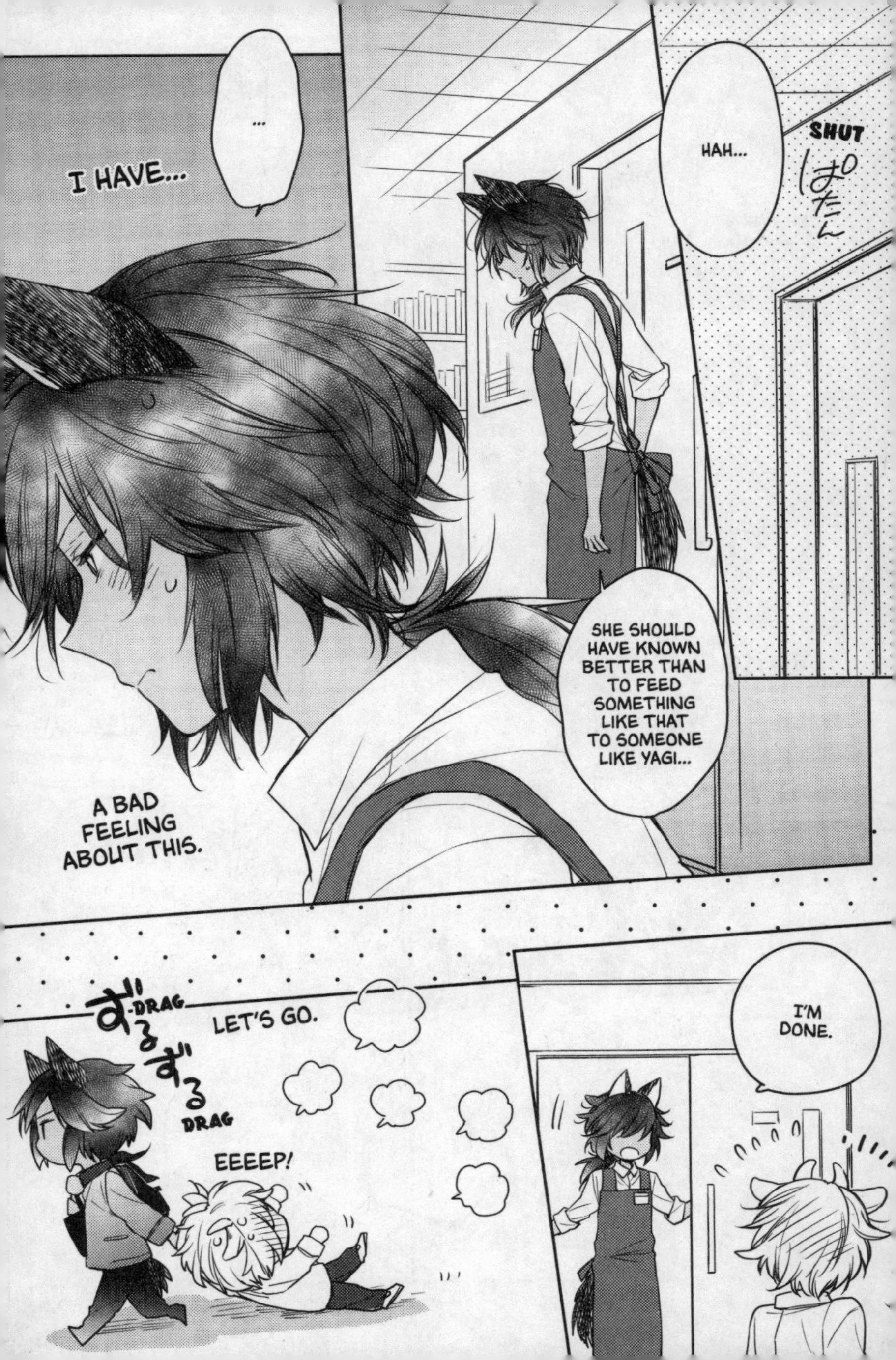

HAH...
SHUT
ぱたん
SHE SHOULD HAVE KNOWN BETTER THAN TO FEED SOMETHING LIKE THAT TO SOMEONE LIKE YAGI...
...
I HAVE...
A BAD FEELING ABOUT THIS.
I'M DONE.
ずる-DRAG
ずる DRAG
LET'S GO.
EEEEP!

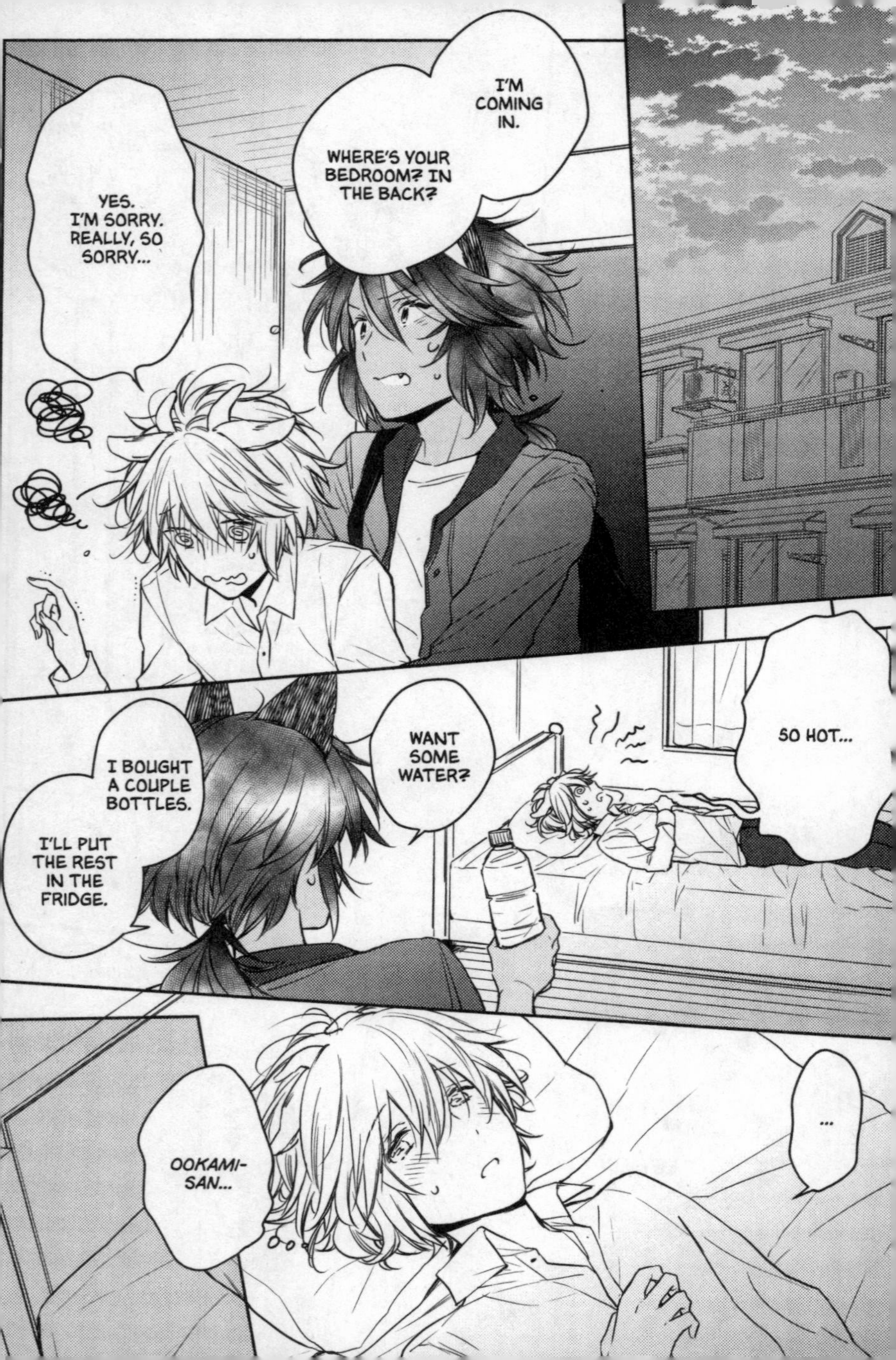
I'M COMING IN.
WHERE'S YOUR BEDROOM? IN THE BACK?
YES. I'M SORRY. REALLY, SO SORRY...
SO HOT...
WANT SOME WATER?
I BOUGHT A COUPLE BOTTLES.
I'LL PUT THE REST IN THE FRIDGE.
...
OOKAMI-SAN...

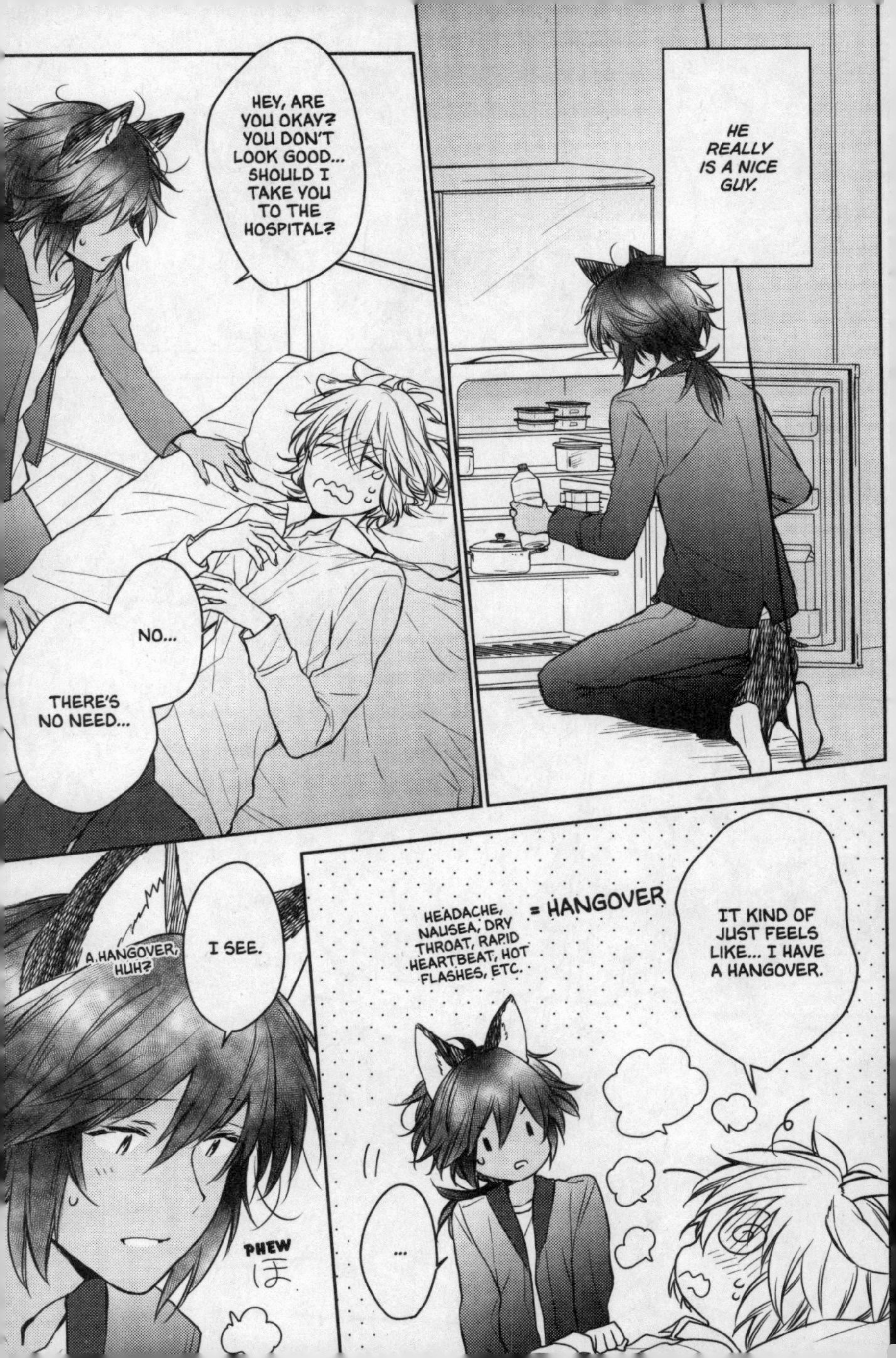
HE REALLY IS A NICE GUY.
HEY, ARE YOU OKAY? YOU DON'T LOOK GOOD... SHOULD I TAKE YOU TO THE HOSPITAL?
NO...
THERE'S NO NEED...
IT KIND OF JUST FEELS LIKE... I HAVE A HANGOVER.
HEADACHE, NAUSEA, DRY THROAT, RAPID HEARTBEAT, HOT FLASHES, ETC.
= HANGOVER
...
I SEE.
A HANGOVER, HUH?
PHEW
ほ

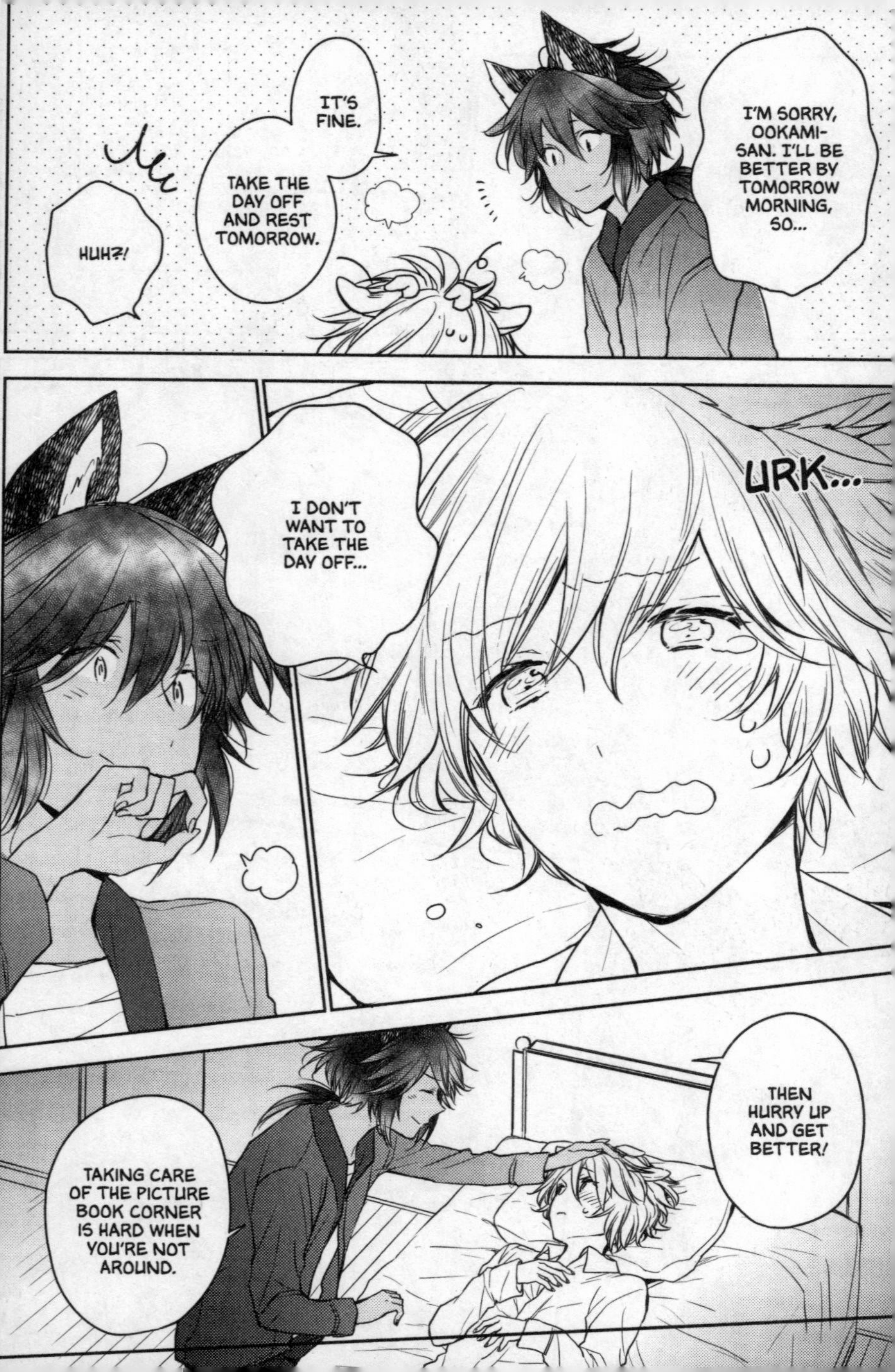
I'M SORRY, OOKAMI-SAN. I'LL BE BETTER BY TOMORROW MORNING, SO...
IT'S FINE.
TAKE THE DAY OFF AND REST TOMORROW.
HUH?!
URK...
I DON'T WANT TO TAKE THE DAY OFF...
THEN HURRY UP AND GET BETTER!
TAKING CARE OF THE PICTURE BOOK CORNER IS HARD WHEN YOU'RE NOT AROUND.

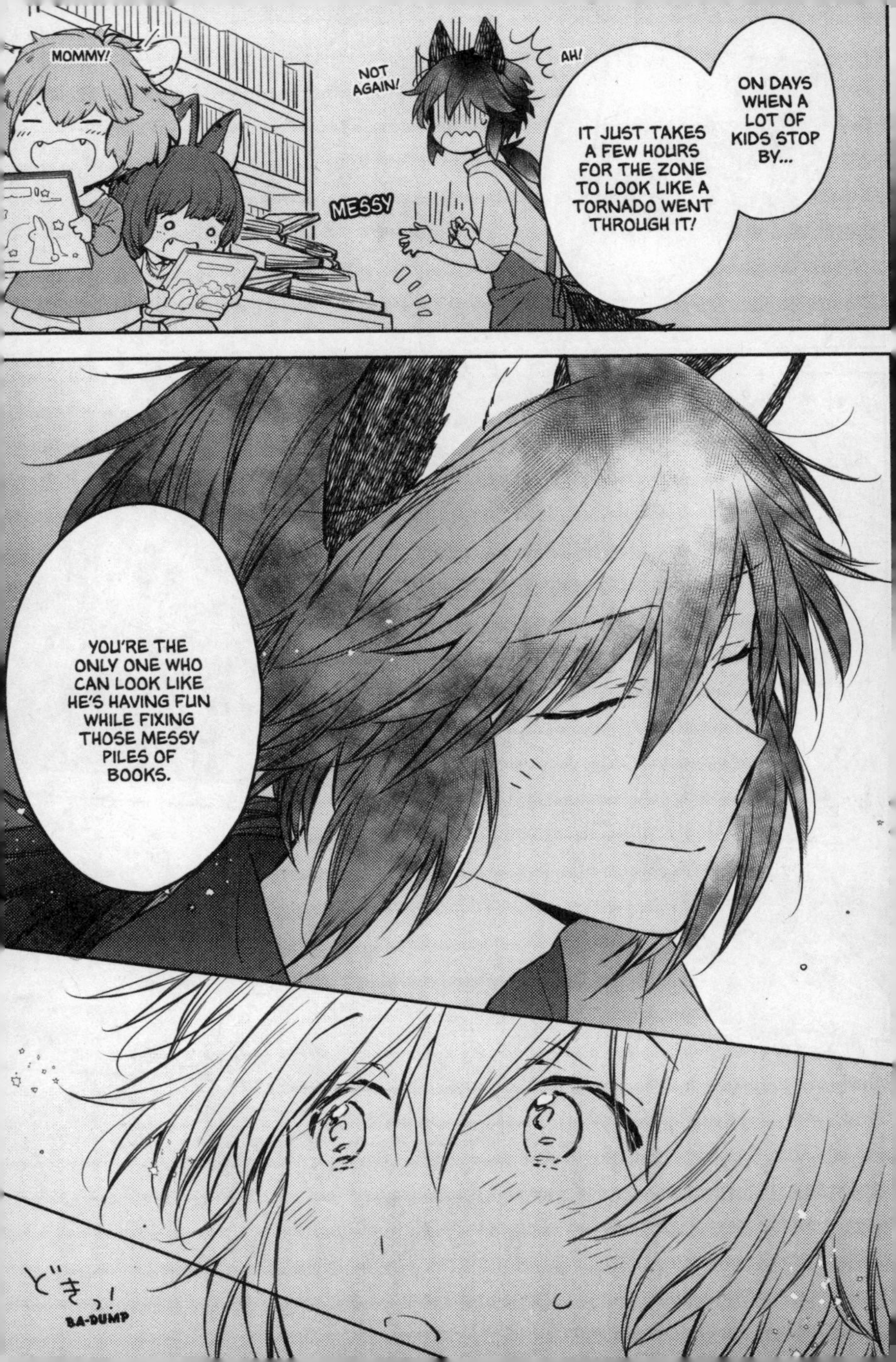
ON DAYS WHEN A LOT OF KIDS STOP BY...
IT JUST TAKES A FEW HOURS FOR THE ZONE TO LOOK LIKE A TORNADO WENT THROUGH IT!
AH!
NOT AGAIN!
MESSY
MOMMY!
YOU'RE THE ONLY ONE WHO CAN LOOK LIKE HE'S HAVING FUN WHILE FIXING THOSE MESSY PILES OF BOOKS.
どきっ!
BA-DUMP

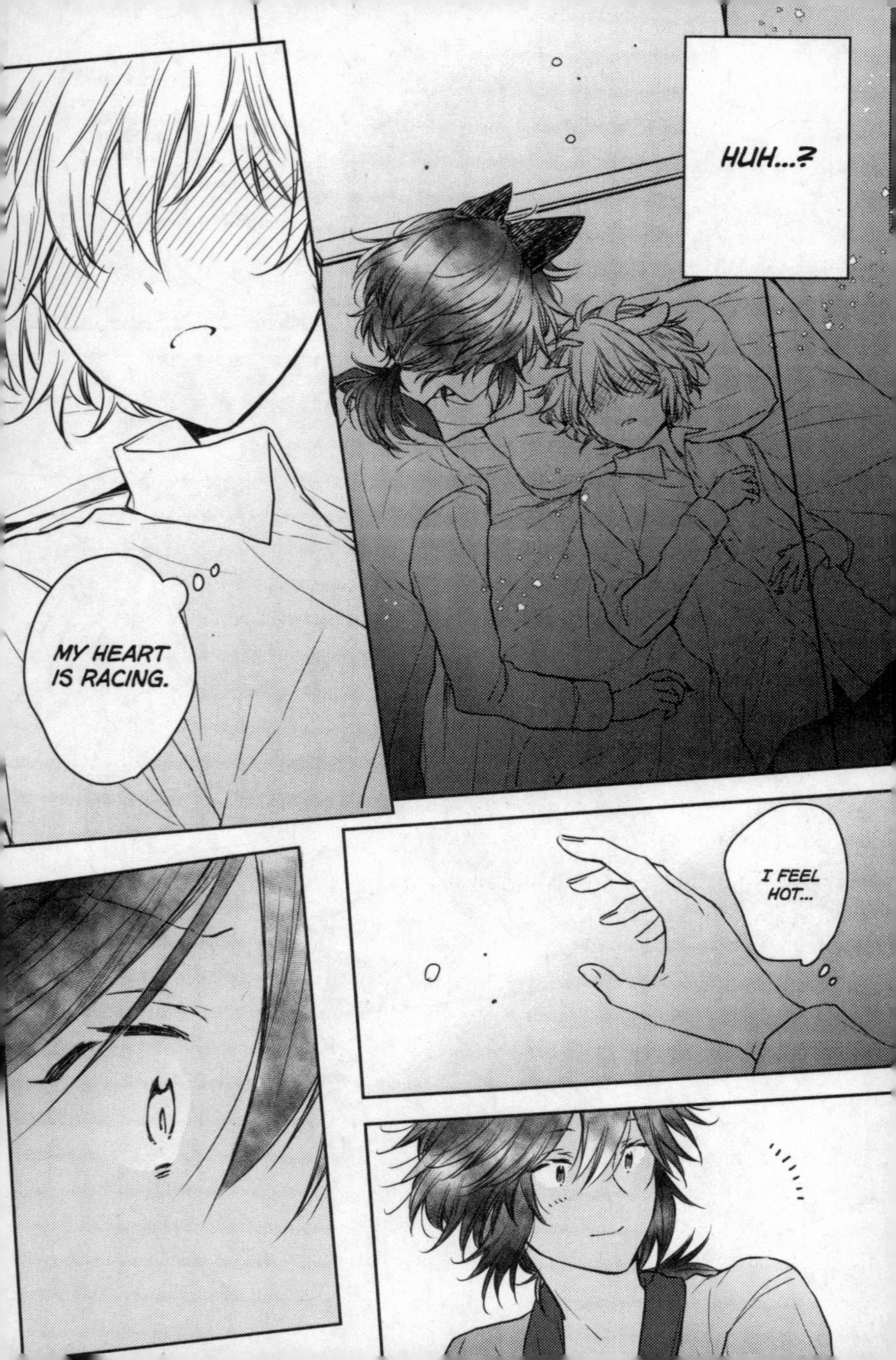
HUH...?
MY HEART IS RACING.
I FEEL HOT...

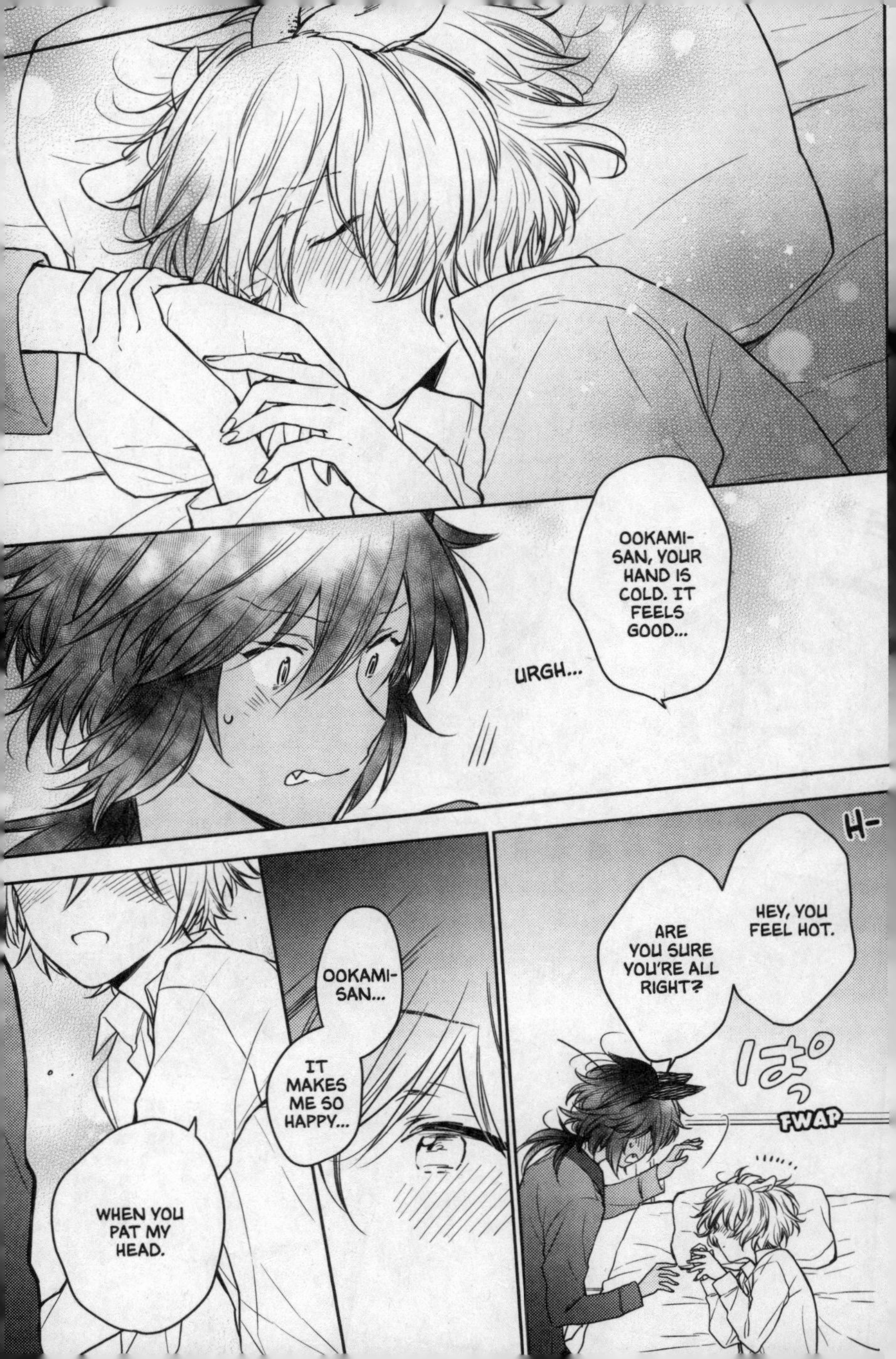
OOKAMI-SAN, YOUR HAND IS COLD. IT FEELS GOOD...
URGH...
H-
HEY, YOU FEEL HOT.
ARE YOU SURE YOU'RE ALL RIGHT?
ぱっ
FWAP
OOKAMI-SAN...
IT MAKES ME SO HAPPY...
WHEN YOU PAT MY HEAD.

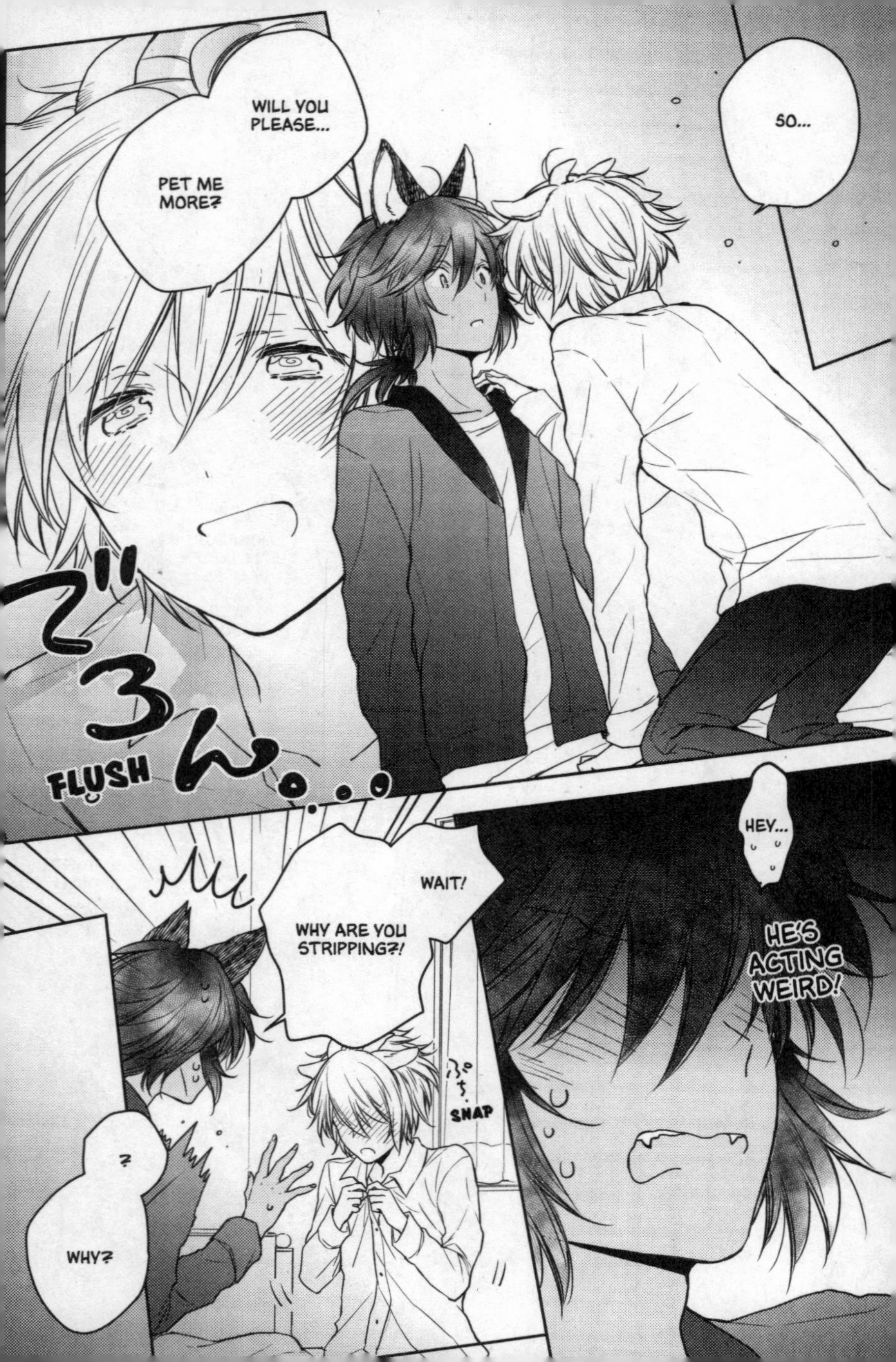
SO...
WILL YOU PLEASE...
PET ME MORE?
でろん。。。
FLUSH
HEY...
HE'S ACTING WEIRD!
WAIT!
WHY ARE YOU STRIPPING?!
ぷち
SNAP
?
WHY?

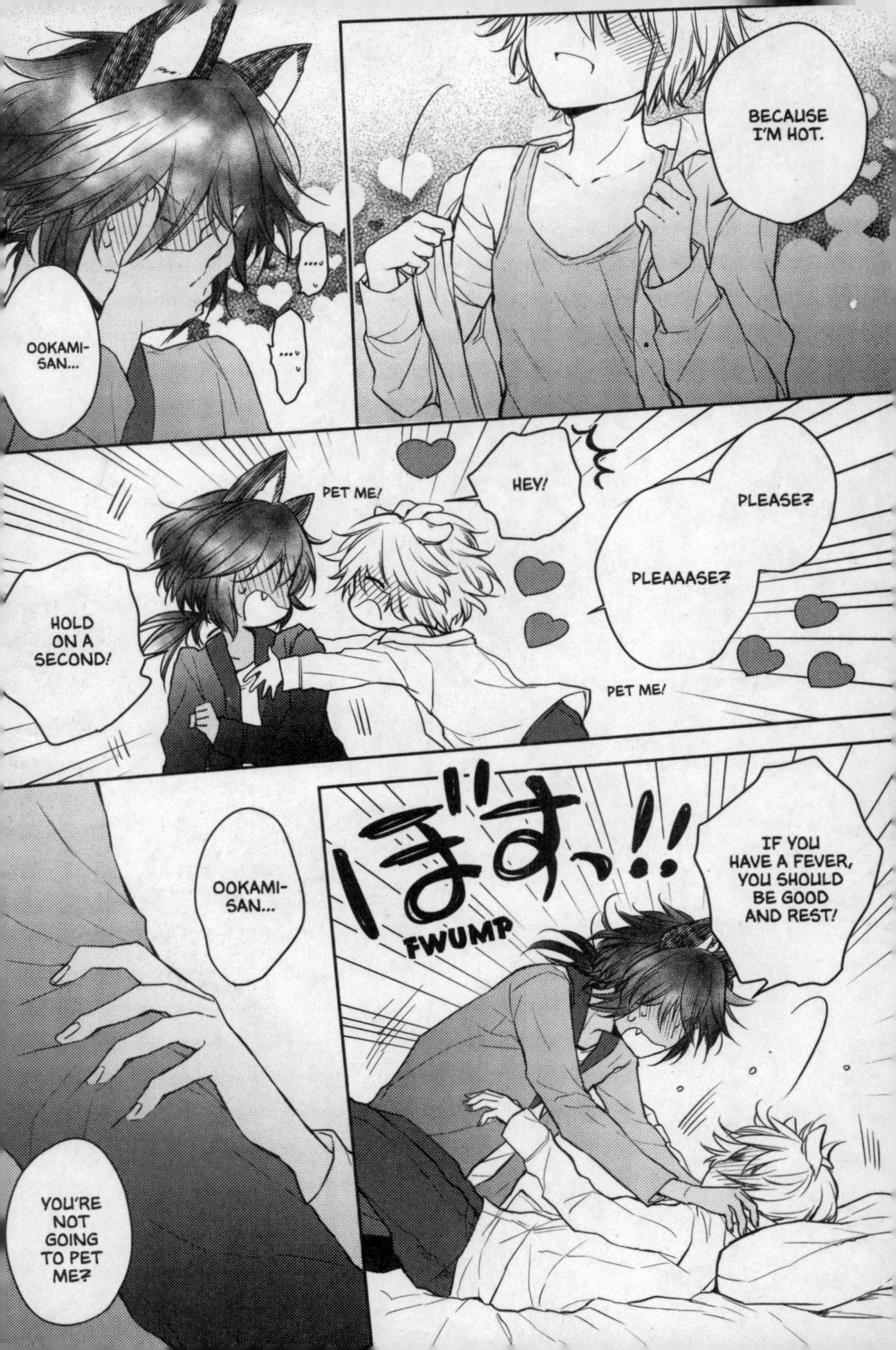
BECAUSE I'M HOT.
....
...
OOKAMI-SAN...
PLEASE? PLEAAASE?
HEY!
PET ME!
PET ME!
HOLD ON A SECOND!
IF YOU HAVE A FEVER, YOU SHOULD BE GOOD AND REST!
ぼすっ!!
FWUMP
OOKAMI-SAN...
YOU'RE NOT GOING TO PET ME?

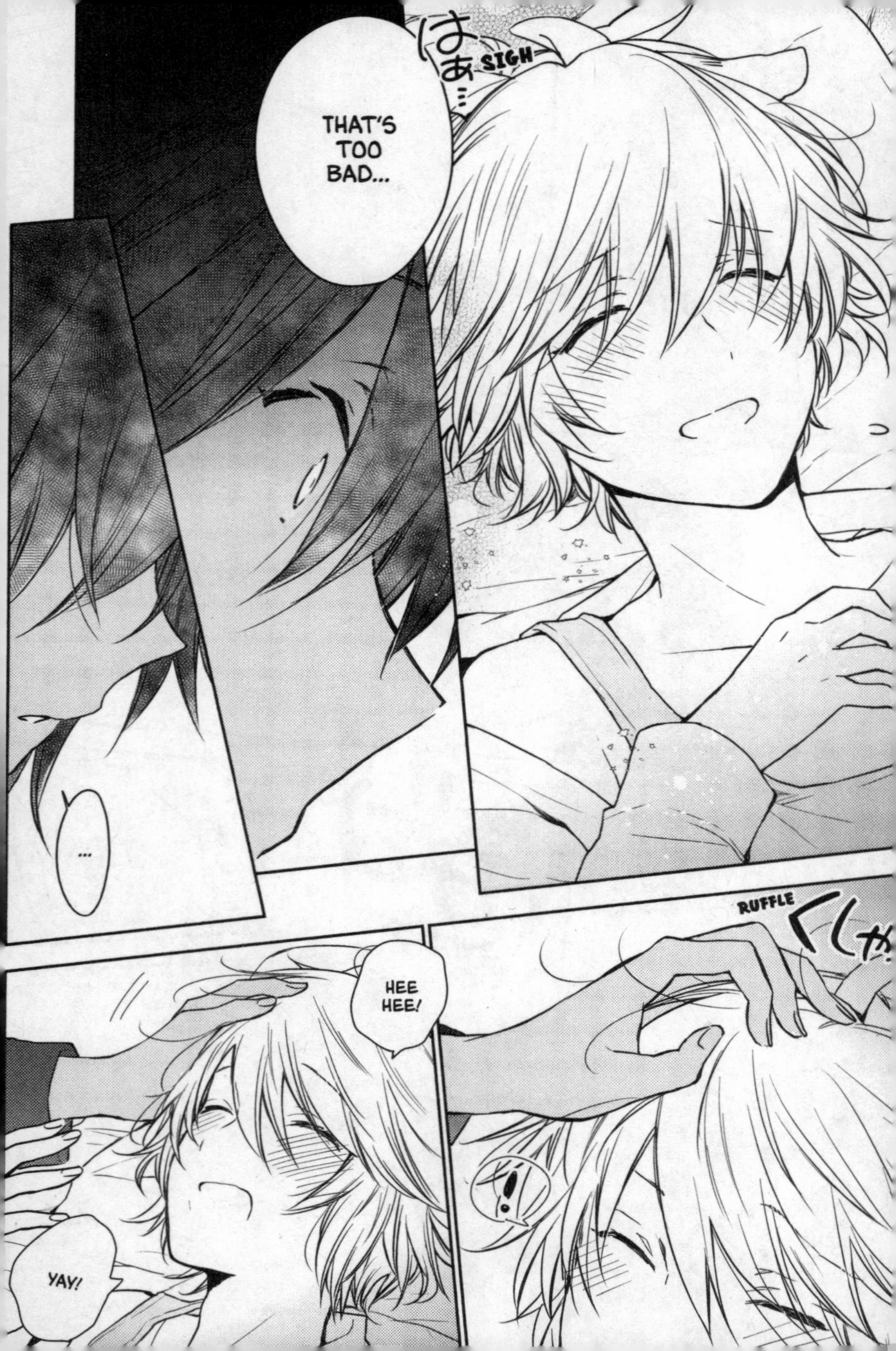
はぁ…
SIGH
THAT'S TOO BAD...
...
RUFFLE
くしゃ
HEE HEE!
YAY!

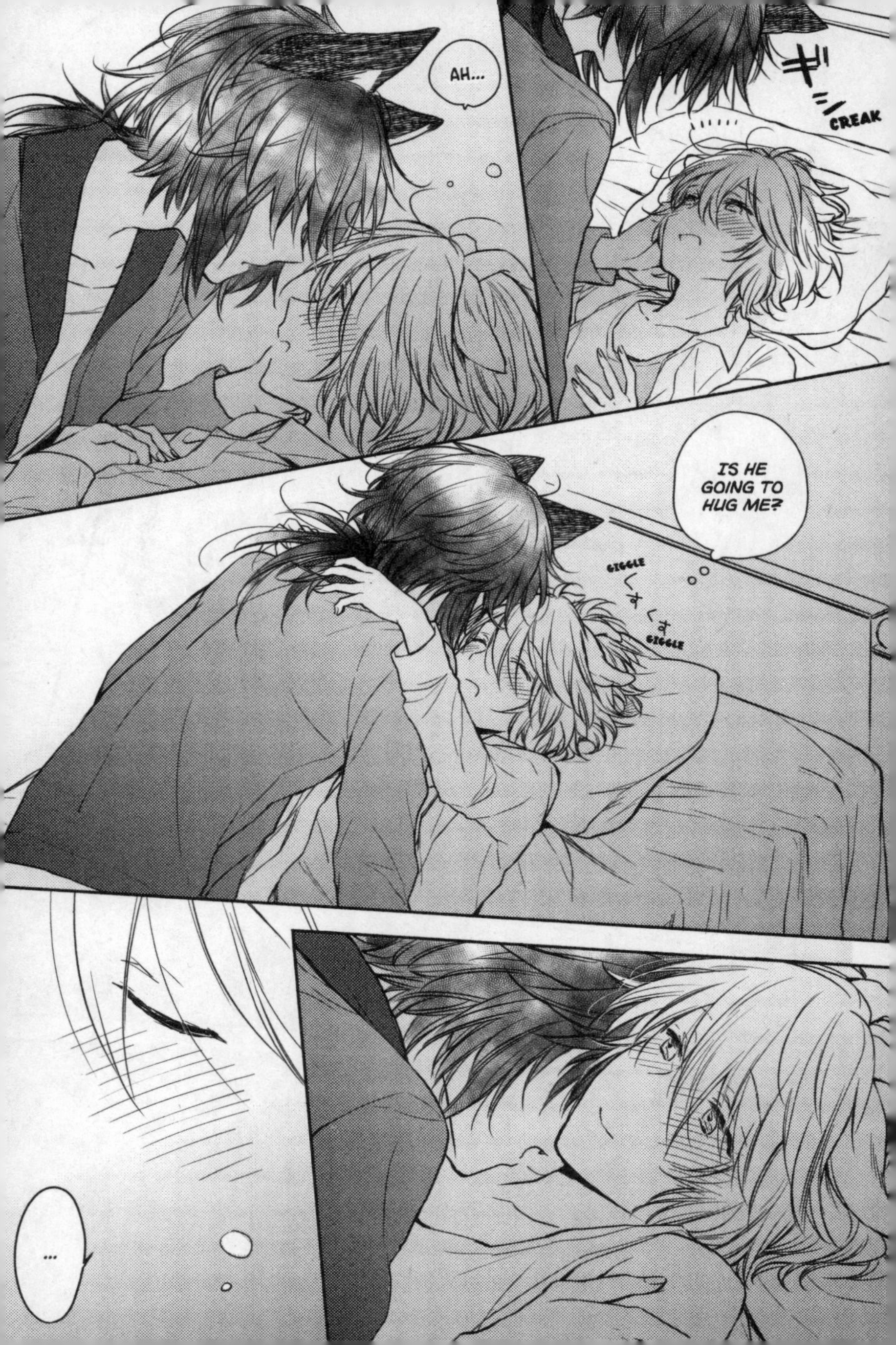
ギシ
CREAK
......
AH...
IS HE GOING TO HUG ME?
GIGGLE
くすくす
GIGGLE
...

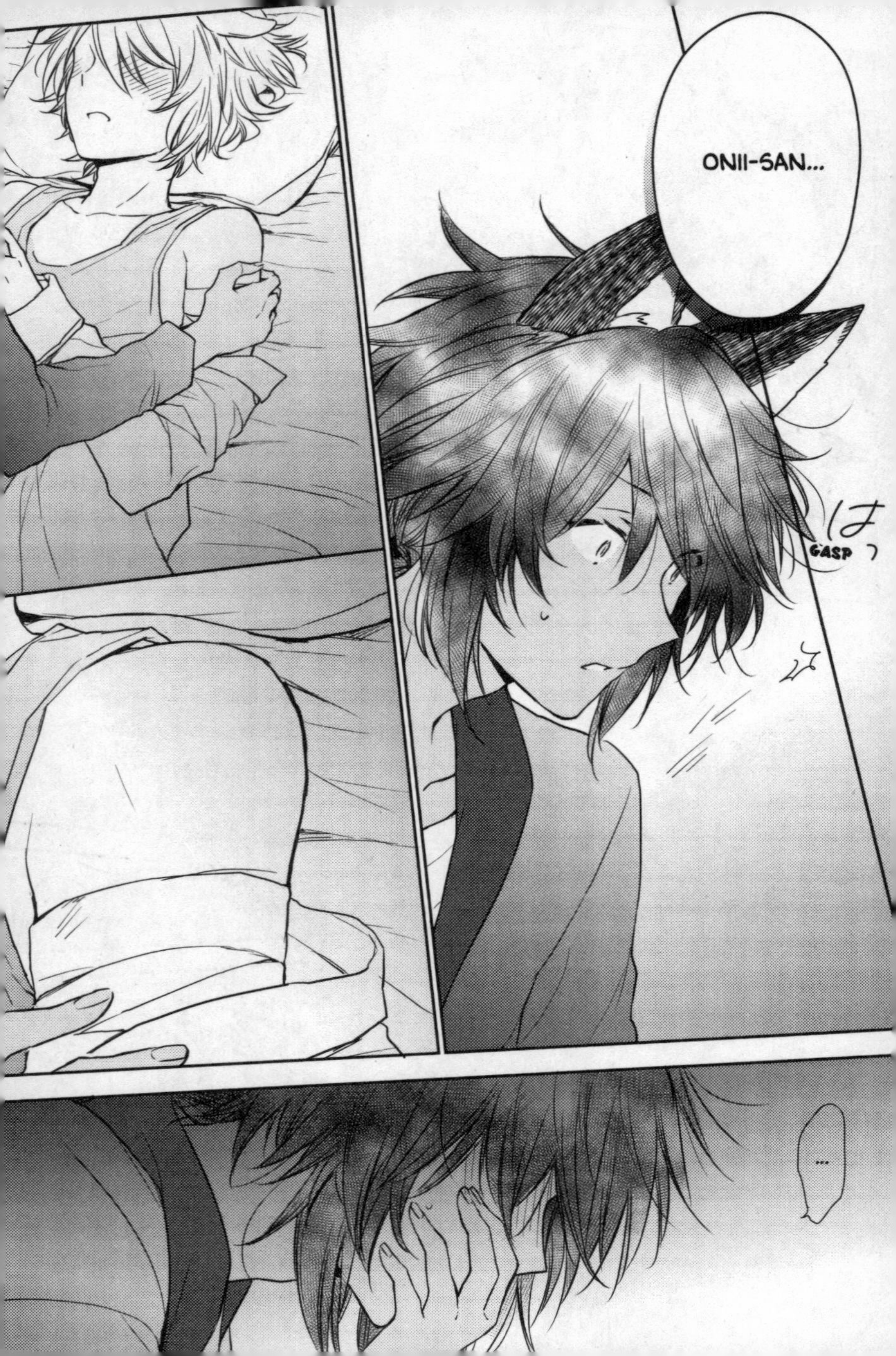
ONII-SAN...
は
GASP
...

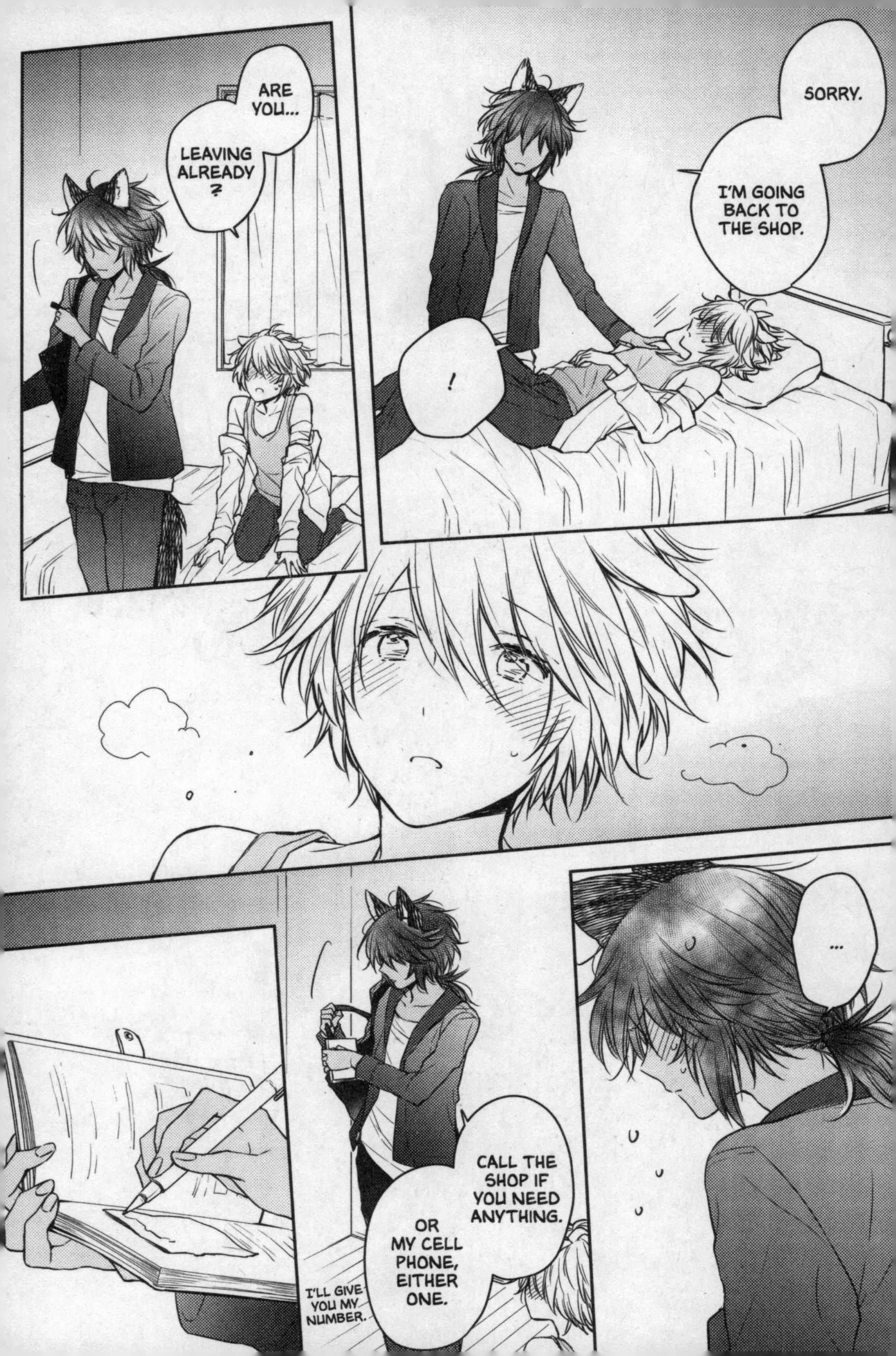
SORRY.
I'M GOING BACK TO THE SHOP.
!
ARE YOU...
LEAVING ALREADY?
...
CALL THE SHOP IF YOU NEED ANYTHING.
OR MY CELL PHONE, EITHER ONE.
I'LL GIVE YOU MY NUMBER.

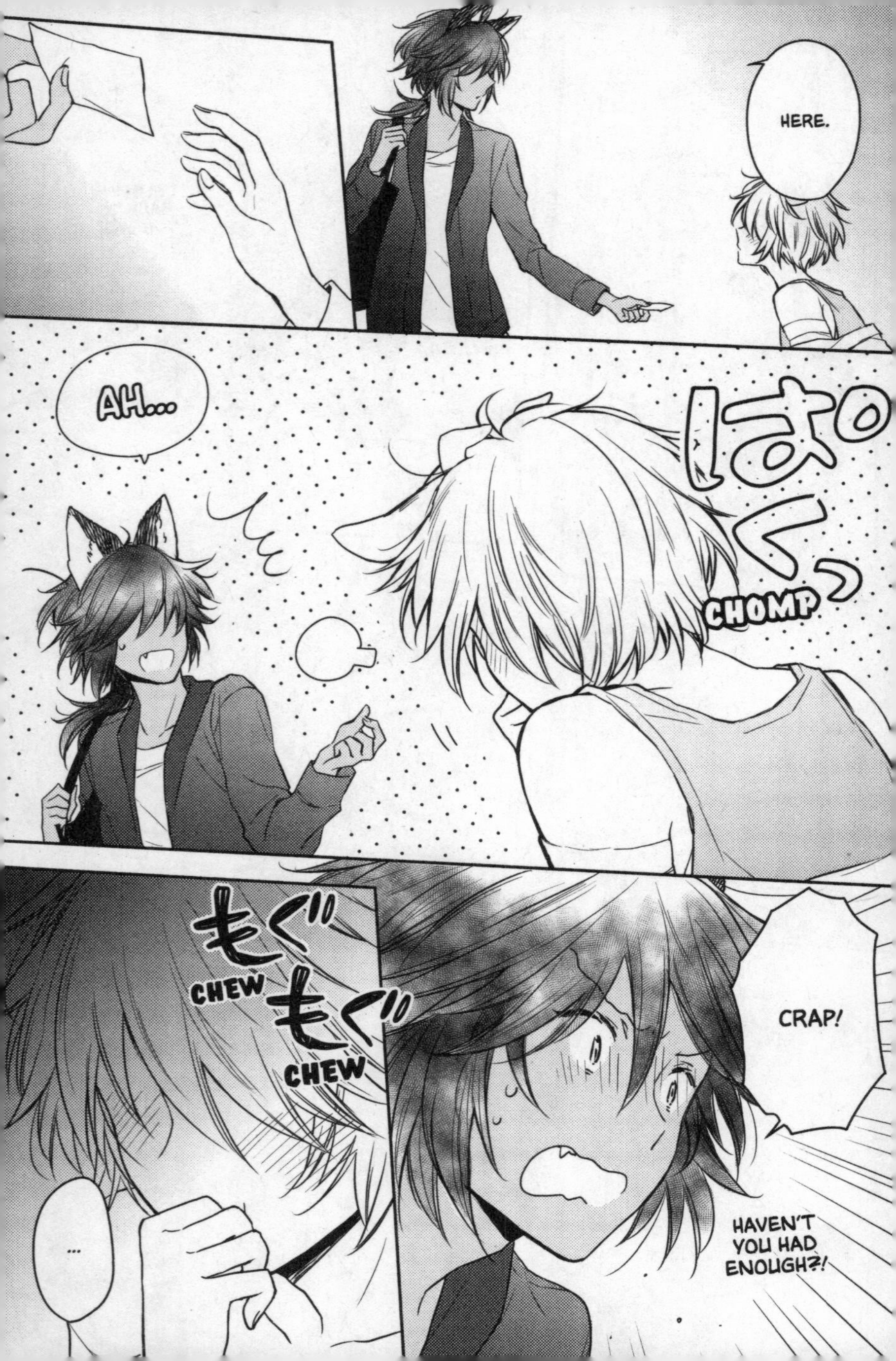
HERE.
はぐっ
CHOMP
AH...
CRAP!
HAVEN'T YOU HAD ENOUGH?!
もぐ
CHEW
もぐ
CHEW
...

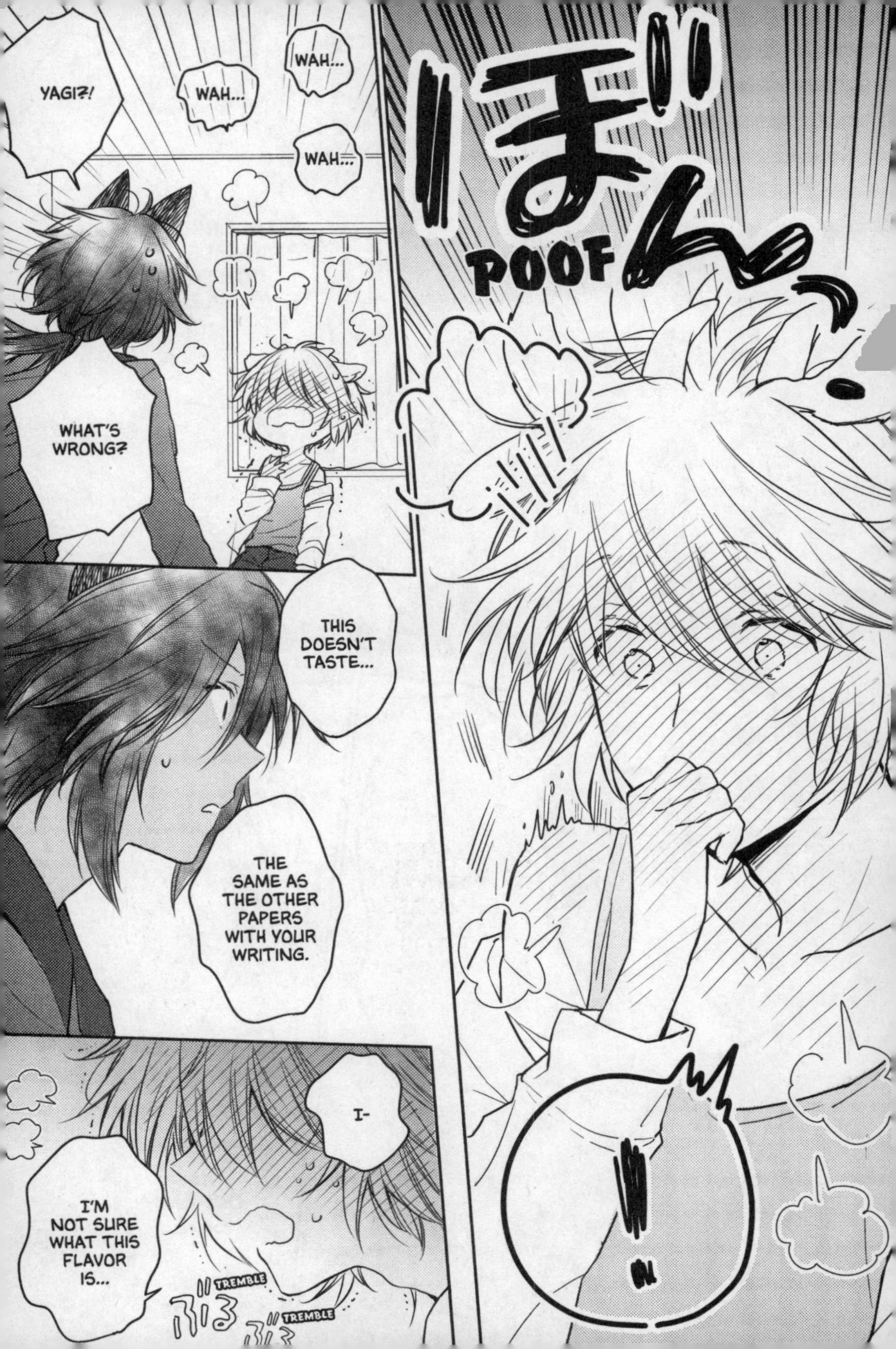
ぼん
POOF
!
WAH...
WAH...
YAGI?!
WAH...
WHAT'S WRONG?
THIS DOESN'T TASTE...
THE SAME AS THE OTHER PAPERS WITH YOUR WRITING.
I-
I'M NOT SURE WHAT THIS FLAVOR IS...
TREMBLE
ぶる
TREMBLE
ぶる

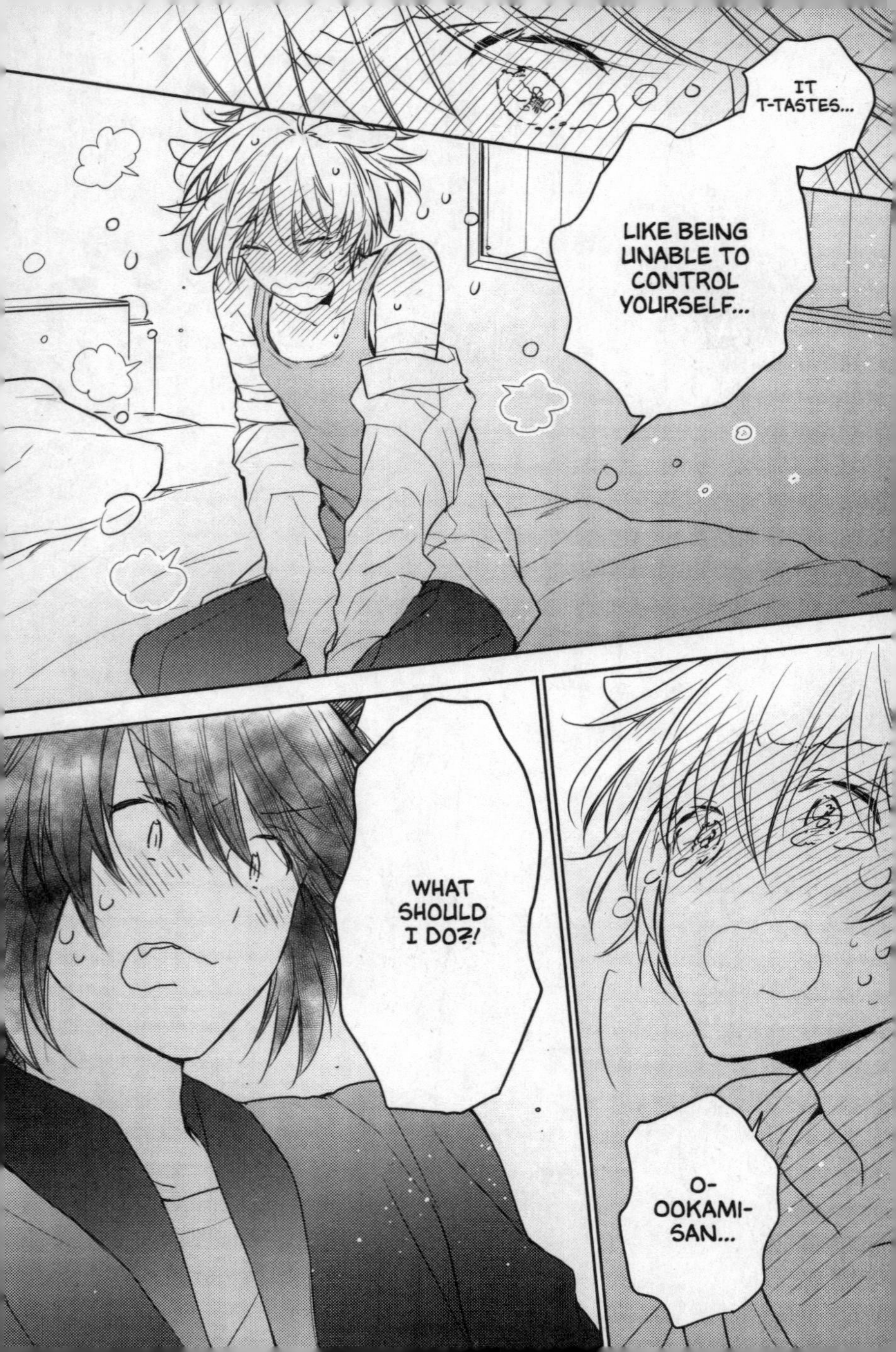
IT T-TASTES...
LIKE BEING UNABLE TO CONTROL YOURSELF...
O-OOKAMI-SAN...
WHAT SHOULD I DO?!

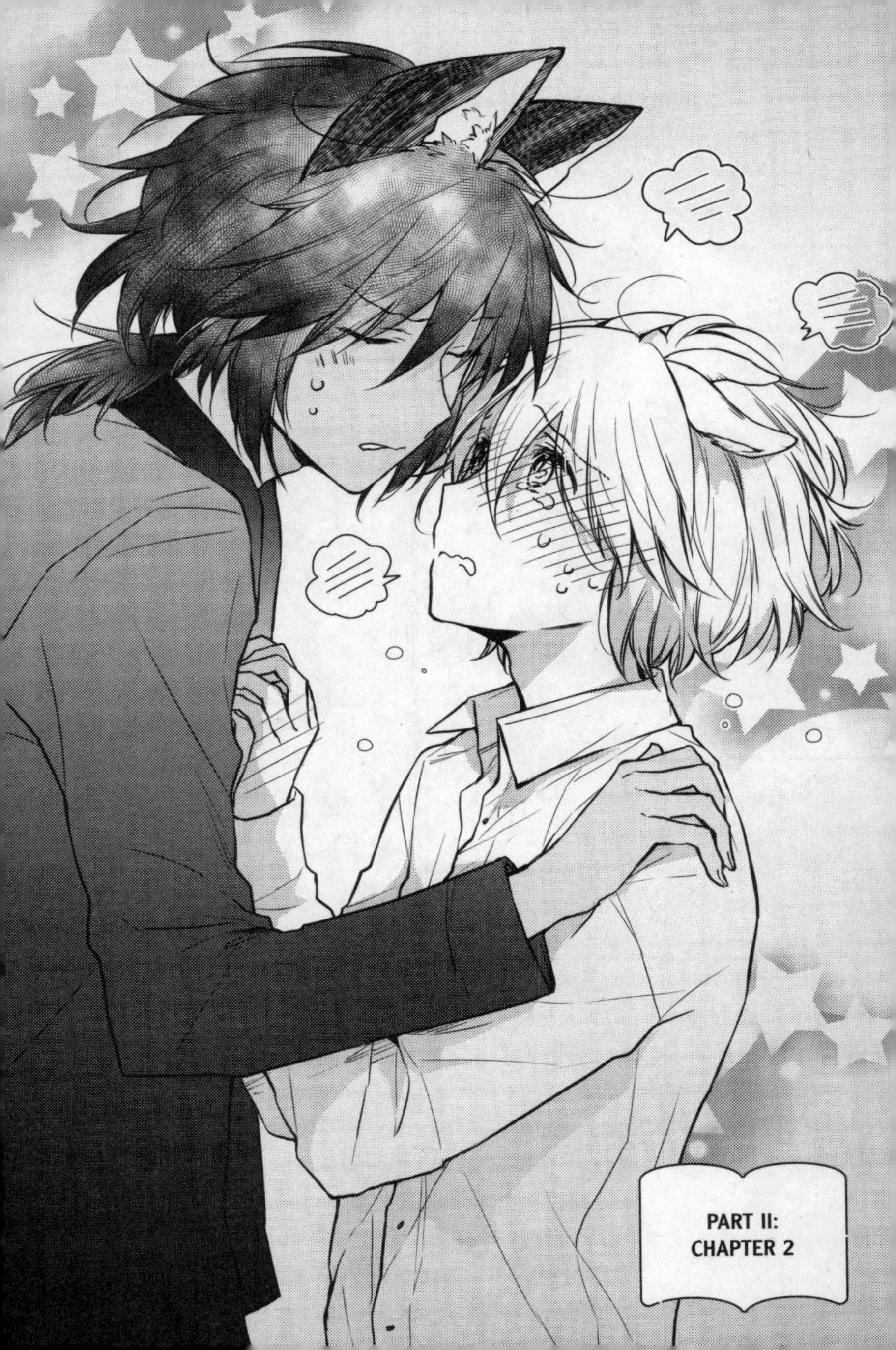
PART II:
CHAPTER 2

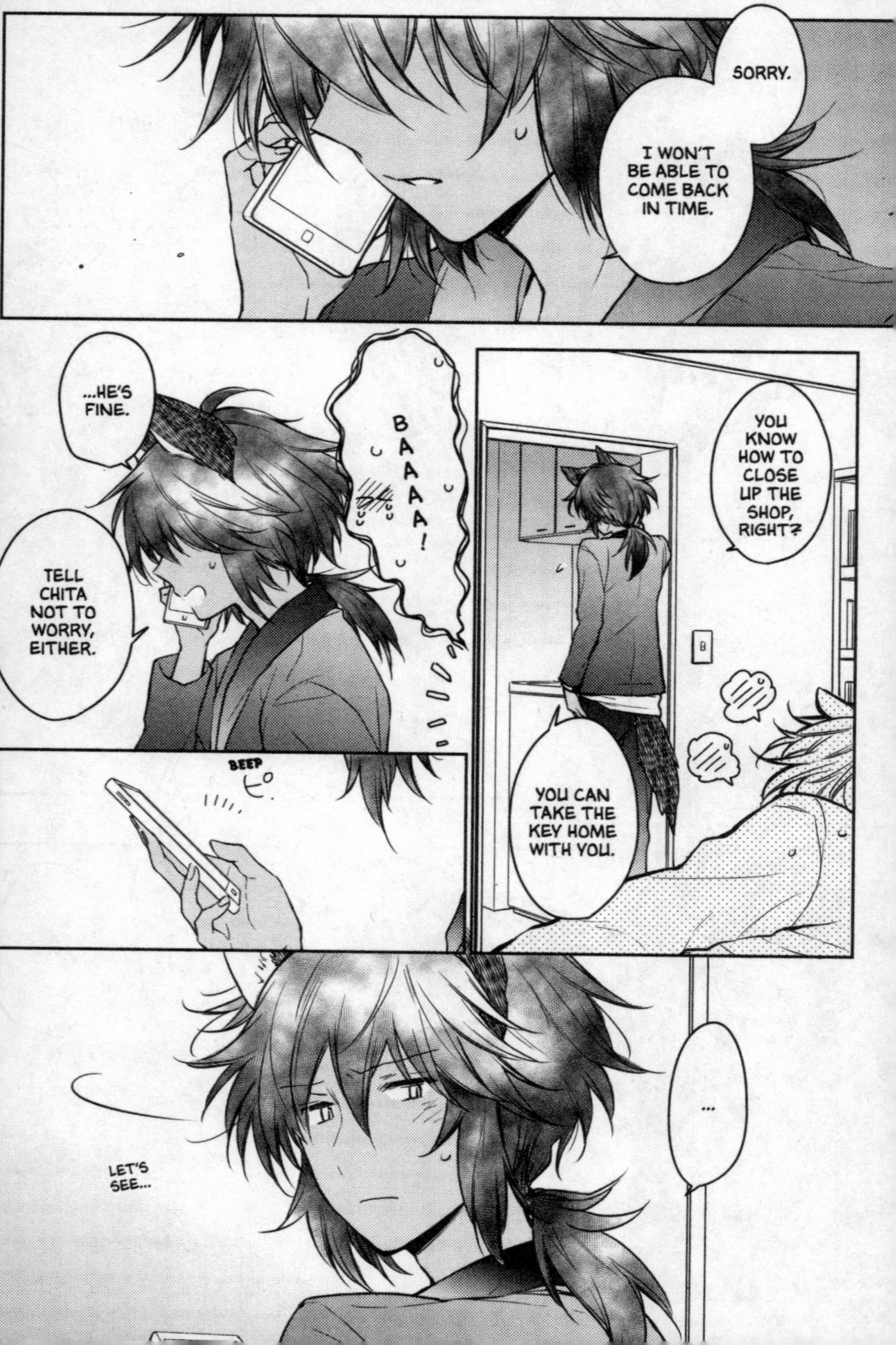

SORRY.
I WON'T BE ABLE TO COME BACK IN TIME.
YOU KNOW HOW TO CLOSE UP THE SHOP, RIGHT?
YOU CAN TAKE THE KEY HOME WITH YOU.
BAAAA!
...HE'S FINE.
TELL CHITA NOT TO WORRY, EITHER.
BEEP
...
LET'S SEE...

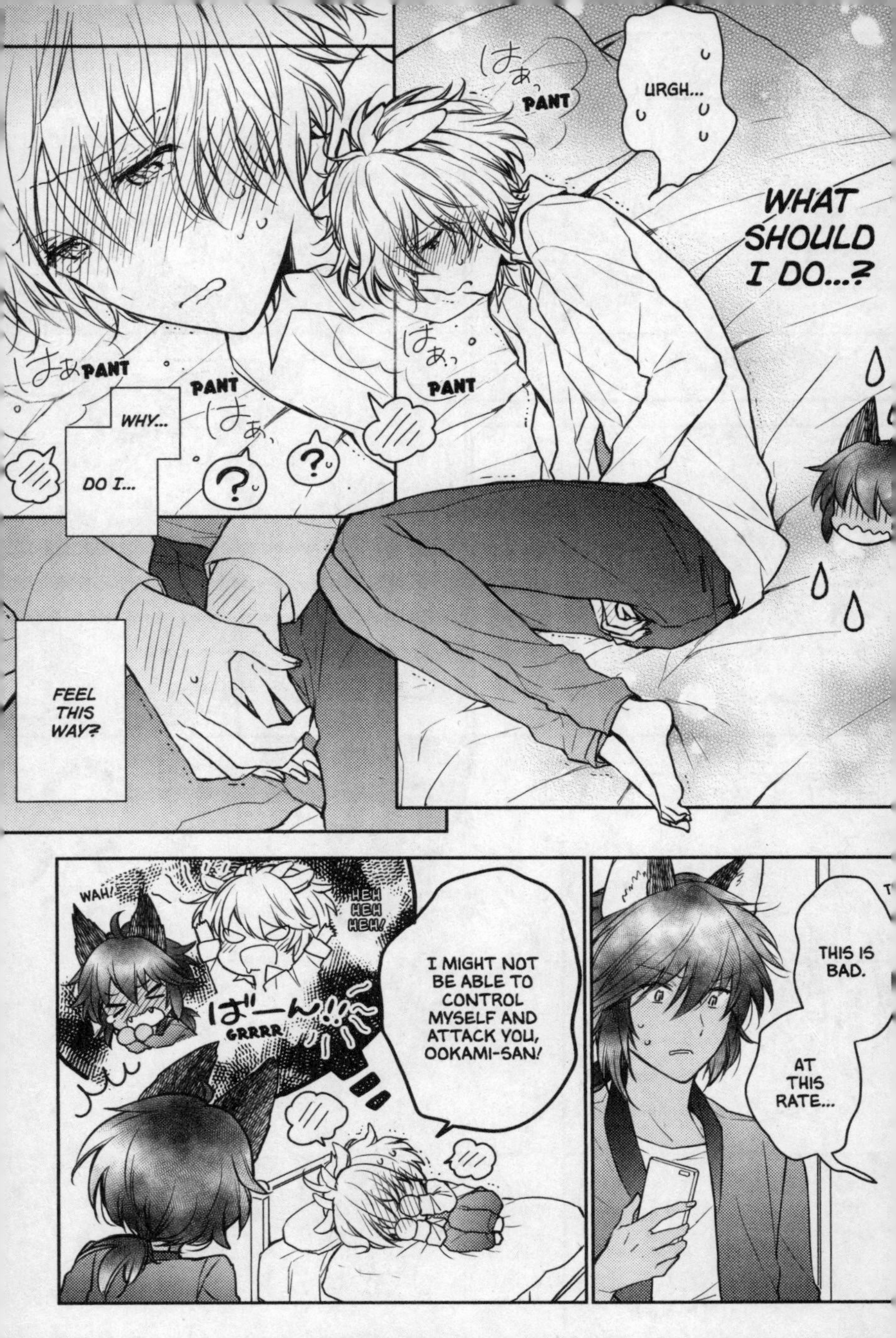
はぁっ
PANT
URGH...
WHAT SHOULD I DO...?
はぁっ
PANT
はあ PANT
PANT はぁ
WHY...
DO I...
FEEL THIS WAY?
THIS IS BAD.
AT THIS RATE...
I MIGHT NOT BE ABLE TO CONTROL MYSELF AND ATTACK YOU, OOKAMI-SAN!
HEH HEH HEH!
WAH!
ばーん!!
GRRRR

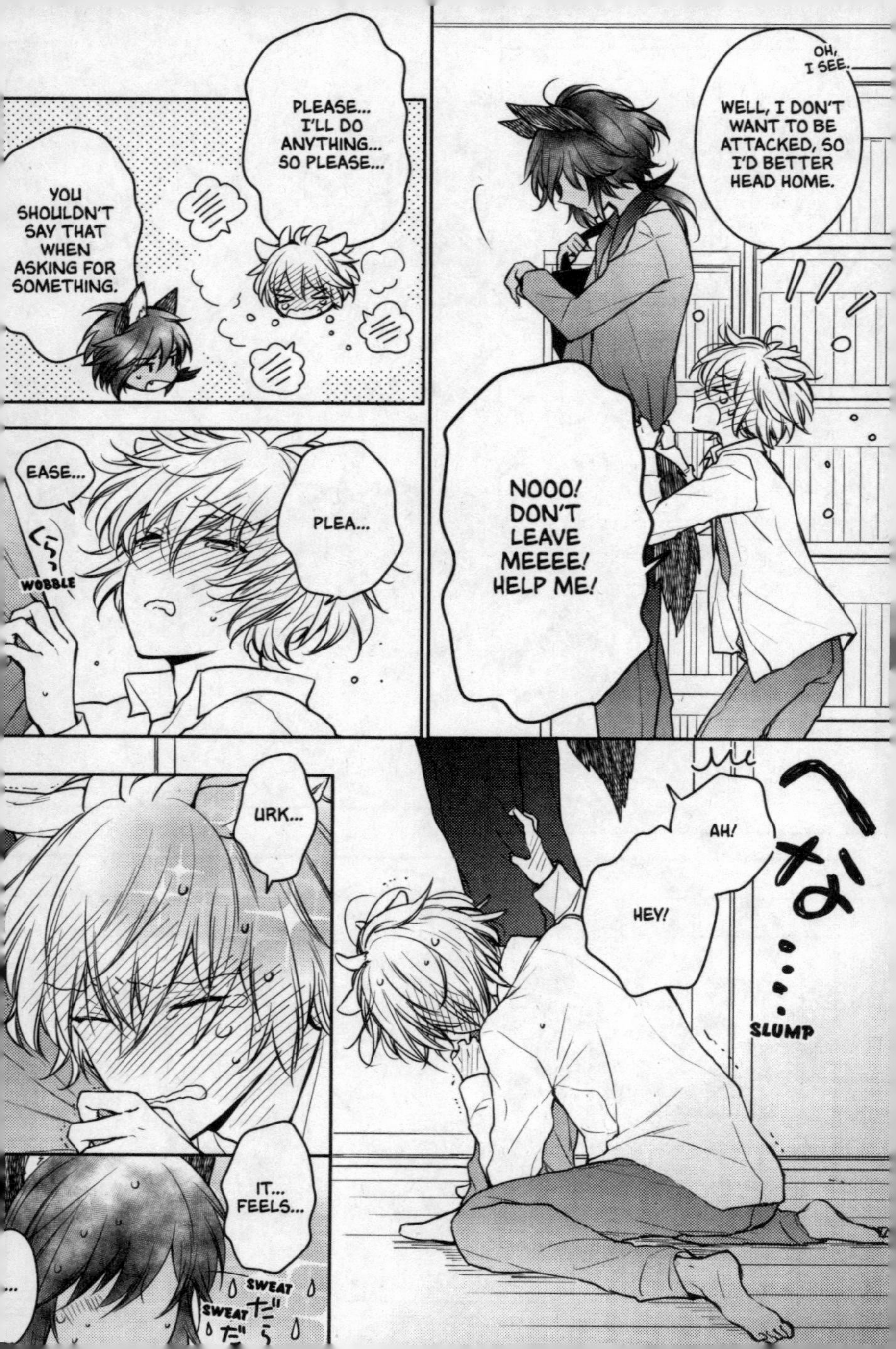
OH, I SEE.
WELL, I DON'T WANT TO BE ATTACKED, SO I'D BETTER HEAD HOME.
NOOO! DON'T LEAVE MEEEE! HELP ME!
PLEASE... I'LL DO ANYTHING... SO PLEASE...
YOU SHOULDN'T SAY THAT WHEN ASKING FOR SOMETHING.
PLEA...
EASE...
くらっ
WOBBLE
へな...
SLUMP
AH!
HEY!
URK...
IT... FEELS...
...
SWEAT だ
SWEAT だ

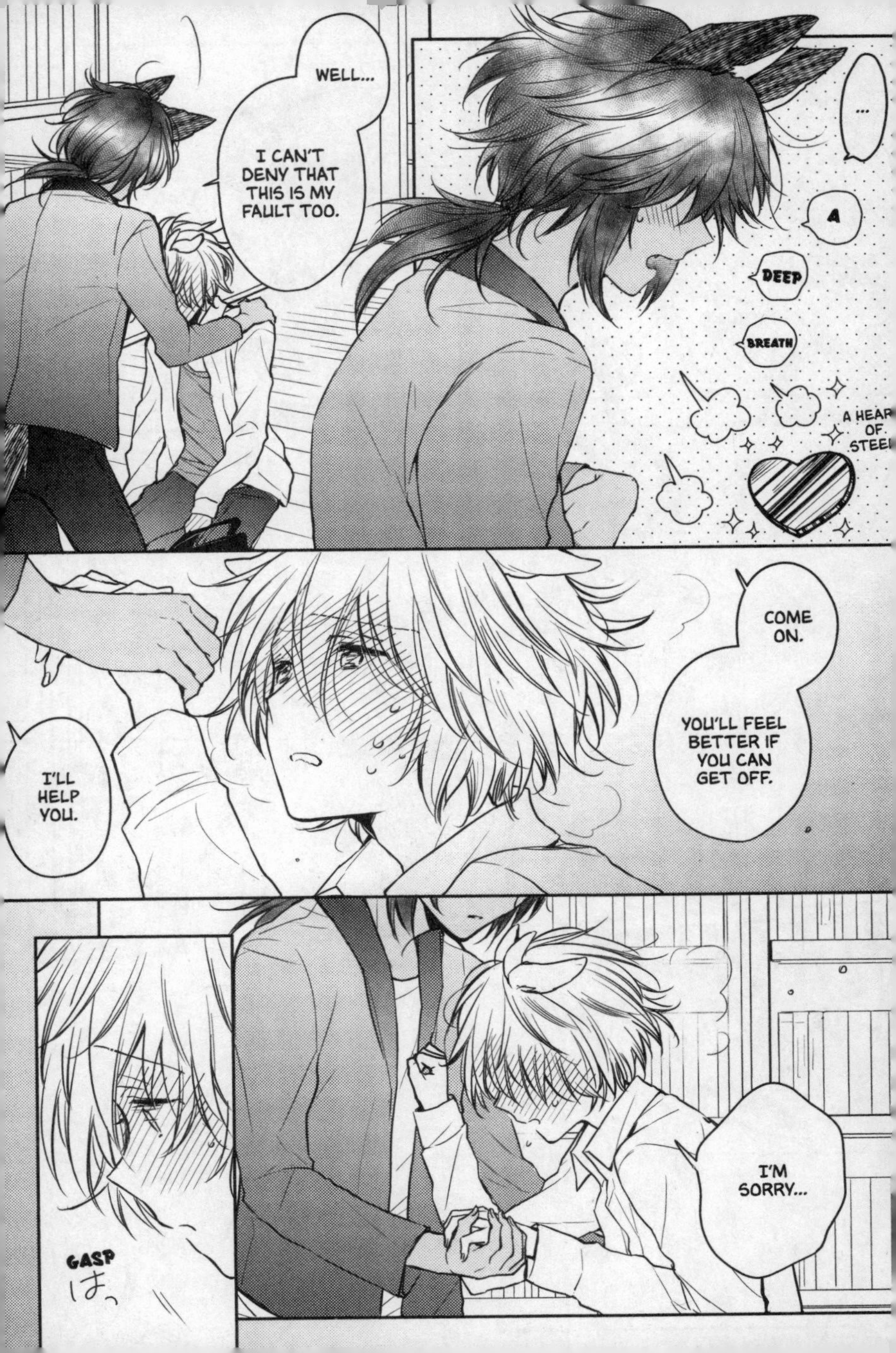
...
A
DEEP
BREATH
A HEAR OF STEE
WELL...
I CAN'T DENY THAT THIS IS MY FAULT TOO.
COME ON.
YOU'LL FEEL BETTER IF YOU CAN GET OFF.
I'LL HELP YOU.
I'M SORRY...
GASP
はっ

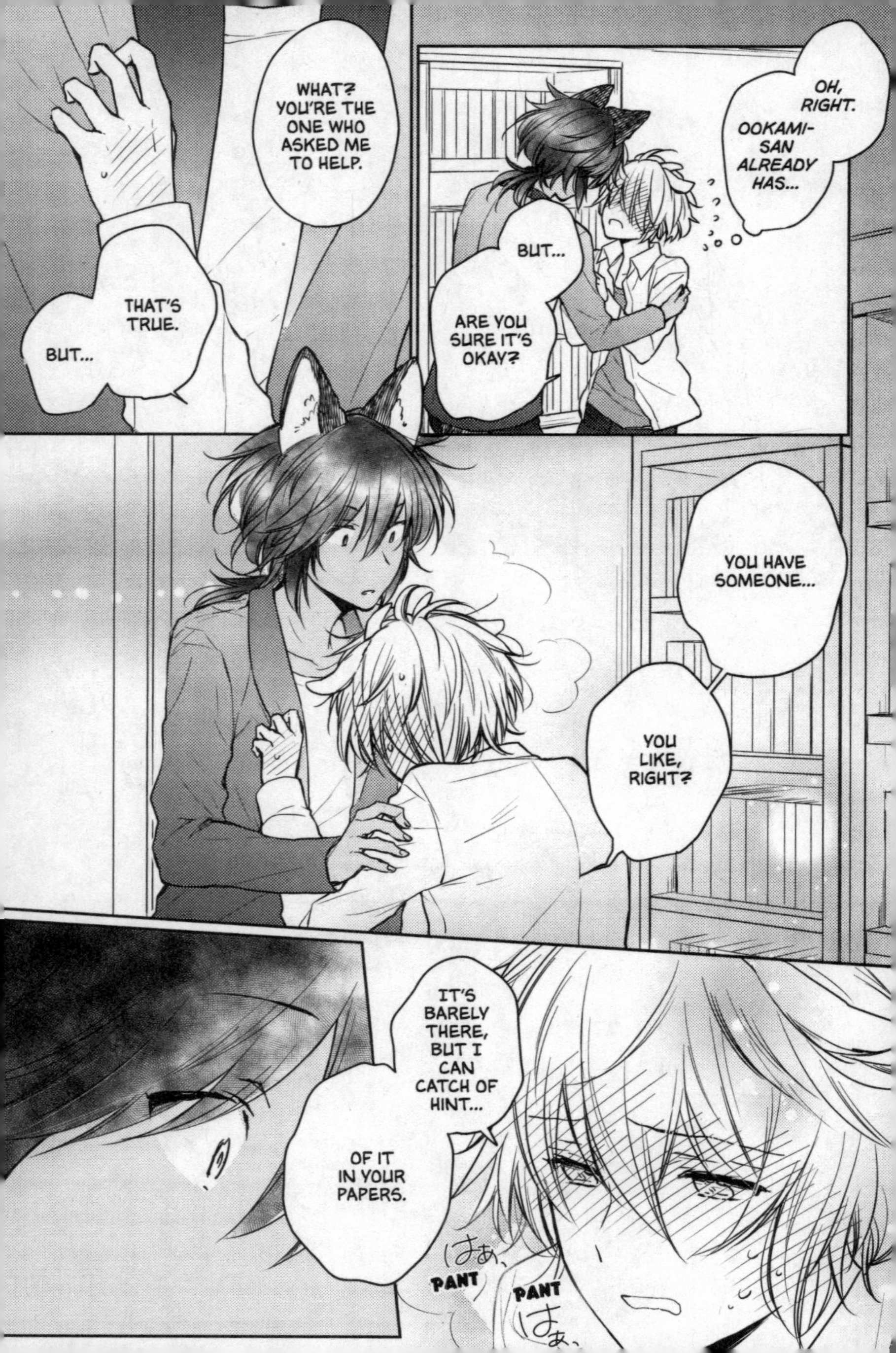

OH, RIGHT.
OOKAMI-SAN ALREADY HAS...
BUT...
ARE YOU SURE IT'S OKAY?
WHAT? YOU'RE THE ONE WHO ASKED ME TO HELP.
THAT'S TRUE.
BUT...
YOU HAVE SOMEONE...
YOU LIKE, RIGHT?
IT'S BARELY THERE, BUT I CAN CATCH OF HINT...
OF IT IN YOUR PAPERS.
はあ、 PANT
PANT はあ、

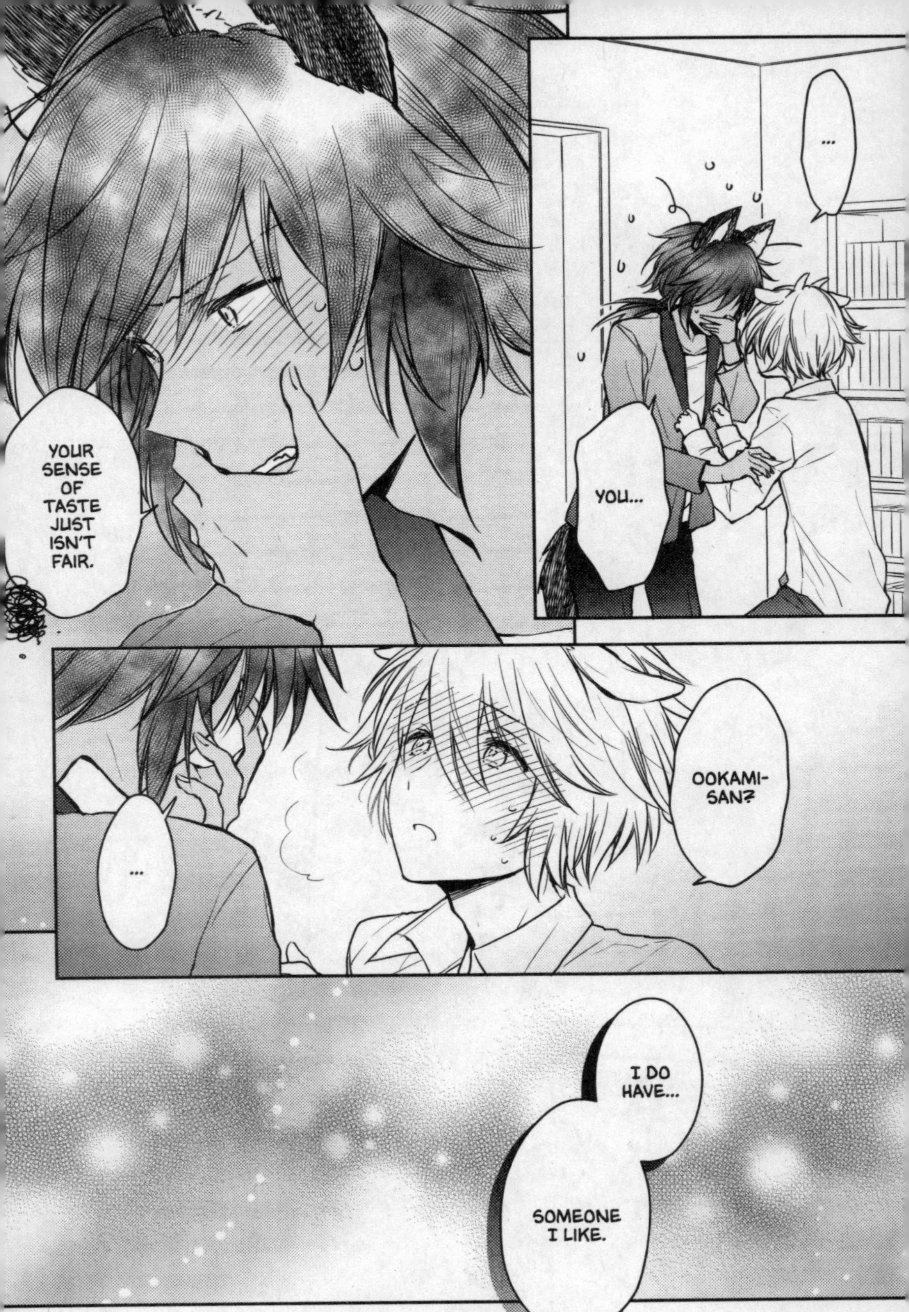
...
YOU...
YOUR SENSE OF TASTE JUST ISN'T FAIR.
OOKAMI-SAN?
...
I DO HAVE...
SOMEONE I LIKE.

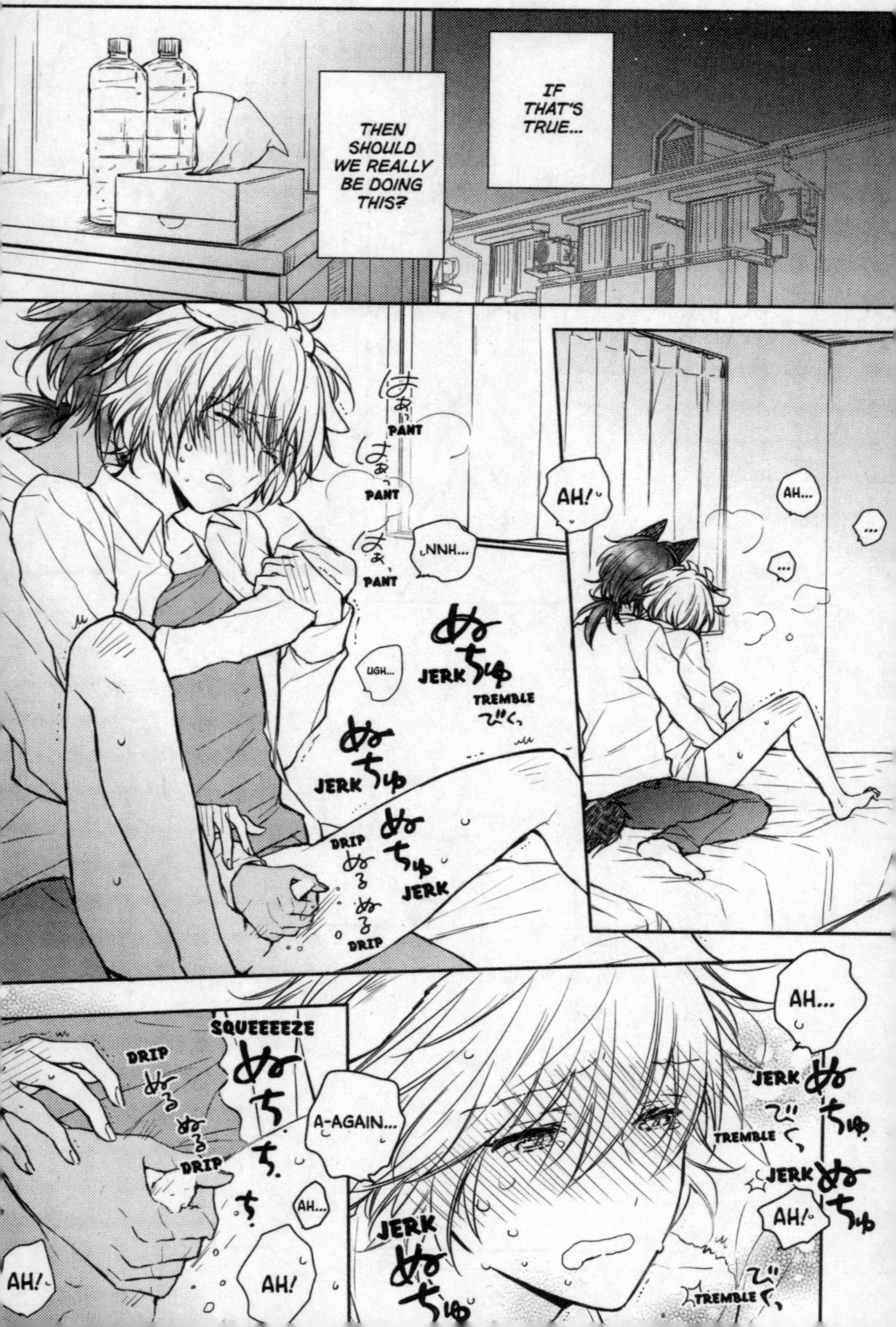

IF THAT'S TRUE...
THEN SHOULD WE REALLY BE DOING THIS?
AH...
...
...
AH!
はぁ PANT
はぁ PANT
はぁ PANT
NNH...
ぬちゅ JERK
TREMBLE びくっ
UGH...
ぬちゅ JERK
ぬちゅ JERK
DRIP ぬるぬる DRIP
AH...
JERK ぬちゅ
TREMBLE びくっ
JERK ぬちゅ
AH!
TREMBLE びくっ
A-AGAIN...
JERK ぬちゅ
SQUEEEEZE ぬちちち
DRIP ぬるぬる DRIP
AH...
AH!
AH!

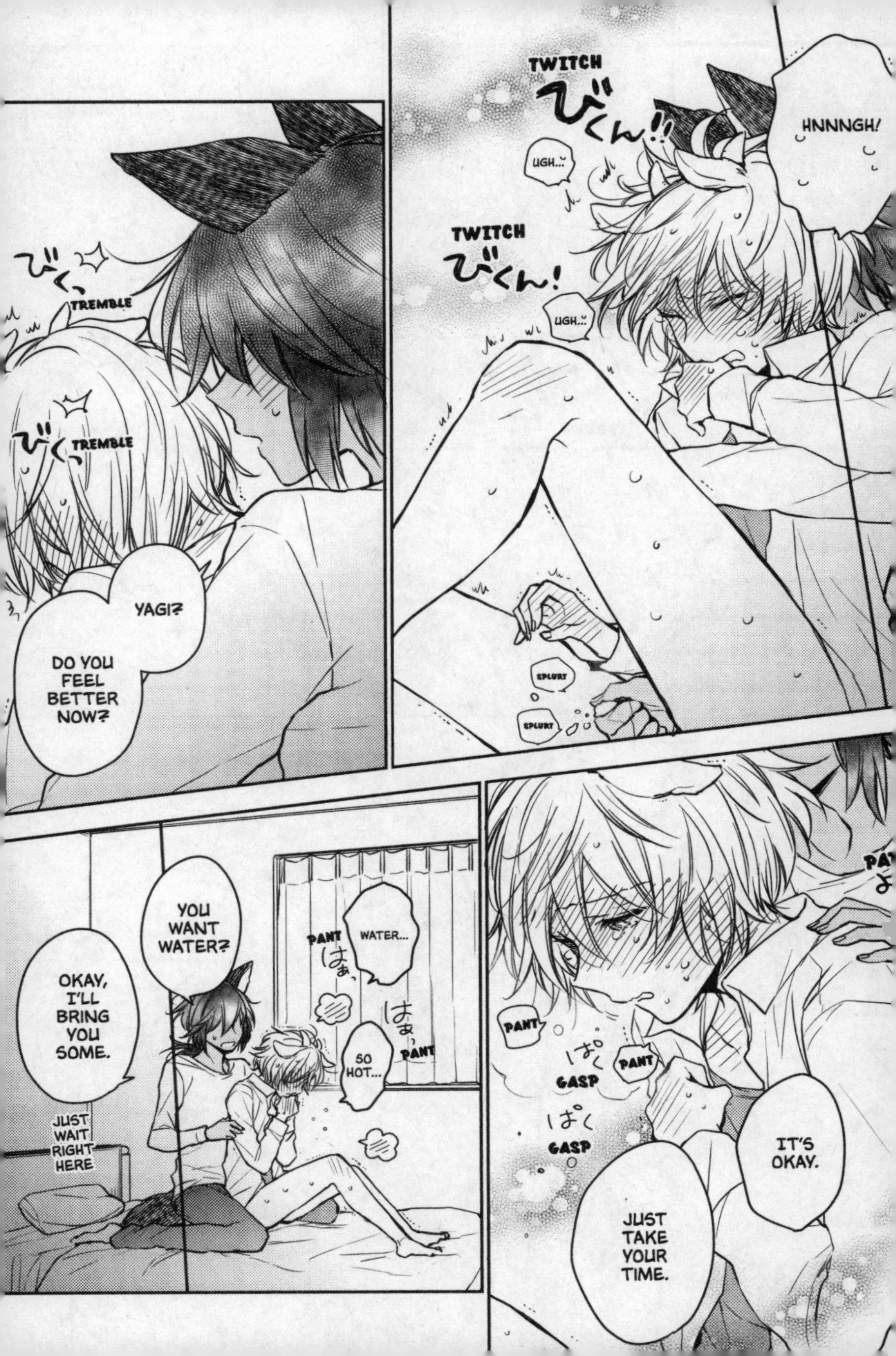
HNNNGH!
TWITCH
びくん!!
UGH...
TWITCH
びくん!
UGH...
SPLURT
SPLURT
びくっ
TREMBLE
びくっ
TREMBLE
YAGI?
DO YOU FEEL BETTER NOW?
PANT
PANT
ぱく
GASP
ぱく
GASP
IT'S OKAY.
JUST TAKE YOUR TIME.
WATER...
PANT
はぁ
はぁ
PANT
SO HOT...
YOU WANT WATER?
OKAY, I'LL BRING YOU SOME.
JUST WAIT RIGHT HERE

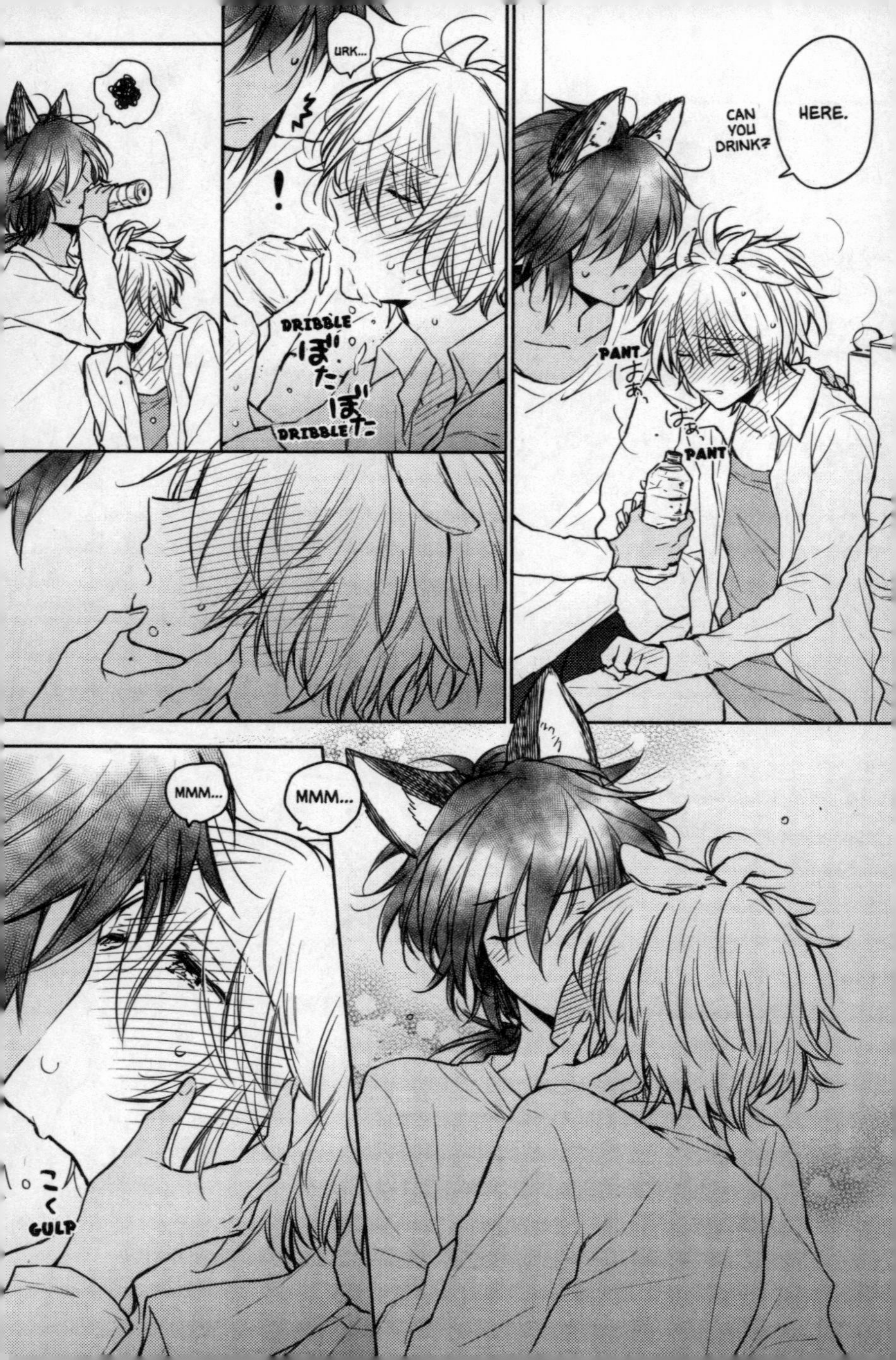
HERE.
CAN YOU DRINK?
PANT
はぁ、
はぁ、
PANT
URK...
!
DRIBBLE
ぼた
ぼた
DRIBBLE
MMM...
MMM...
こく
GULP

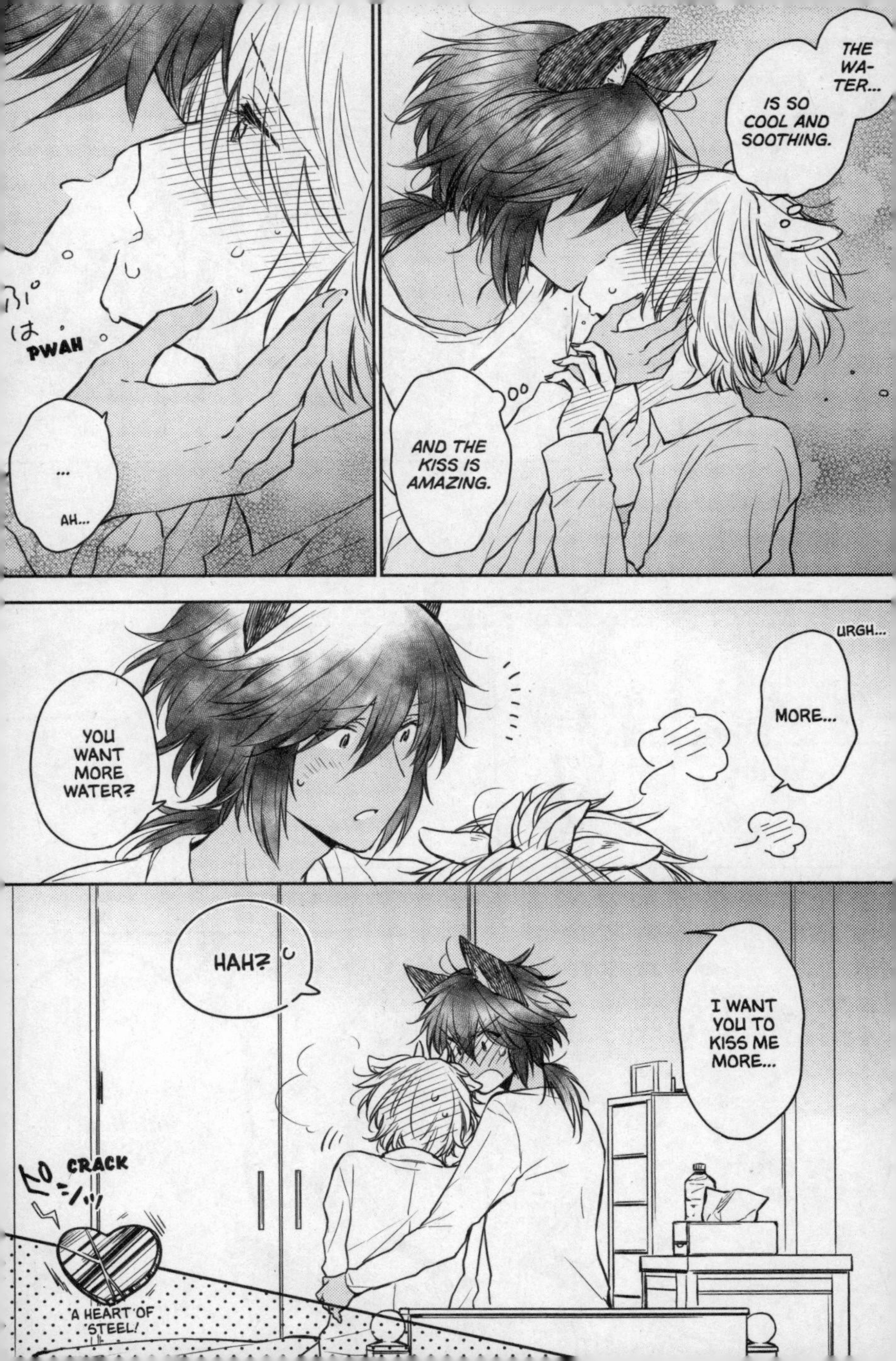
THE WATER... IS SO COOL AND SOOTHING.
AND THE KISS IS AMAZING.
ぷは
PWAH
...
AH...
URGH...
MORE...
YOU WANT MORE WATER?
I WANT YOU TO KISS ME MORE...
HAH?
CRACK
A HEART OF STEEL!

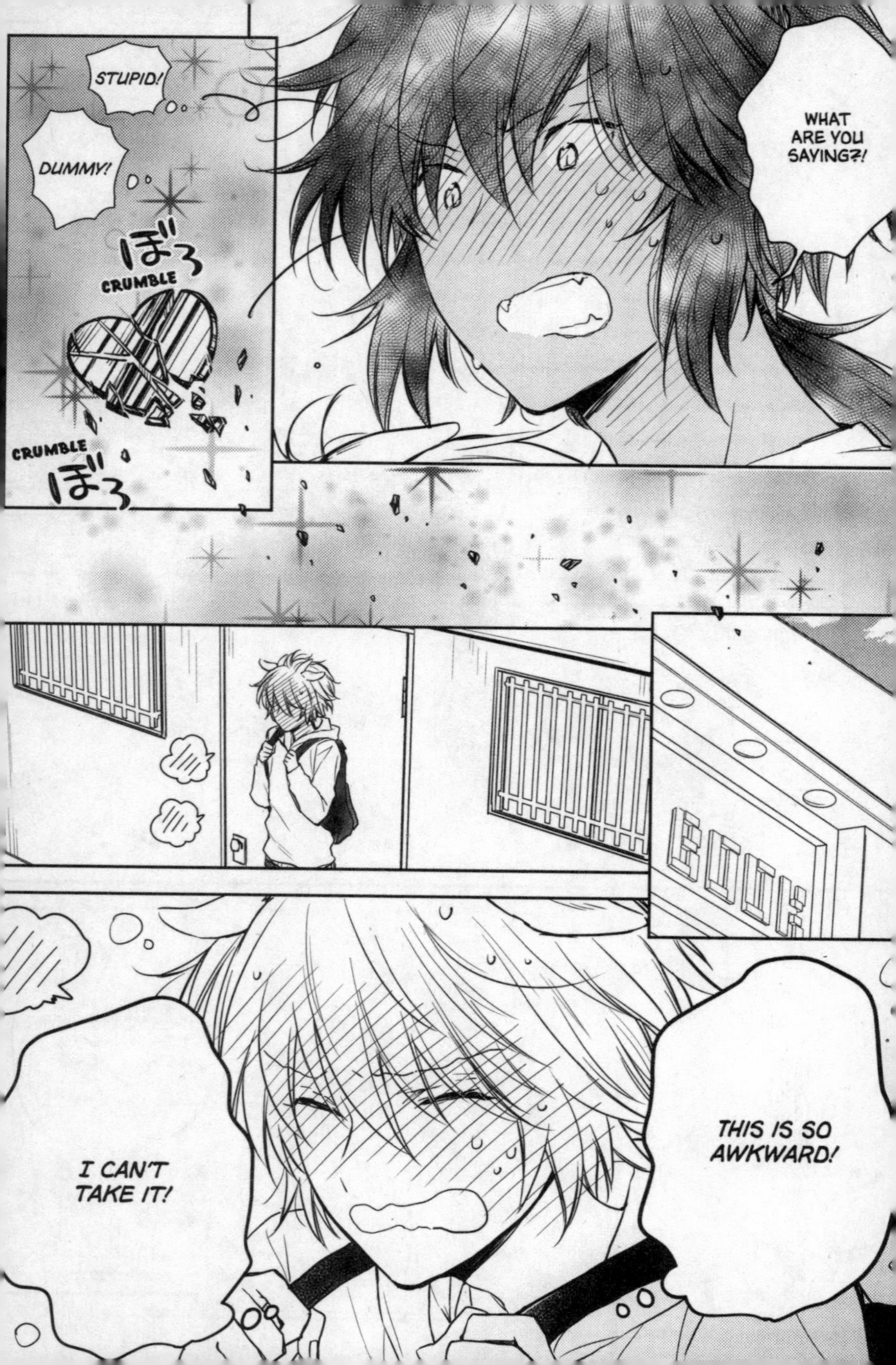
WHAT ARE YOU SAYING?!
STUPID!
DUMMY!
ぼろ
CRUMBLE
CRUMBLE
ぼろ
THIS IS SO AWKWARD!
I CAN'T TAKE IT!

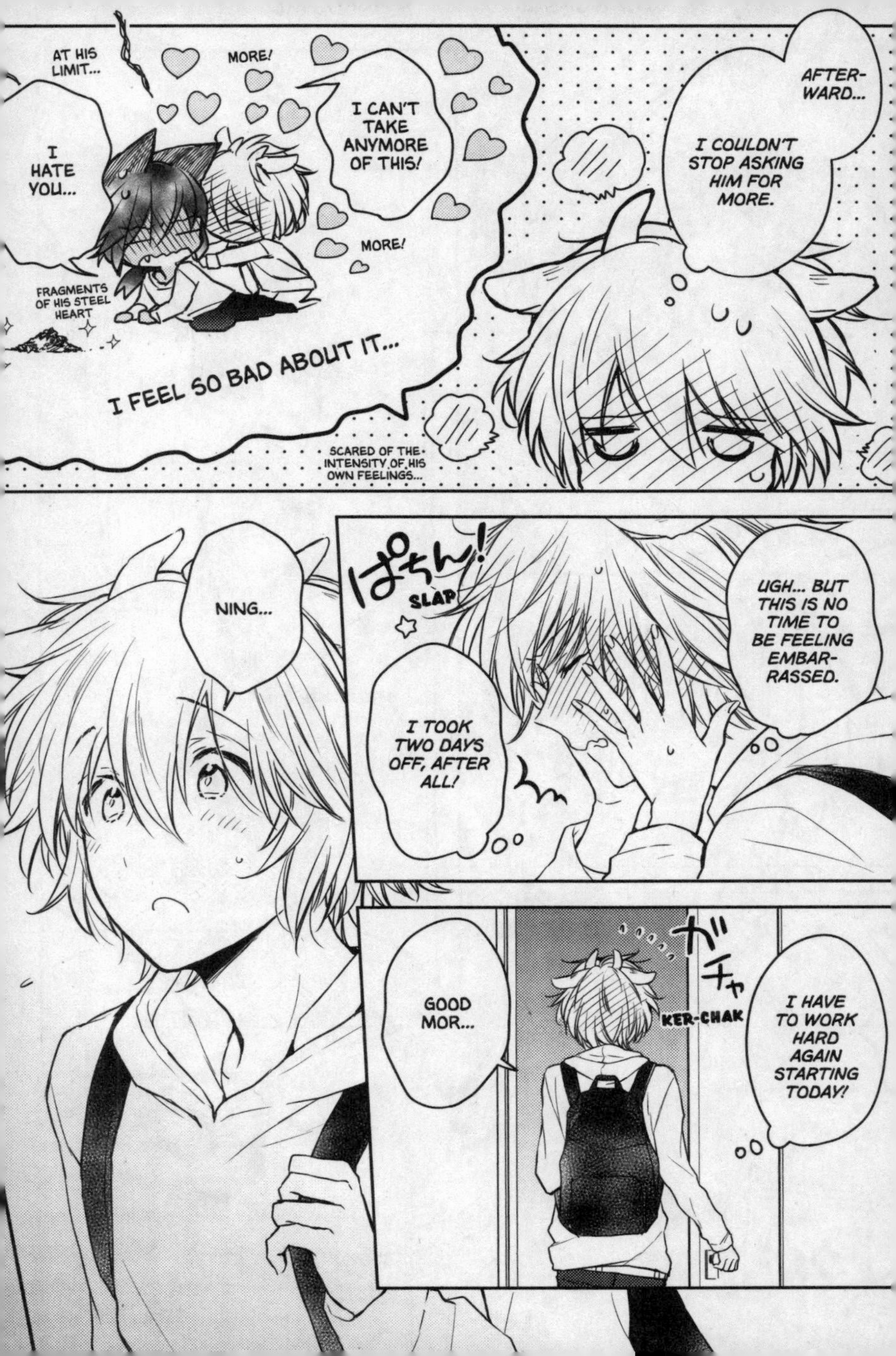
AFTER-WARD... I COULDN'T STOP ASKING HIM FOR MORE.
I CAN'T TAKE ANYMORE OF THIS!
MORE!
MORE!
AT HIS LIMIT...
I HATE YOU...
FRAGMENTS OF HIS STEEL HEART
I FEEL SO BAD ABOUT IT...
SCARED OF THE INTENSITY OF HIS OWN FEELINGS...
UGH... BUT THIS IS NO TIME TO BE FEELING EMBARRASSED.
ぱちん! SLAP
I TOOK TWO DAYS OFF, AFTER ALL!
I HAVE TO WORK HARD AGAIN STARTING TODAY!
ガチャ KER-CHAK
GOOD MOR...
NING...

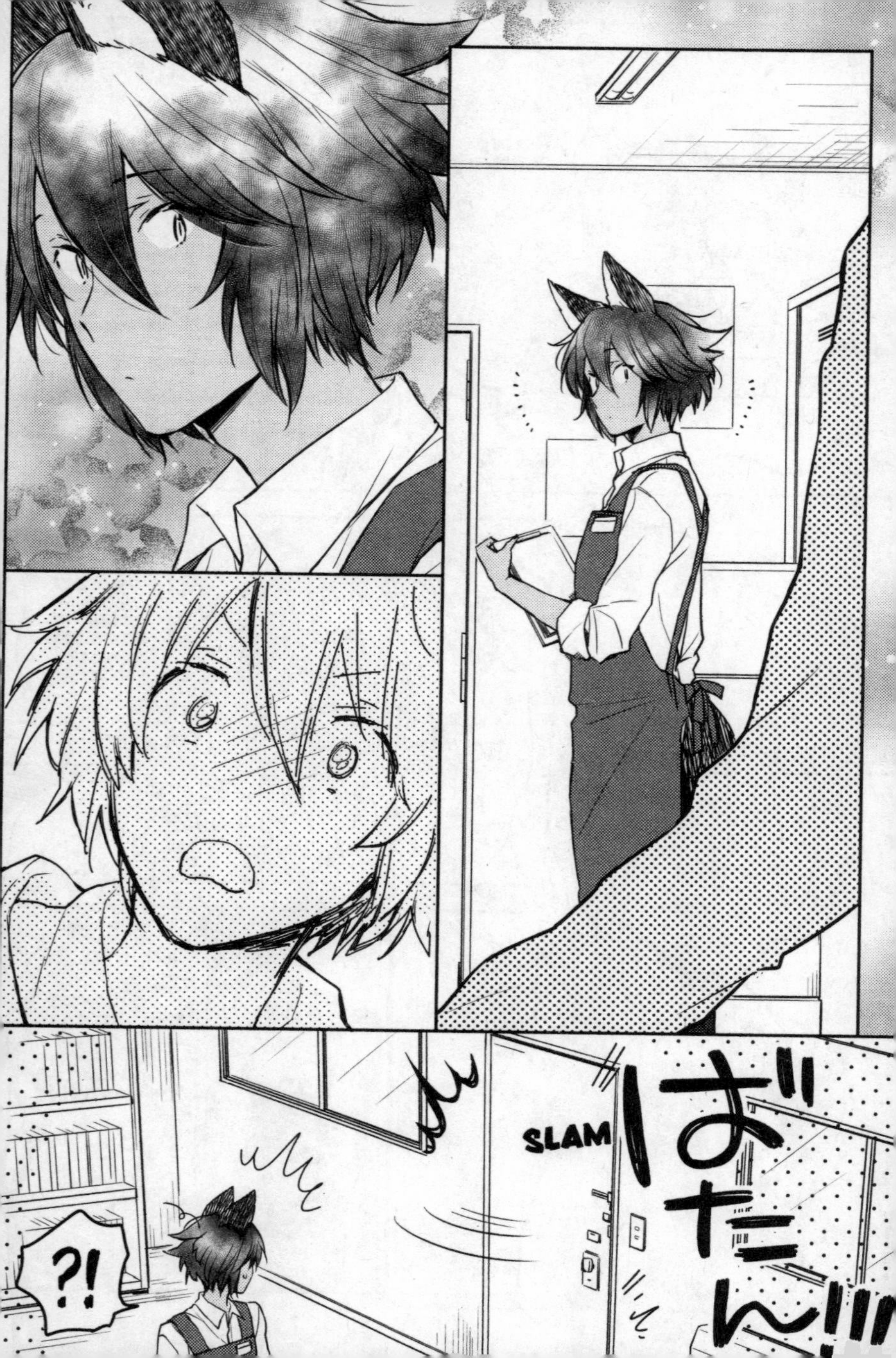
ばたん!!!
SLAM
?!

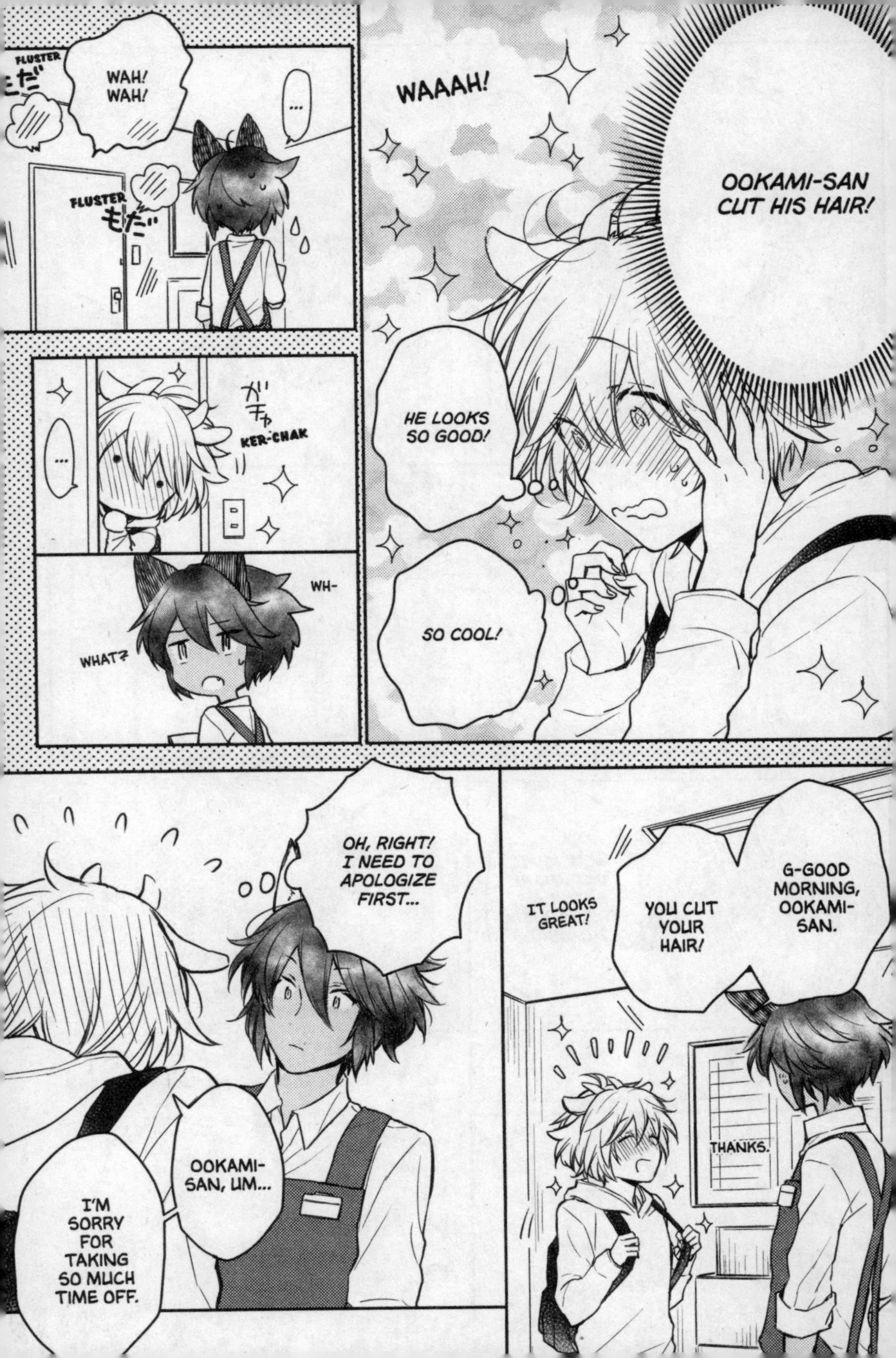
OOKAMI-SAN CUT HIS HAIR!
WAAAH!
HE LOOKS SO GOOD!
SO COOL!
...
WAH! WAH!
FLUSTER
FLUSTER もだ
ガチャ KER-CHAK
...
WH-
WHAT?
G-GOOD MORNING, OOKAMI-SAN.
YOU CUT YOUR HAIR!
IT LOOKS GREAT!
THANKS.
OH, RIGHT! I NEED TO APOLOGIZE FIRST...
OOKAMI-SAN, UM...
I'M SORRY FOR TAKING SO MUCH TIME OFF.

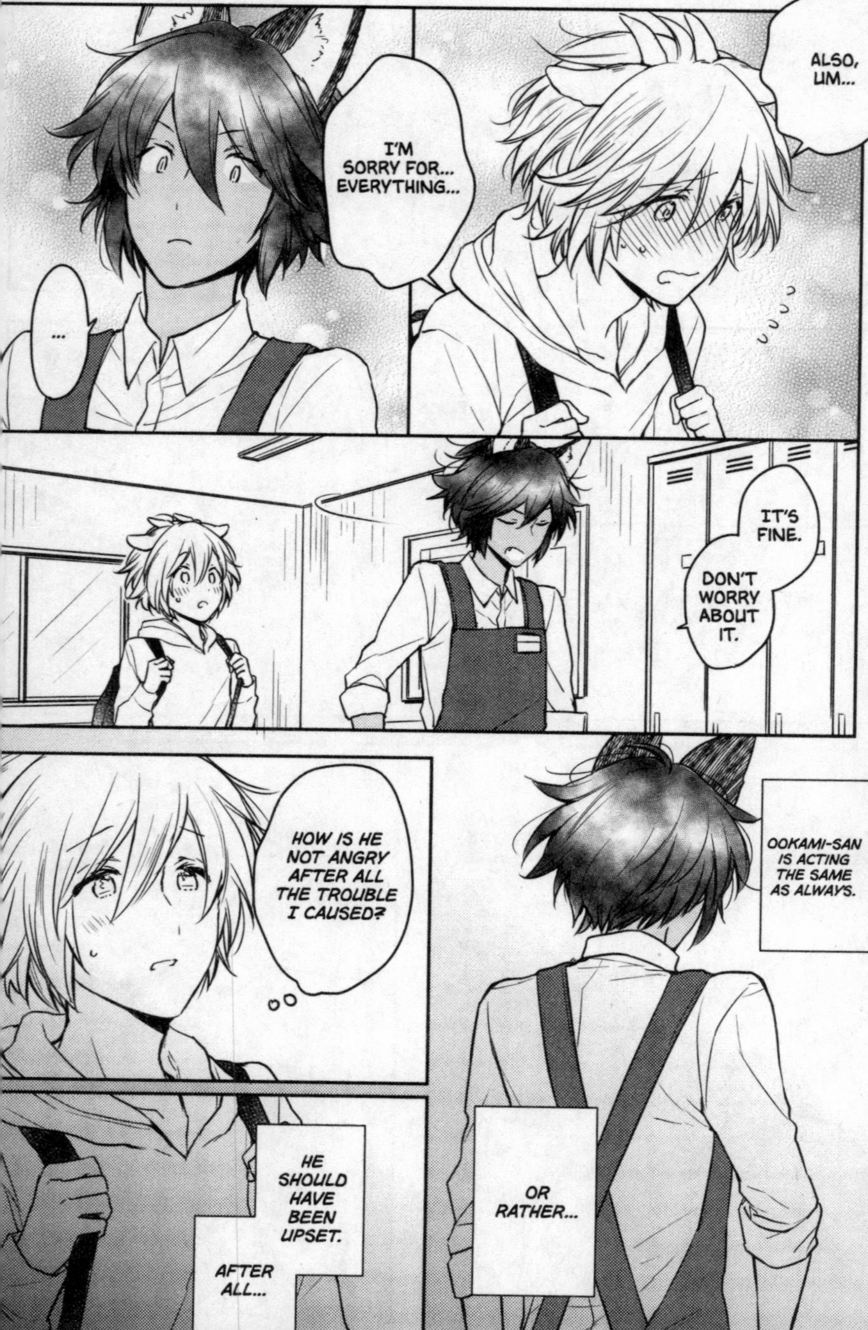

ALSO, UM...
I'M SORRY FOR... EVERYTHING...
...
IT'S FINE.
DON'T WORRY ABOUT IT.
OOKAMI-SAN IS ACTING THE SAME AS ALWAYS.
OR RATHER...
HOW IS HE NOT ANGRY AFTER ALL THE TROUBLE I CAUSED?
HE SHOULD HAVE BEEN UPSET.
AFTER ALL...

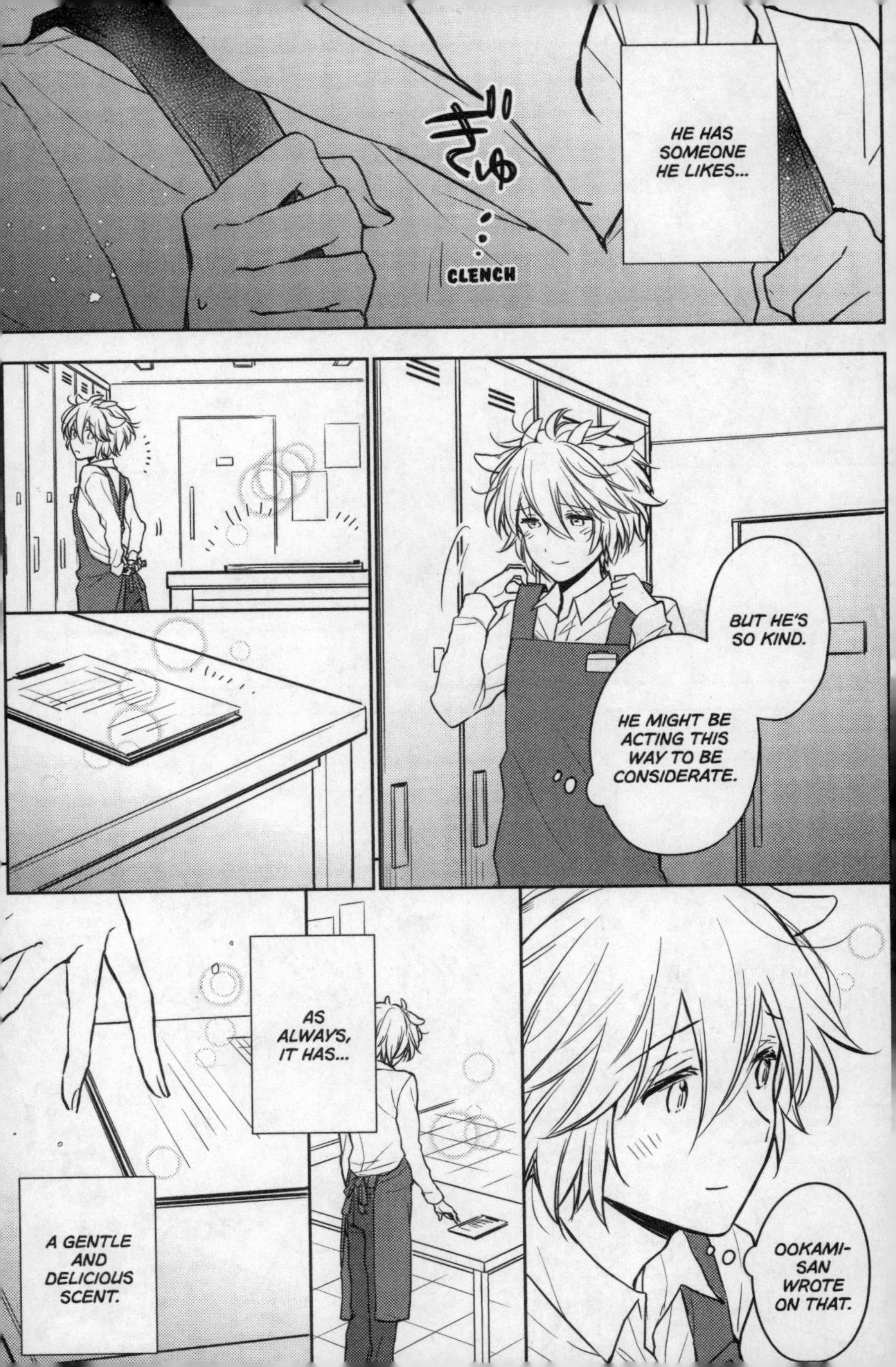
HE HAS SOMEONE HE LIKES...
ぎゅ
CLENCH
BUT HE'S SO KIND.
HE MIGHT BE ACTING THIS WAY TO BE CONSIDERATE.
OOKAMI-SAN WROTE ON THAT.
AS ALWAYS, IT HAS...
A GENTLE AND DELICIOUS SCENT.

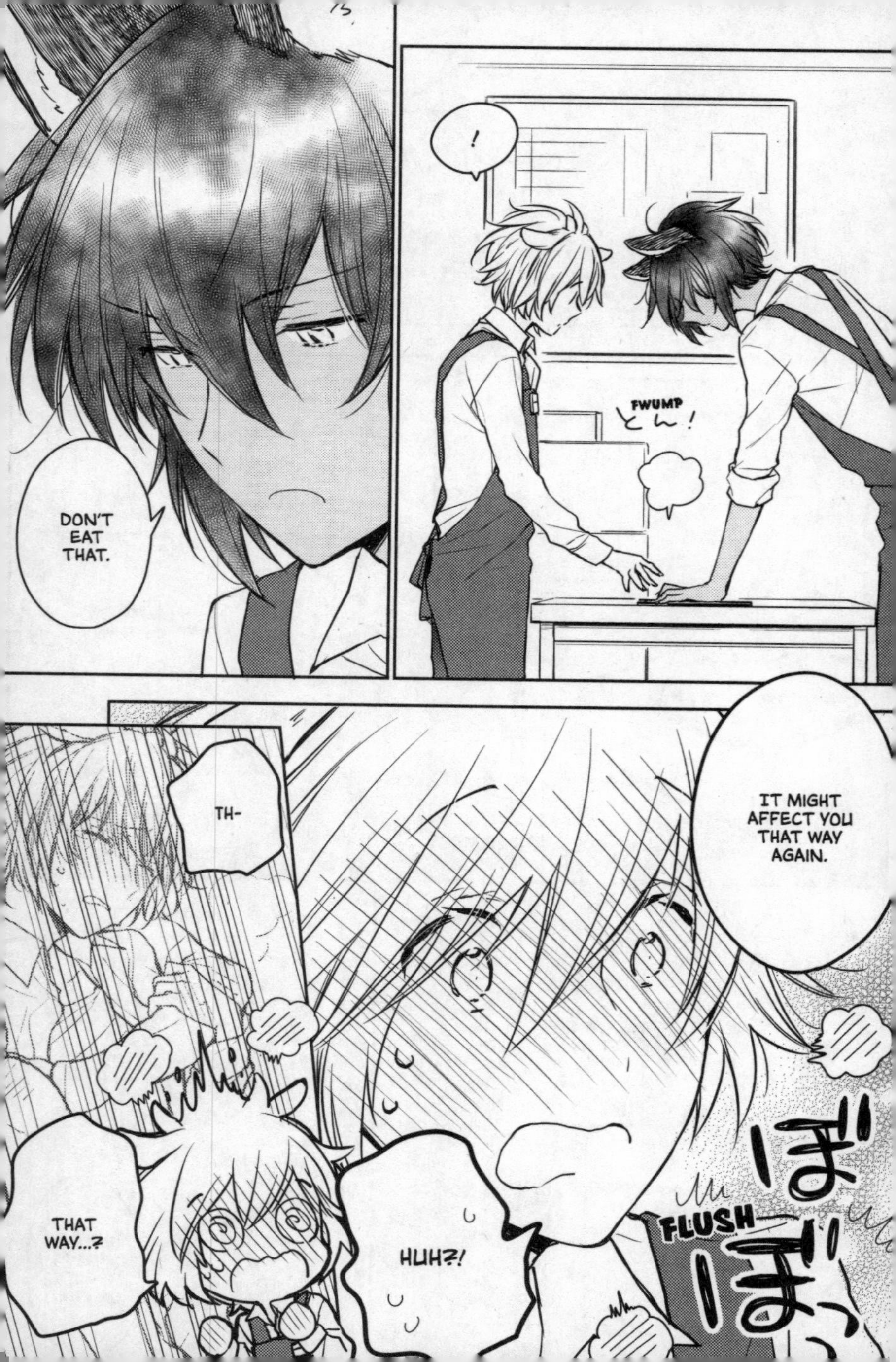
!
FWUMP
とん！
DON'T EAT THAT.
IT MIGHT AFFECT YOU THAT WAY AGAIN.
FLUSH
ぼぼっ
HUH?!
TH-
THAT WAY...?

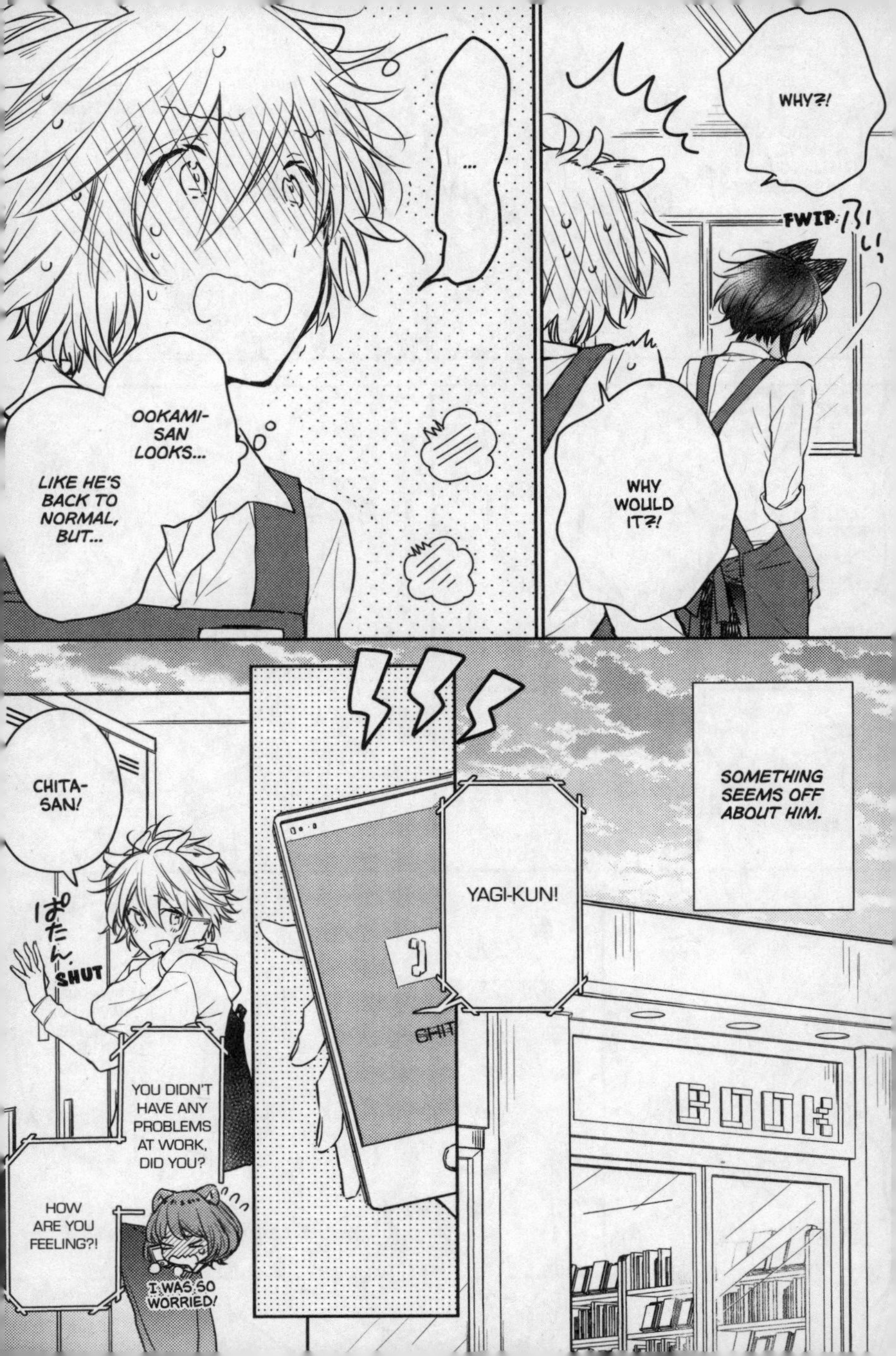
WHY?!
FWIP
WHY WOULD IT?!
...
OOKAMI-SAN LOOKS...
LIKE HE'S BACK TO NORMAL, BUT...
SOMETHING SEEMS OFF ABOUT HIM.
YAGI-KUN!
CHITA-SAN!
ぱたん
SHUT
YOU DIDN'T HAVE ANY PROBLEMS AT WORK, DID YOU?
HOW ARE YOU FEELING?!
I WAS SO WORRIED!

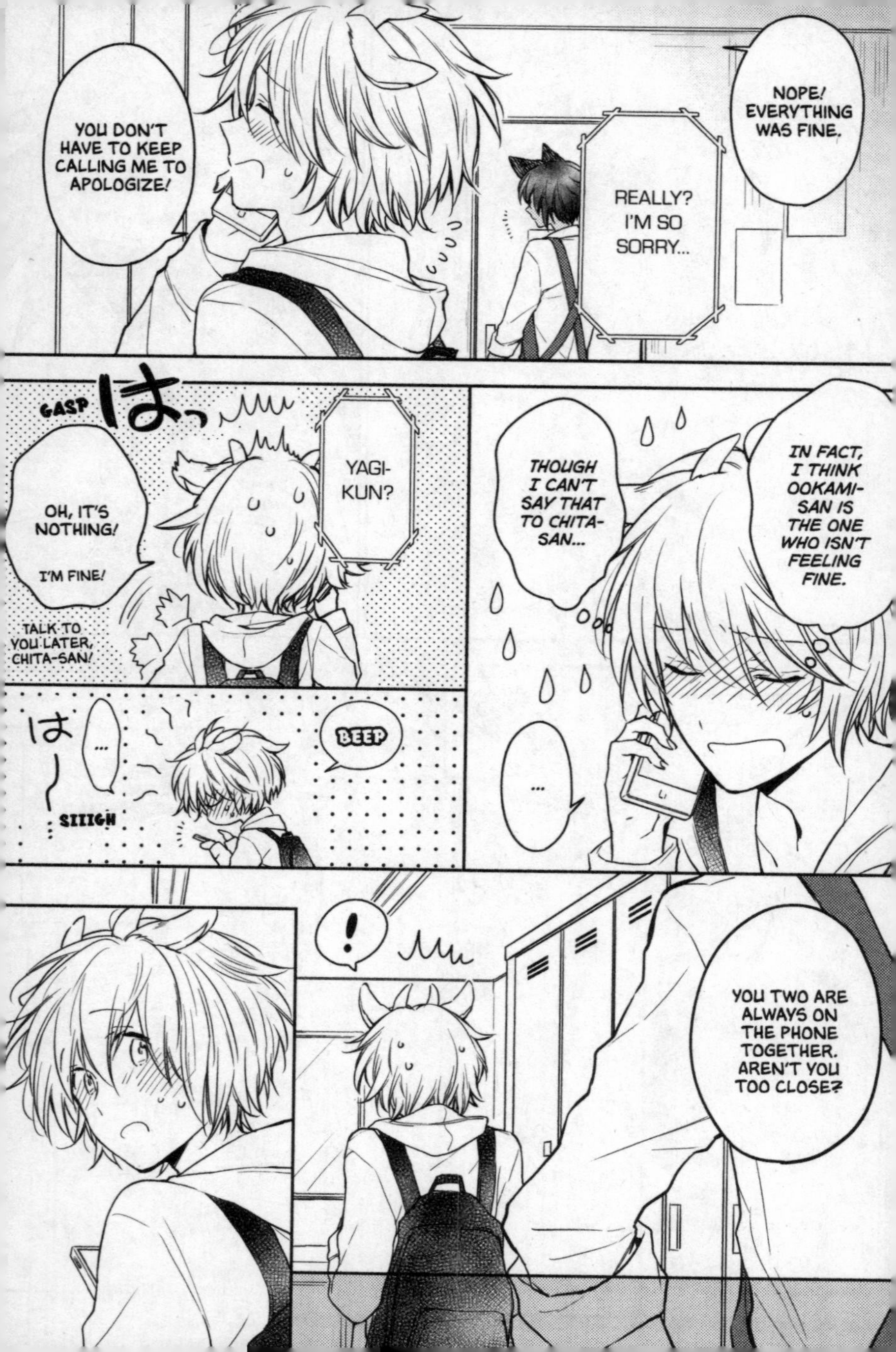
NOPE! EVERYTHING WAS FINE.
REALLY? I'M SO SORRY...
YOU DON'T HAVE TO KEEP CALLING ME TO APOLOGIZE!
IN FACT, I THINK OOKAMI-SAN IS THE ONE WHO ISN'T FEELING FINE.
THOUGH I CAN'T SAY THAT TO CHITA-SAN...
...
YAGI-KUN?
はっ
GASP
OH, IT'S NOTHING! I'M FINE!
TALK TO YOU LATER, CHITA-SAN!
BEEP
...
はー
SIIIGH
YOU TWO ARE ALWAYS ON THE PHONE TOGETHER. AREN'T YOU TOO CLOSE?
!

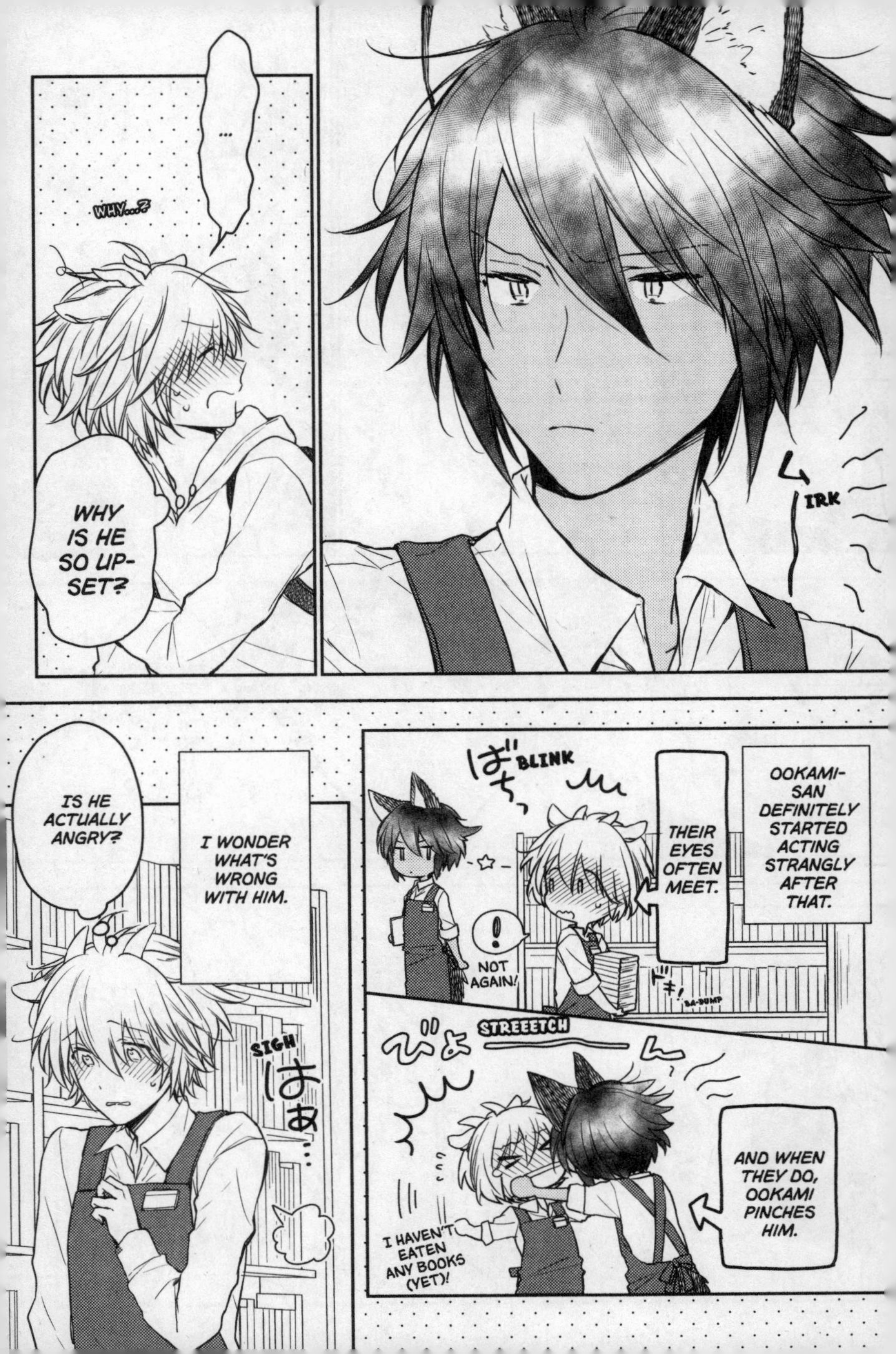
ム
IRK
...
WHY...?
WHY IS HE SO UPSET?
OOKAMI-SAN DEFINITELY STARTED ACTING STRANGLY AFTER THAT.
THEIR EYES OFTEN MEET.
ぱちっ
BLINK
!
NOT AGAIN!
ドキ!
BA-DUMP
AND WHEN THEY DO, OOKAMI PINCHES HIM.
びよーん
STREEETCH
I HAVEN'T EATEN ANY BOOKS (YET)!
I WONDER WHAT'S WRONG WITH HIM.
IS HE ACTUALLY ANGRY?
SIGH
はぁ…

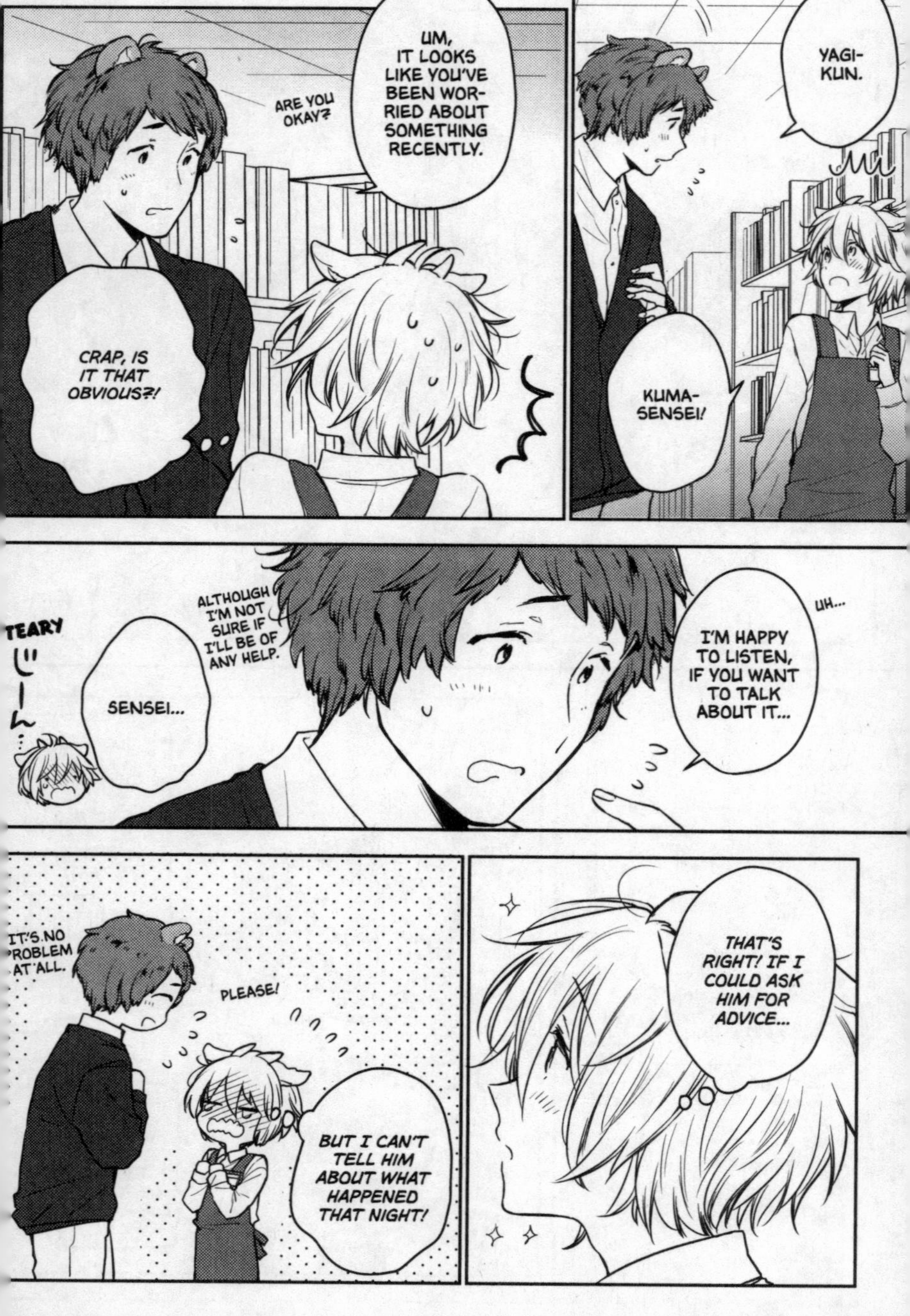
YAGI-KUN.
KUMA-SENSEI!
UM, IT LOOKS LIKE YOU'VE BEEN WOR-RIED ABOUT SOMETHING RECENTLY.
ARE YOU OKAY?
CRAP, IS IT THAT OBVIOUS?!
UH...
I'M HAPPY TO LISTEN, IF YOU WANT TO TALK ABOUT IT...
ALTHOUGH I'M NOT SURE IF I'LL BE OF ANY HELP.
SENSEI...
TEARY
じーん...
THAT'S RIGHT! IF I COULD ASK HIM FOR ADVICE...
IT'S NO PROBLEM AT ALL.
PLEASE!
BUT I CAN'T TELL HIM ABOUT WHAT HAPPENED THAT NIGHT!

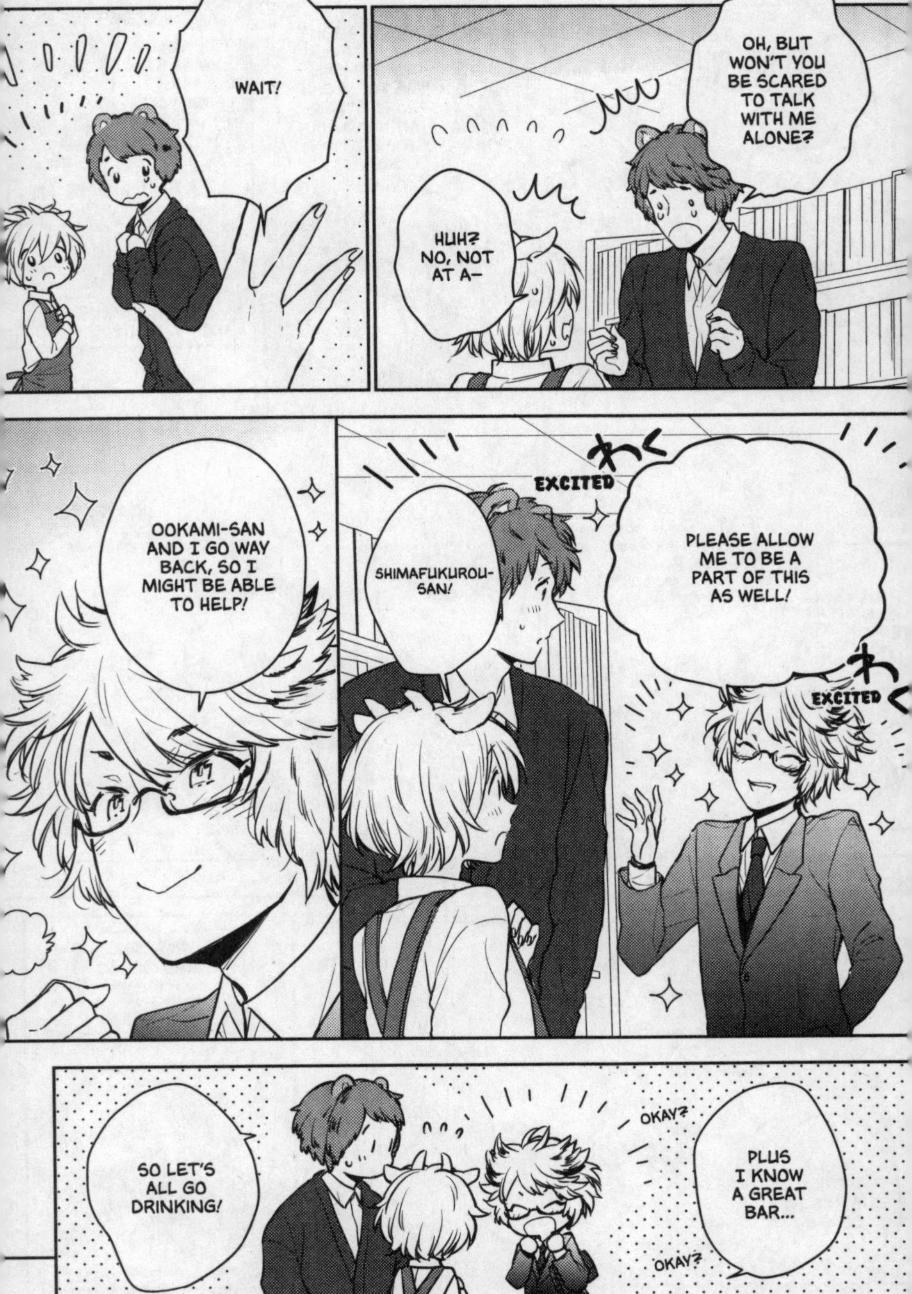
OH, BUT WON'T YOU BE SCARED TO TALK WITH ME ALONE?
HUH? NO, NOT AT A—
WAIT!
わく
EXCITED
PLEASE ALLOW ME TO BE A PART OF THIS AS WELL!
SHIMAFUKUROU-SAN!
わく
EXCITED
OOKAMI-SAN AND I GO WAY BACK, SO I MIGHT BE ABLE TO HELP!
OKAY?
PLUS I KNOW A GREAT BAR...
OKAY?
SO LET'S ALL GO DRINKING!

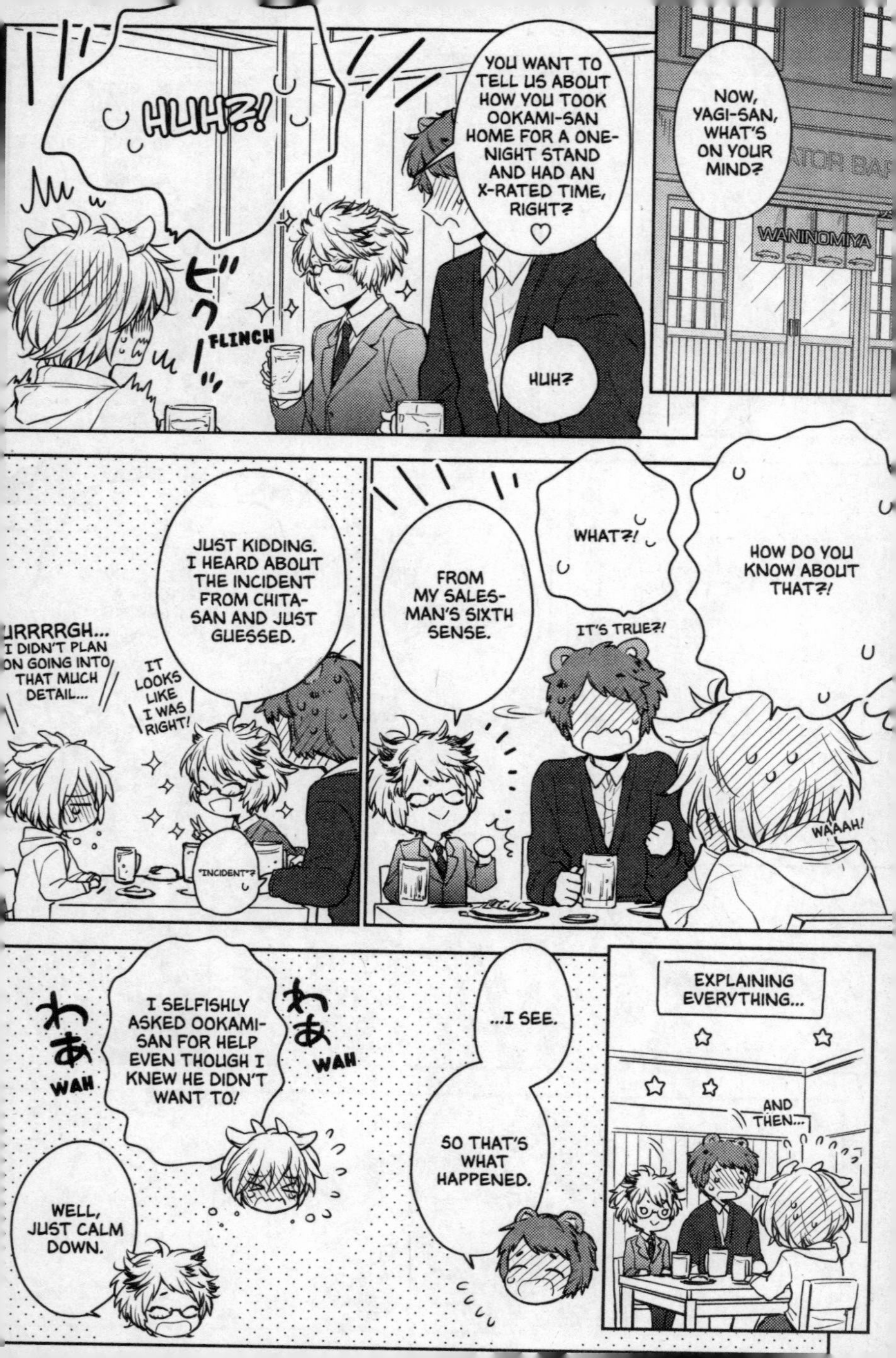
NOW, YAGI-SAN, WHAT'S ON YOUR MIND?
WANINOMIYA
YOU WANT TO TELL US ABOUT HOW YOU TOOK OOKAMI-SAN HOME FOR A ONE-NIGHT STAND AND HAD AN X-RATED TIME, RIGHT? ♡
HUH?
HUH?!
ビク
FLINCH
WHAT?!
HOW DO YOU KNOW ABOUT THAT?!
IT'S TRUE?!
FROM MY SALES-MAN'S SIXTH SENSE.
WAAAH!
JUST KIDDING. I HEARD ABOUT THE INCIDENT FROM CHITA-SAN AND JUST GUESSED.
IT LOOKS LIKE I WAS RIGHT!
"INCIDENT"?
URRRRGH... I DIDN'T PLAN ON GOING INTO THAT MUCH DETAIL...
EXPLAINING EVERYTHING...
AND THEN...
...I SEE.
SO THAT'S WHAT HAPPENED.
わあ
WAH
I SELFISHLY ASKED OOKAMI-SAN FOR HELP EVEN THOUGH I KNEW HE DIDN'T WANT TO!
わあ
WAH
WELL, JUST CALM DOWN.

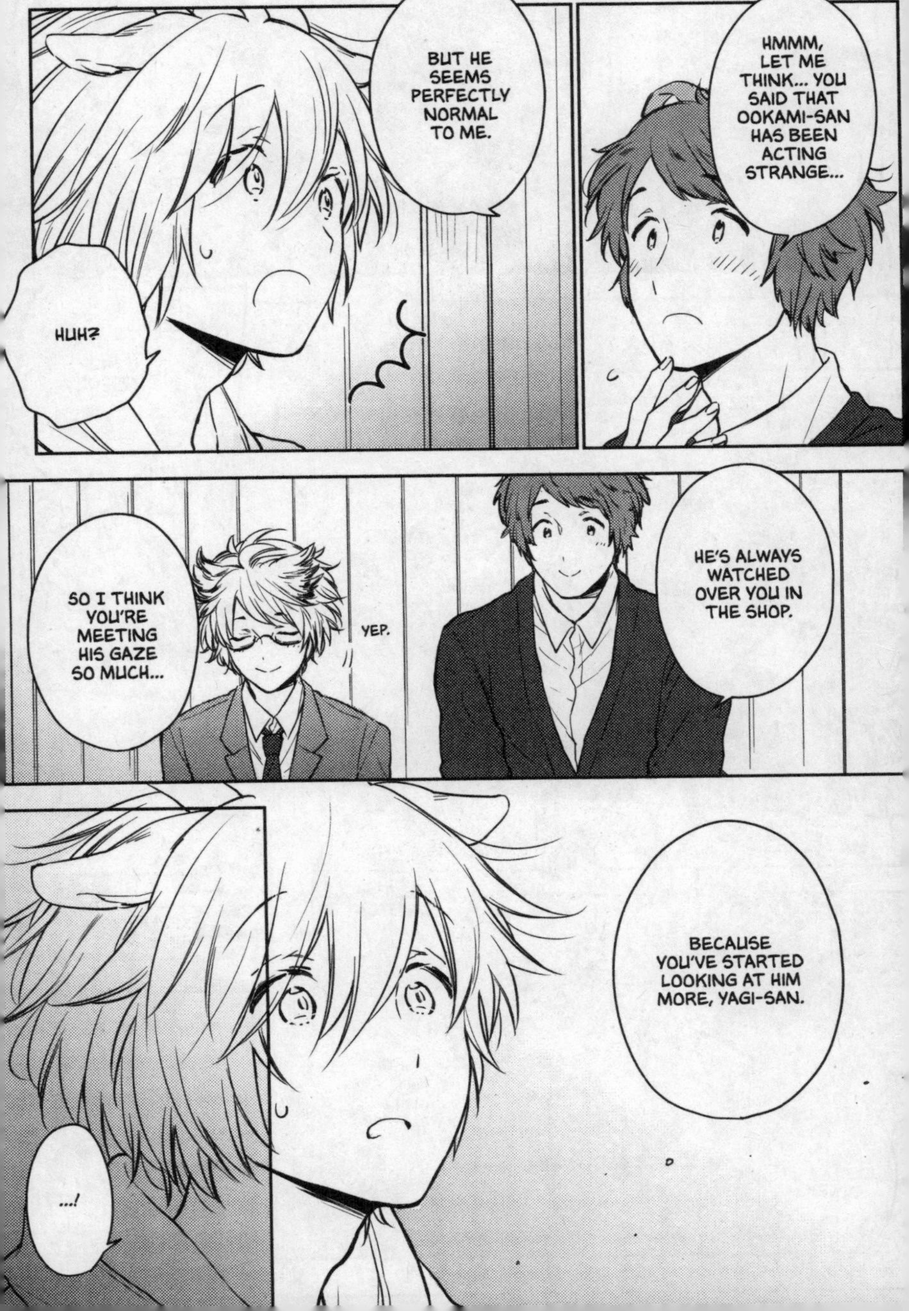
HMMM, LET ME THINK... YOU SAID THAT OOKAMI-SAN HAS BEEN ACTING STRANGE...
BUT HE SEEMS PERFECTLY NORMAL TO ME.
HUH?
HE'S ALWAYS WATCHED OVER YOU IN THE SHOP.
YEP.
SO I THINK YOU'RE MEETING HIS GAZE SO MUCH...
BECAUSE YOU'VE STARTED LOOKING AT HIM MORE, YAGI-SAN.
...!

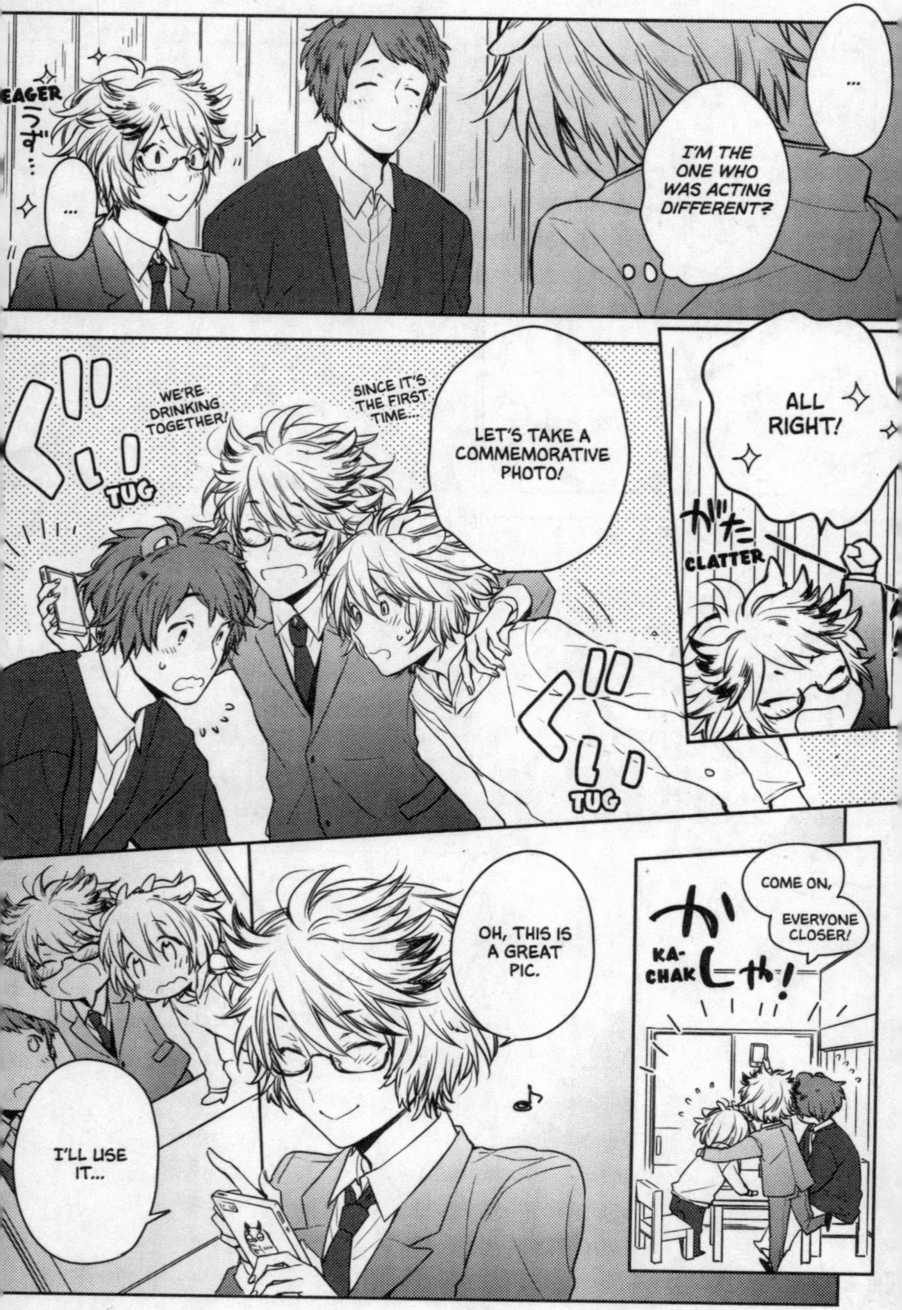
...
I'M THE ONE WHO WAS ACTING DIFFERENT?
EAGER
うず…
...
ALL RIGHT!
がたっ
CLATTER
LET'S TAKE A COMMEMORATIVE PHOTO!
SINCE IT'S THE FIRST TIME...
WE'RE DRINKING TOGETHER!
くい
TUG
くい
TUG
COME ON, EVERYONE CLOSER!
かしゃ!
KA-CHAK
OH, THIS IS A GREAT PIC.
I'LL USE IT...

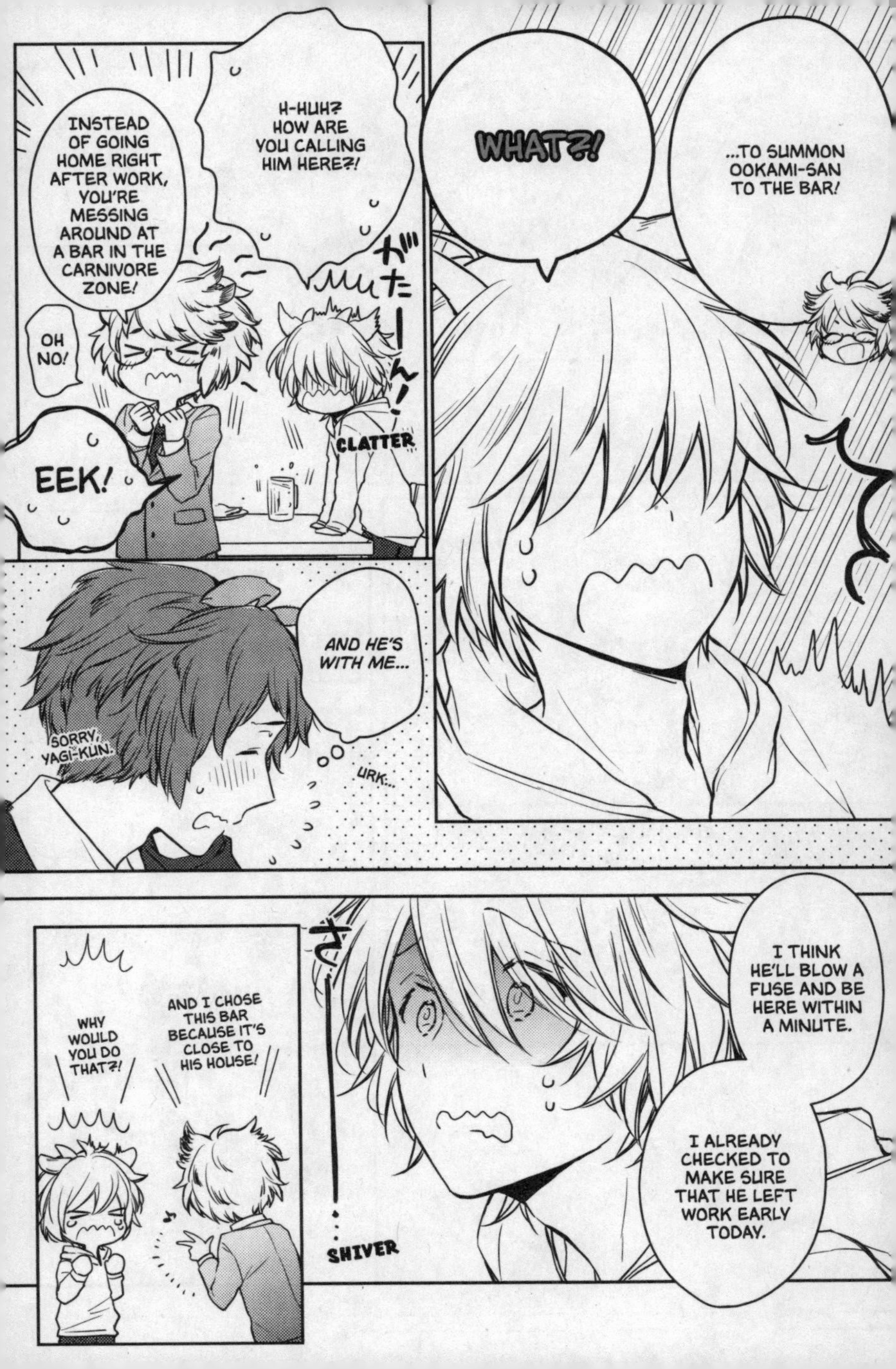
...TO SUMMON OOKAMI-SAN TO THE BAR!
WHAT?!
H-HUH? HOW ARE YOU CALLING HIM HERE?!
がたーん!
CLATTER
INSTEAD OF GOING HOME RIGHT AFTER WORK, YOU'RE MESSING AROUND AT A BAR IN THE CARNIVORE ZONE!
OH NO!
EEK!
AND HE'S WITH ME...
URK...
SORRY, YAGI-KUN.
I THINK HE'LL BLOW A FUSE AND BE HERE WITHIN A MINUTE.
I ALREADY CHECKED TO MAKE SURE THAT HE LEFT WORK EARLY TODAY.
SHIVER
AND I CHOSE THIS BAR BECAUSE IT'S CLOSE TO HIS HOUSE!
WHY WOULD YOU DO THAT?!

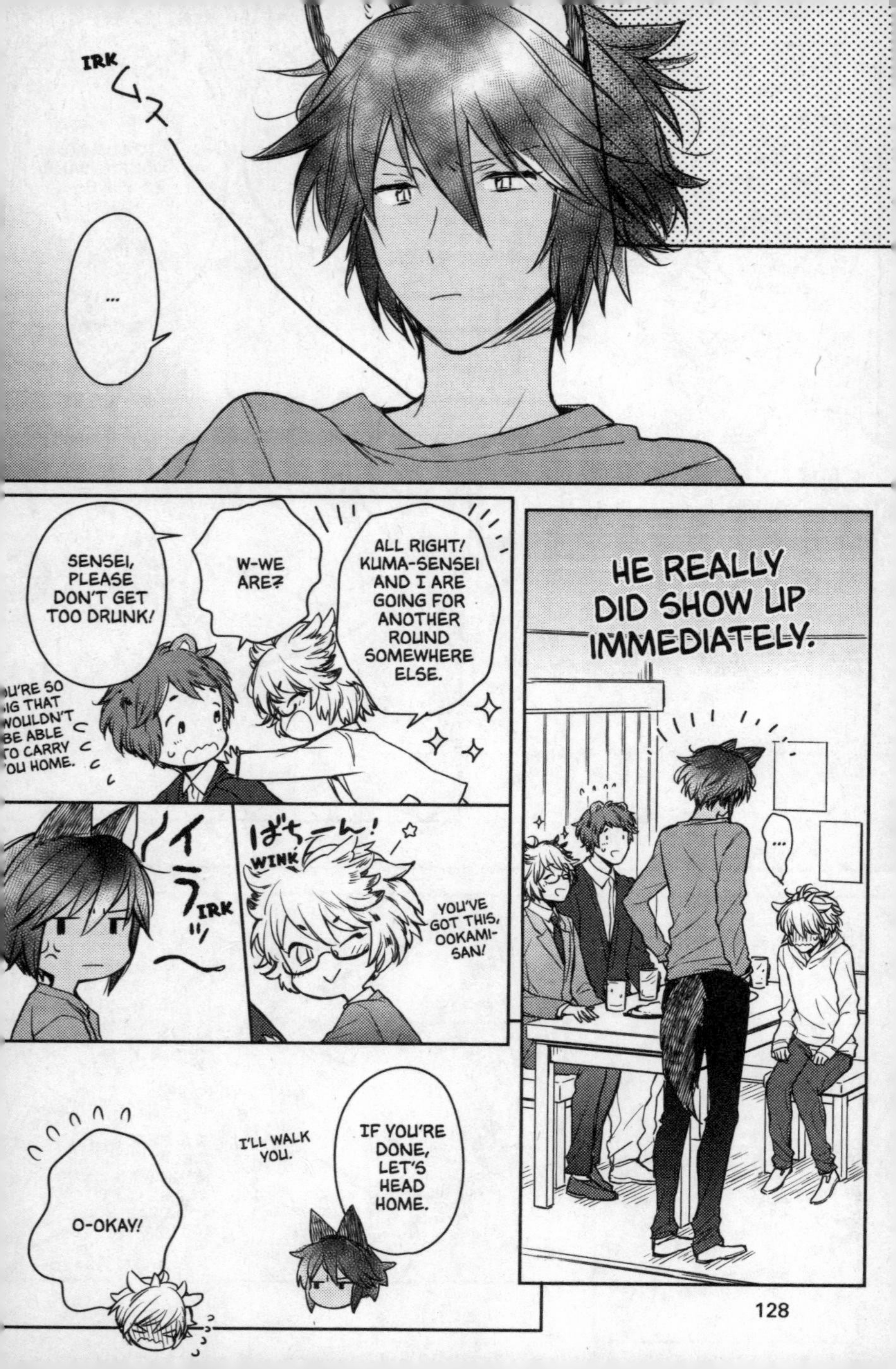

ムス
IRK
...
HE REALLY DID SHOW UP IMMEDIATELY.
...
ALL RIGHT! KUMA-SENSEI AND I ARE GOING FOR ANOTHER ROUND SOMEWHERE ELSE.
W-WE ARE?
SENSEI, PLEASE DON'T GET TOO DRUNK!
U'RE SO IG THAT WOULDN'T BE ABLE TO CARRY OU HOME.
ばちーん!
WINK
YOU'VE GOT THIS, OOKAMI-SAN!
イラ
IRK
IF YOU'RE DONE, LET'S HEAD HOME.
I'LL WALK YOU.
O-OKAY!

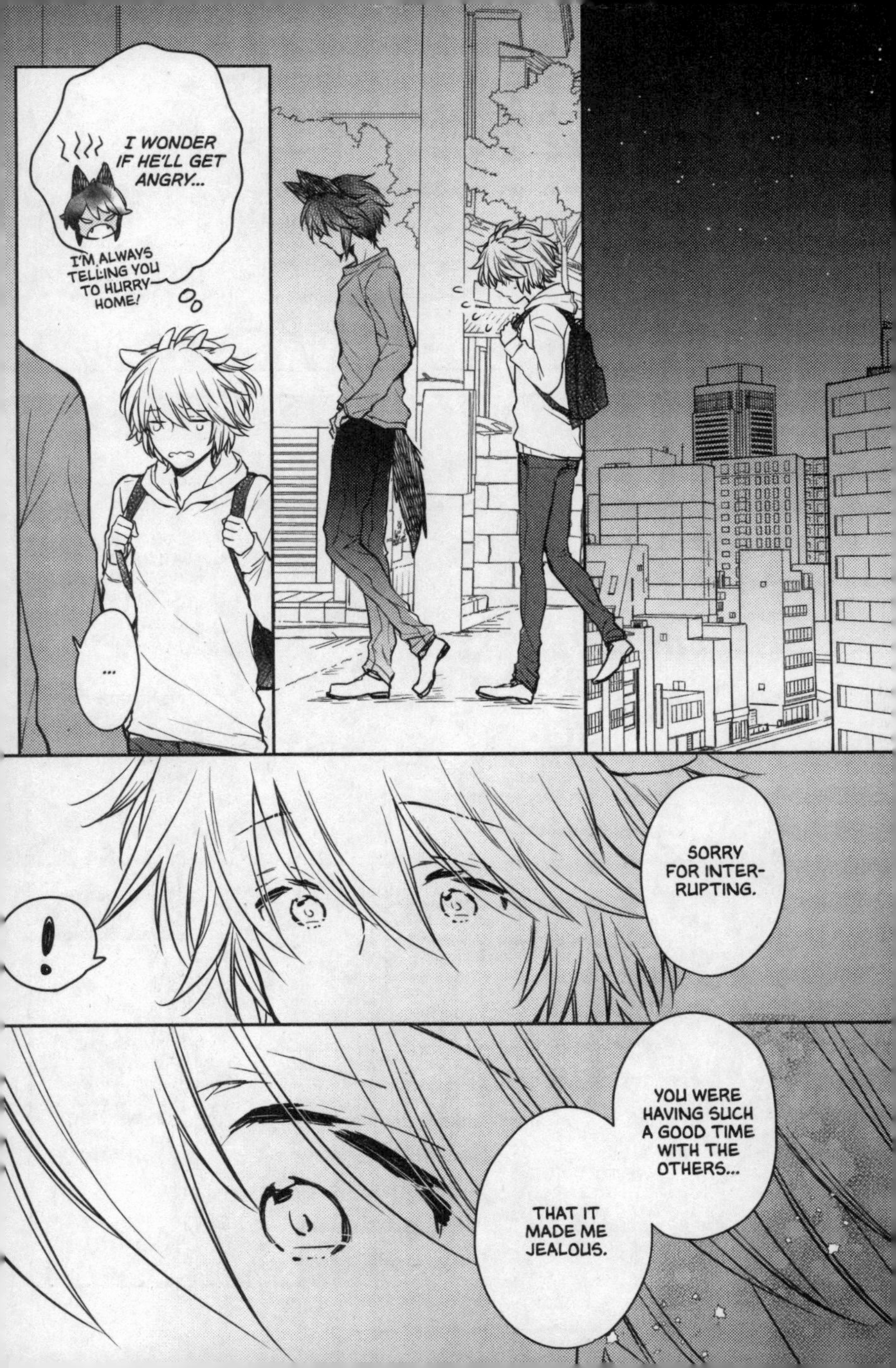
I WONDER IF HE'LL GET ANGRY...
I'M ALWAYS TELLING YOU TO HURRY HOME!
...
SORRY FOR INTER-RUPTING.
!
YOU WERE HAVING SUCH A GOOD TIME WITH THE OTHERS...
THAT IT MADE ME JEALOUS.

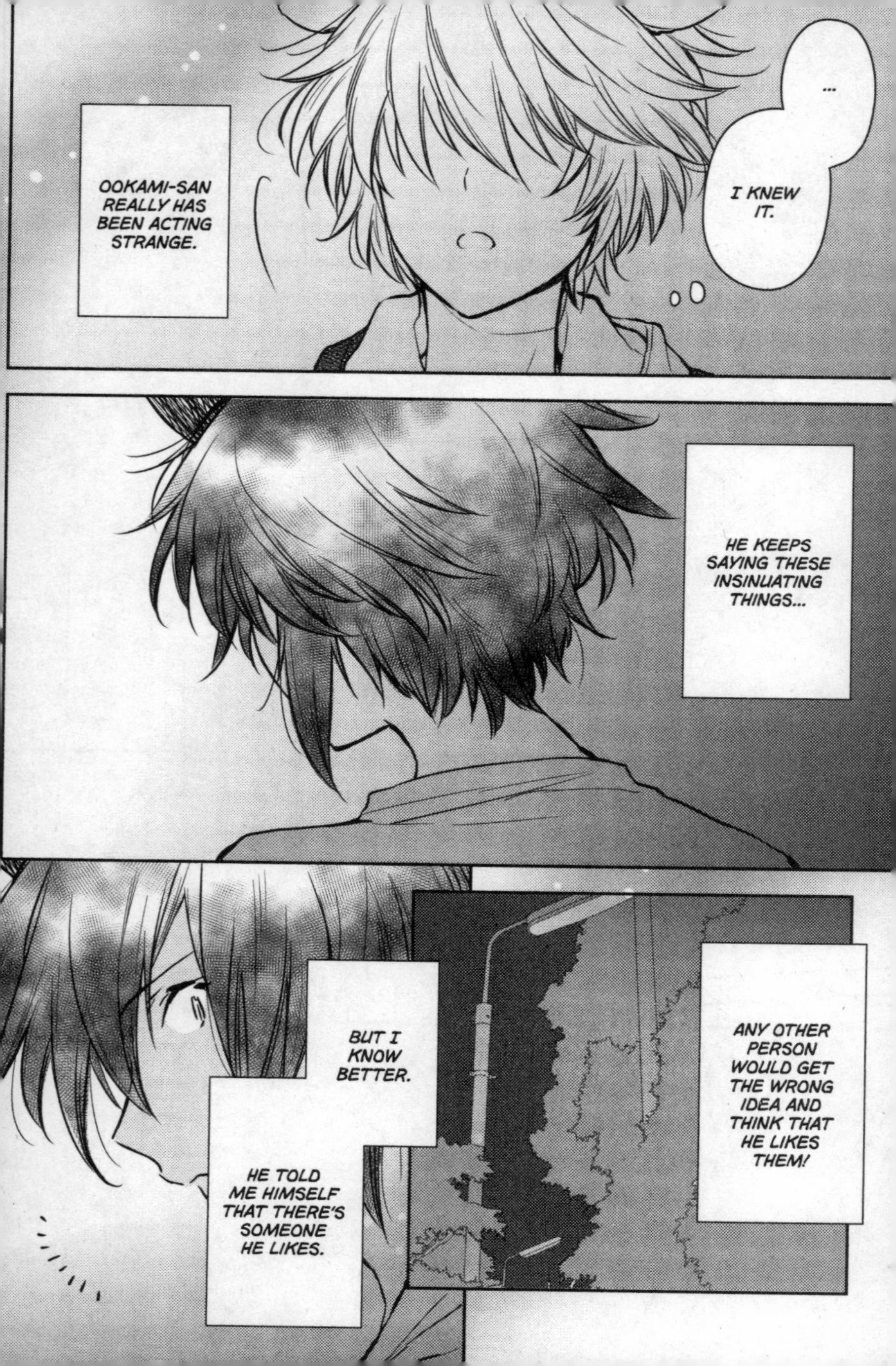
...
I KNEW IT.
OOKAMI-SAN REALLY HAS BEEN ACTING STRANGE.
HE KEEPS SAYING THESE INSINUATING THINGS...
ANY OTHER PERSON WOULD GET THE WRONG IDEA AND THINK THAT HE LIKES THEM!
BUT I KNOW BETTER.
HE TOLD ME HIMSELF THAT THERE'S SOMEONE HE LIKES.

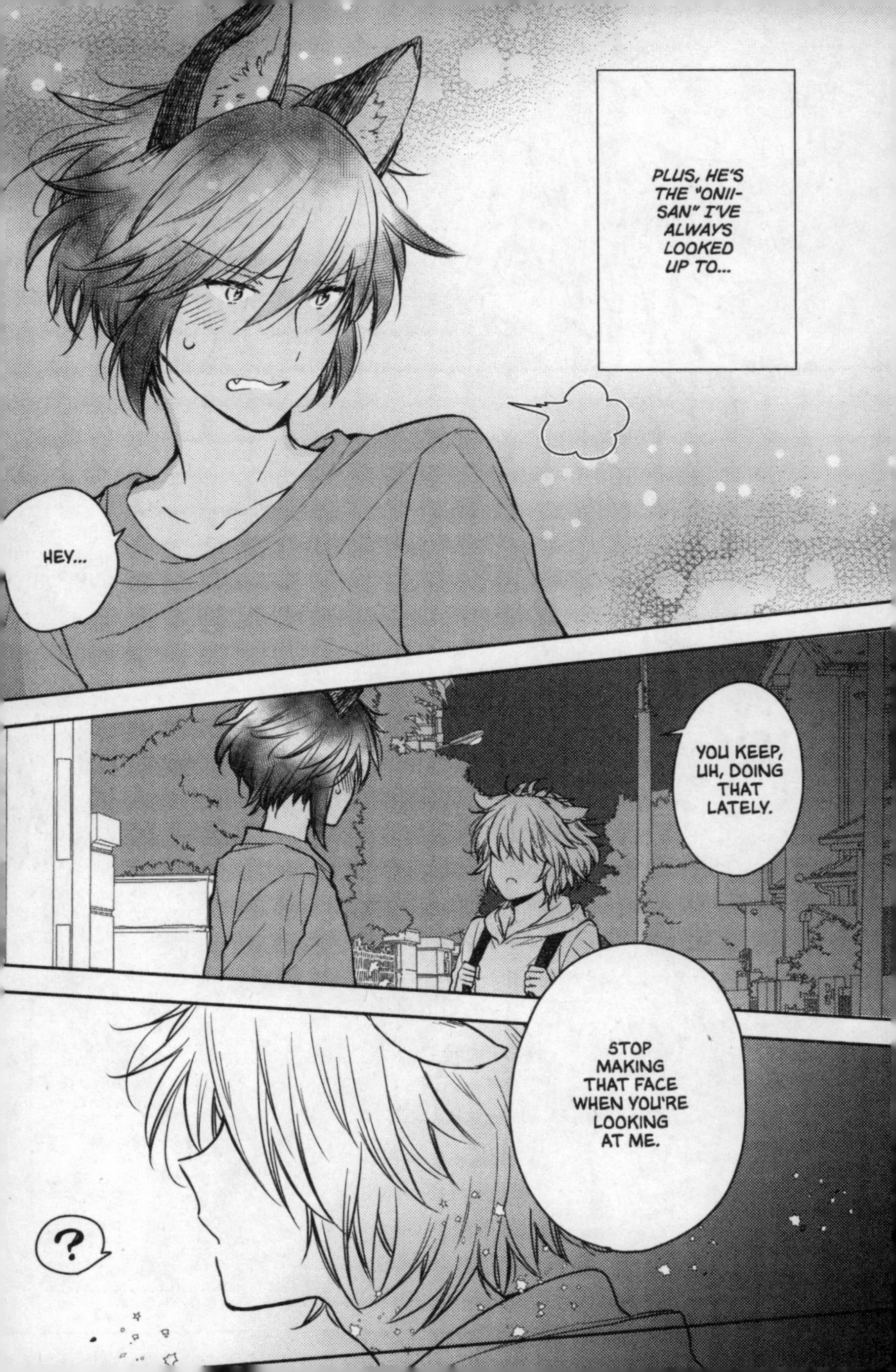
PLUS, HE'S THE "ONII-SAN" I'VE ALWAYS LOOKED UP TO...
HEY...
YOU KEEP, UH, DOING THAT LATELY.
STOP MAKING THAT FACE WHEN YOU'RE LOOKING AT ME.
?

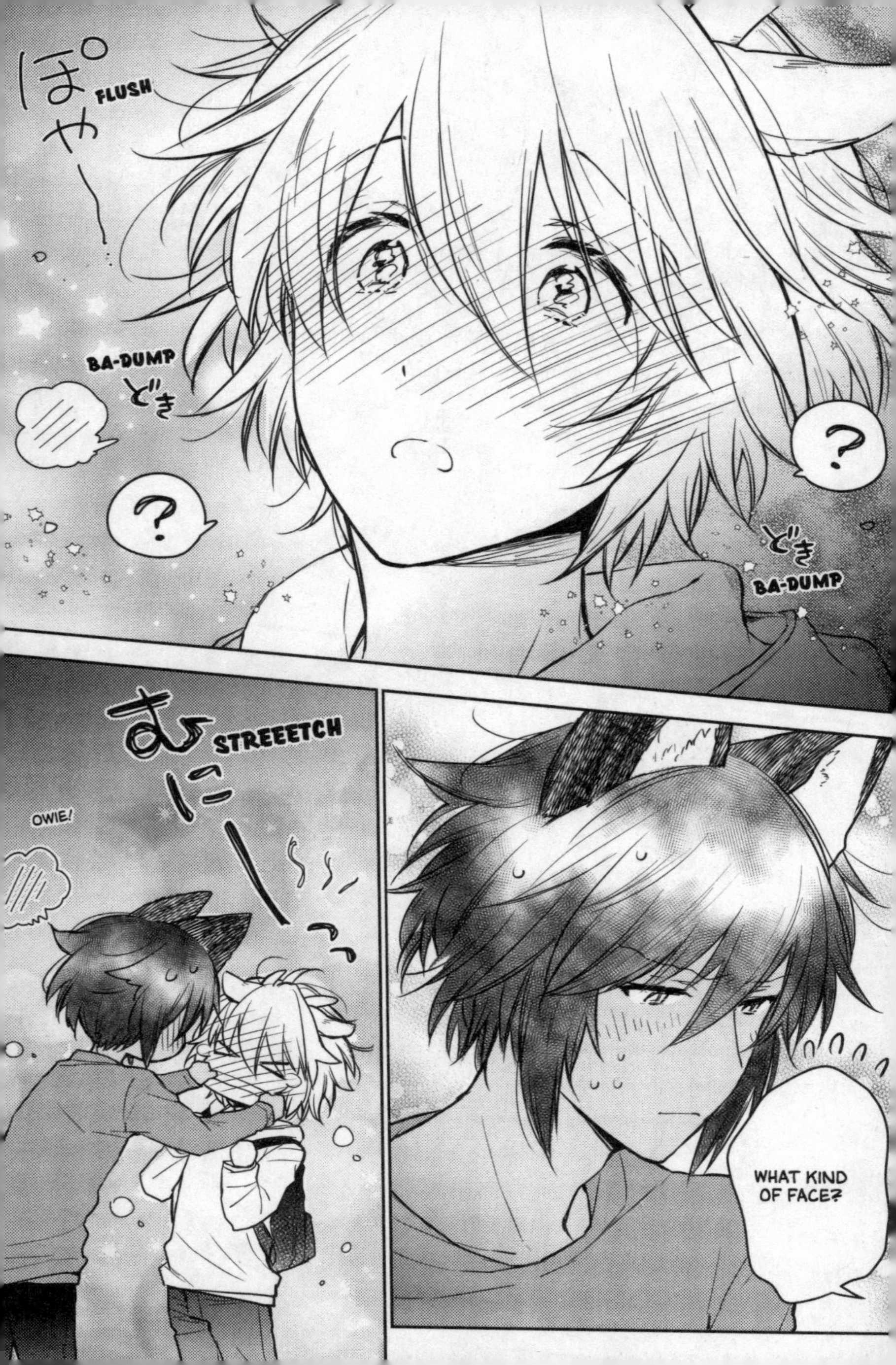
ぽやー
FLUSH
?
どき
BA-DUMP
BA-DUMP
どき
?
WHAT KIND OF FACE?
むにーー
STREEETCH
OWIE!

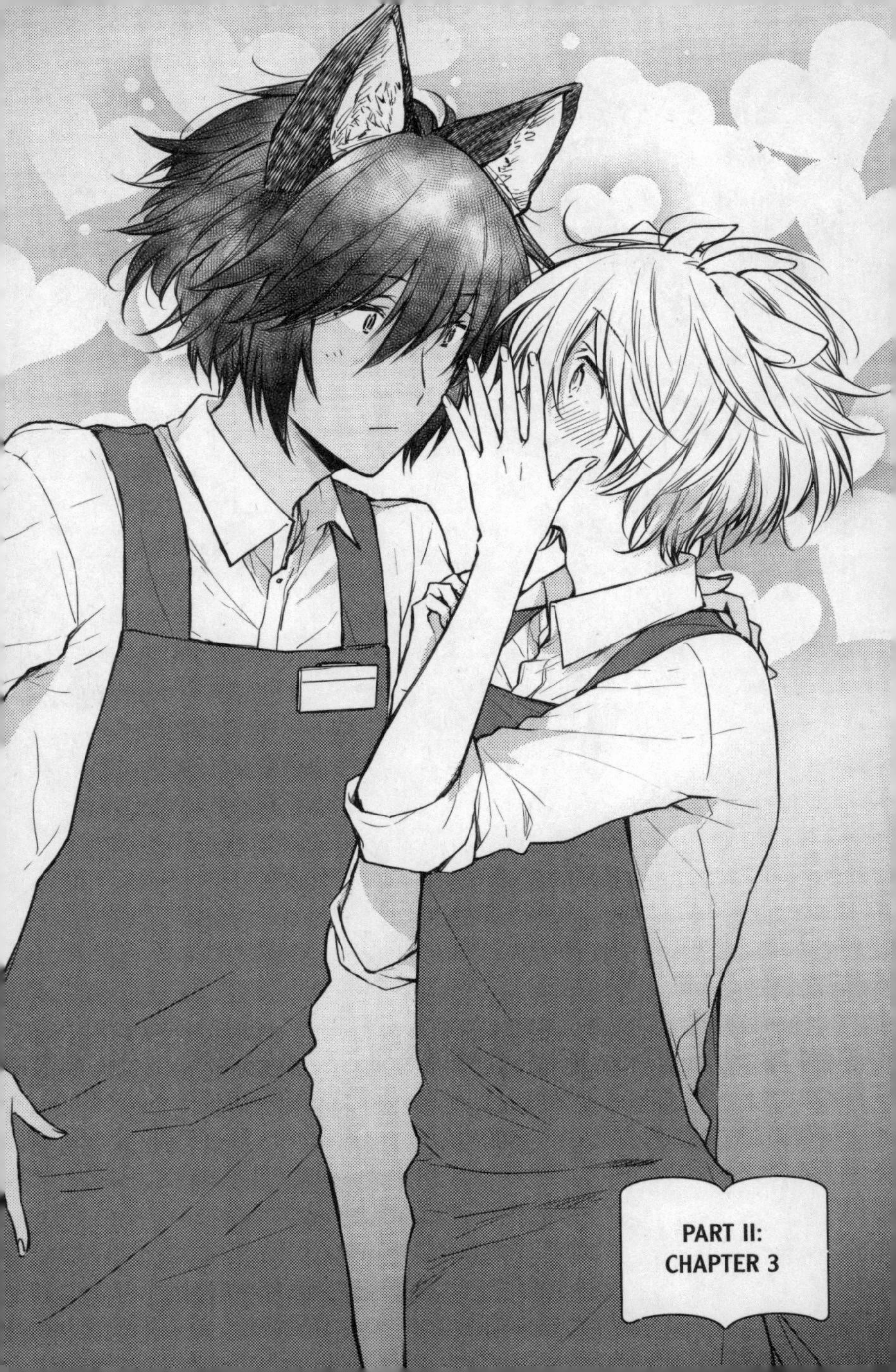
PART II:
CHAPTER 3

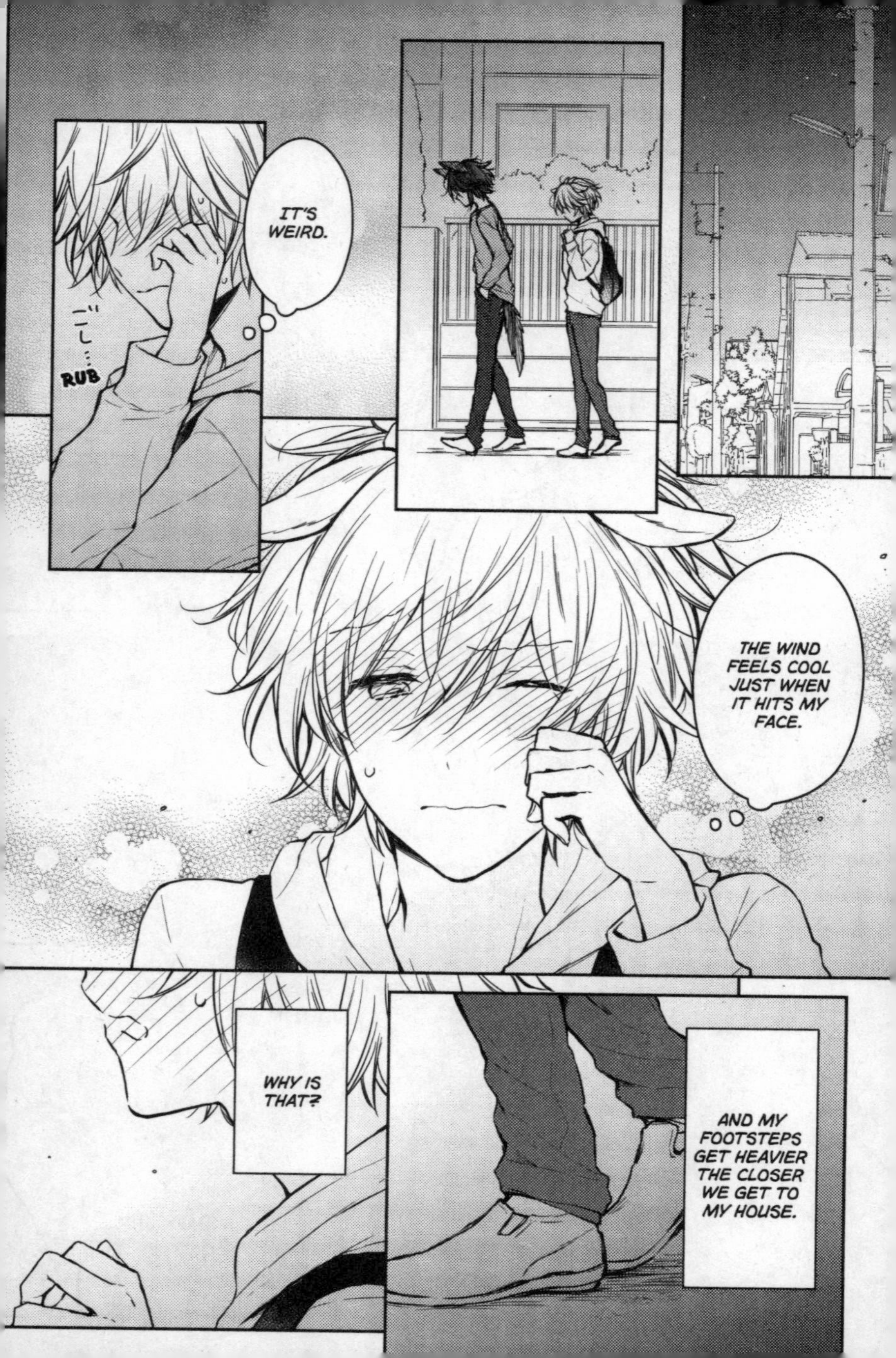
IT'S WEIRD.
ごし…
RUB
THE WIND FEELS COOL JUST WHEN IT HITS MY FACE.
AND MY FOOTSTEPS GET HEAVIER THE CLOSER WE GET TO MY HOUSE.
WHY IS THAT?

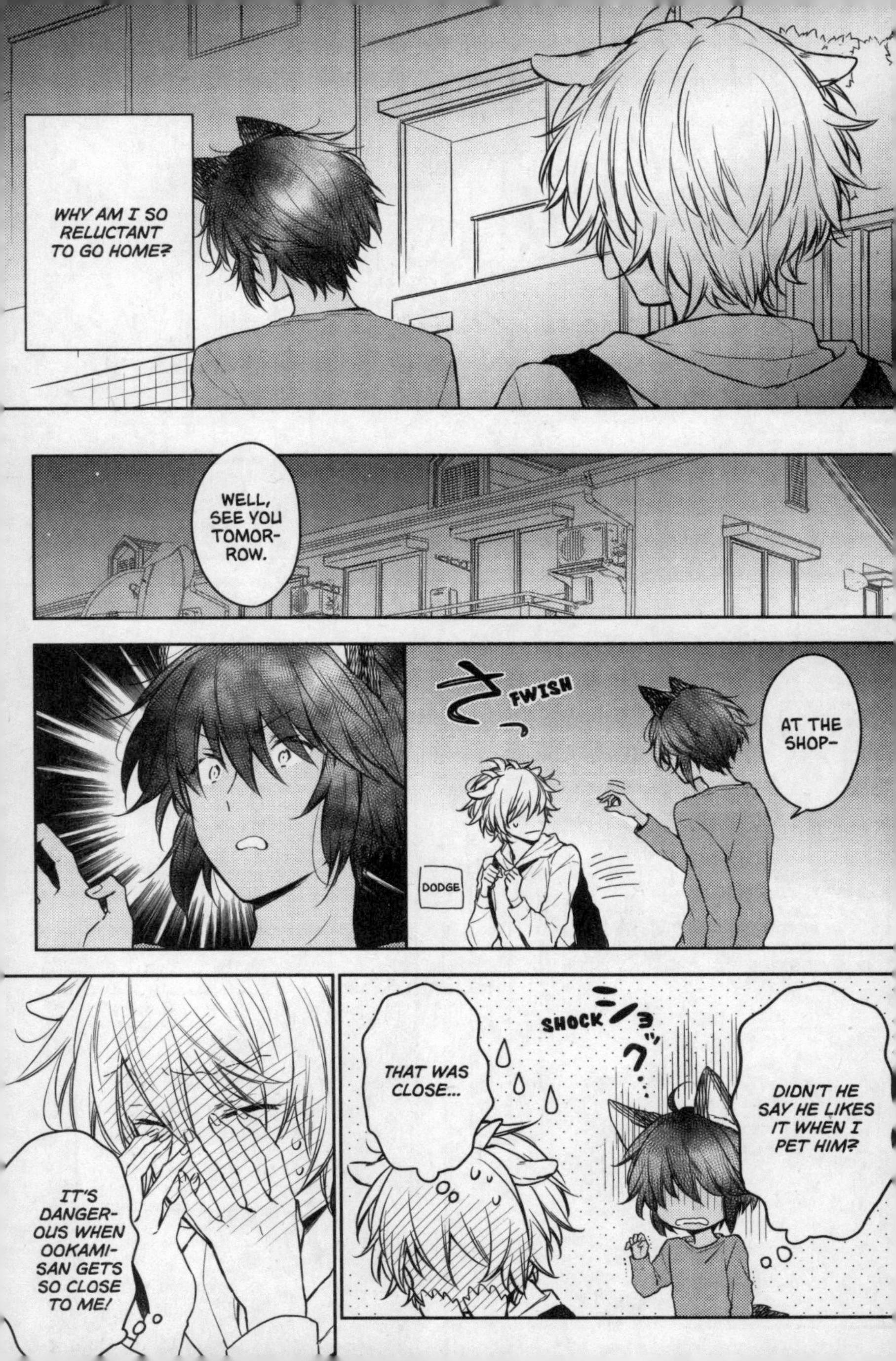
WHY AM I SO RELUCTANT TO GO HOME?
WELL, SEE YOU TOMORROW.
AT THE SHOP-
さっ
FWISH
DODGE
DIDN'T HE SAY HE LIKES IT WHEN I PET HIM?
ショック
SHOCK
THAT WAS CLOSE...
IT'S DANGEROUS WHEN OOKAMI-SAN GETS SO CLOSE TO ME!

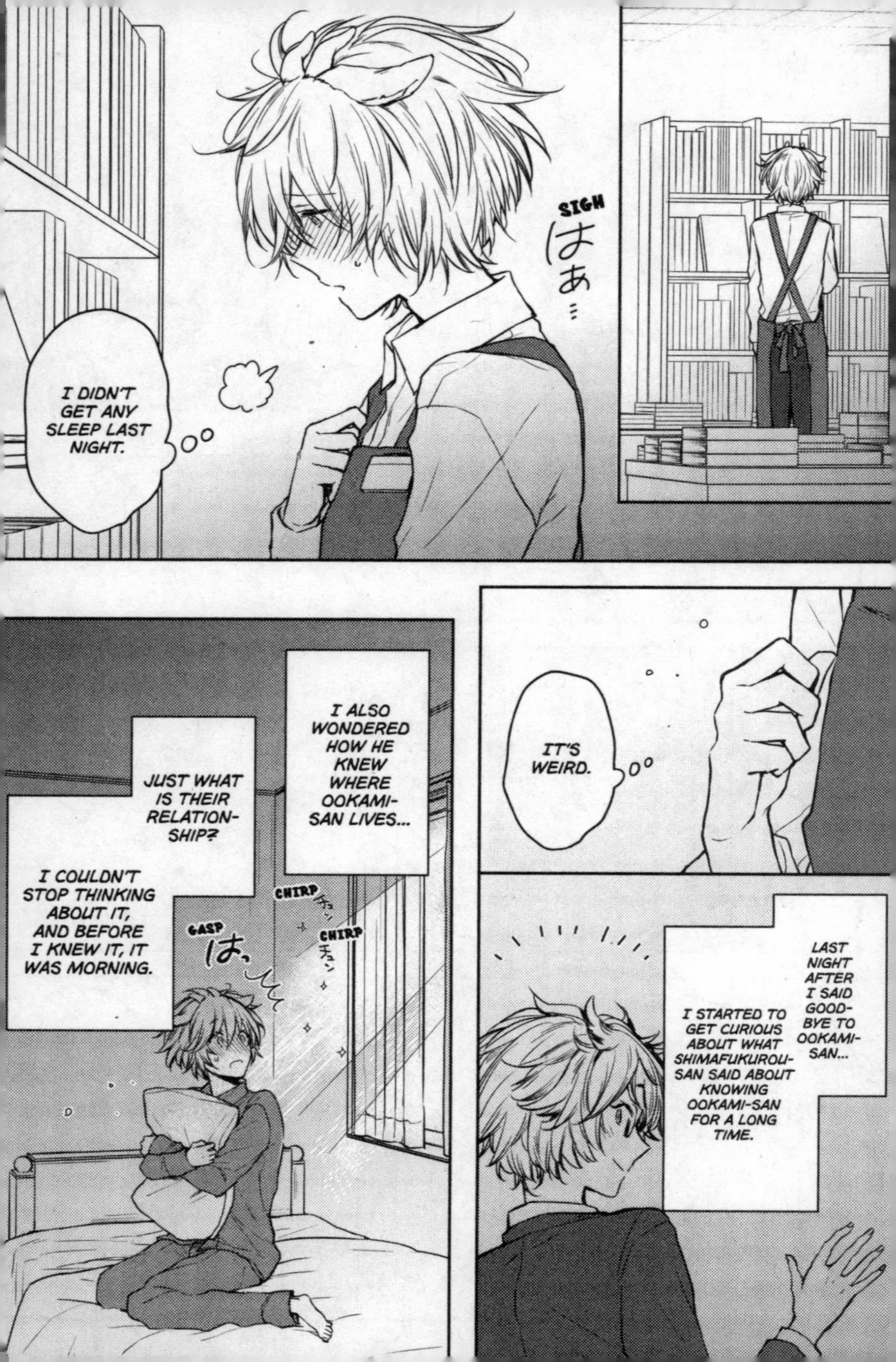
SIGH
はぁ…
I DIDN'T GET ANY SLEEP LAST NIGHT.
IT'S WEIRD.
LAST NIGHT AFTER I SAID GOOD-BYE TO OOKAMI-SAN...
I STARTED TO GET CURIOUS ABOUT WHAT SHIMAFUKUROU-SAN SAID ABOUT KNOWING OOKAMI-SAN FOR A LONG TIME.
I ALSO WONDERED HOW HE KNEW WHERE OOKAMI-SAN LIVES...
JUST WHAT IS THEIR RELATION-SHIP?
I COULDN'T STOP THINKING ABOUT IT, AND BEFORE I KNEW IT, IT WAS MORNING.
CHIRP
チュン
CHIRP
チュン
GASP
は

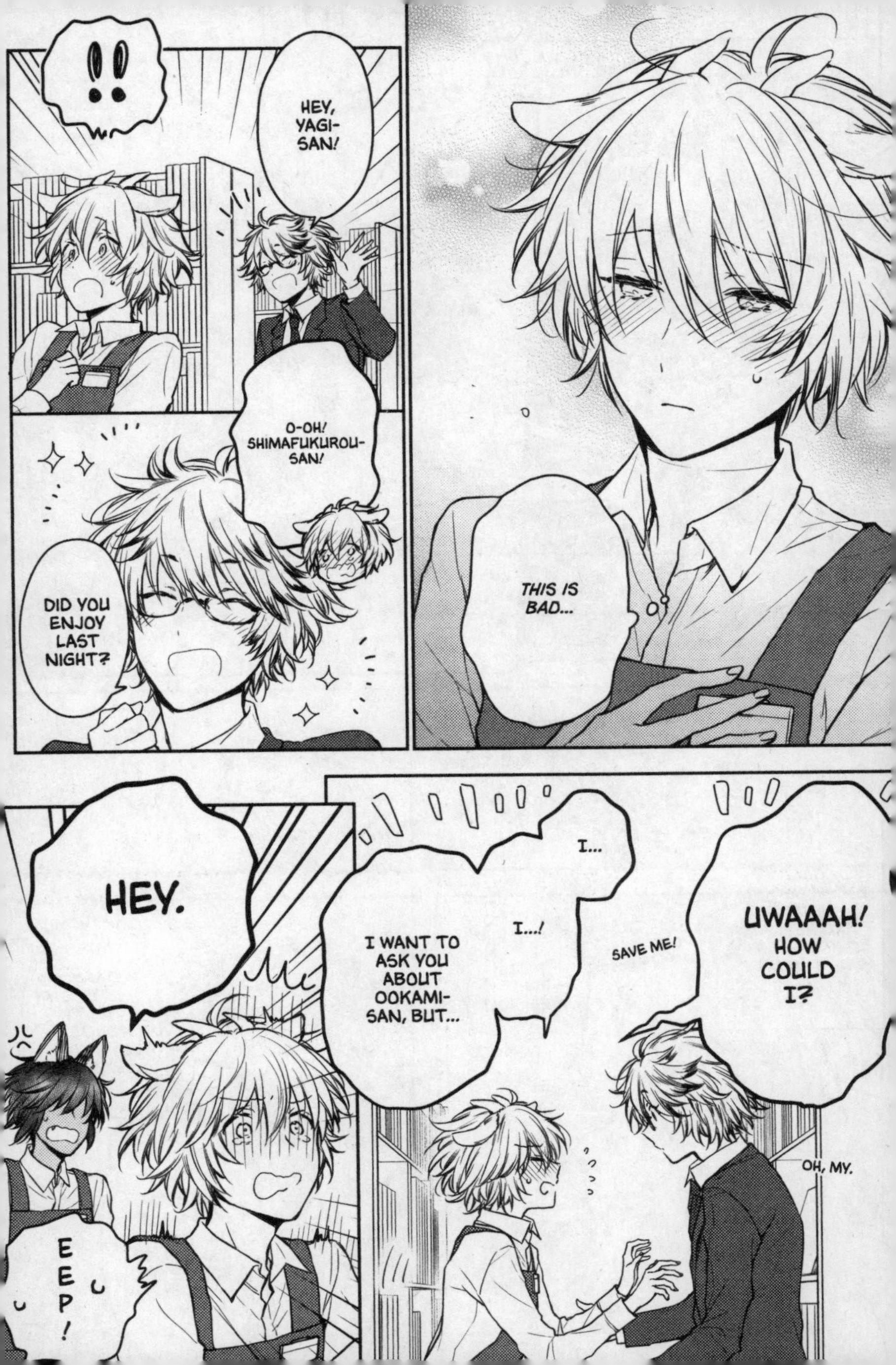

THIS IS BAD...
!!
HEY, YAGI-SAN!
O-OH! SHIMAFUKUROU-SAN!
DID YOU ENJOY LAST NIGHT?
UWAAAH! HOW COULD I?
I...
SAVE ME!
I...!
I WANT TO ASK YOU ABOUT OOKAMI-SAN, BUT...
OH, MY.
HEY.
EEP!

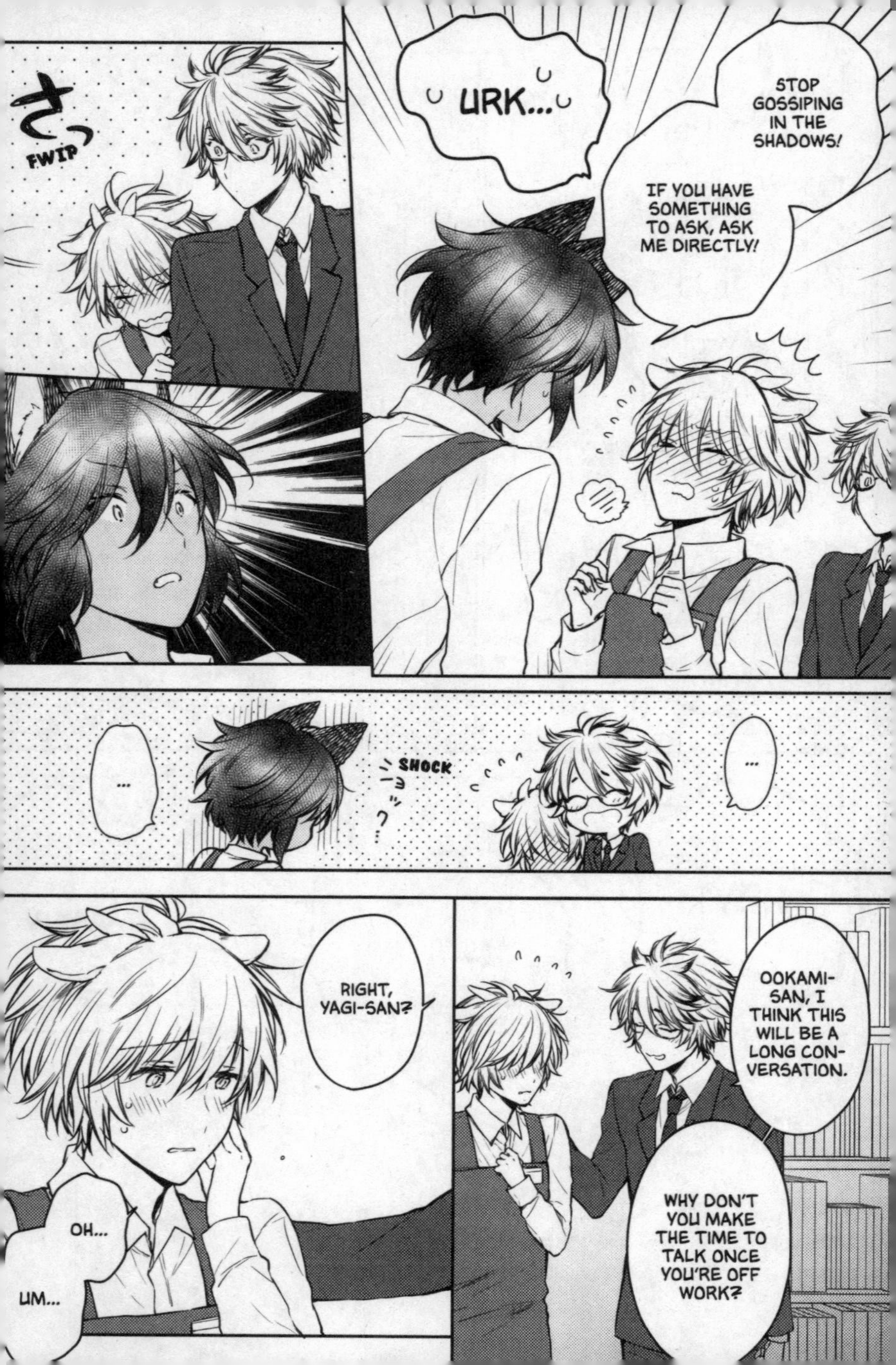
STOP GOSSIPING IN THE SHADOWS!
URK...
IF YOU HAVE SOMETHING TO ASK, ASK ME DIRECTLY!
さっ
FWIP
...
SHOCK
...
OOKAMI-SAN, I THINK THIS WILL BE A LONG CONVERSATION.
WHY DON'T YOU MAKE THE TIME TO TALK ONCE YOU'RE OFF WORK?
RIGHT, YAGI-SAN?
OH...
UM...

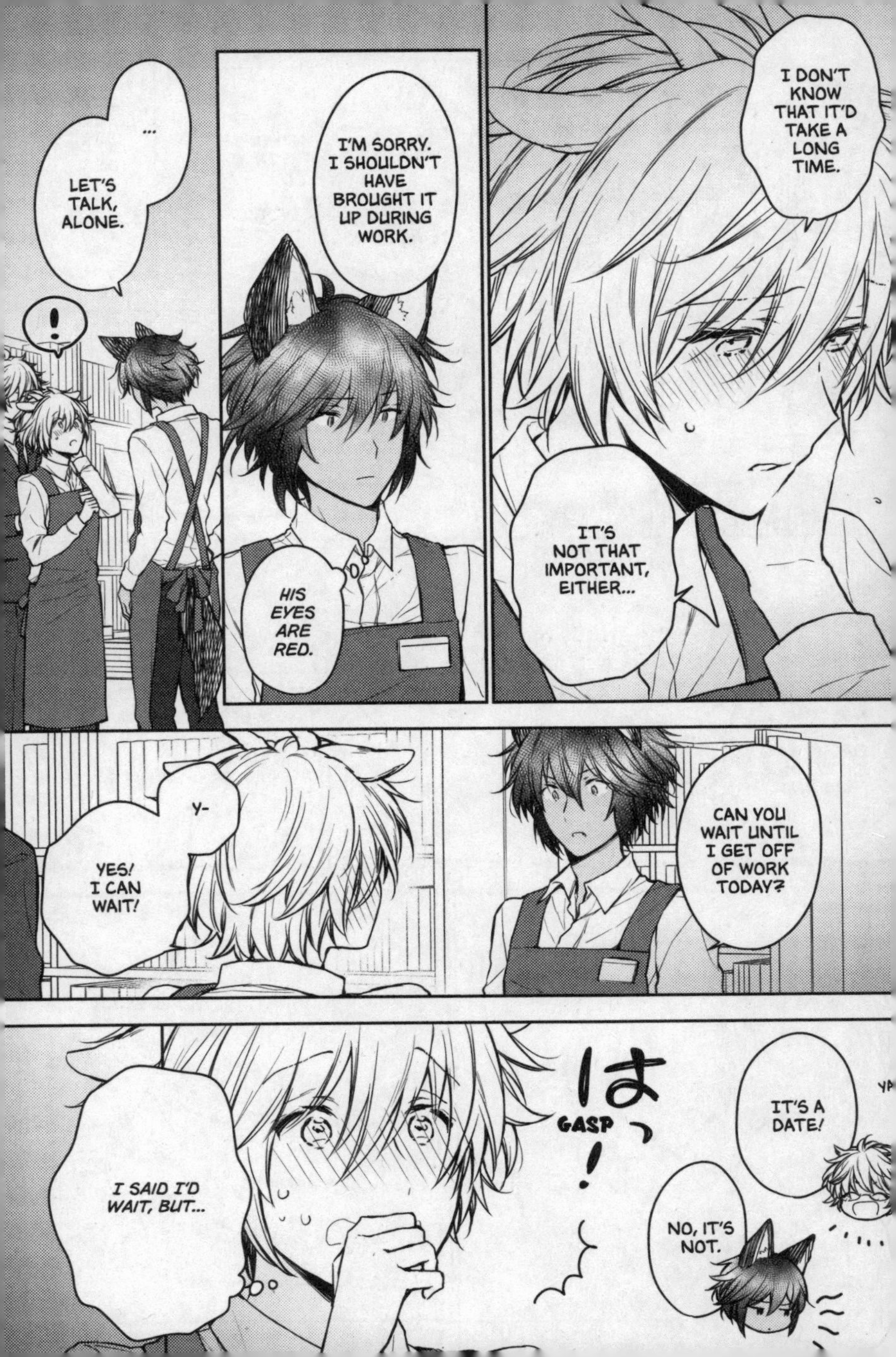
I DON'T KNOW THAT IT'D TAKE A LONG TIME.
IT'S NOT THAT IMPORTANT, EITHER...
I'M SORRY. I SHOULDN'T HAVE BROUGHT IT UP DURING WORK.
HIS EYES ARE RED.
...
LET'S TALK, ALONE.
!
CAN YOU WAIT UNTIL I GET OFF OF WORK TODAY?
Y-
YES! I CAN WAIT!
IT'S A DATE!
NO, IT'S NOT.
はっ!
GASP
I SAID I'D WAIT, BUT...

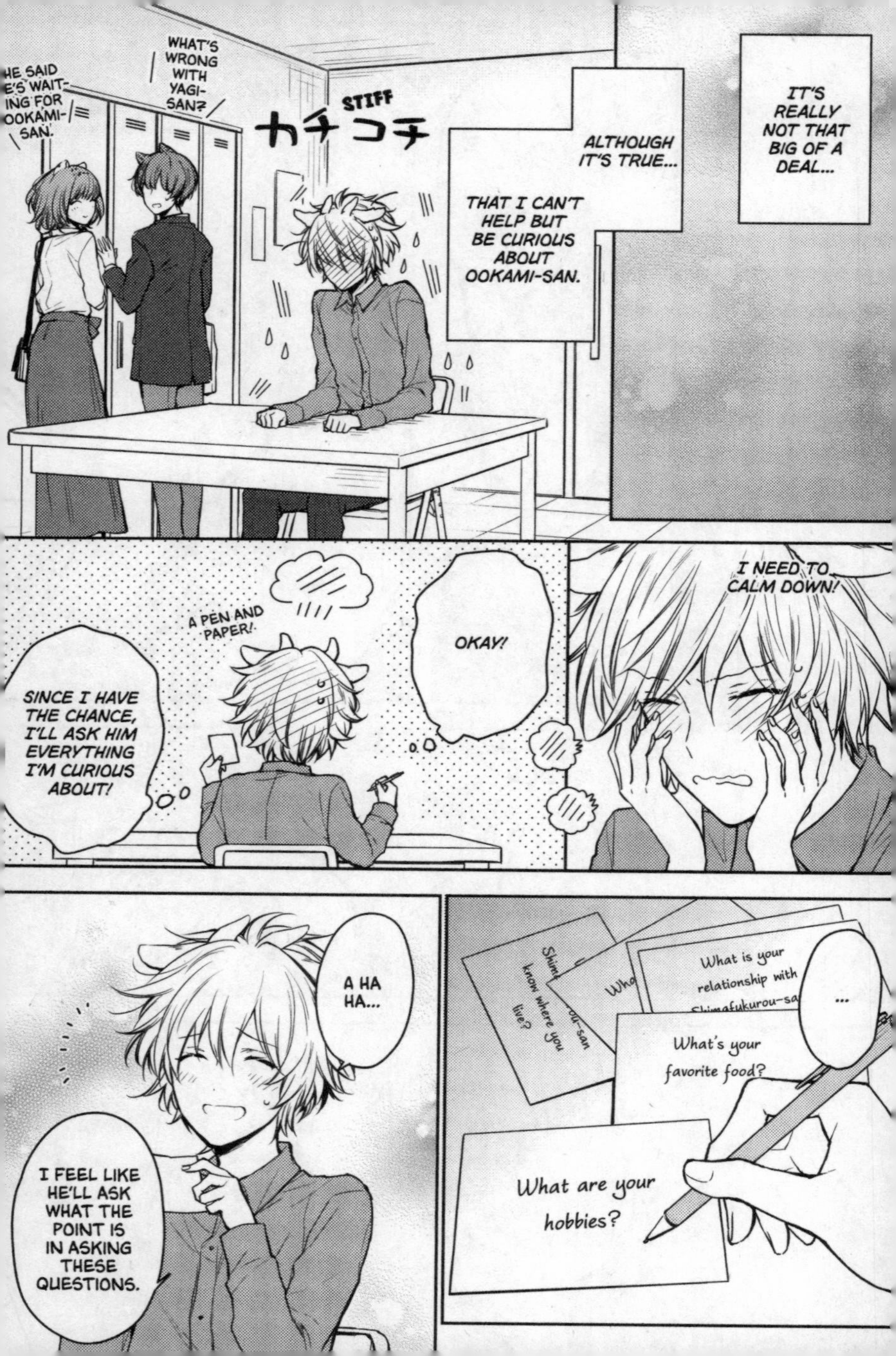
IT'S REALLY NOT THAT BIG OF A DEAL...
ALTHOUGH IT'S TRUE...
THAT I CAN'T HELP BUT BE CURIOUS ABOUT OOKAMI-SAN.
STIFF
カチコチ
WHAT'S WRONG WITH YAGI-SAN?
HE SAID E'S WAIT-ING FOR OOKAMI-SAN.
I NEED TO CALM DOWN!
OKAY!
A PEN AND PAPER!
SINCE I HAVE THE CHANCE, I'LL ASK HIM EVERYTHING I'M CURIOUS ABOUT!
...
What is your relationship with
know where you live?
What's your favorite food?
What are your hobbies?
A HA HA...
I FEEL LIKE HE'LL ASK WHAT THE POINT IS IN ASKING THESE QUESTIONS.

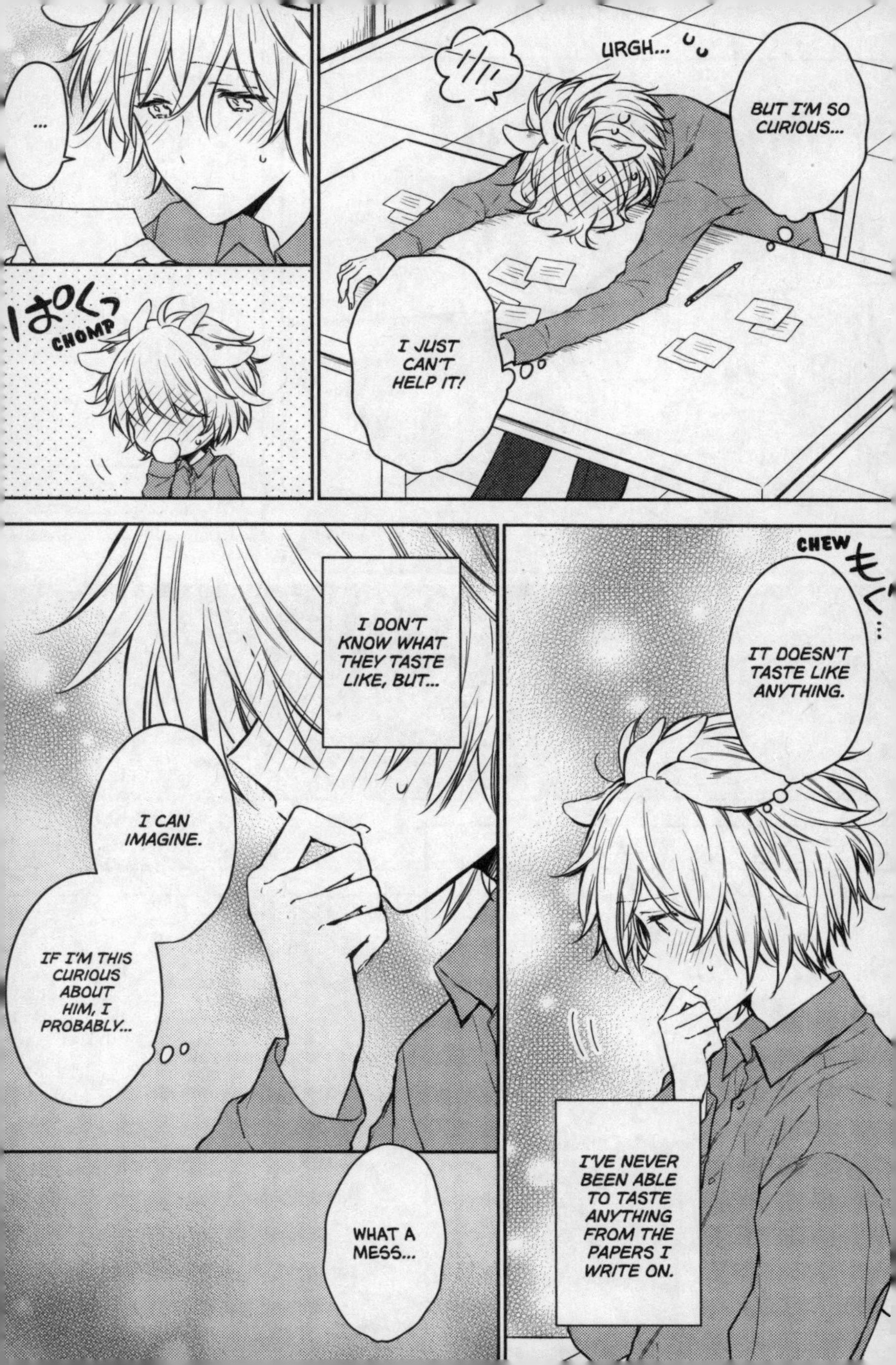
URGH...
BUT I'M SO CURIOUS...
I JUST CAN'T HELP IT!
...
はくっ
CHOMP
CHEW
もぐ…
IT DOESN'T TASTE LIKE ANYTHING.
I'VE NEVER BEEN ABLE TO TASTE ANYTHING FROM THE PAPERS I WRITE ON.
I DON'T KNOW WHAT THEY TASTE LIKE, BUT...
I CAN IMAGINE.
IF I'M THIS CURIOUS ABOUT HIM, I PROBABLY...
WHAT A MESS...

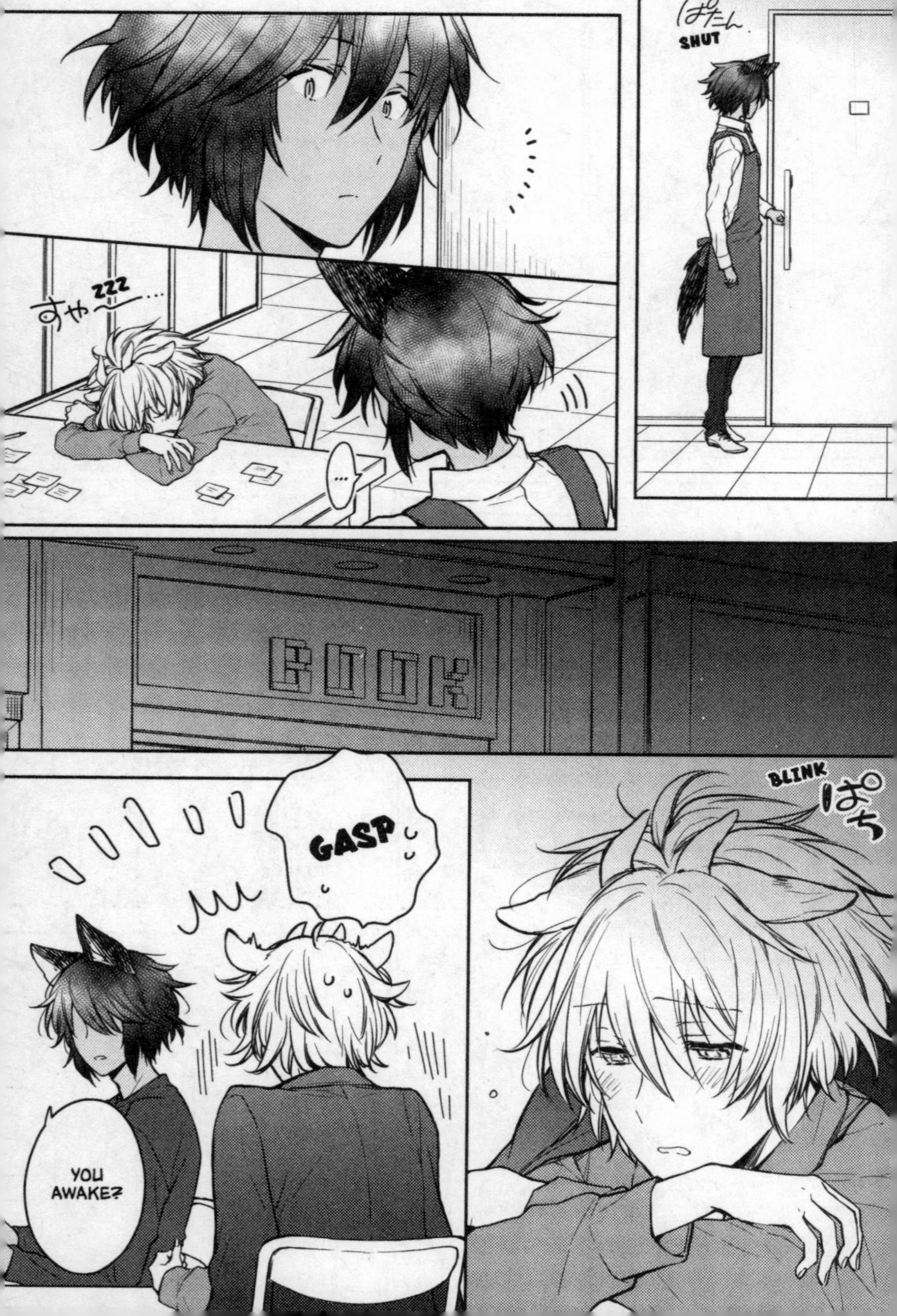
ぱたん
SHUT
すや～
zzz
…
…
BLINK
ぱち
GASP
YOU AWAKE?

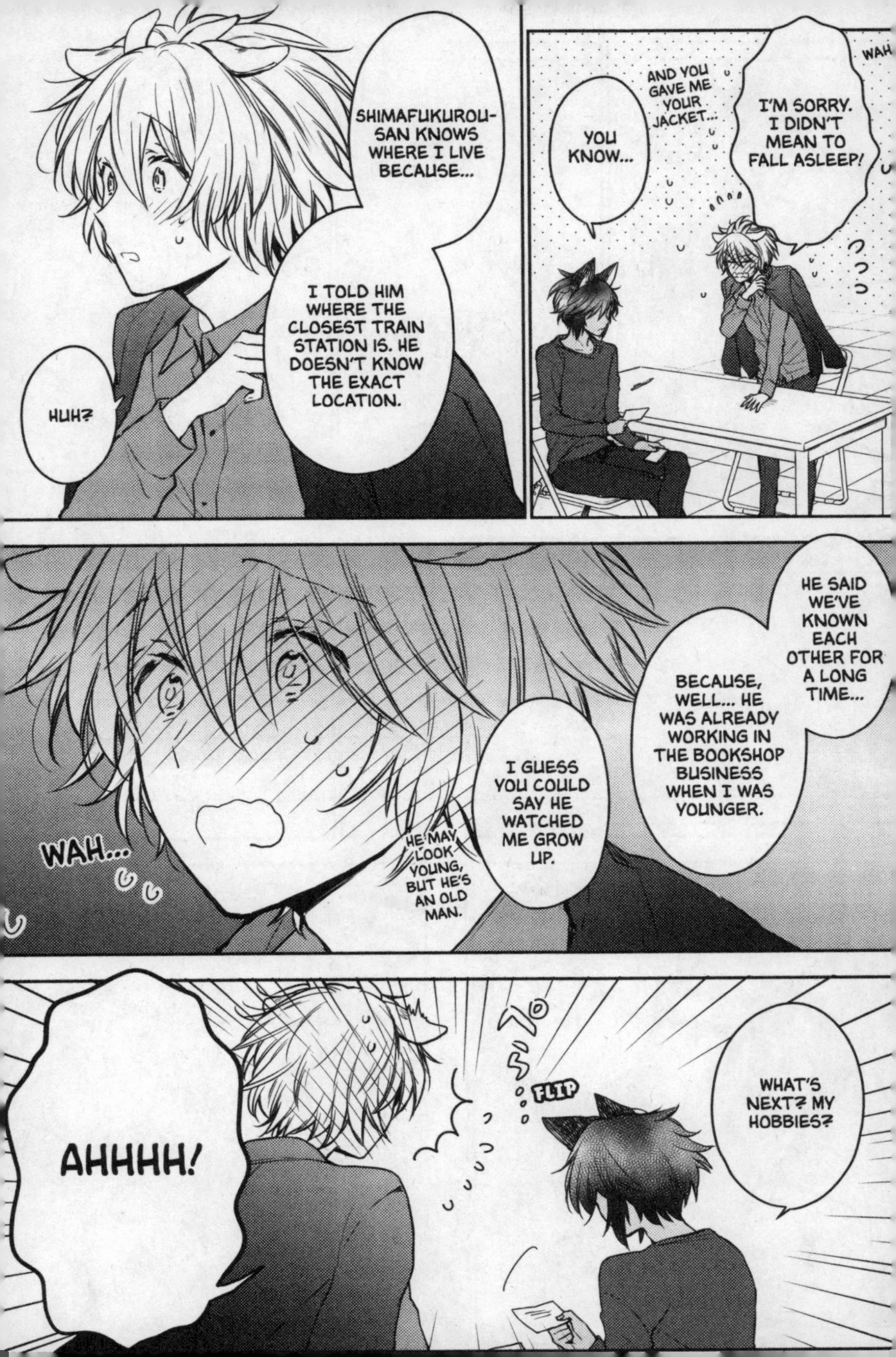
WAH
I'M SORRY. I DIDN'T MEAN TO FALL ASLEEP!
AND YOU GAVE ME YOUR JACKET...
YOU KNOW...
SHIMAFUKUROU-SAN KNOWS WHERE I LIVE BECAUSE...
I TOLD HIM WHERE THE CLOSEST TRAIN STATION IS. HE DOESN'T KNOW THE EXACT LOCATION.
HUH?
HE SAID WE'VE KNOWN EACH OTHER FOR A LONG TIME...
BECAUSE, WELL... HE WAS ALREADY WORKING IN THE BOOKSHOP BUSINESS WHEN I WAS YOUNGER.
I GUESS YOU COULD SAY HE WATCHED ME GROW UP.
HE MAY LOOK YOUNG, BUT HE'S AN OLD MAN.
WAH...
WHAT'S NEXT? MY HOBBIES?
FLIP
AHHHH!

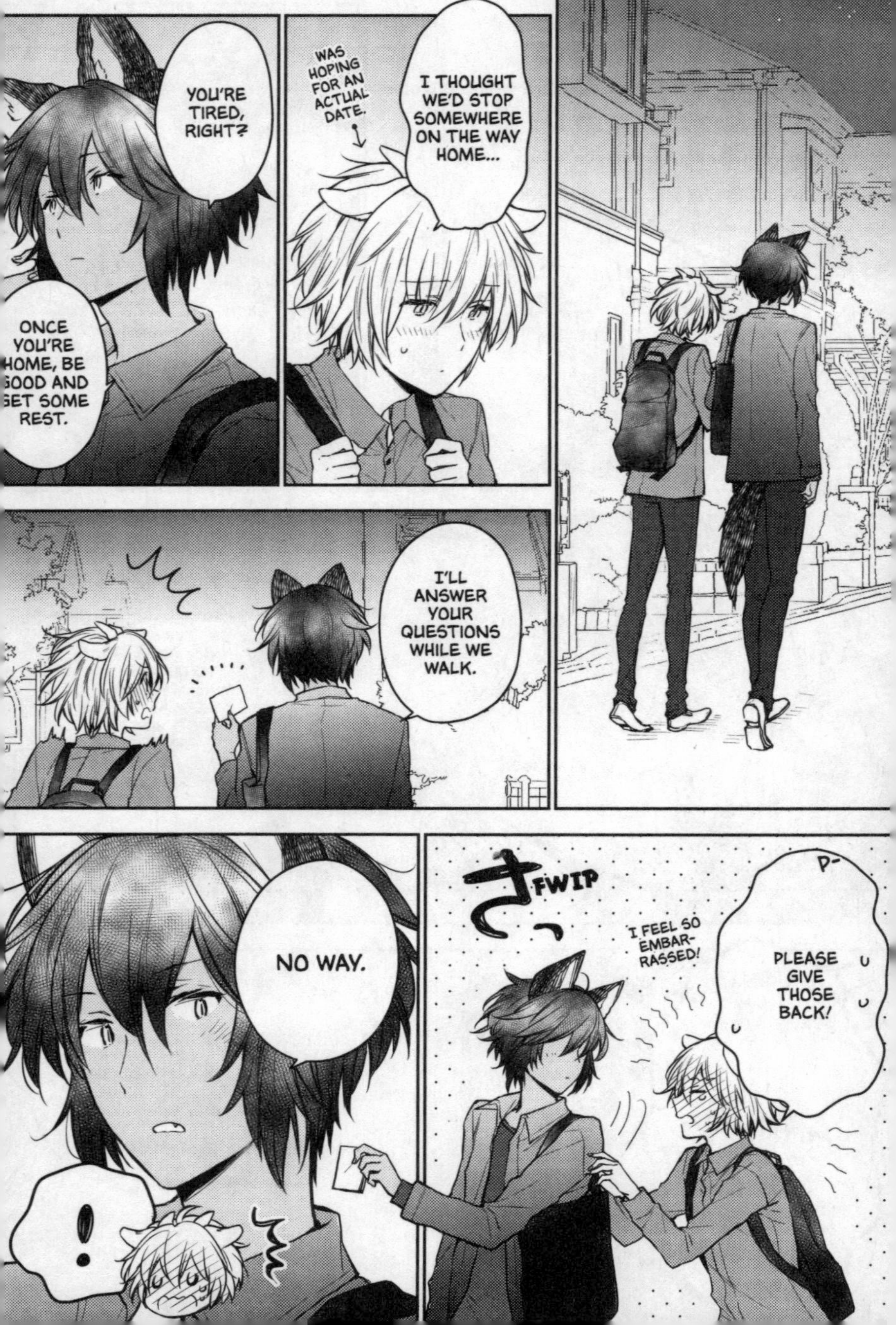

I THOUGHT WE'D STOP SOMEWHERE ON THE WAY HOME...
WAS HOPING FOR AN ACTUAL DATE.
YOU'RE TIRED, RIGHT?
ONCE YOU'RE HOME, BE GOOD AND GET SOME REST.
I'LL ANSWER YOUR QUESTIONS WHILE WE WALK.
FWIP
P- PLEASE GIVE THOSE BACK!
I FEEL SO EMBARRASSED!
NO WAY.
!

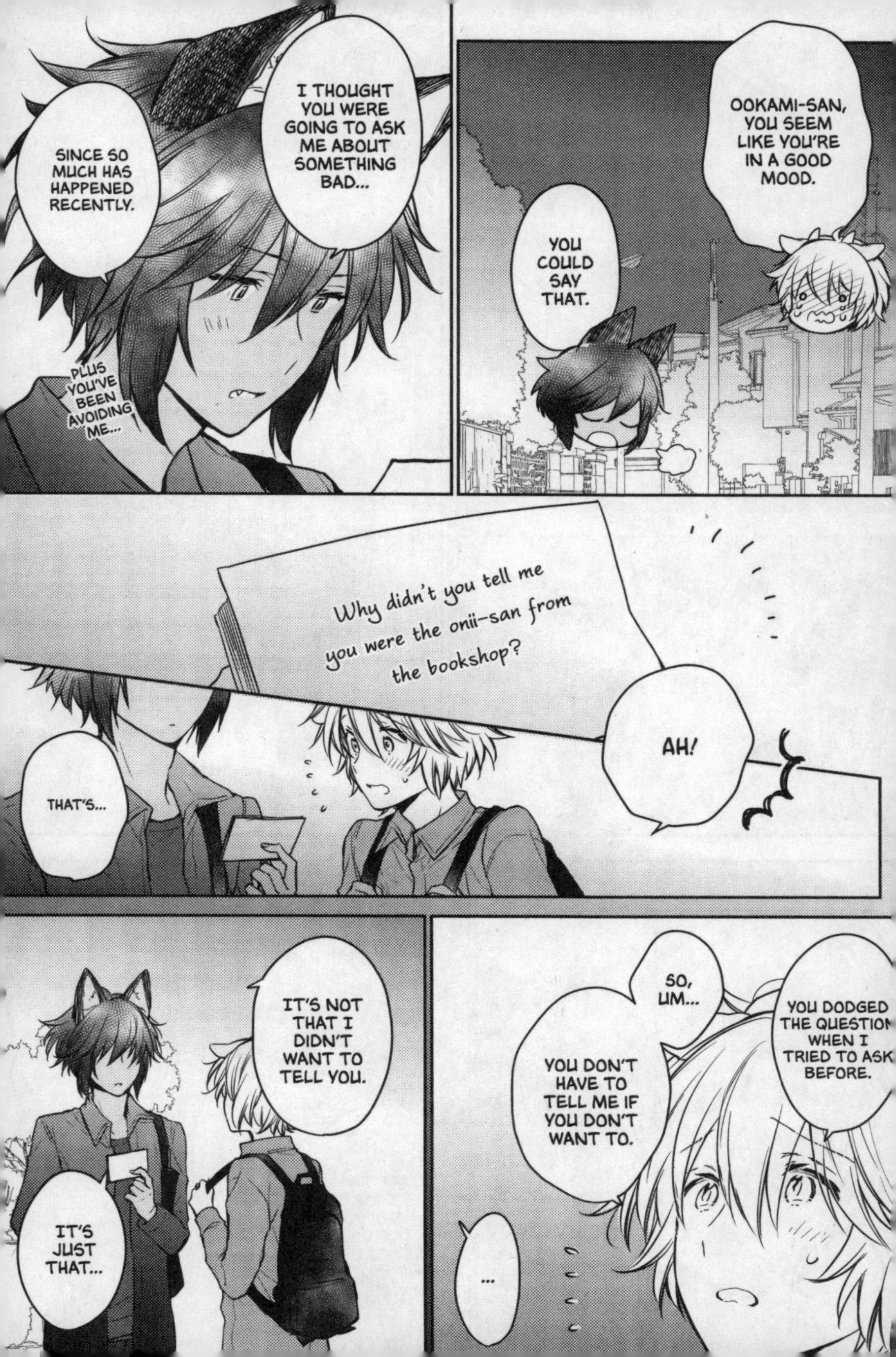
OOKAMI-SAN, YOU SEEM LIKE YOU'RE IN A GOOD MOOD.
YOU COULD SAY THAT.
I THOUGHT YOU WERE GOING TO ASK ME ABOUT SOMETHING BAD...
SINCE SO MUCH HAS HAPPENED RECENTLY.
PLUS YOU'VE BEEN AVOIDING ME...
Why didn't you tell me you were the onii-san from the bookshop?
AH!
THAT'S...
YOU DODGED THE QUESTION WHEN I TRIED TO ASK BEFORE.
SO, UM...
YOU DON'T HAVE TO TELL ME IF YOU DON'T WANT TO.
...
IT'S NOT THAT I DIDN'T WANT TO TELL YOU.
IT'S JUST THAT...

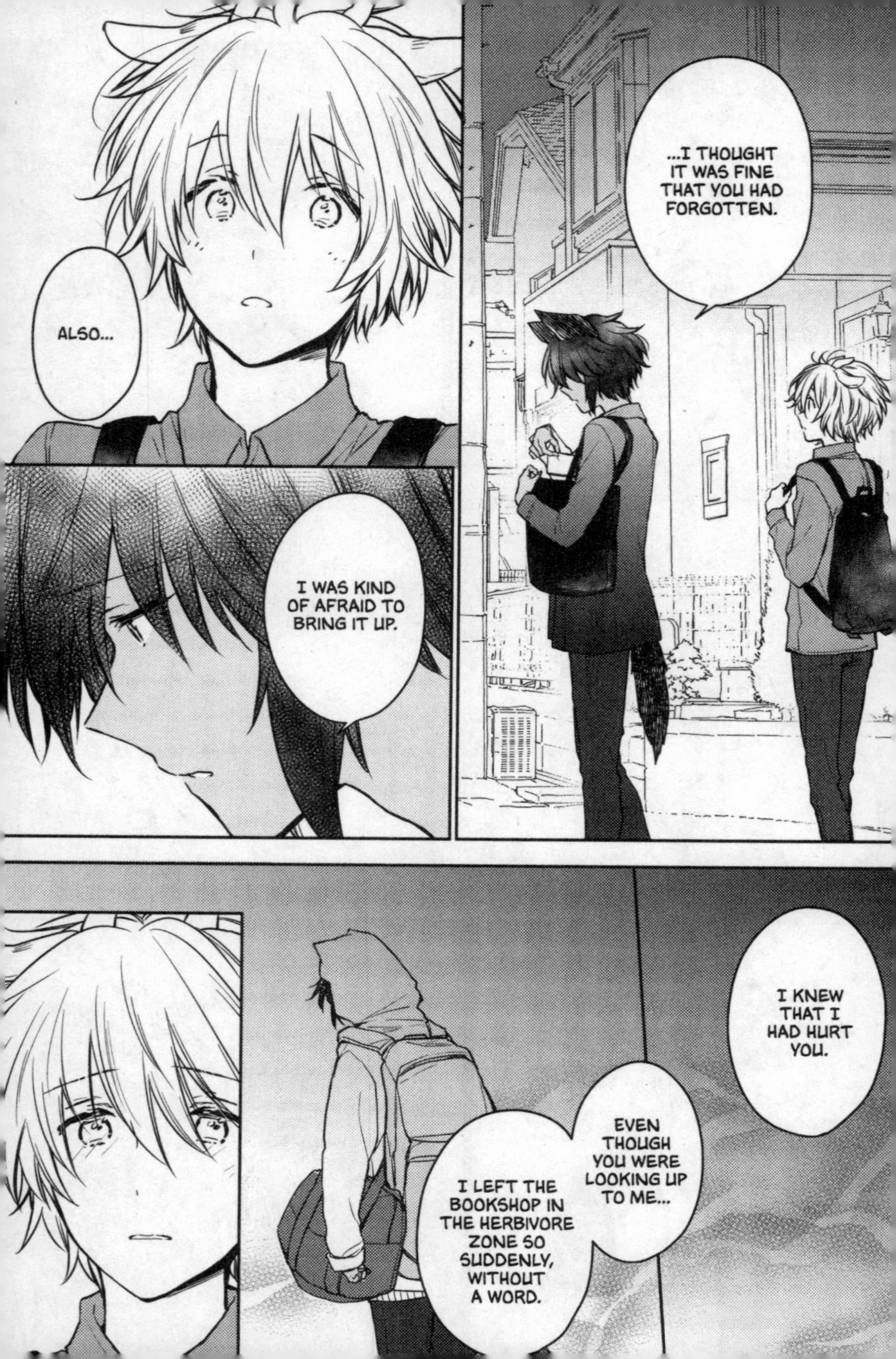
...I THOUGHT IT WAS FINE THAT YOU HAD FORGOTTEN.
ALSO...
I WAS KIND OF AFRAID TO BRING IT UP.
I KNEW THAT I HAD HURT YOU.
EVEN THOUGH YOU WERE LOOKING UP TO ME...
I LEFT THE BOOKSHOP IN THE HERBIVORE ZONE SO SUDDENLY, WITHOUT A WORD.

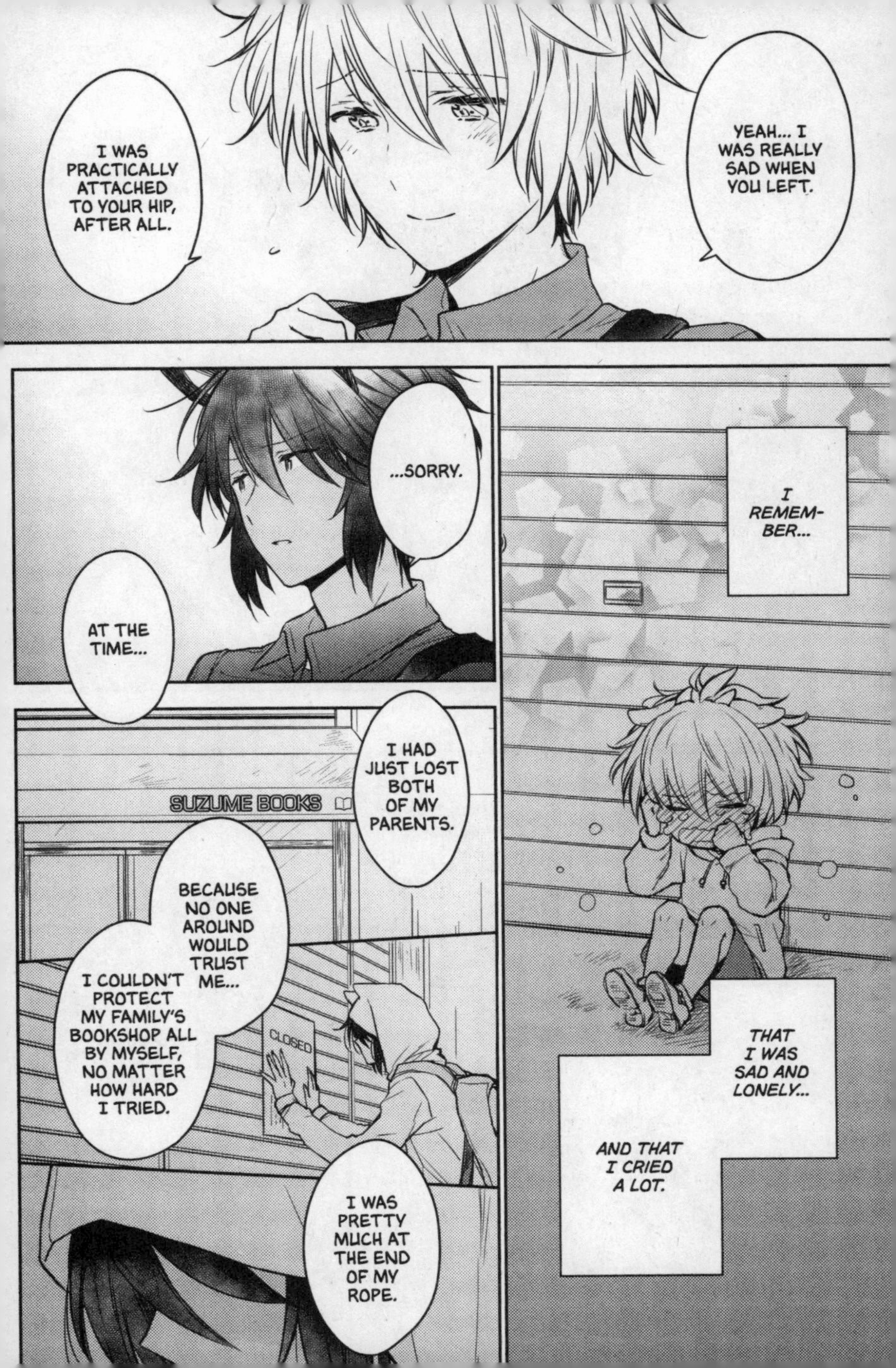
YEAH... I WAS REALLY SAD WHEN YOU LEFT.
I WAS PRACTICALLY ATTACHED TO YOUR HIP, AFTER ALL.
I REMEMBER...
THAT I WAS SAD AND LONELY...
AND THAT I CRIED A LOT.
...SORRY.
AT THE TIME...
I HAD JUST LOST BOTH OF MY PARENTS.
SUZUME BOOKS
BECAUSE NO ONE AROUND WOULD TRUST ME...
I COULDN'T PROTECT MY FAMILY'S BOOKSHOP ALL BY MYSELF, NO MATTER HOW HARD I TRIED.
CLOSED
I WAS PRETTY MUCH AT THE END OF MY ROPE.

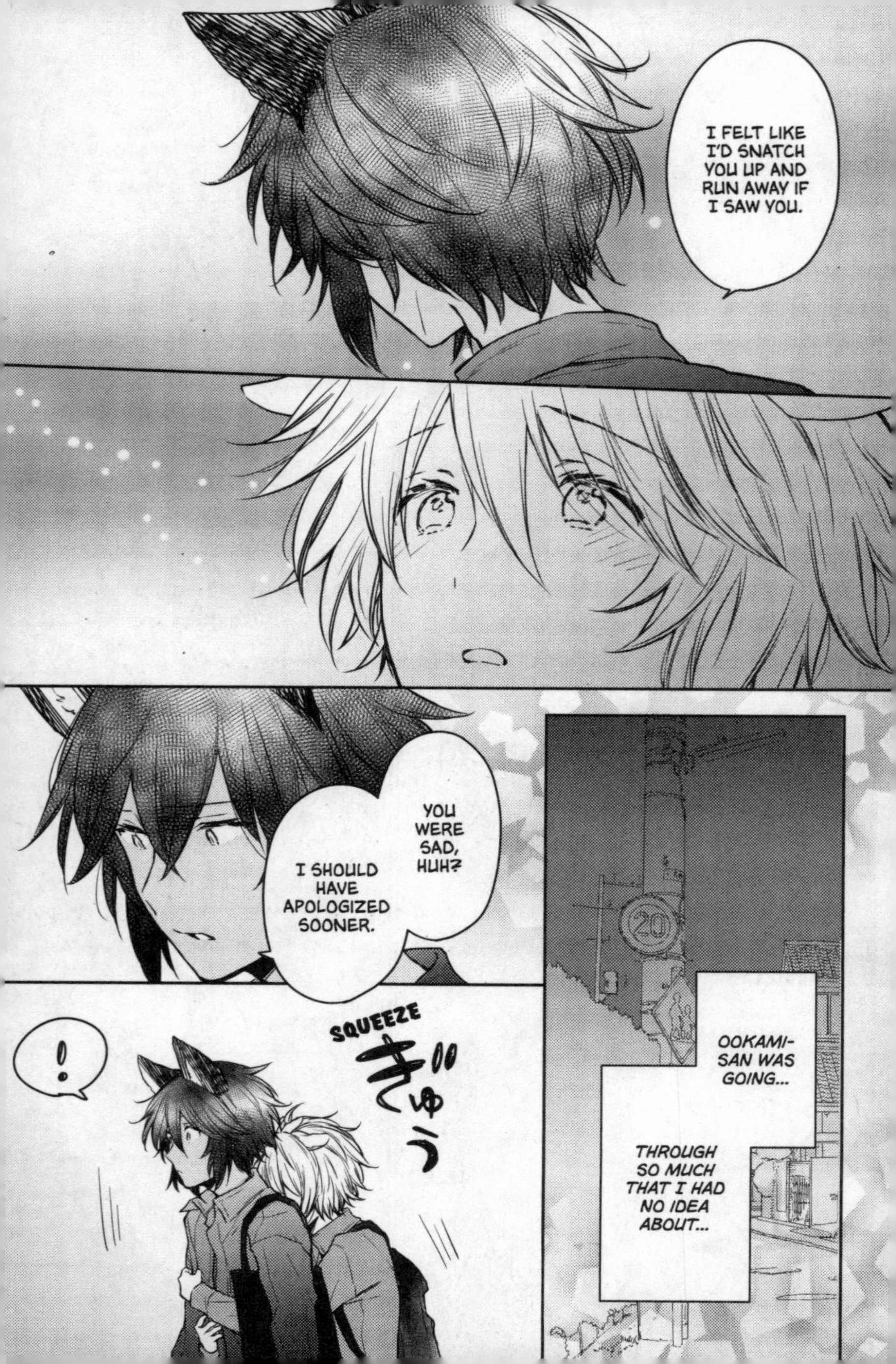
I FELT LIKE I'D SNATCH YOU UP AND RUN AWAY IF I SAW YOU.
OOKAMI-SAN WAS GOING...
THROUGH SO MUCH THAT I HAD NO IDEA ABOUT...
YOU WERE SAD, HUH?
I SHOULD HAVE APOLOGIZED SOONER.
SQUEEZE
ぎゅう
!

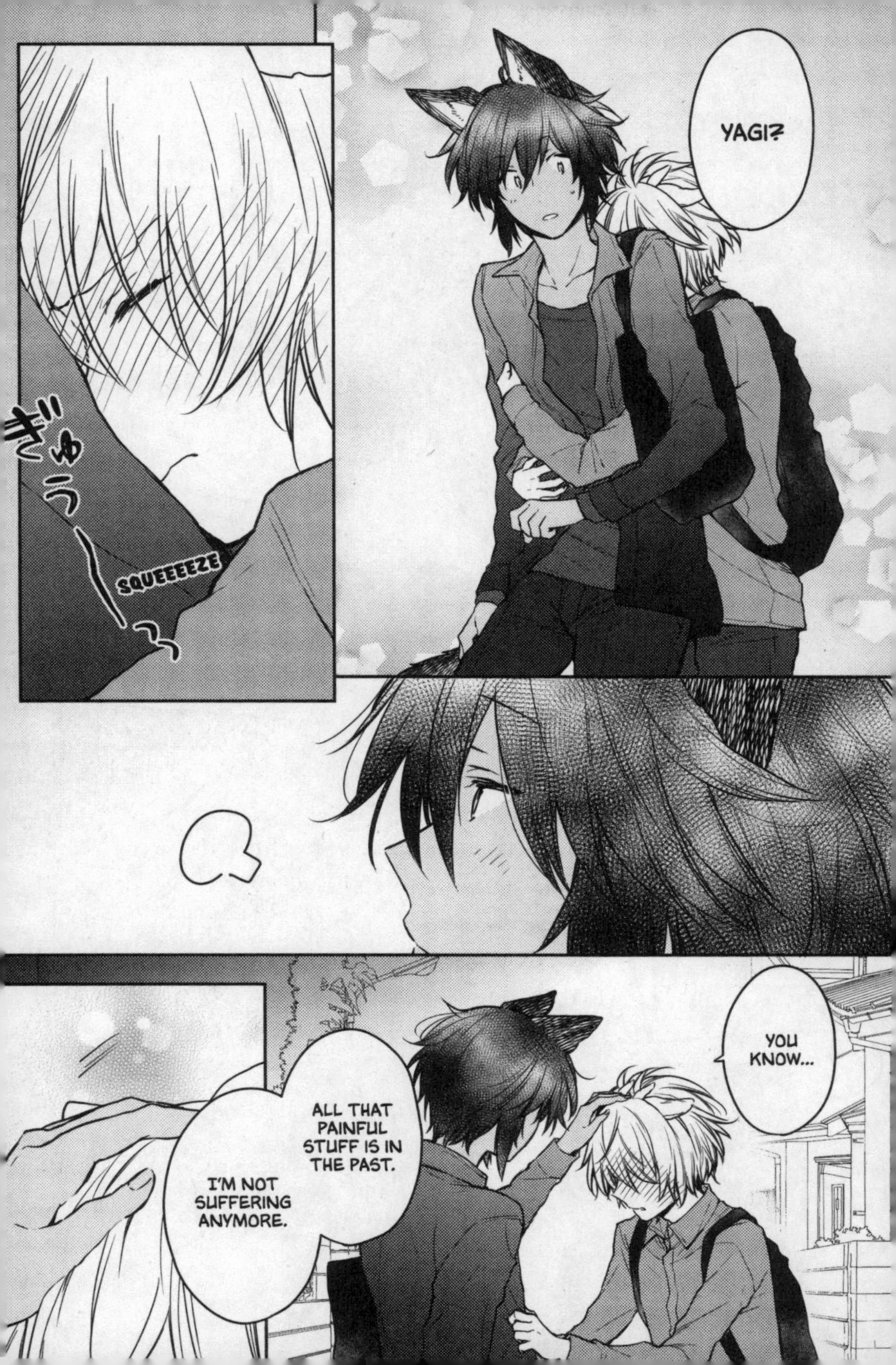
YAGI?
ぎゅうーっ
SQUEEEEZE
YOU KNOW...
ALL THAT PAINFUL STUFF IS IN THE PAST.
I'M NOT SUFFERING ANYMORE.

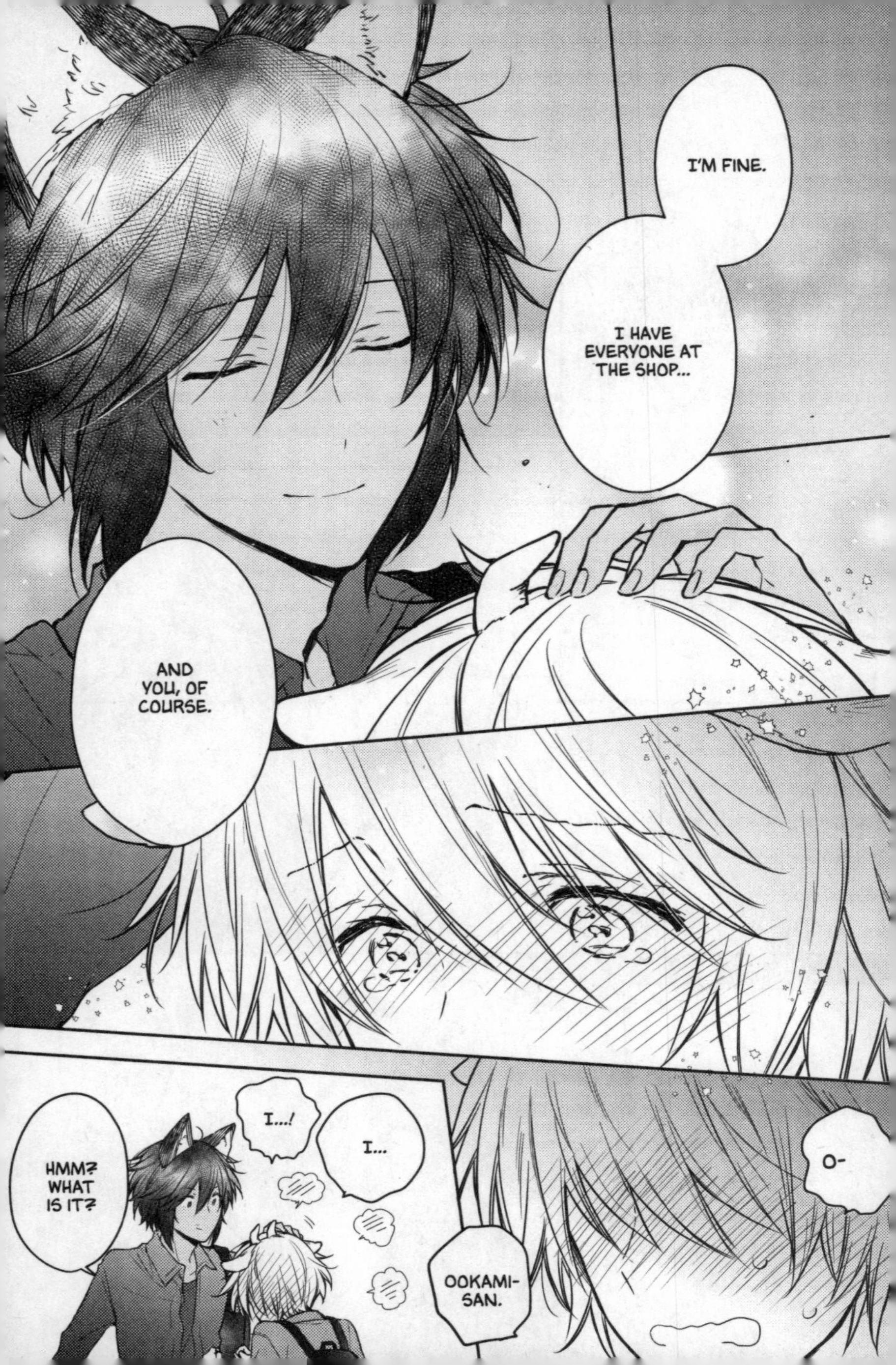
I'M FINE.
I HAVE EVERYONE AT THE SHOP...
AND YOU, OF COURSE.
O-
OOKAMI-SAN.
I...
I...!
HMM? WHAT IS IT?

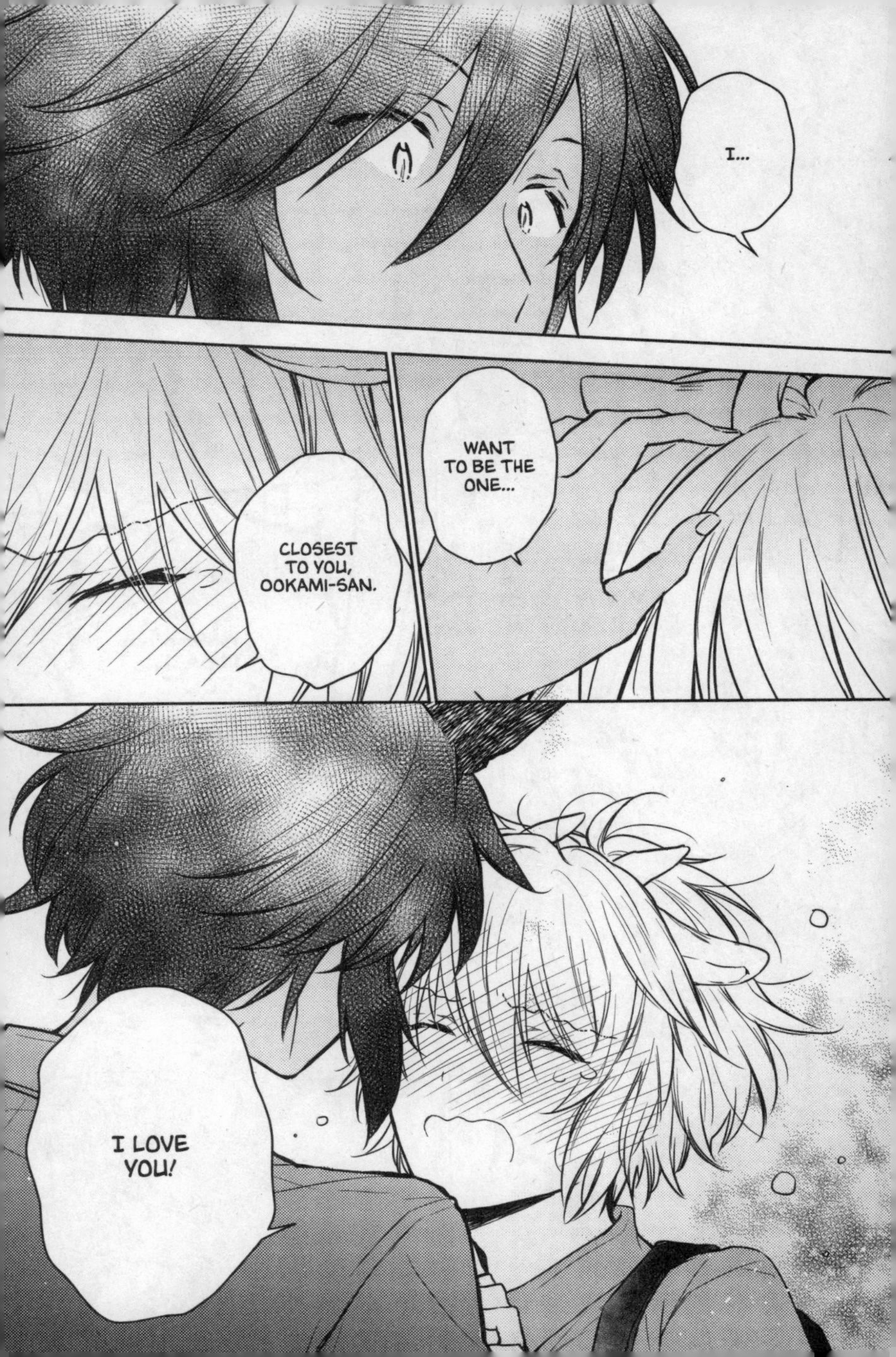
I...
WANT TO BE THE ONE...
CLOSEST TO YOU, OOKAMI-SAN.
I LOVE YOU!

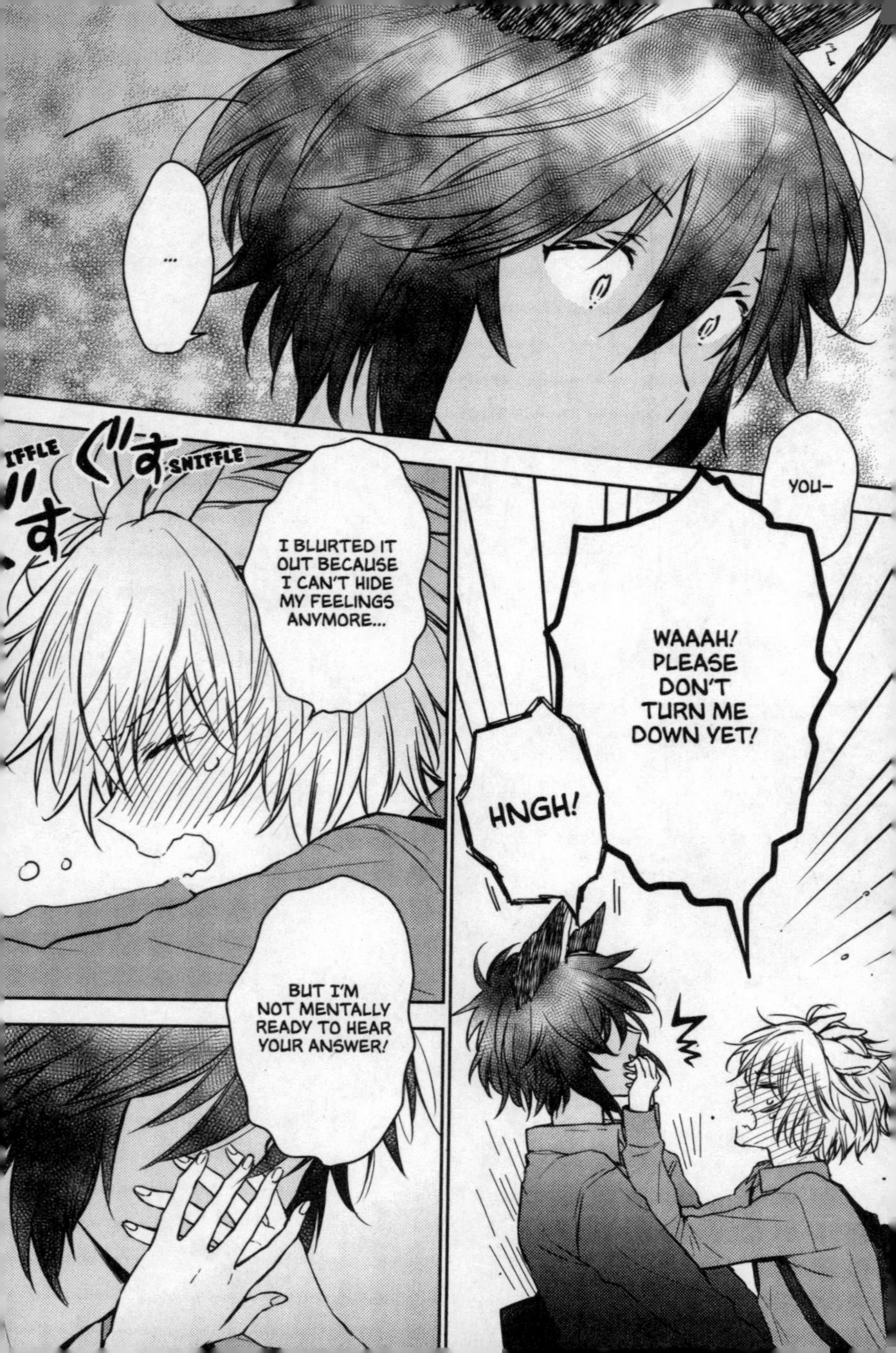
...
YOU–
WAAAH! PLEASE DON'T TURN ME DOWN YET!
HNGH!
ぐす SNIFFLE
I BLURTED IT OUT BECAUSE I CAN'T HIDE MY FEELINGS ANYMORE...
BUT I'M NOT MENTALLY READY TO HEAR YOUR ANSWER!

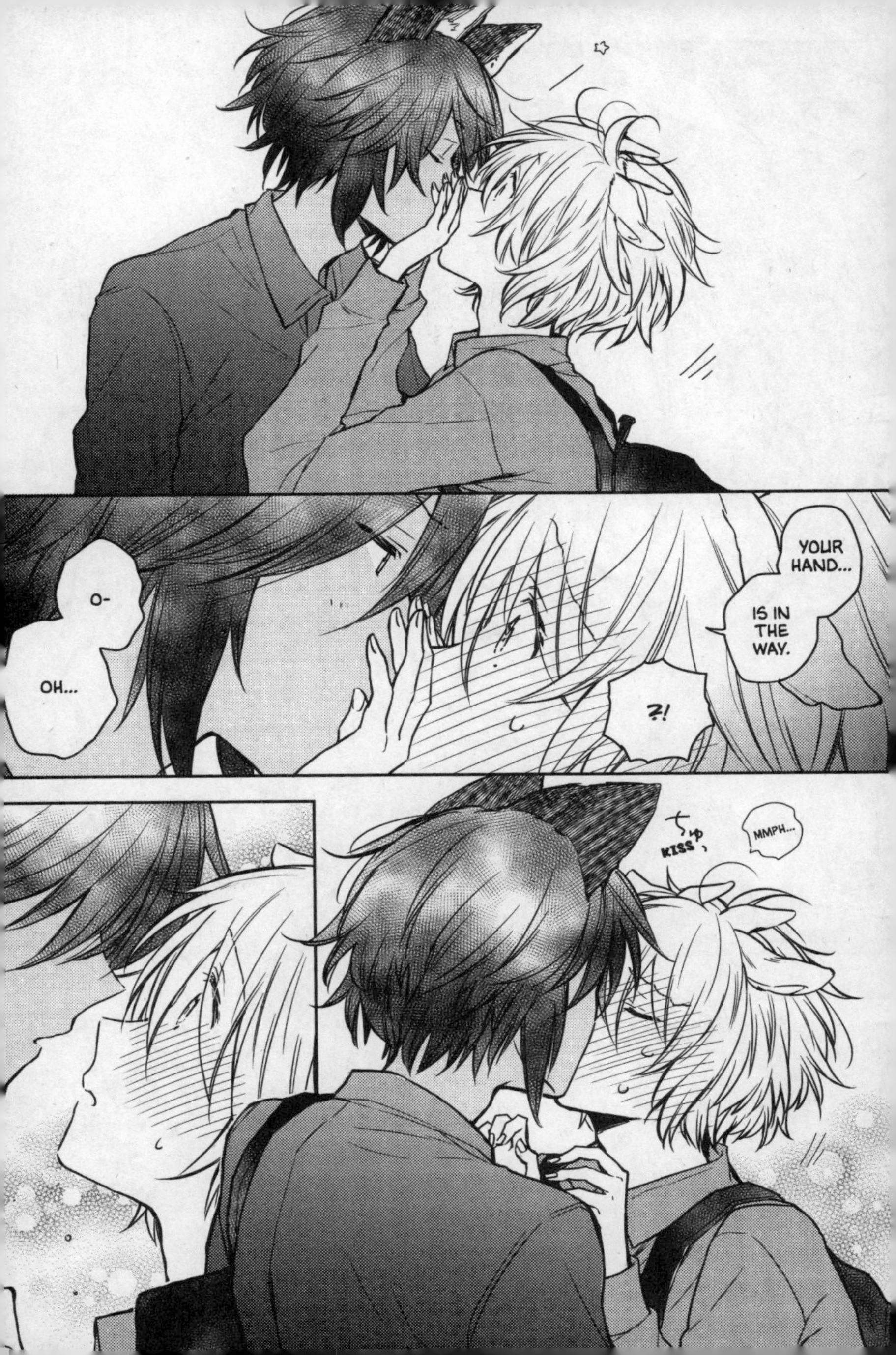
YOUR HAND...
IS IN THE WAY.
?!
O-
OH...
MMPH...
ちゅ
KISS

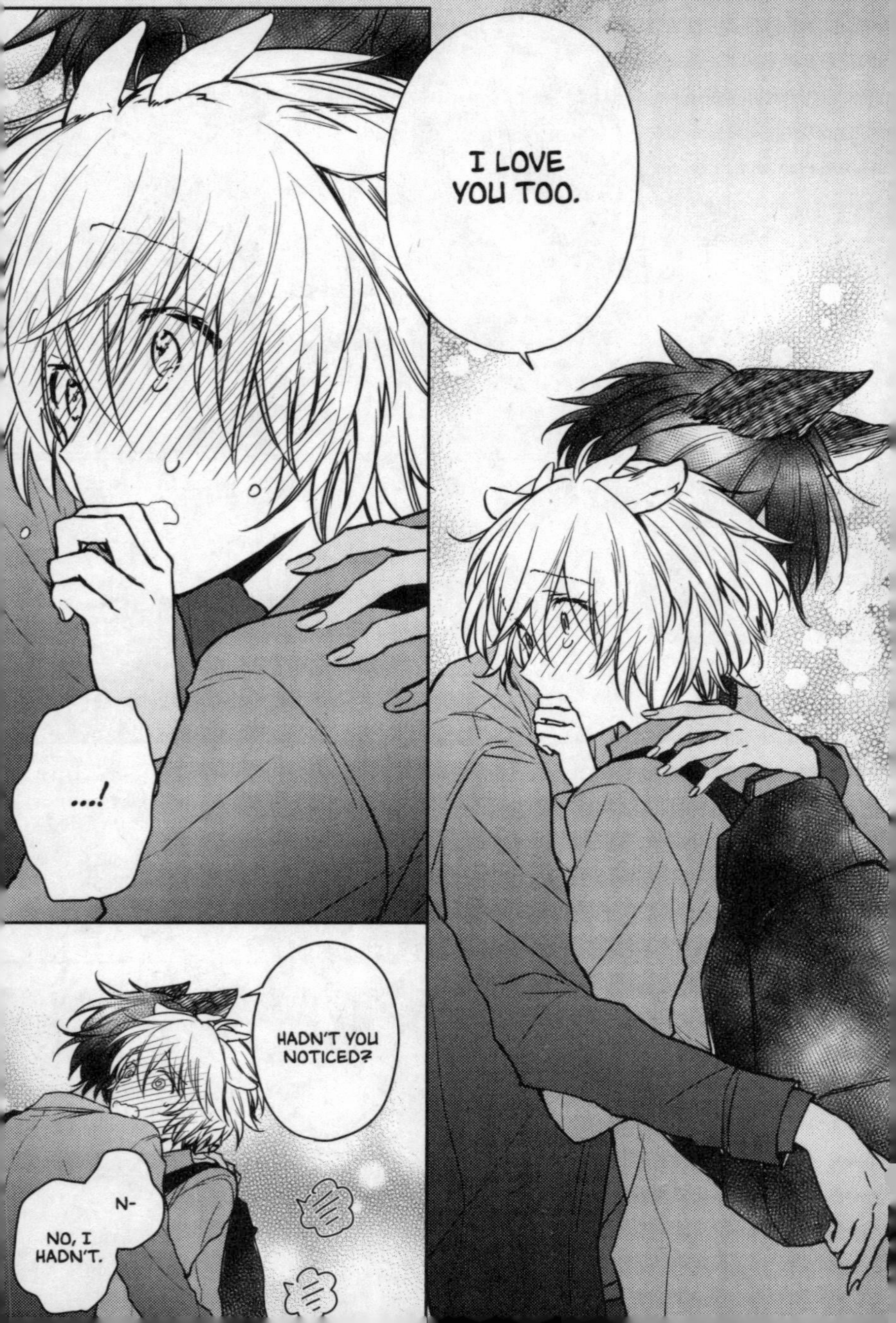
I LOVE YOU TOO.
...!
HADN'T YOU NOTICED?
N- NO, I HADN'T.

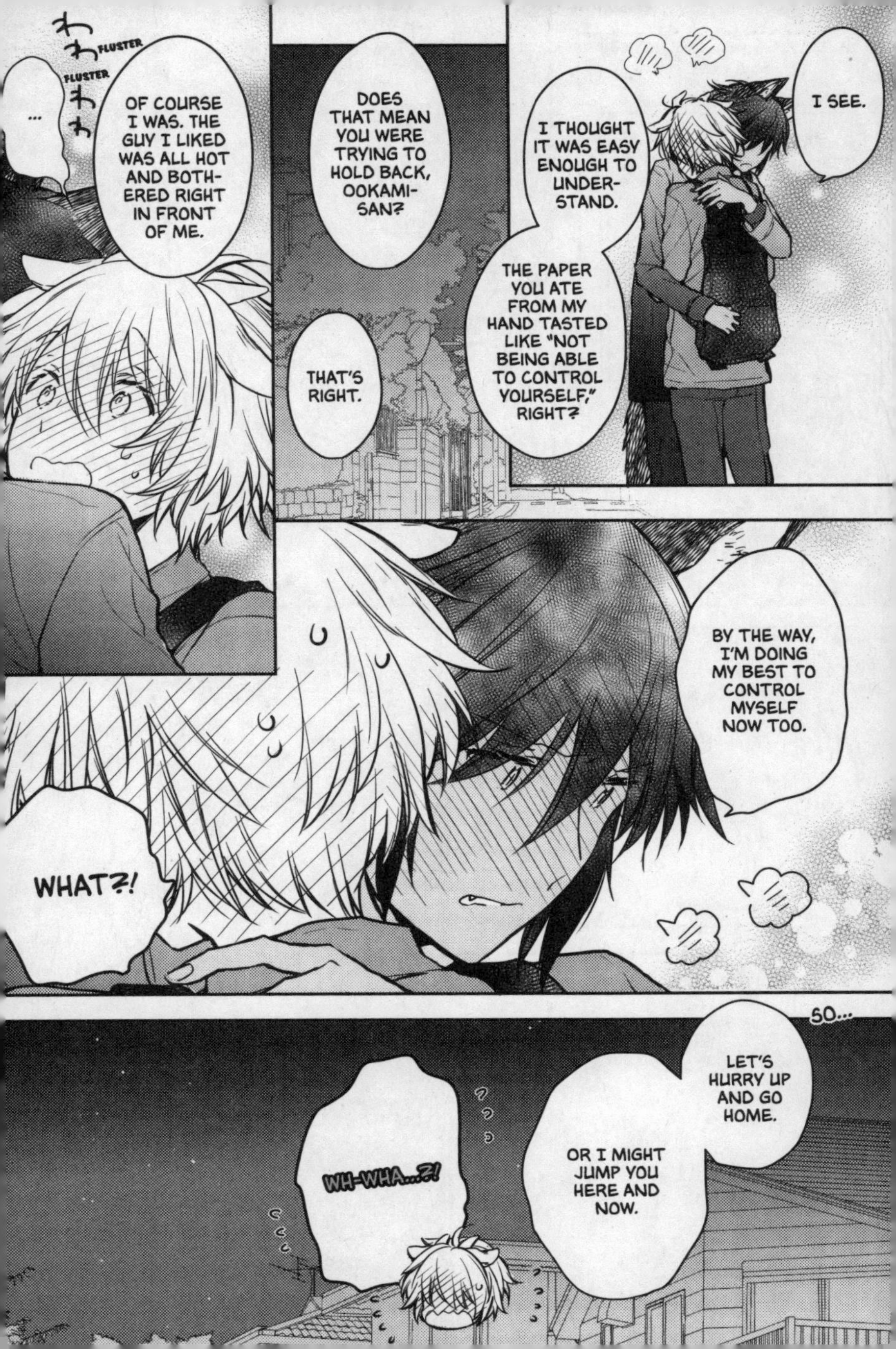
I SEE.
I THOUGHT IT WAS EASY ENOUGH TO UNDER-STAND.
THE PAPER YOU ATE FROM MY HAND TASTED LIKE "NOT BEING ABLE TO CONTROL YOURSELF," RIGHT?
DOES THAT MEAN YOU WERE TRYING TO HOLD BACK, OOKAMI-SAN?
THAT'S RIGHT.
わわ FLUSTER
FLUSTER わわ
OF COURSE I WAS. THE GUY I LIKED WAS ALL HOT AND BOTH-ERED RIGHT IN FRONT OF ME.
...
BY THE WAY, I'M DOING MY BEST TO CONTROL MYSELF NOW TOO.
WHAT?!
SO...
LET'S HURRY UP AND GO HOME.
OR I MIGHT JUMP YOU HERE AND NOW.
WH-WHA...?!

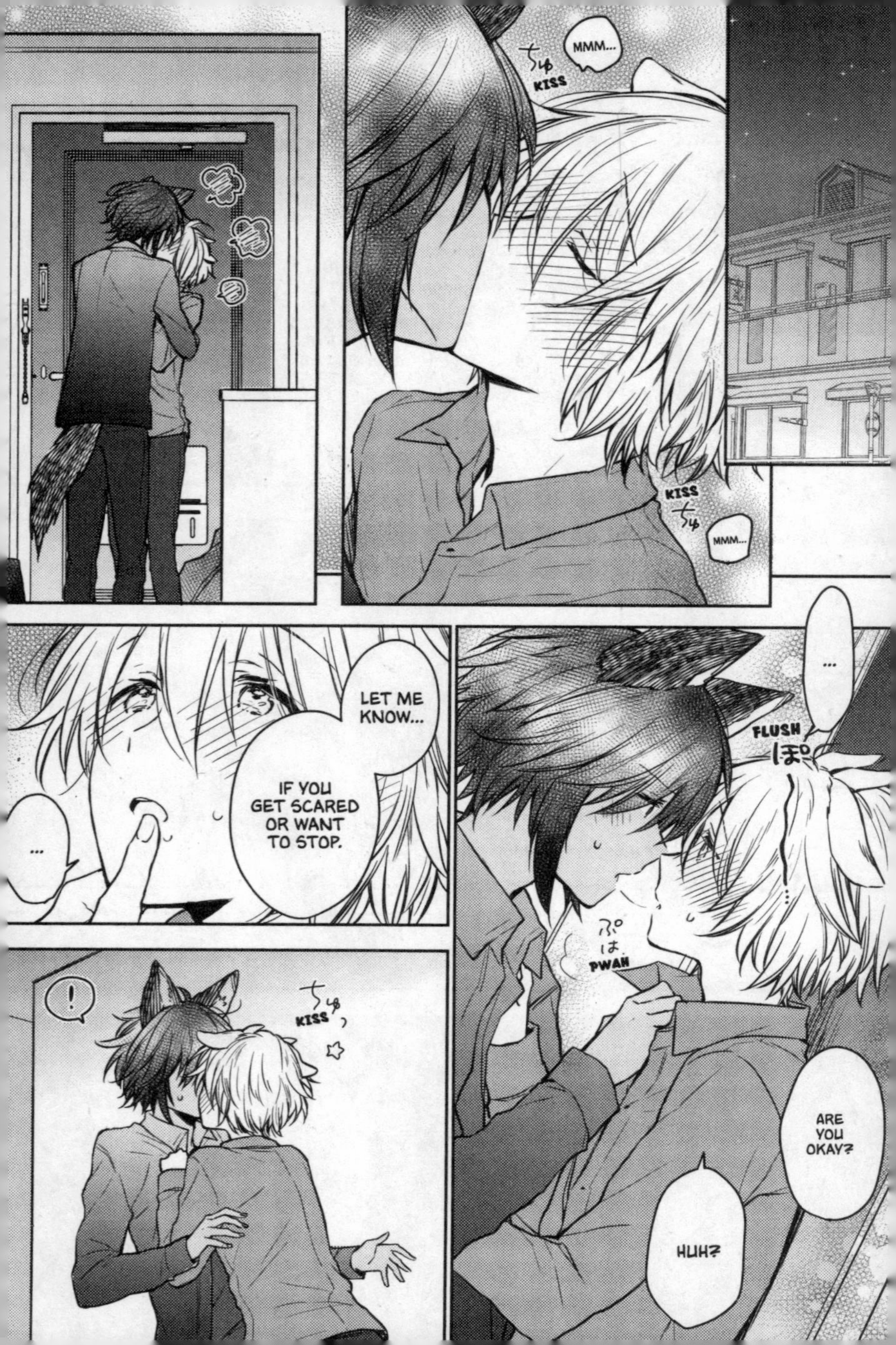
ちゅ KISS
MMM...
KISS ちゅ
MMM...
...
FLUSH ぽ
ぷは PWAH
ARE YOU OKAY?
HUH?
LET ME KNOW...
IF YOU GET SCARED OR WANT TO STOP.
...
!
ちゅ KISS

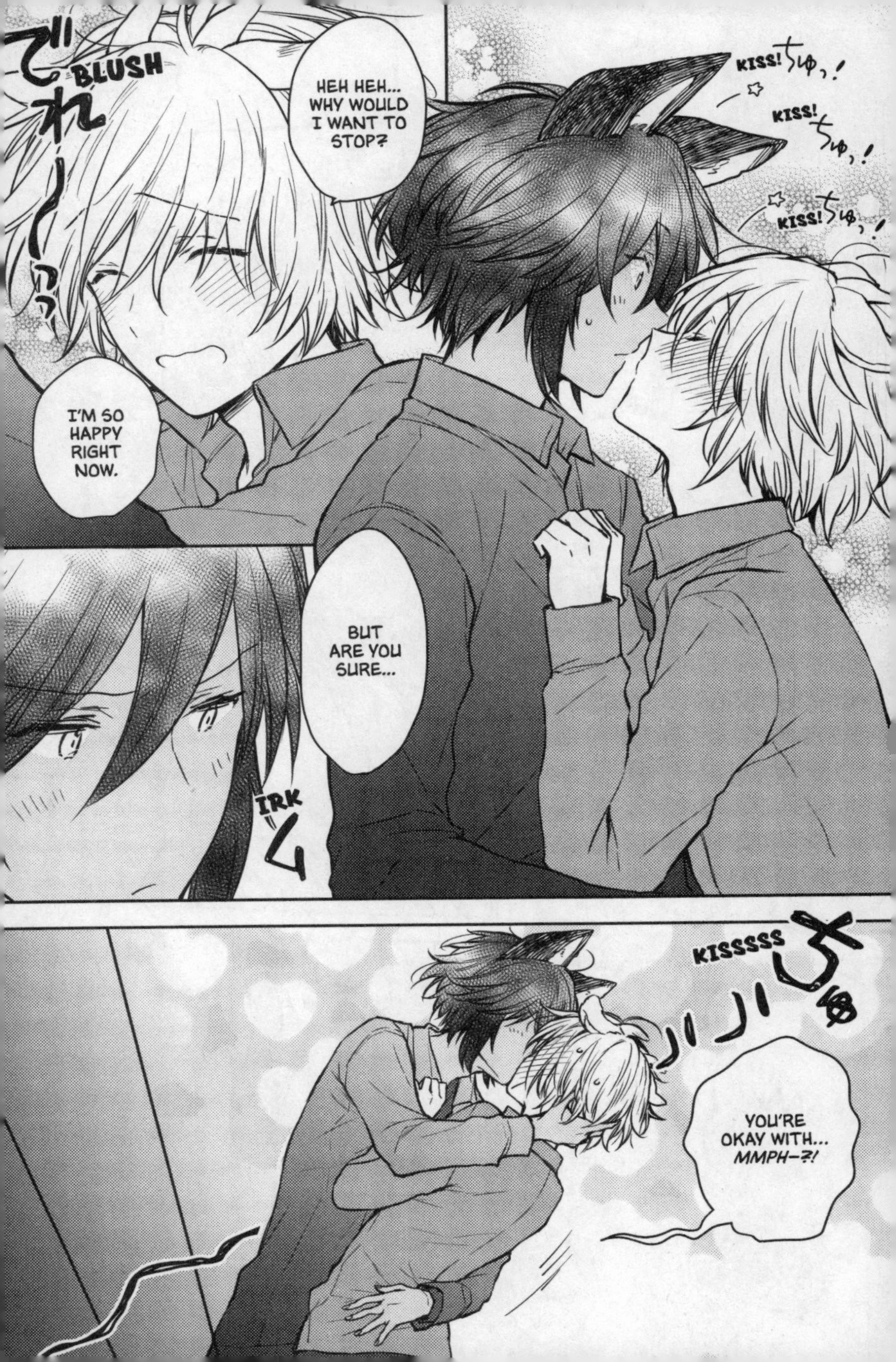
KISS! ちゅっ!
KISS! ちゅっ!
KISS! ちゅっ!
HEH HEH... WHY WOULD I WANT TO STOP?
BLUSH
I'M SO HAPPY RIGHT NOW.
BUT ARE YOU SURE...
IRK
KISSSSS
YOU'RE OKAY WITH... *MMPH*-?!

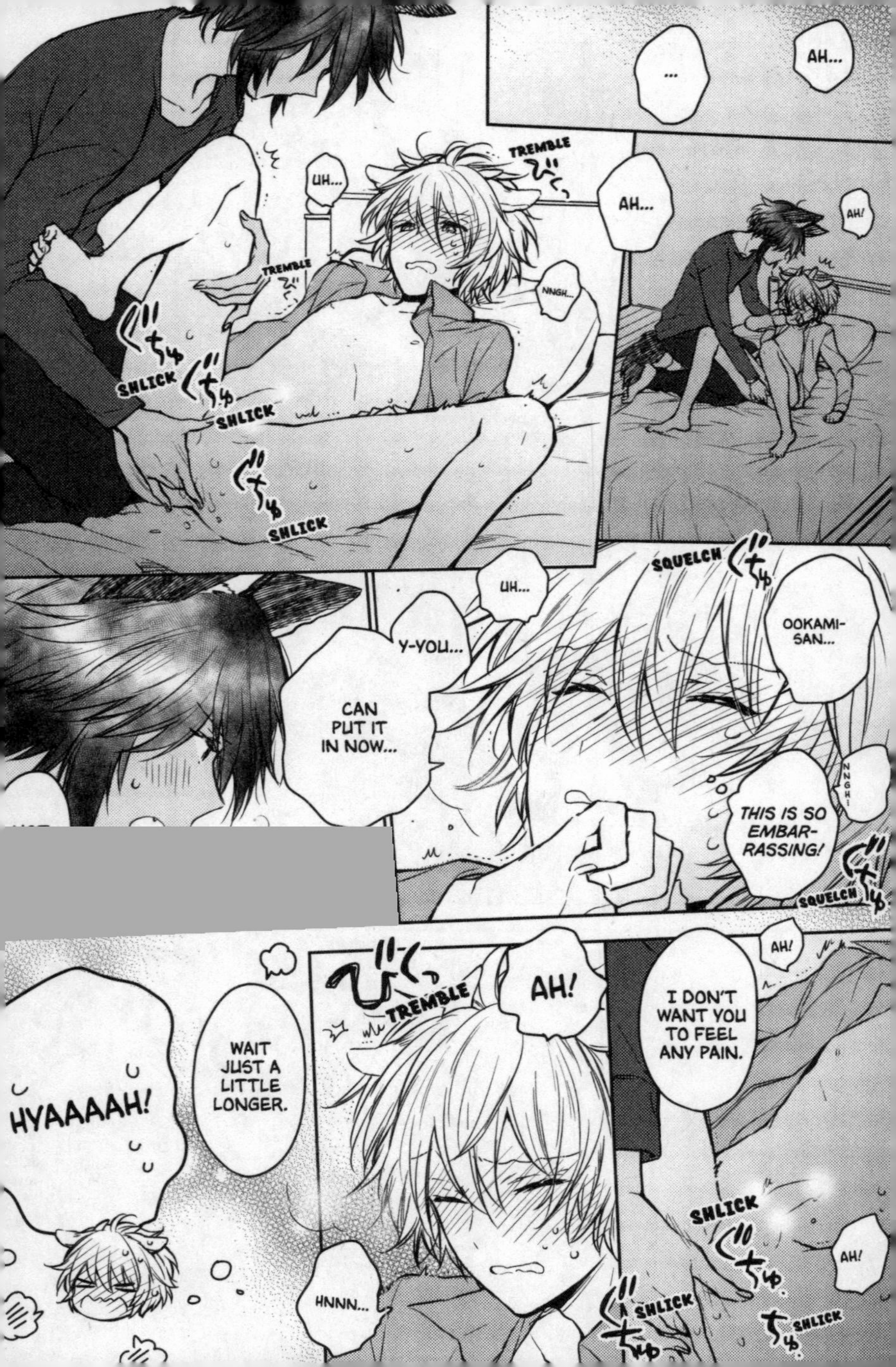
AH...
...
AH!
AH...
TREMBLE
UH...
NNGH...
TREMBLE
SHLICK
SHLICK
SHLICK
SQUELCH
OOKAMI-SAN...
UH...
Y-YOU...
CAN PUT IT IN NOW...
NNGH!
THIS IS SO EMBARRASSING!
SQUELCH
AH!
I DON'T WANT YOU TO FEEL ANY PAIN.
SHLICK
AH!
SHLICK
SHLICK
AH!
TREMBLE
HNNN...
WAIT JUST A LITTLE LONGER.
HYAAAAH!

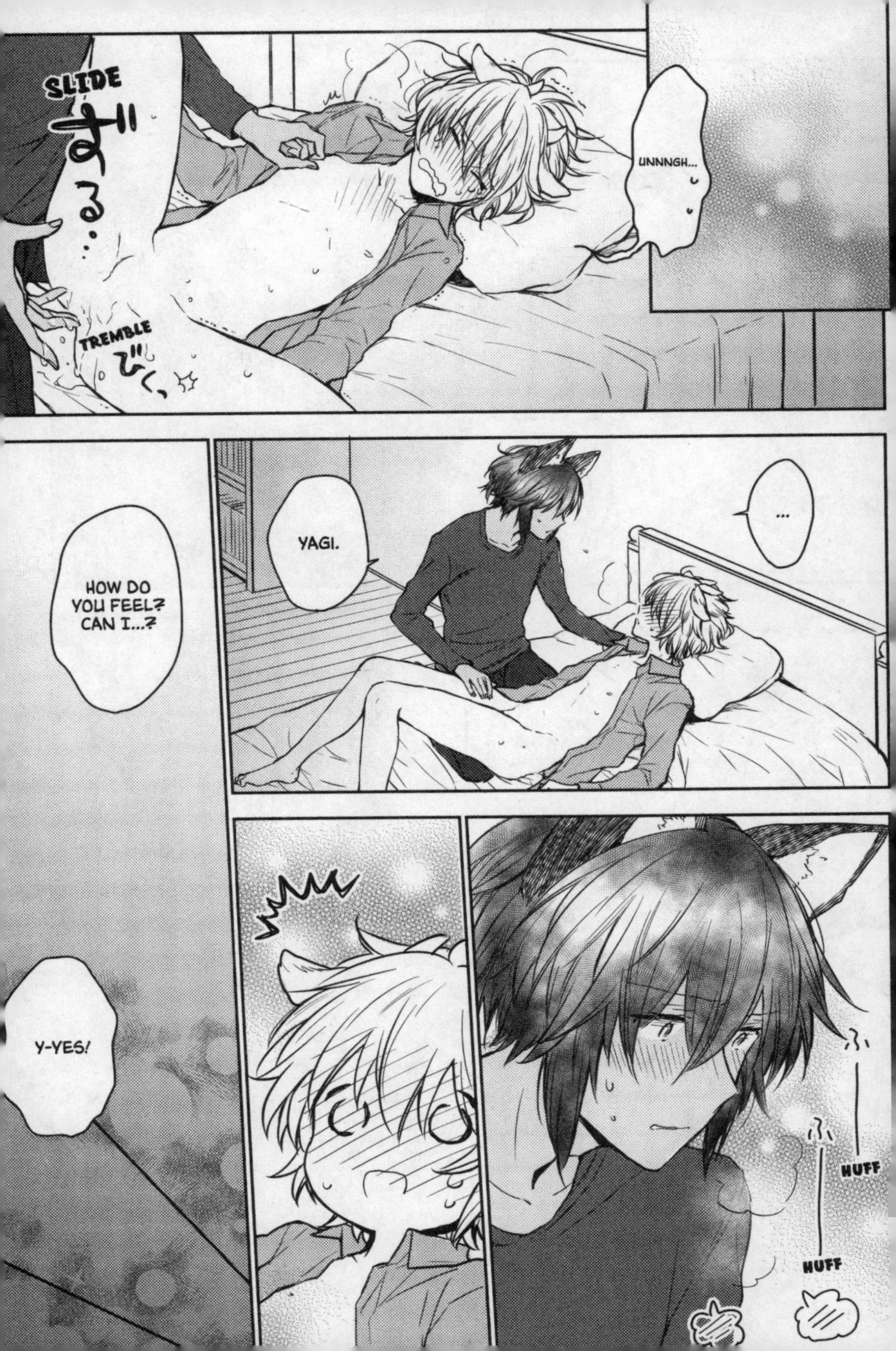
UNNNGH...
SLIDE
する...
TREMBLE
びく、
...
YAGI.
ふー
HUFF
ふー
HUFF
HOW DO YOU FEEL? CAN I...?
Y-YES!

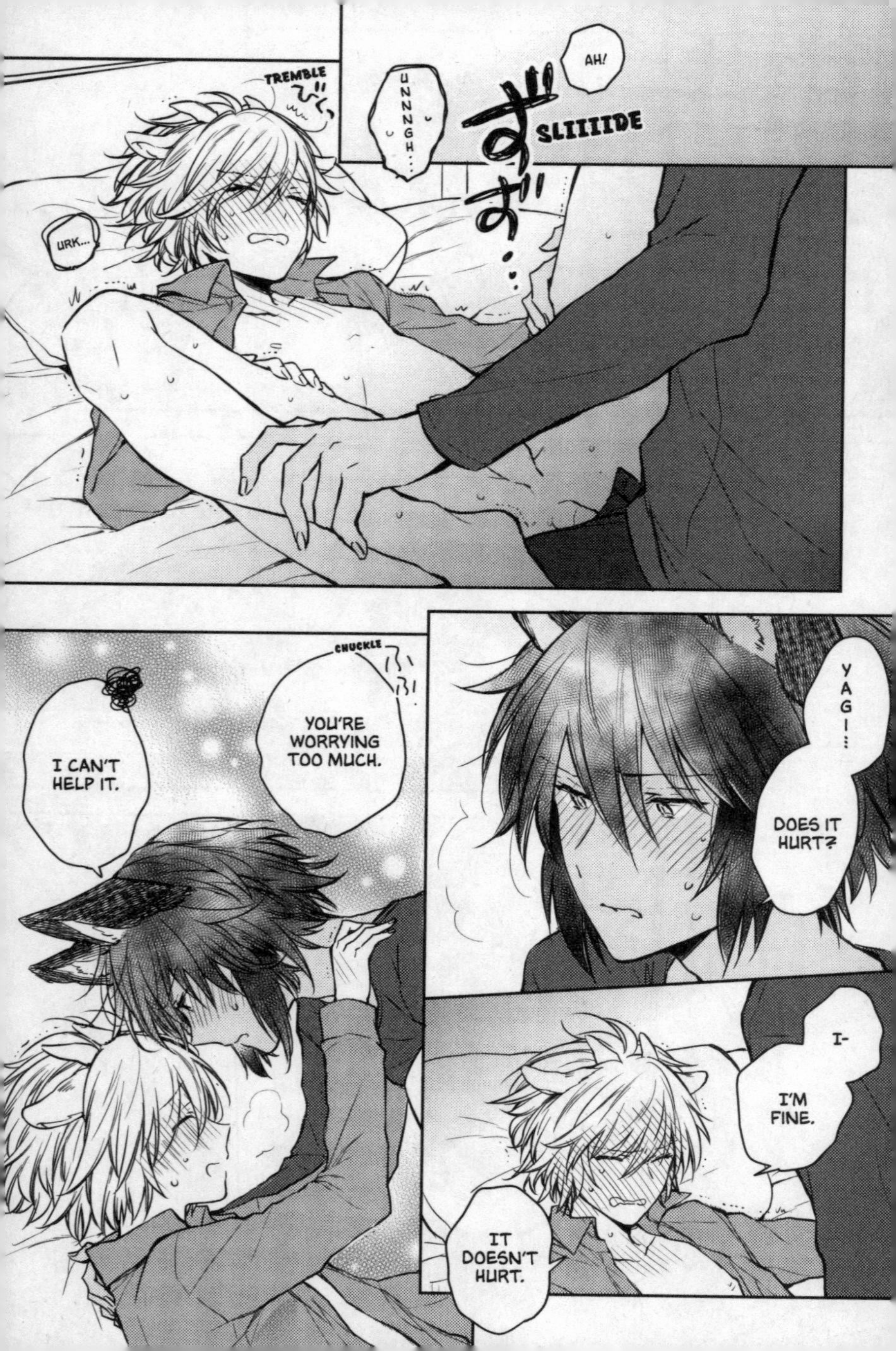
AH!
SLIIIIDE
UNNNGH...
TREMBLE
URK...
YAGI...
DOES IT HURT?
I-
I'M FINE.
IT DOESN'T HURT.
CHUCKLE
YOU'RE WORRYING TOO MUCH.
I CAN'T HELP IT.

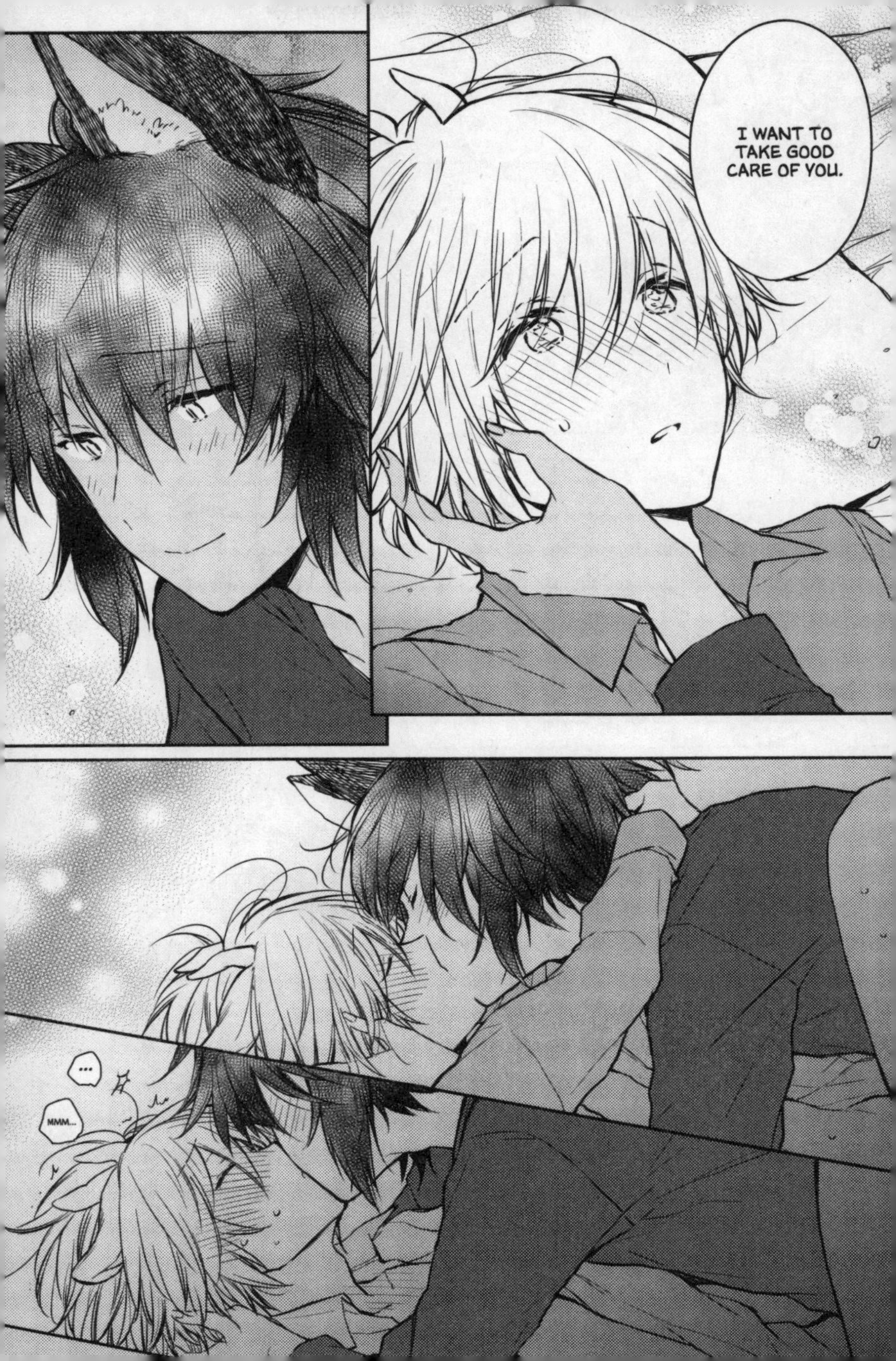
I WANT TO TAKE GOOD CARE OF YOU.
...
MMM...

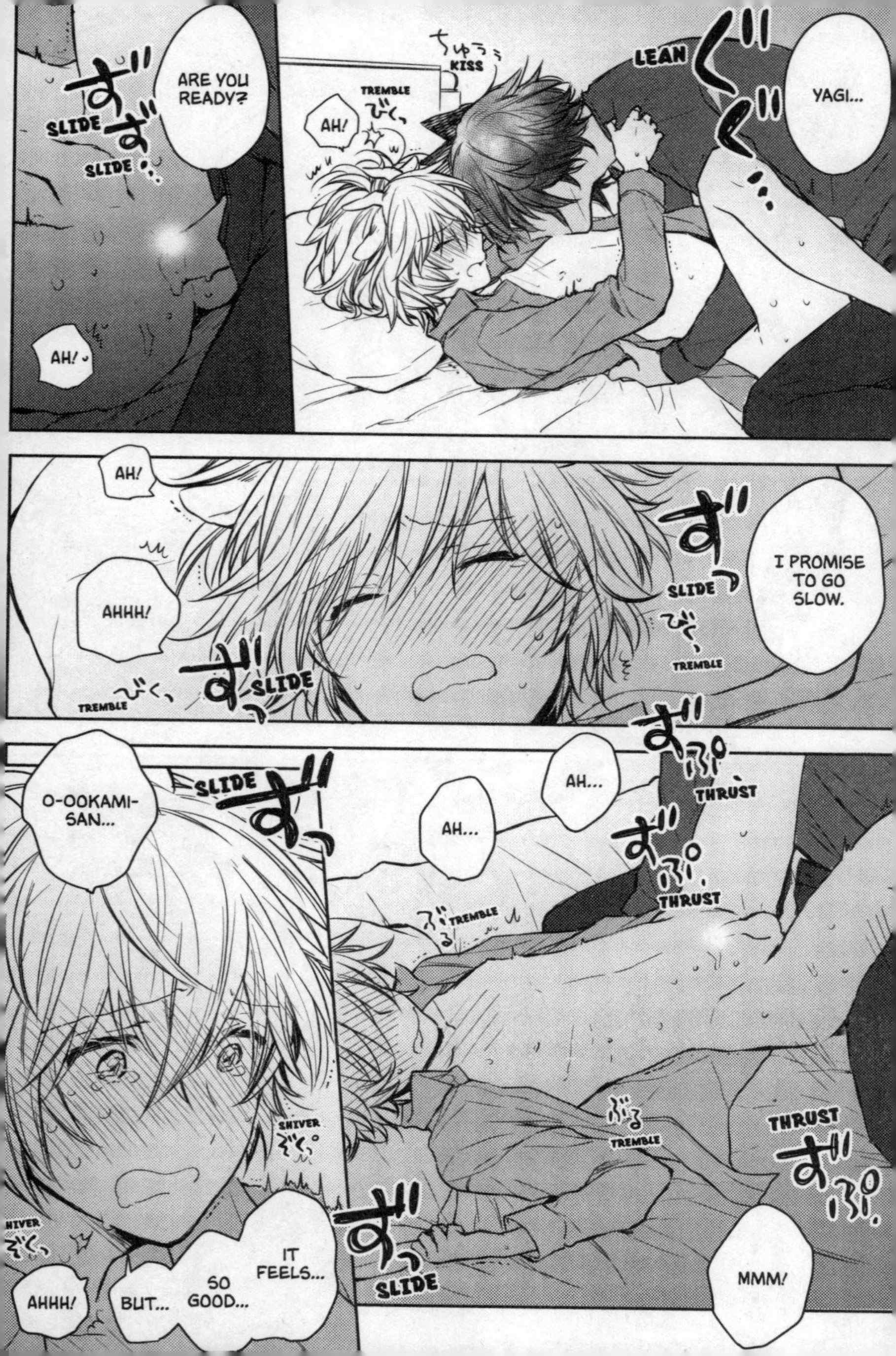
LEAN ぐぐぐ...
YAGI...
ちゅうぅ KISS
TREMBLE びくっ
AH!
ARE YOU READY?
ずず SLIDE
SLIDE...
AH!
I PROMISE TO GO SLOW.
ずっ SLIDE
びくっ TREMBLE
AH!
AHHH!
ずっ SLIDE
びくっ TREMBLE
AH...
ずぷ THRUST
AH...
ずぷ THRUST
ぷる TREMBLE
ぷる TREMBLE
THRUST ずぷ
MMM!
ずっ SLIDE
O-OOKAMI-SAN...
SLIDE ずっ
SHIVER ぞくっ
SHIVER ぞくっ
IT FEELS... SO GOOD...
BUT...
AHHH!

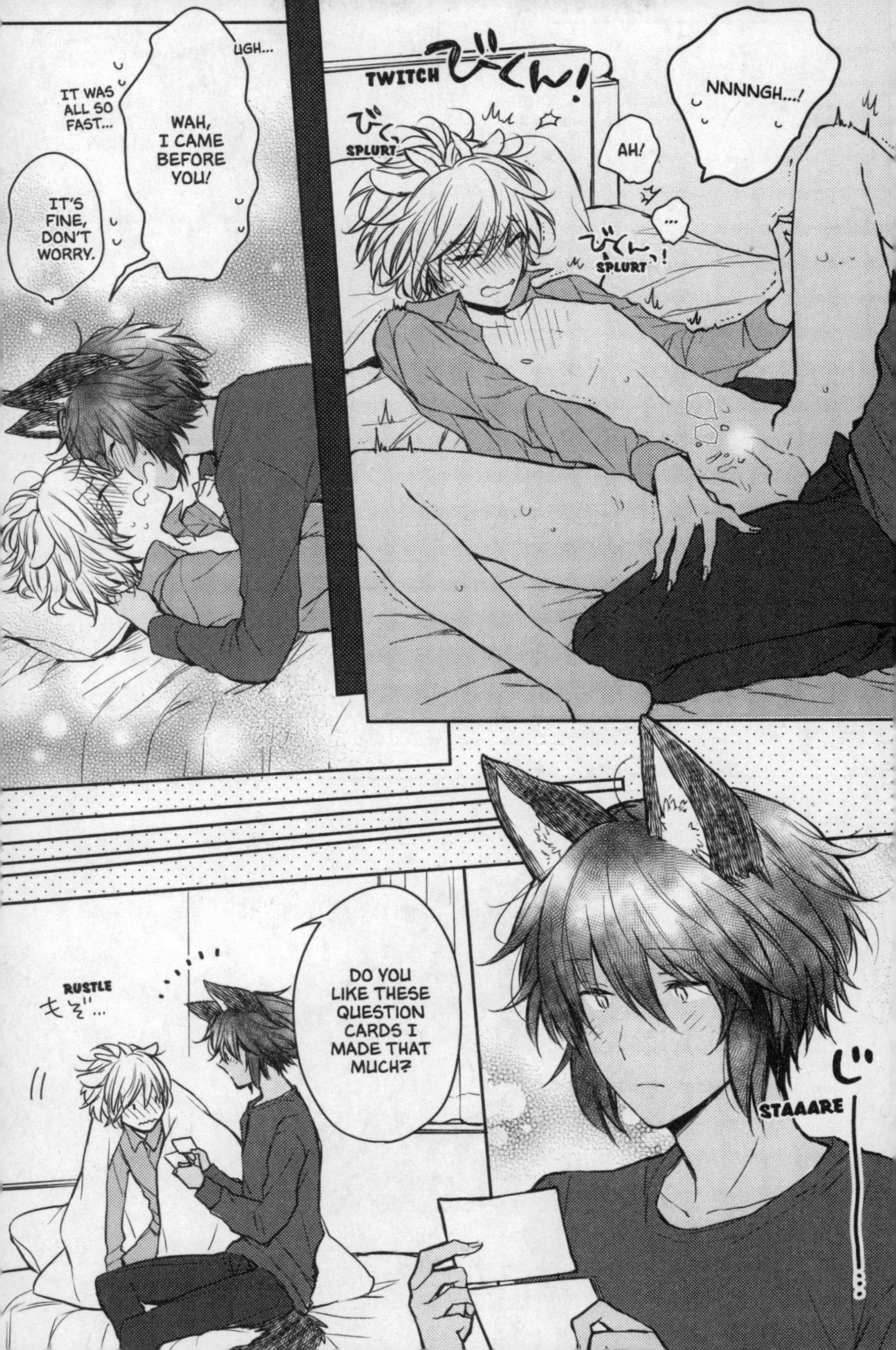
NNNNGH...!
AH!
TWITCH
びくん!
...
SPLURT
SPLURT
UGH...
WAH, I CAME BEFORE YOU!
IT WAS ALL SO FAST...
IT'S FINE, DON'T WORRY.
STAAARE
DO YOU LIKE THESE QUESTION CARDS I MADE THAT MUCH?
RUSTLE

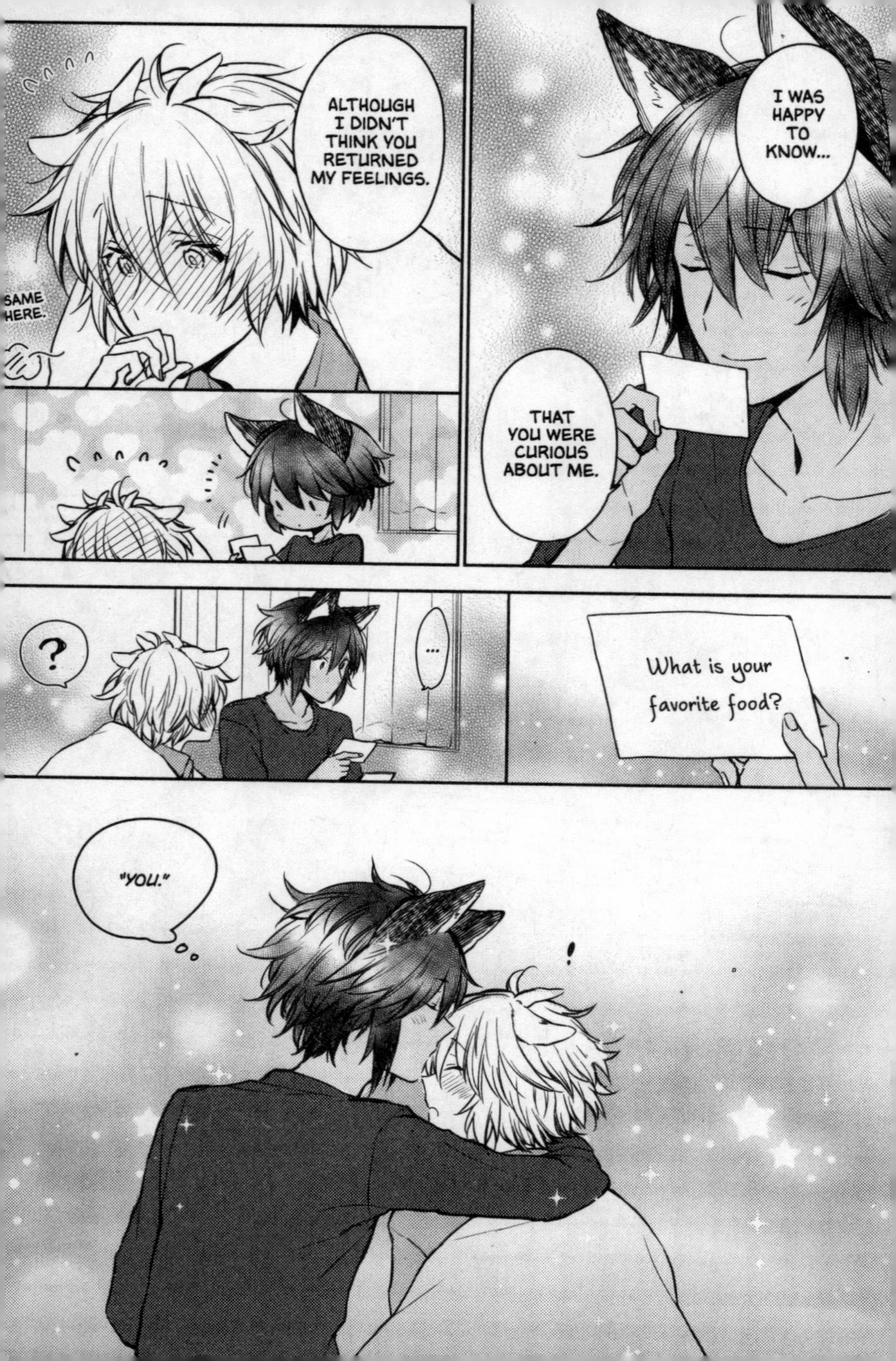
I WAS HAPPY TO KNOW...
THAT YOU WERE CURIOUS ABOUT ME.
ALTHOUGH I DIDN'T THINK YOU RETURNED MY FEELINGS.
SAME HERE.
What is your favorite food?
...
?
"YOU."

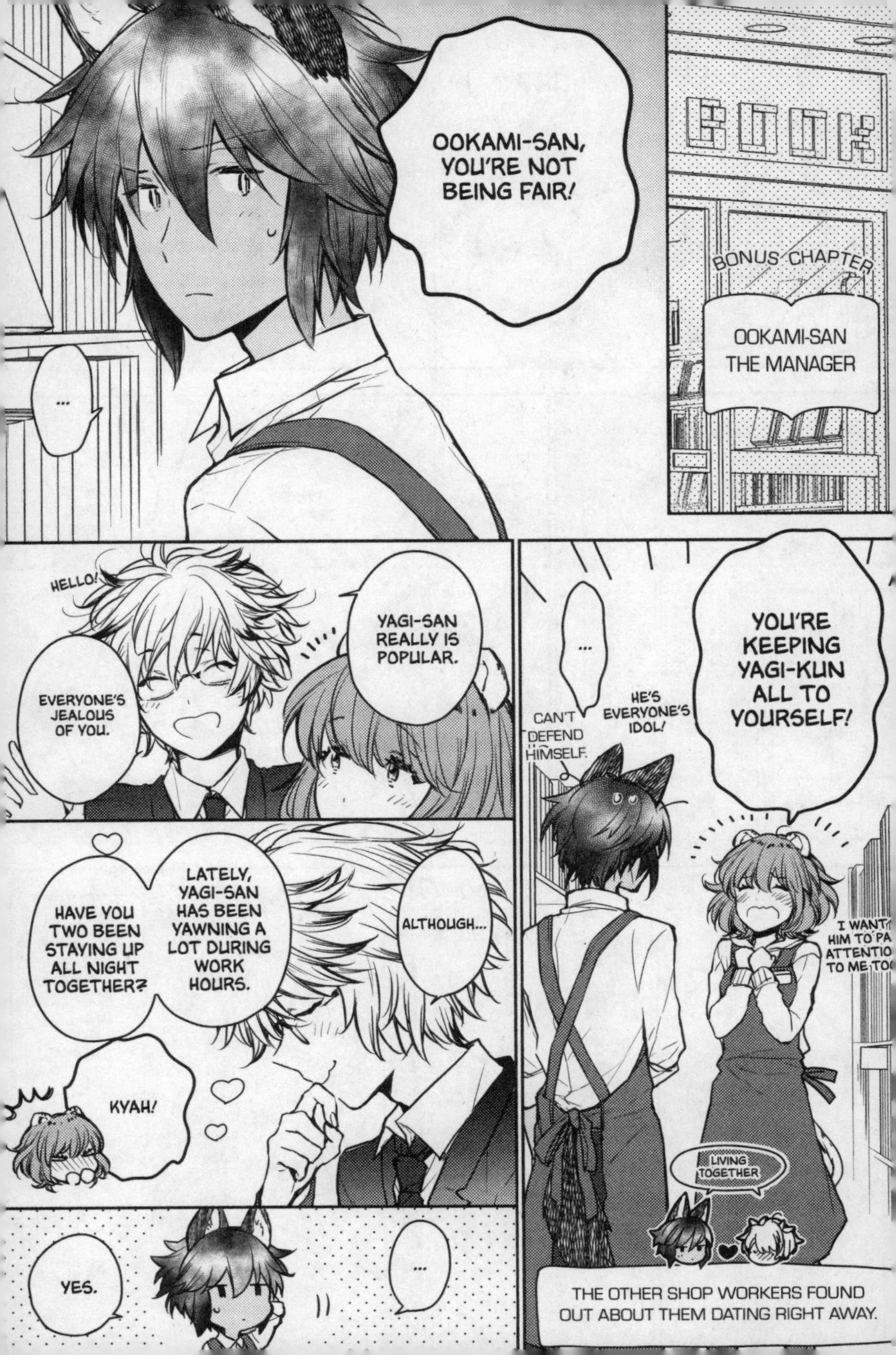
BOOK
BONUS CHAPTER
OOKAMI-SAN THE MANAGER
OOKAMI-SAN, YOU'RE NOT BEING FAIR!
...
YOU'RE KEEPING YAGI-KUN ALL TO YOURSELF!
...
HE'S EVERYONE'S IDOL!
CAN'T DEFEND HIMSELF.
I WANT HIM TO PA ATTENTIO TO ME TO
LIVING TOGETHER
THE OTHER SHOP WORKERS FOUND OUT ABOUT THEM DATING RIGHT AWAY.
YAGI-SAN REALLY IS POPULAR.
HELLO!
EVERYONE'S JEALOUS OF YOU.
ALTHOUGH...
LATELY, YAGI-SAN HAS BEEN YAWNING A LOT DURING WORK HOURS.
HAVE YOU TWO BEEN STAYING UP ALL NIGHT TOGETHER?
KYAH!
...
YES.

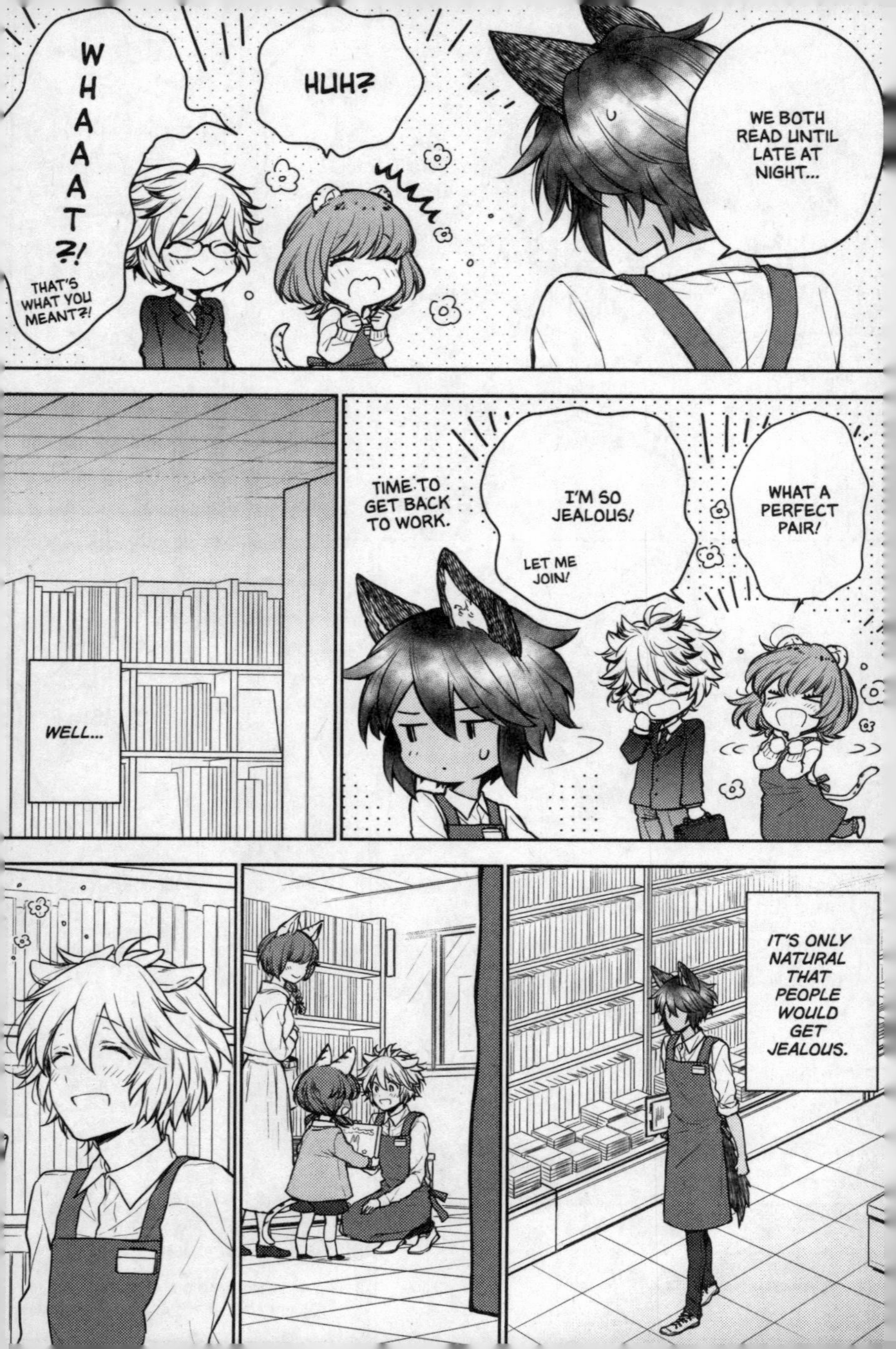

WE BOTH READ UNTIL LATE AT NIGHT...
HUH?
WHAAAT?!
THAT'S WHAT YOU MEANT?!
WHAT A PERFECT PAIR!
I'M SO JEALOUS!
LET ME JOIN!
TIME TO GET BACK TO WORK.
WELL...
IT'S ONLY NATURAL THAT PEOPLE WOULD GET JEALOUS.

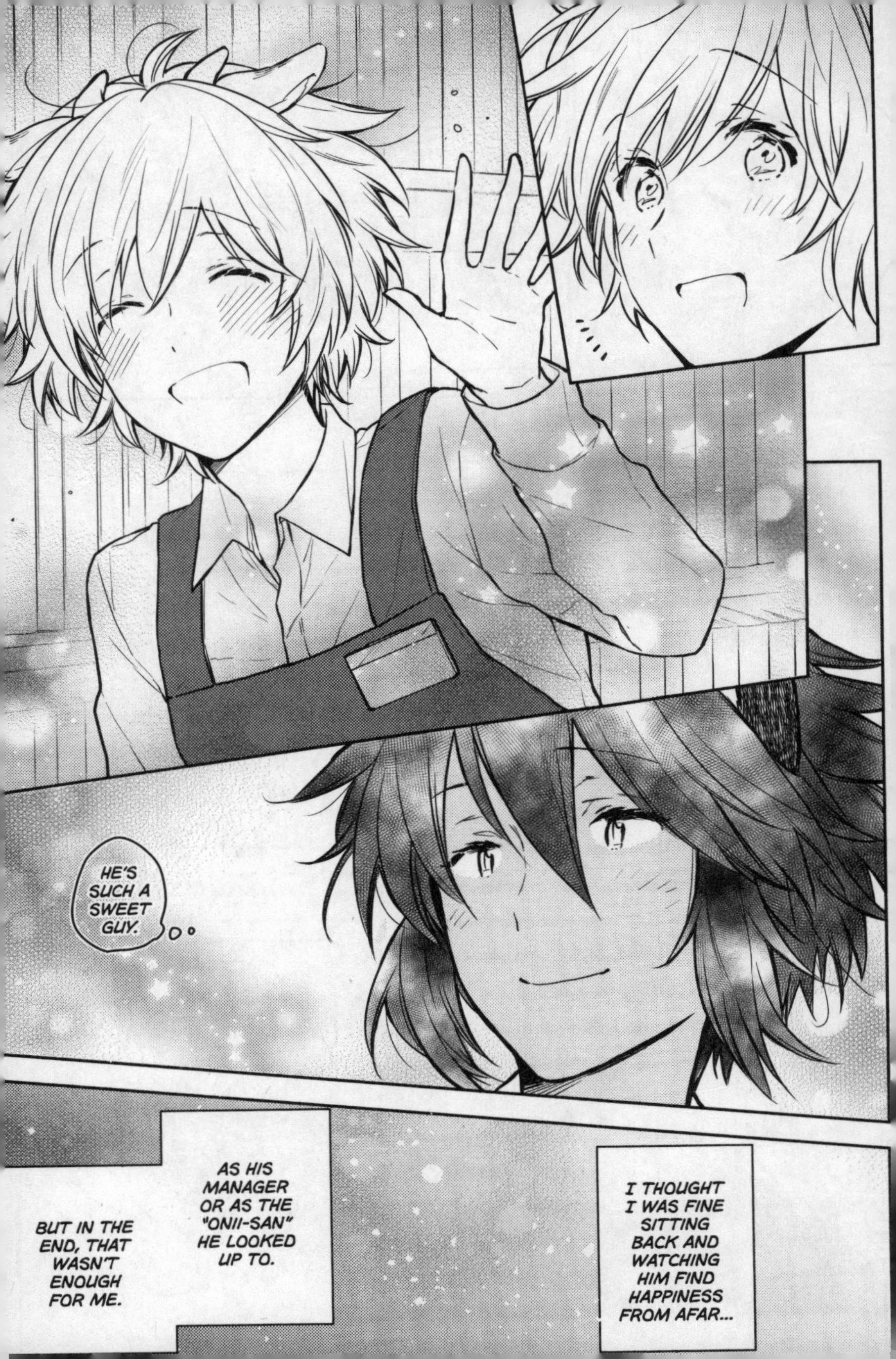
HE'S SUCH A SWEET GUY.
I THOUGHT I WAS FINE SITTING BACK AND WATCHING HIM FIND HAPPINESS FROM AFAR...
AS HIS MANAGER OR AS THE "ONII-SAN" HE LOOKED UP TO.
BUT IN THE END, THAT WASN'T ENOUGH FOR ME.

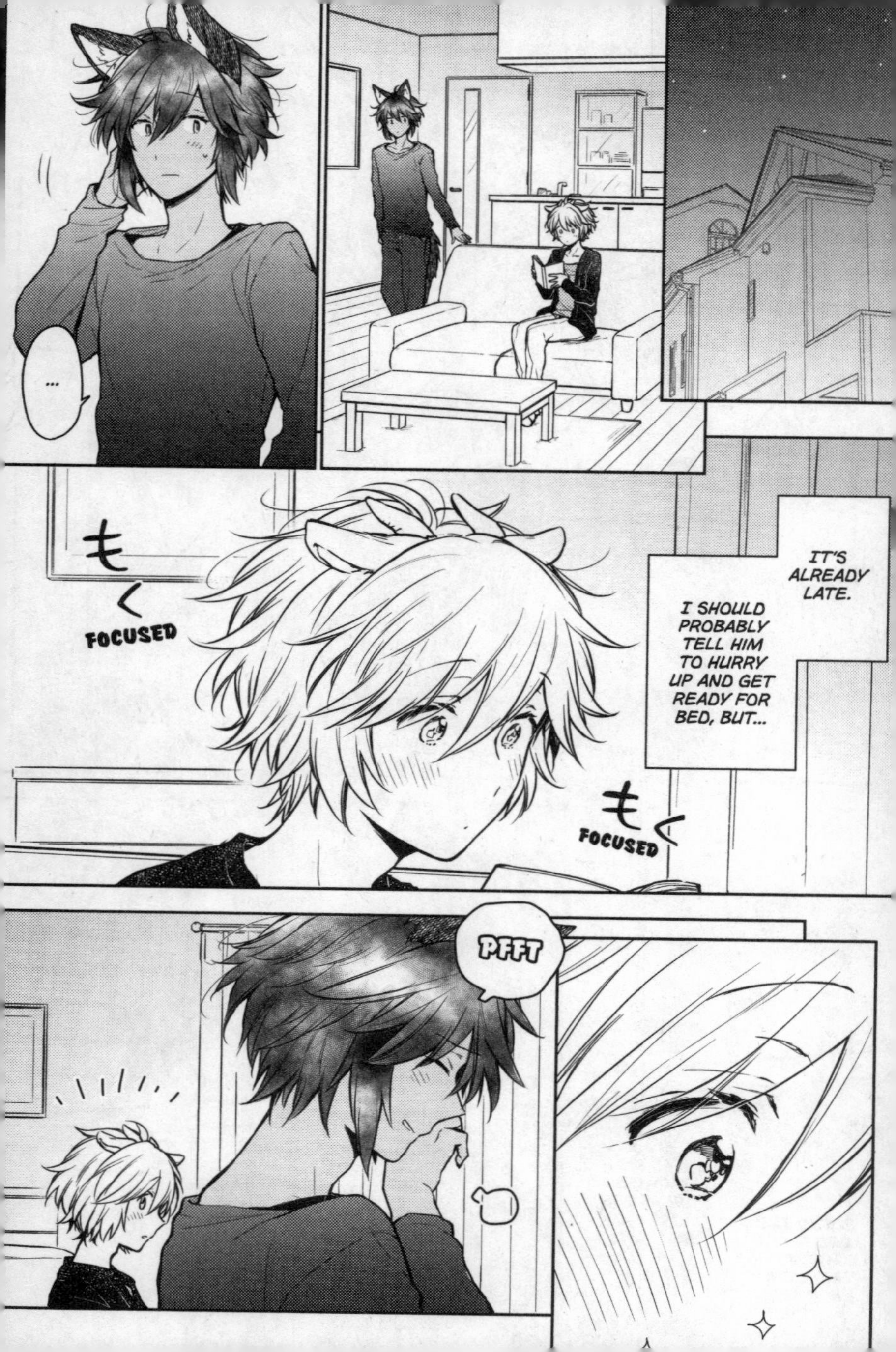
...
IT'S ALREADY LATE.
I SHOULD PROBABLY TELL HIM TO HURRY UP AND GET READY FOR BED, BUT...
もく
FOCUSED
もく
FOCUSED
PFFT

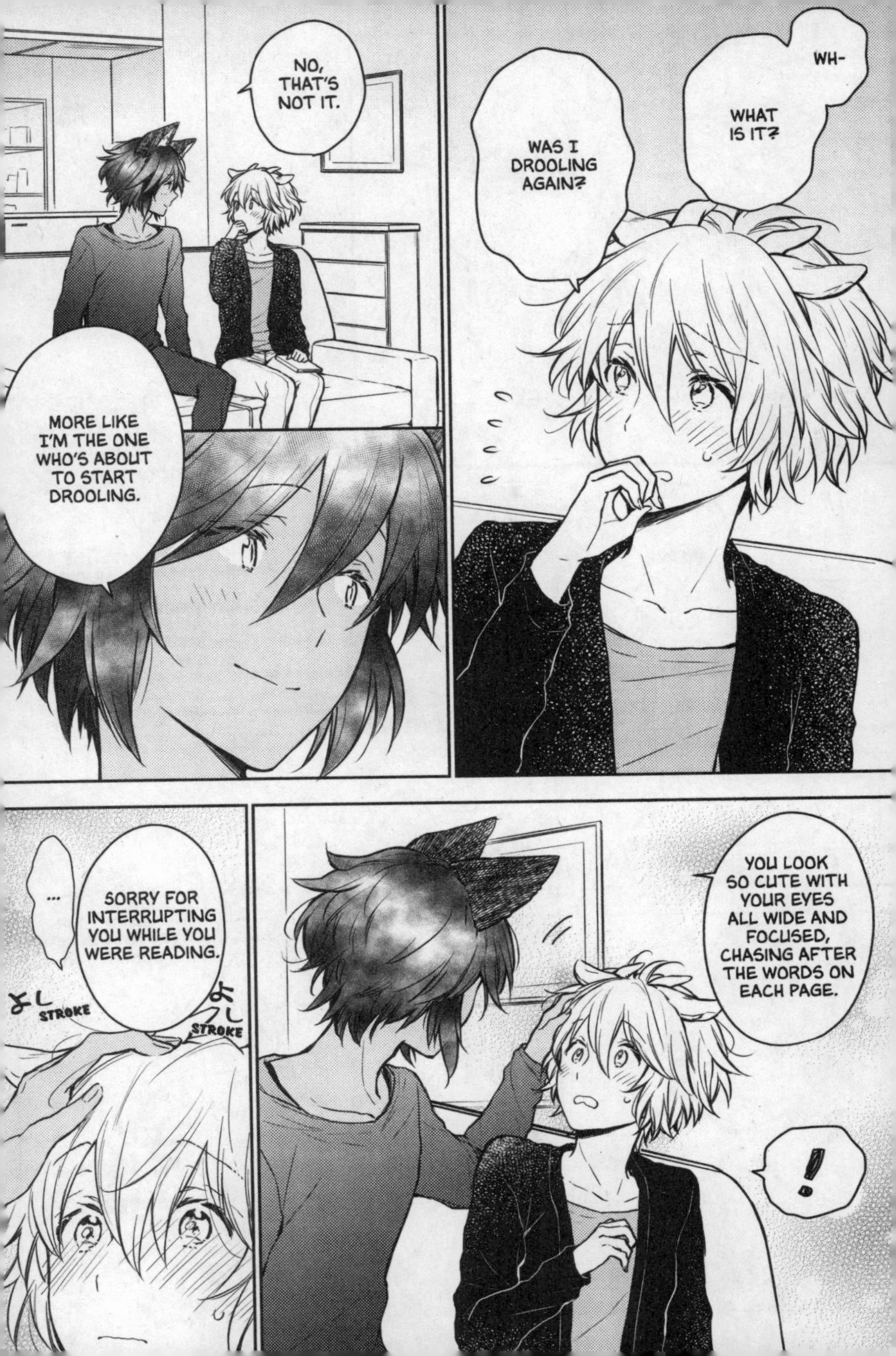
WH-
WHAT IS IT?
WAS I DROOLING AGAIN?
NO, THAT'S NOT IT.
MORE LIKE I'M THE ONE WHO'S ABOUT TO START DROOLING.
YOU LOOK SO CUTE WITH YOUR EYES ALL WIDE AND FOCUSED, CHASING AFTER THE WORDS ON EACH PAGE.
!
SORRY FOR INTERRUPTING YOU WHILE YOU WERE READING.
よし STROKE
よし STROKE
...

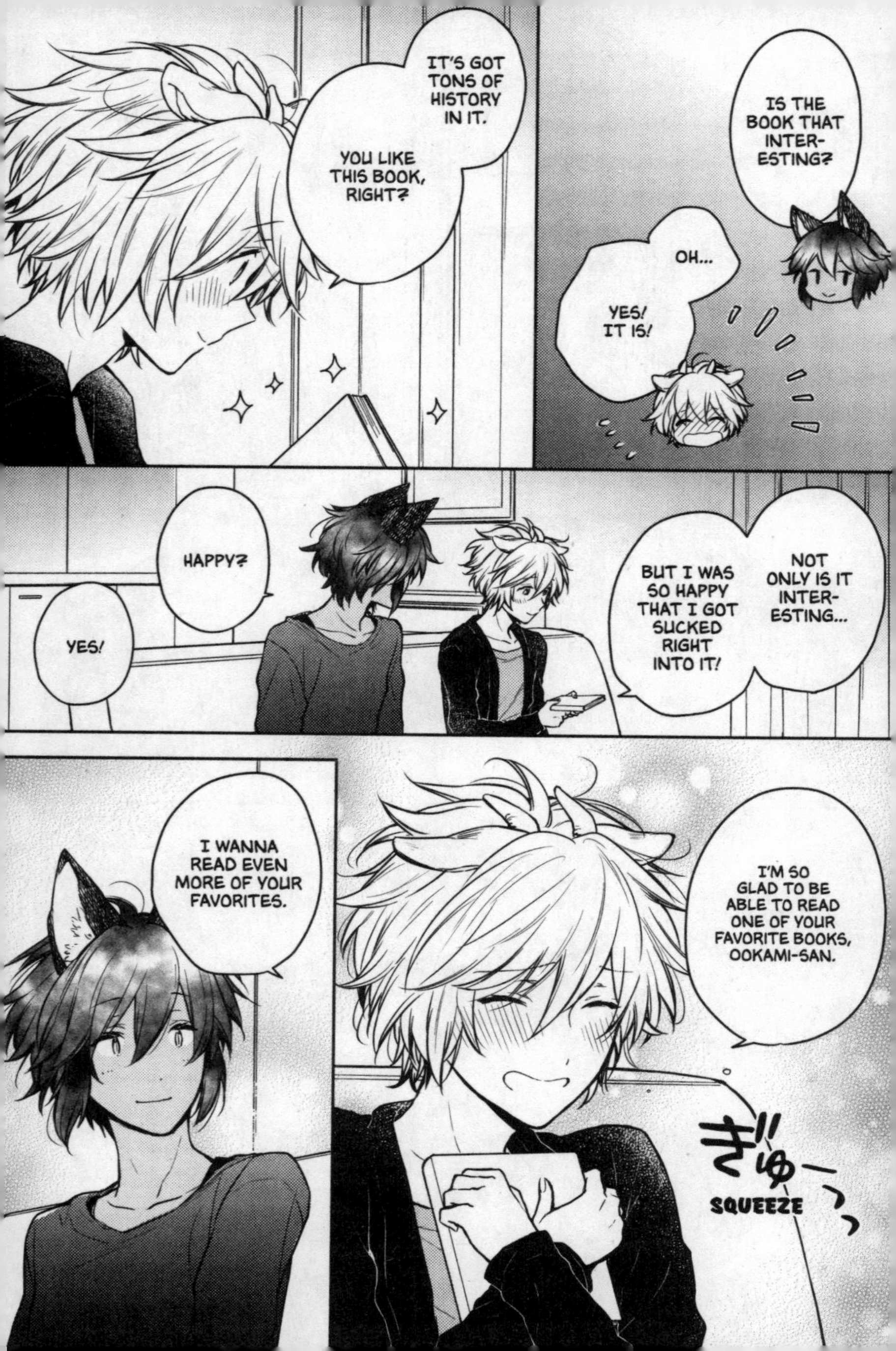
IS THE BOOK THAT INTERESTING?
OH...
YES! IT IS!
IT'S GOT TONS OF HISTORY IN IT.
YOU LIKE THIS BOOK, RIGHT?
NOT ONLY IS IT INTERESTING...
BUT I WAS SO HAPPY THAT I GOT SUCKED RIGHT INTO IT!
HAPPY?
YES!
I'M SO GLAD TO BE ABLE TO READ ONE OF YOUR FAVORITE BOOKS, OOKAMI-SAN.
ぎゅー
SQUEEZE
I WANNA READ EVEN MORE OF YOUR FAVORITES.

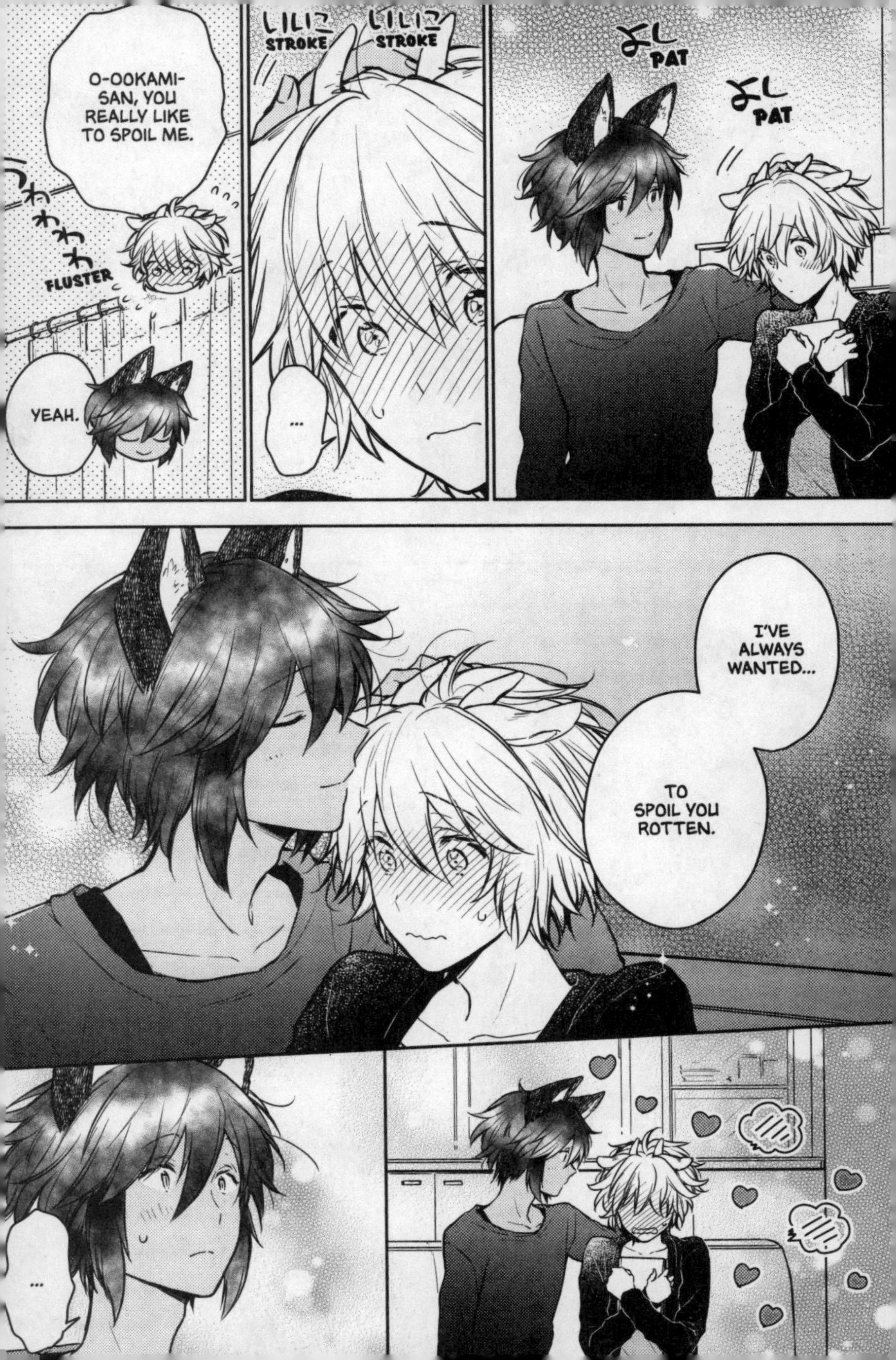
よし
PAT
よし
PAT
いいこ
STROKE
いいこ
STROKE
...
O-OOKAMI-SAN, YOU REALLY LIKE TO SPOIL ME.
うわわわわ
FLUSTER
YEAH.
I'VE ALWAYS WANTED...
TO SPOIL YOU ROTTEN.
...

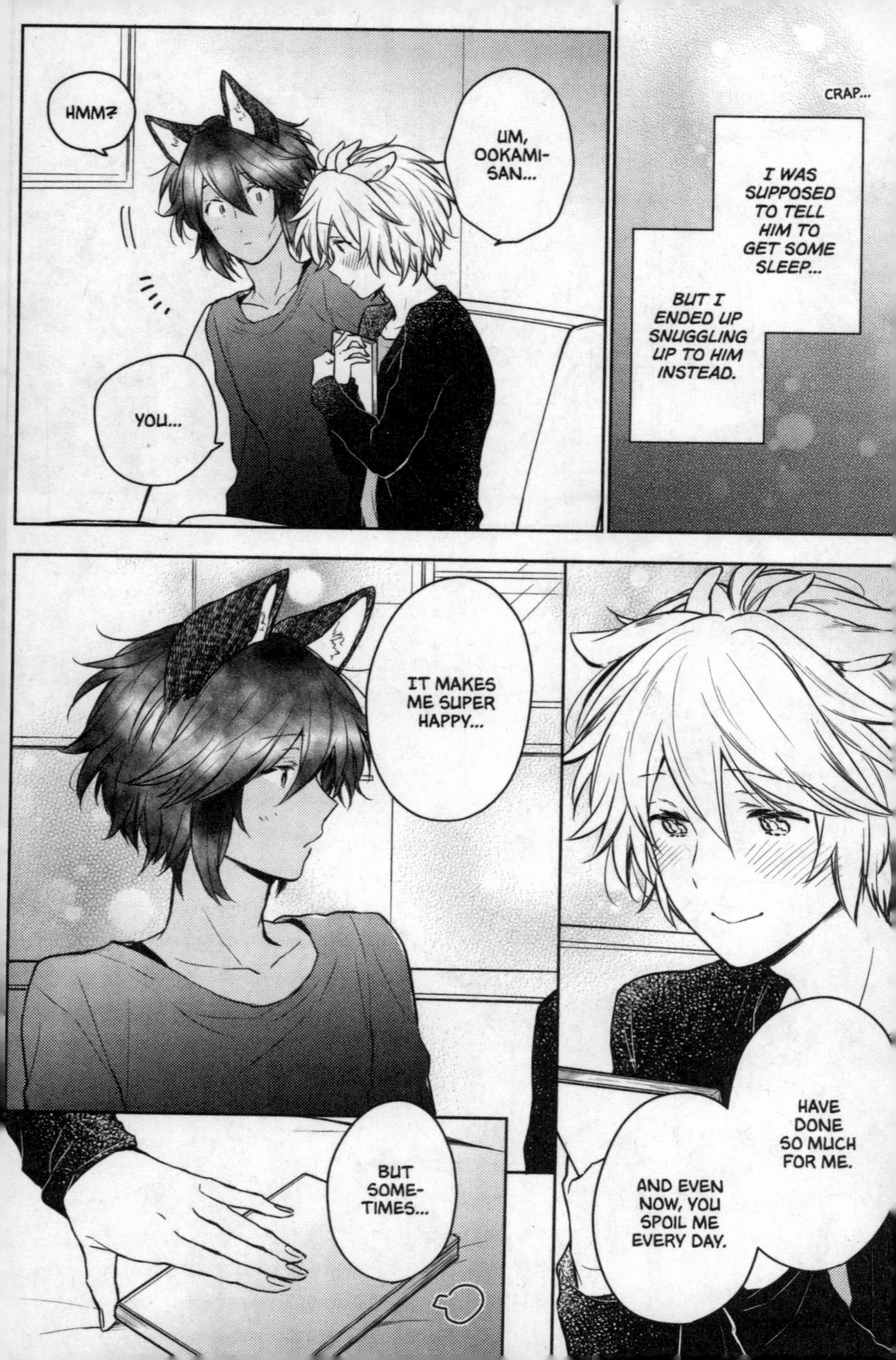
CRAP...
I WAS SUPPOSED TO TELL HIM TO GET SOME SLEEP...
BUT I ENDED UP SNUGGLING UP TO HIM INSTEAD.
UM, OOKAMI-SAN...
HMM?
YOU...
HAVE DONE SO MUCH FOR ME.
AND EVEN NOW, YOU SPOIL ME EVERY DAY.
IT MAKES ME SUPER HAPPY...
BUT SOME-TIMES...

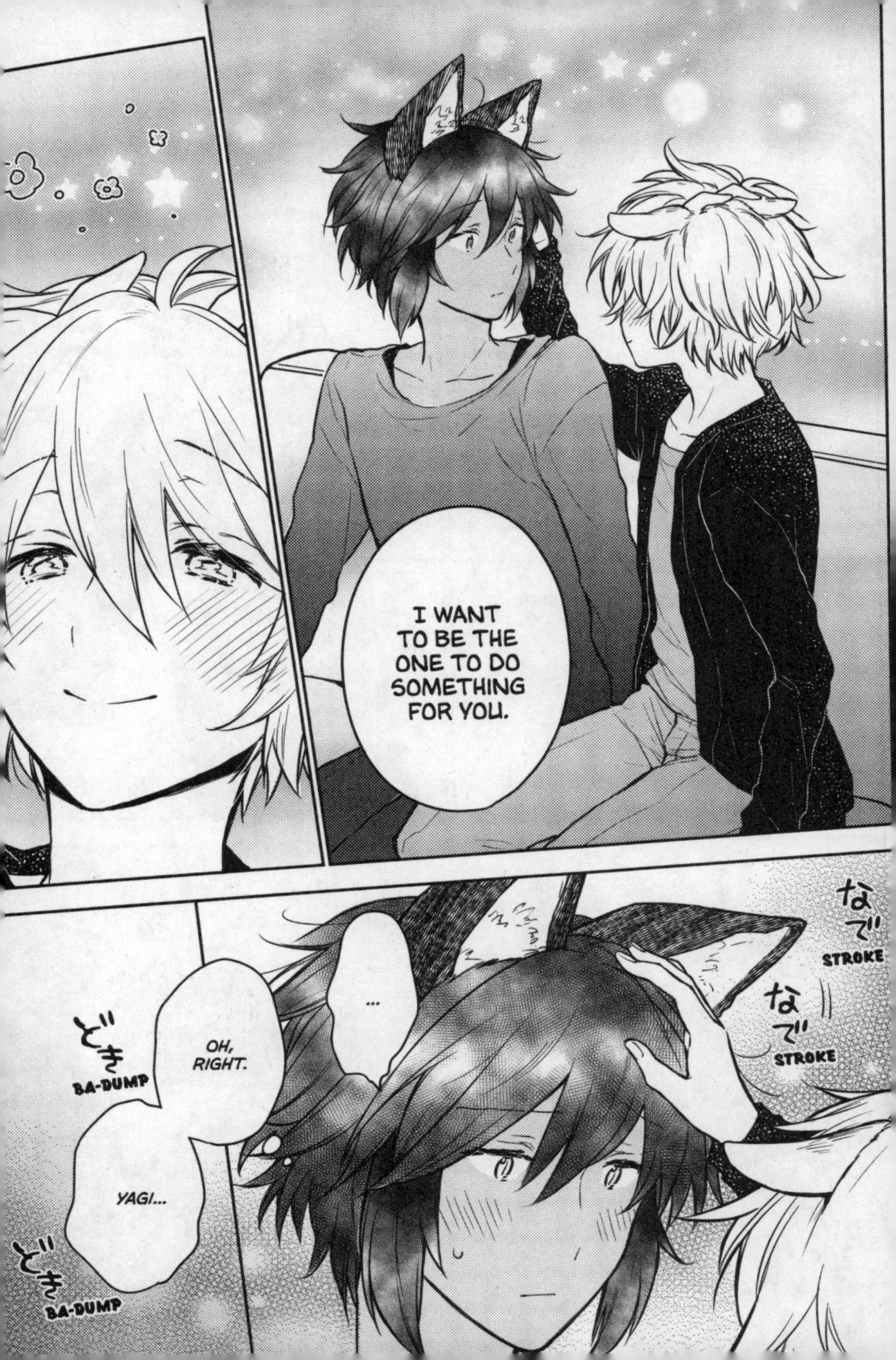
I WANT TO BE THE ONE TO DO SOMETHING FOR YOU.
なで STROKE
なで STROKE
...
OH, RIGHT.
どき BA-DUMP
YAGI...
どき BA-DUMP

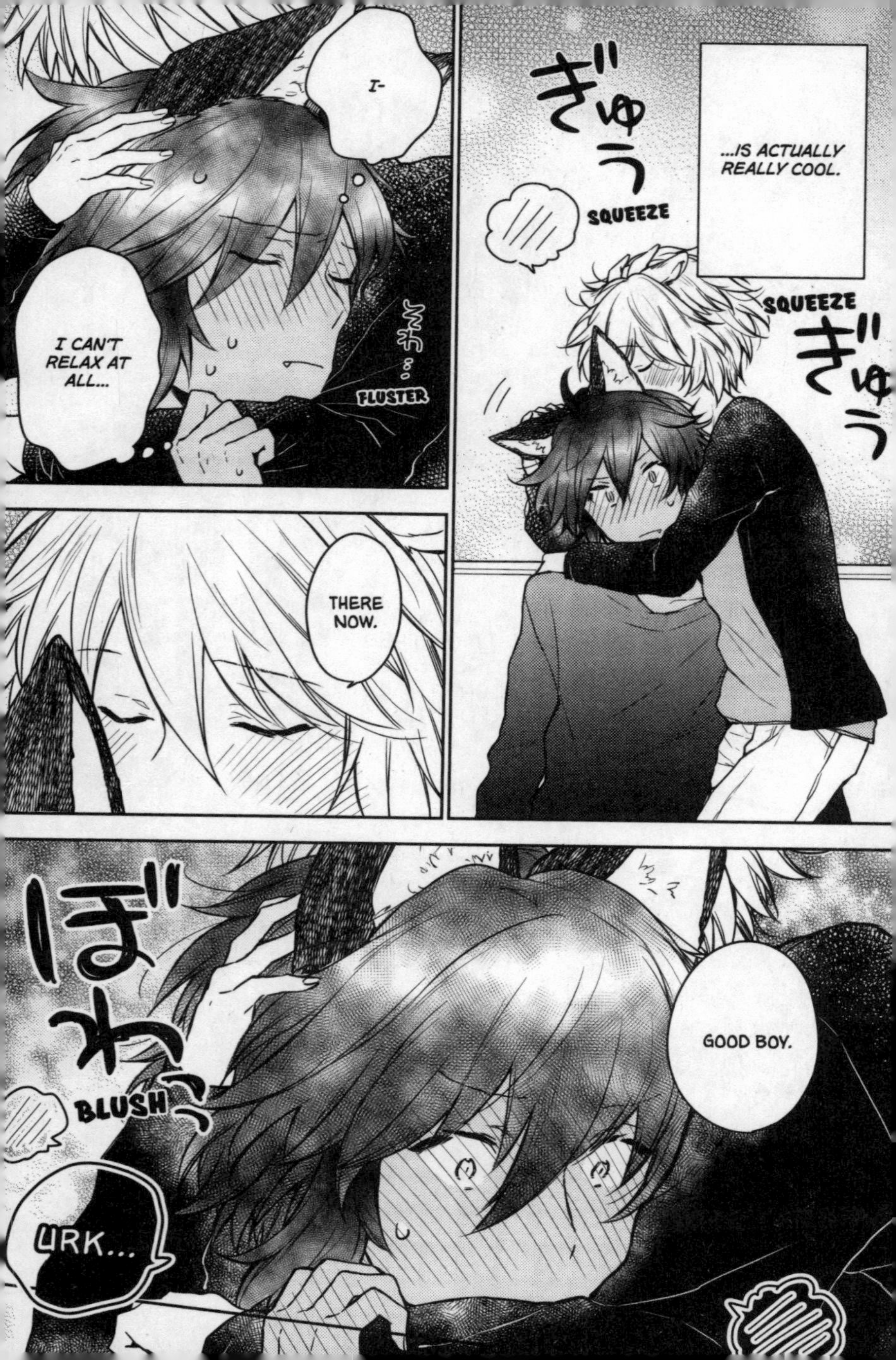

...IS ACTUALLY REALLY COOL.
ぎゅう
SQUEEZE
SQUEEZE
ぎゅう
I-
そわ・・
FLUSTER
I CAN'T RELAX AT ALL...
THERE NOW.
GOOD BOY.
ぼわっ
BLUSH
URK...

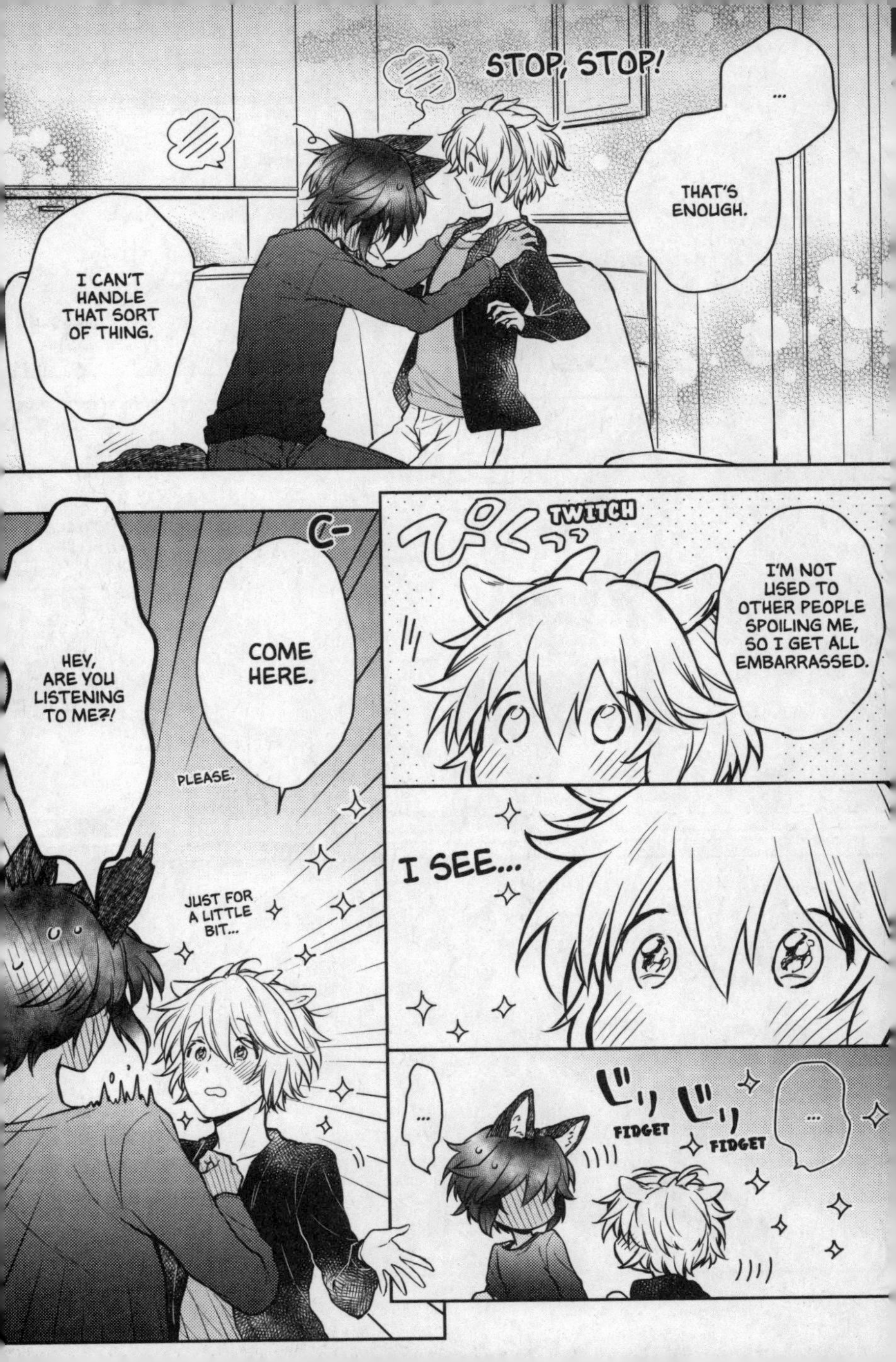
...
THAT'S ENOUGH.
STOP, STOP!
I CAN'T HANDLE THAT SORT OF THING.
ぴくっ
TWITCH
I'M NOT USED TO OTHER PEOPLE SPOILING ME, SO I GET ALL EMBARRASSED.
I SEE...
...
じりじり
FIDGET FIDGET
...
C-
COME HERE.
HEY, ARE YOU LISTENING TO ME?!
PLEASE.
JUST FOR A LITTLE BIT...

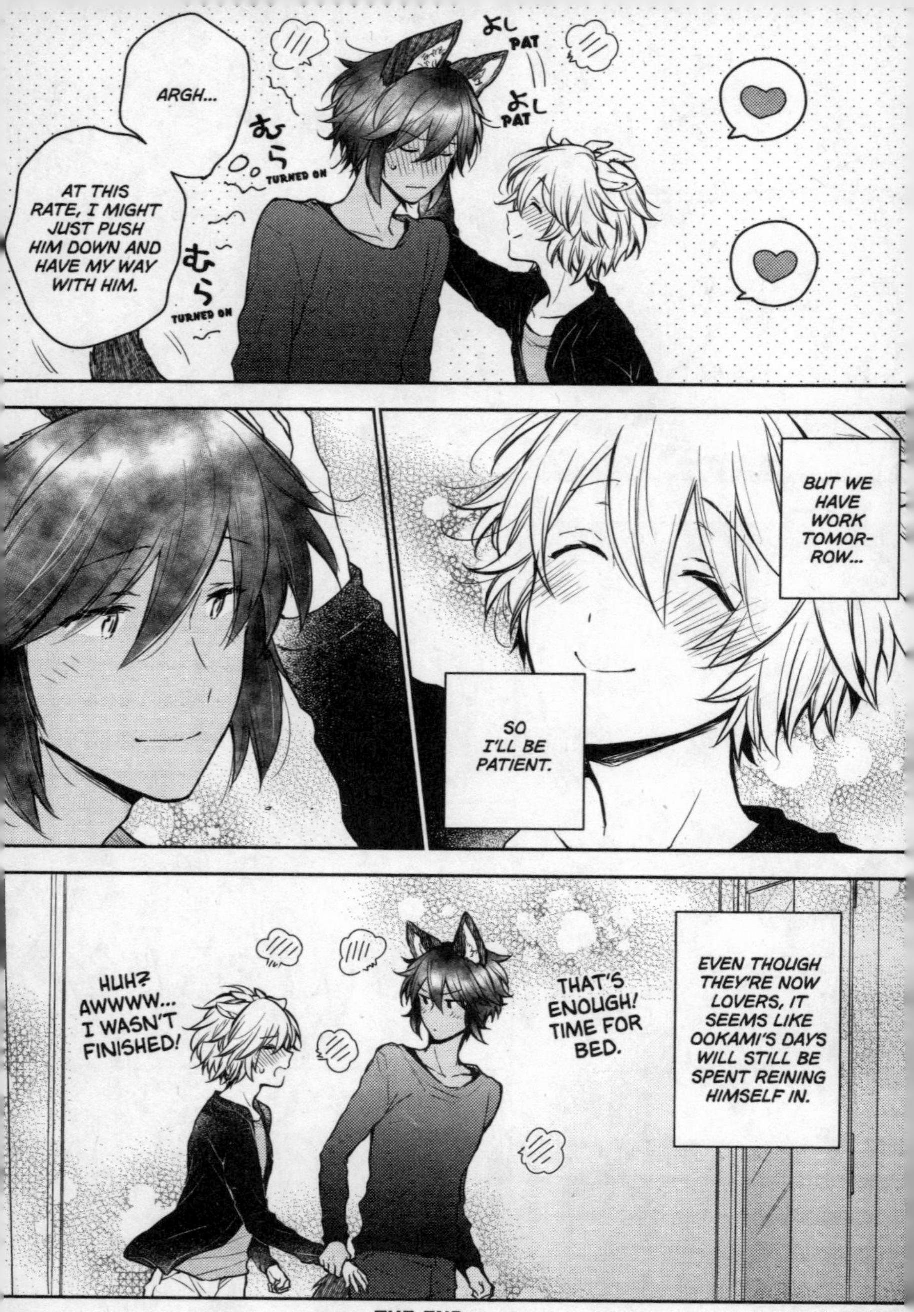
よし PAT
よし PAT
ARGH...
AT THIS RATE, I MIGHT JUST PUSH HIM DOWN AND HAVE MY WAY WITH HIM.
むら TURNED ON
むら TURNED ON
BUT WE HAVE WORK TOMOR-ROW...
SO I'LL BE PATIENT.
EVEN THOUGH THEY'RE NOW LOVERS, IT SEEMS LIKE OOKAMI'S DAYS WILL STILL BE SPENT REINING HIMSELF IN.
THAT'S ENOUGH! TIME FOR BED.
HUH? AWWWW... I WASN'T FINISHED!

THE END

YAGI
THE
BOOKSHOP GOAT

BONUS COMIC

OOKAMI-SAN!
どき BA-DUMP
I-
どき BA-DUMP
I WANT TO SLEEP WITH YOU!
PLEASE!
HAS ULTERIOR MOTIVES
AH!
SHUT ぱたん!
YOU...!
ぽわ。
BLUSH
?
DID YOU EAT ONE OF MY NOTES AGAIN?!
I TOLD YOU TO CUT IT OUT SINCE IT ALWAYS GETS YOU TURNED ON!
!

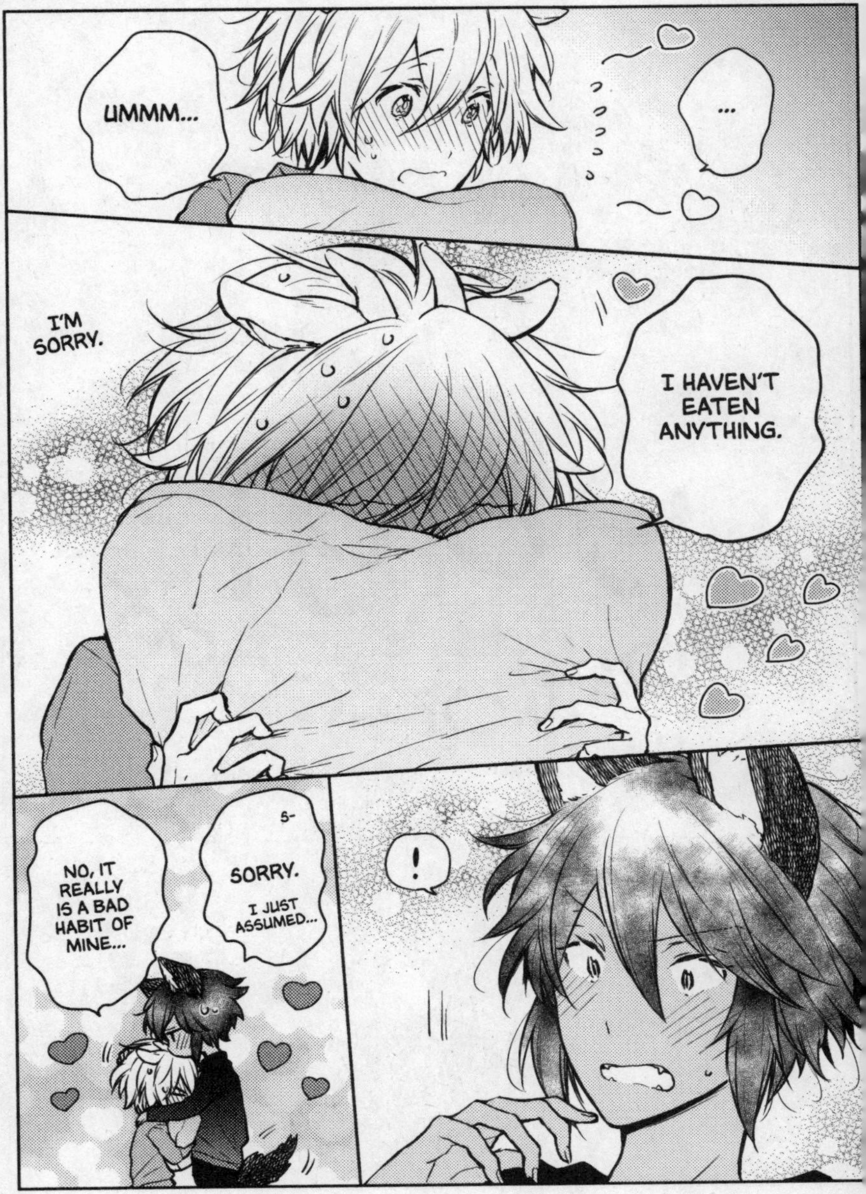
...
UMMM...
I HAVEN'T EATEN ANYTHING.
I'M SORRY.
!
S-
SORRY.
I JUST ASSUMED...
NO, IT REALLY IS A BAD HABIT OF MINE...

yägi

the

BOOKShOP GOAT

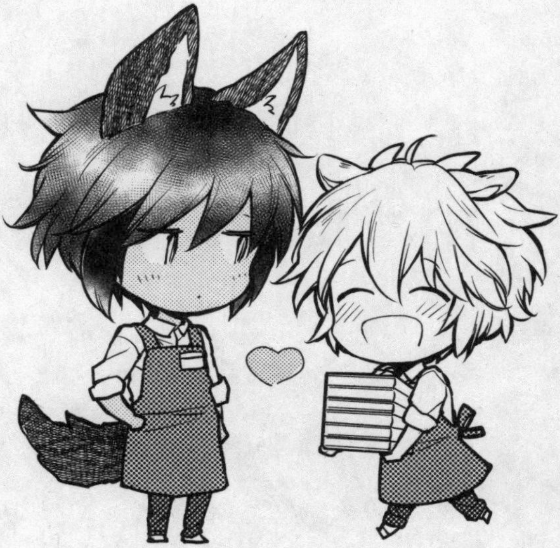

I enjoyed drawing Yagi-kun and Ookami-san's story so much.

I am so grateful to everyone involved in its production, my friends who gave me advice and helped me out, as well as all of my readers.

Thank you so much!

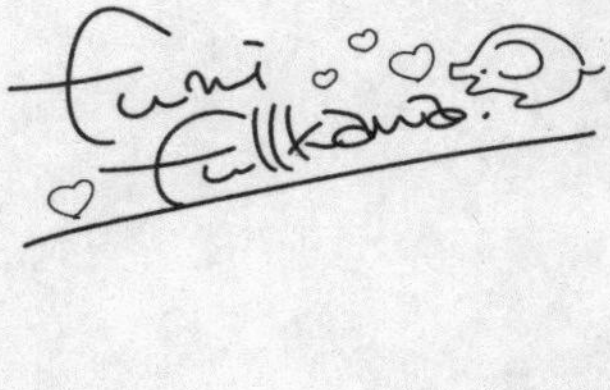

TOKYOPOP believes all types of romances deserve to be celebrated. *LOVE x LOVE* was born from that idea and our commitment to representing a variety of stories and voices as diverse as our fans.

FANGS

1

Billy Balibally

FANGS, VOL 1
Billy Balibally

TOKYOPOP®

δLOVE-x-LOVEδ   MATURE 18+

"What kind of guy is unlucky enough to get bitten... and survive?"
As the sole survivor of a vampire attack, En wakes up to find that his
hair has gone white as snow — and worse, he's developed a craving
for blood! Fortunately, the vampire health and welfare organization
FANGS is there to help with the transition, and the handsome Ichii
steps up as his guardian and mentor.

KATAKOI LAMP
Kyohei Azumi

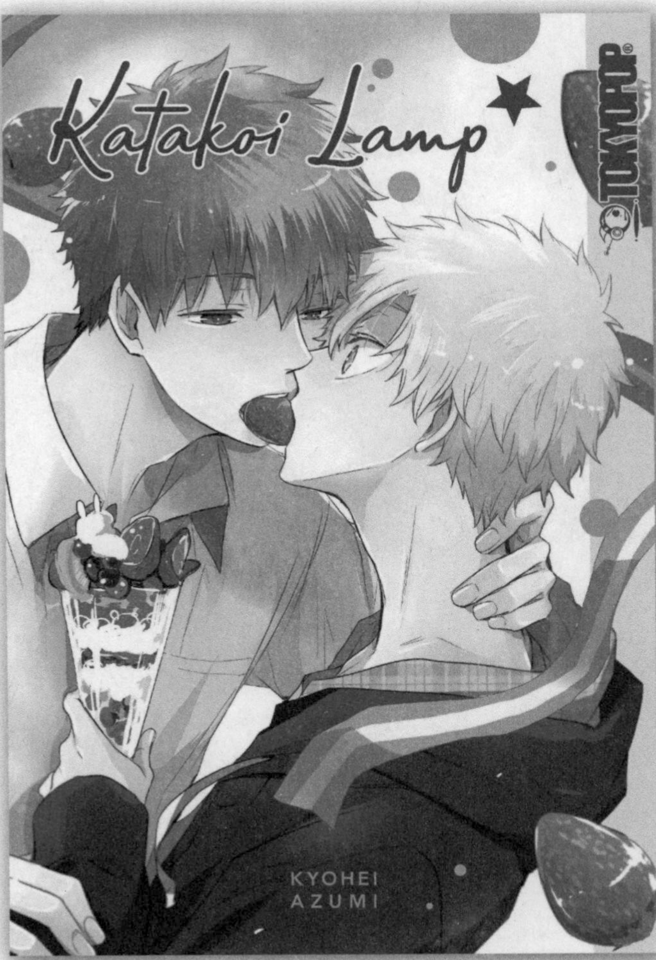
Katakoi Lamp
TOKYOPOP
KYOHEI AZUMI

LOVE x LOVE

TOKYOPOP

Kazuto Muronoi runs a cute little coffee shop, where many people enjoy doing some work or writing papers for school. Among his coffee shop's regulars is a college student named Jun, who often studies there. It was love at first sight for Kazuto! Will Kazuto be able to find the courage to confess his crush before Jun graduates college and stops frequenting the shop? And to make matters even more complicated... it seems Jun has his sights set on another worker at the café!

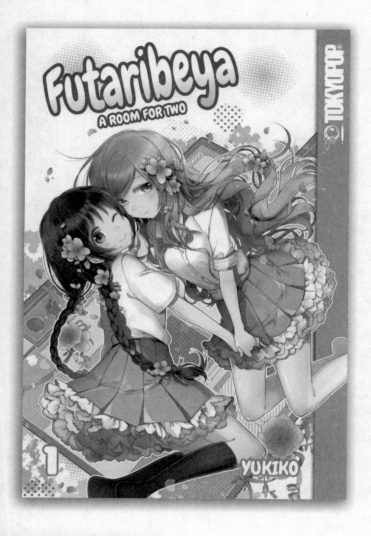

Futaribeya
A ROOM FOR TWO
TOKYOPOP
1
YUKIKO

FUTARIBEYA: A ROOM FOR TWO, VOL 1

Yukiko

♀LOVE-x-LOVE♀

As her exciting first year of high school begins, Sakurako Kawawa settles into her new lodgings. There, she meets her roommate — the stunningly beautiful Kasumi Yamabuki, who lives life at her own pace. From day one, responsible, level-headed Sakurako and lazy, easygoing Kasumi find themselves at odds with one another... But with their matching mugs and one bed to share, Sakurako and Kasumi's friendship is just beginning!

TOKYOPOP

THE CAT PROPOSED

Dento Hayane

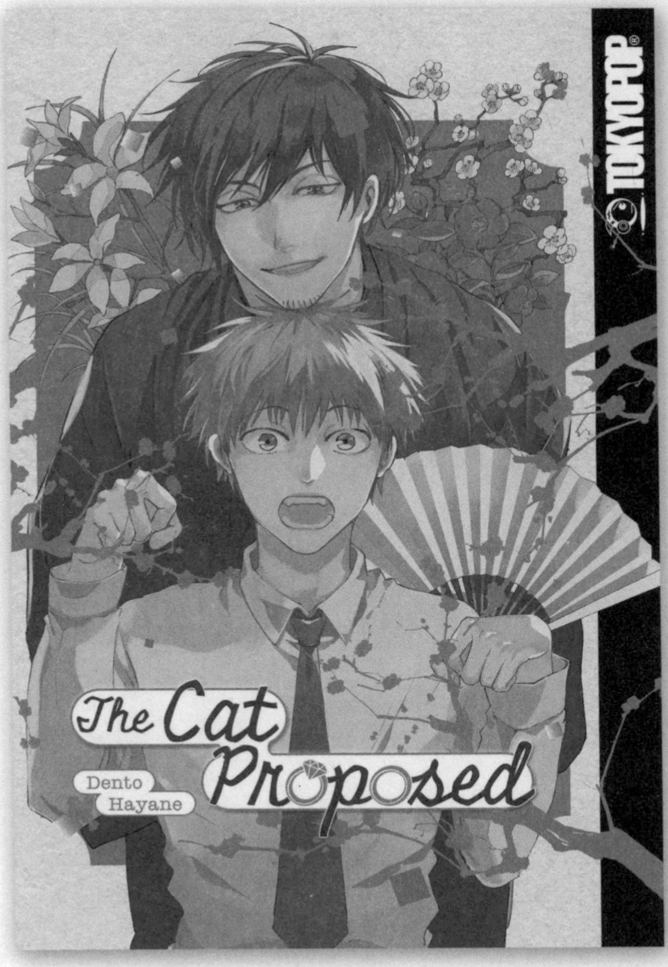

TOKYOPOP
The Cat Proposed
Dento Hayane

LOVE x LOVE

Matoi Souta is an overworked office worker tired of his life. Then, on his way home from a long day of work one day, he decides to watch a traditional Japanese play. But something strange happens. He could have sworn he saw one of the actors has cat ears. It turns out that the man is actually a bakeneko — a shapeshifting cat from Japanese folklore. And then, the cat speaks: "From now on, you will be my mate."

TOKYOPOP

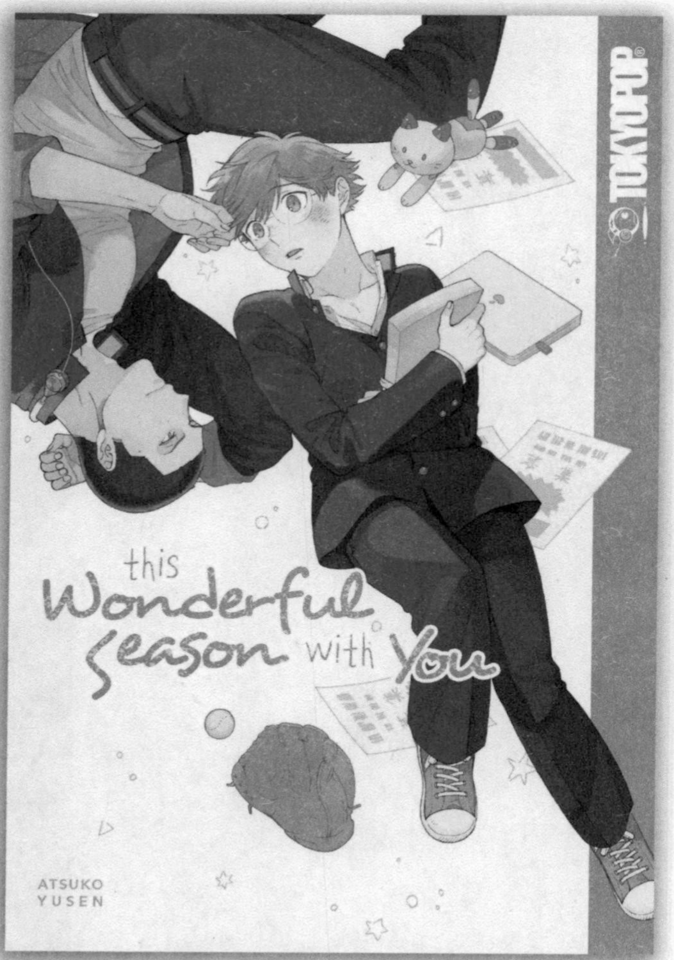
TOKYOPOP
this Wonderful season with You
ATSUKO YUSEN

THIS WONDERFUL SEASON WITH YOU

Atsuko Yusen

LOVE-x-LOVE MATURE 18+

Enoki is practically the poster-boy for what a typical nerd looks like: short and slight, complete with big round glasses and social awkwardness. His main hobby is making video games, and he's used to not having many friends at school. Then, he meets Shirataki, a former member of the baseball club and his exact opposite; tall, muscular and sporty. Despite their many differences, the spark of friendship between the two boys begins to grow into something more...

TOKYOPOP

THE TREASURE OF THE KING AND THE CAT
You Kajika

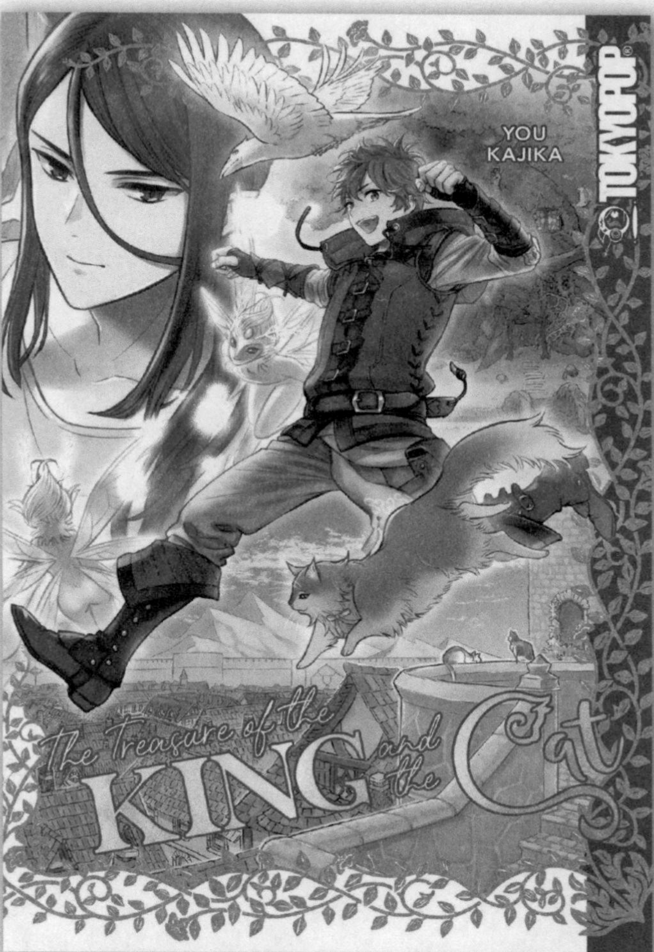
TOKYOPOP
YOU
KAJIKA
The Treasure of the KING and the Cat

LOVE-x-LOVE

One day, a large number of people suddenly disappeared in the royal capital. When young King Castio goes out to investigate this occurrence, he comes across the culprit... but the criminal puts a spell on him! To help him out, the king calls the wizard O'Feuille to his castle, along with Prince Volks and his loyal retainer Nios. Together, they're determined to solve this strange, fluffy mystery full of cats, swords and magic!

TOKYOPOP

MAME COORDINATE, VOLUME 1

Sachi Miyabe

SLICE OF LIFE

She loves meat and fried foods, and eats only karaage bento. Wearing exclusively clothes with weird characters printed on them, her fashion sense is practically non-existent. No confidence in her own looks. Extreme social anxiety. She speaks with a country drawl, and even her name is unusual. But then Mame (born in Tottori prefecture) was discovered by an intimidating, bespectacled rookie manager, and now begins the arduous task of getting her ready for auditions! The road to Top Model looks awfully steep from here.

Yagi the Bookshop Goat
Manga by Fumi Furukawa

Editor	-	Lena Atanassova
Marketing Associate	-	Janae Young
Translator	-	Katie Kimura
Copy Editor	-	Tina Tseng
Quality Check	-	Shingo Nemoto
Proof Reader	-	Claudia Takizawa
Editorial Associate	-	Janae Young
Licensing Specialist	-	Arika Yanaka
Graphic Designer	-	Sol DeLeo
Retouching and Lettering	-	Vibrraant Publishing Studio
Editor-in-Chief & Publisher	-	Stu Levy

A  Manga

TOKYOPOP and 🐸 are trademarks or registered trademarks of TOKYOPOP Inc.

TOKYOPOP inc.
5200 W Century Blvd
Suite 705
Los Angeles, CA 90045 USA

E-mail: info@TOKYOPOP.com
Come visit us online at www.TOKYOPOP.com

f www.facebook.com/TOKYOPOP
🐦 www.twitter.com/TOKYOPOP
📷 www.instagram.com/TOKYOPOP

ISBN: 978-1-4278-6889-3
First TOKYOPOP Printing: February 2022
Printed in CANADA

STOP

THIS IS THE BACK OF THE BOOK!

How do you read manga-style? It's simple! Let's practice -- just start in the top right panel and follow the numbers below!

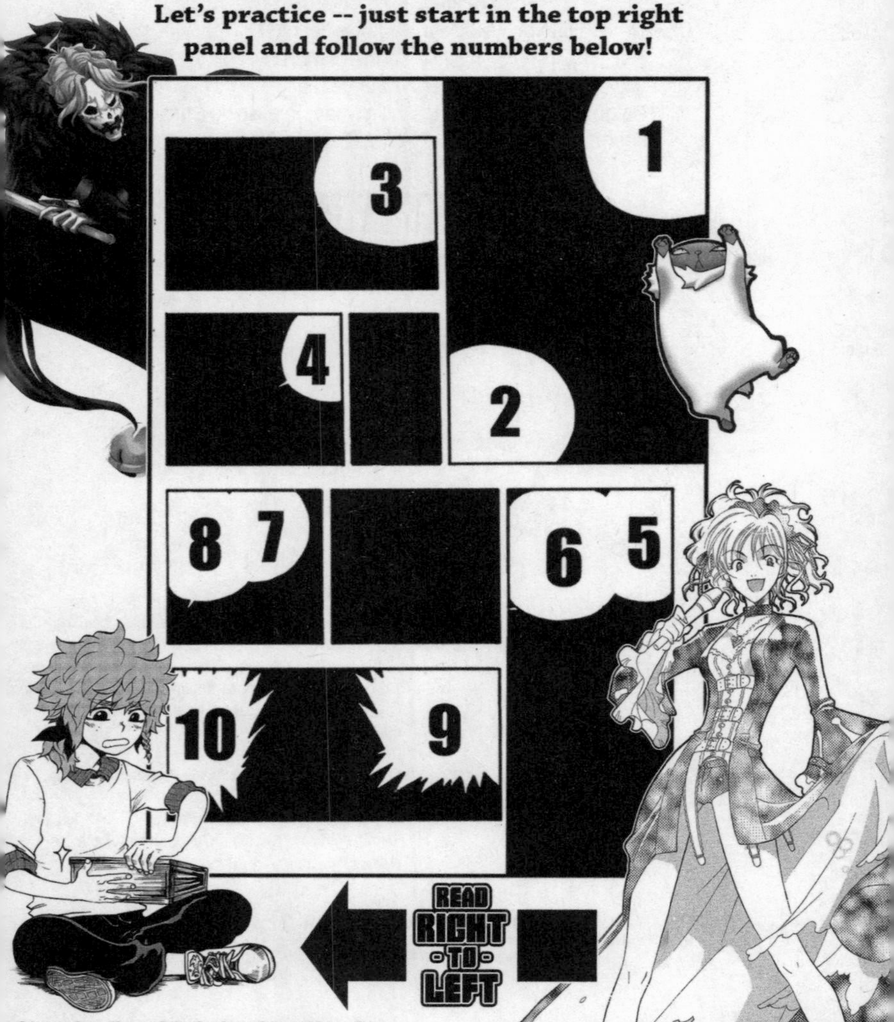

1
2
3
4
5
6
7
8
9
10
READ
RIGHT
-TO-
LEFT

Crimson from ***Kamo*** / Fairy Cat from ***Grimms Manga Tales***
Morrey from ***Goldfisch*** / Princess Ai from ***Princess Ai***

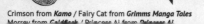

KONOHANA KITAN, VOLUME 1

Sakuya Amano

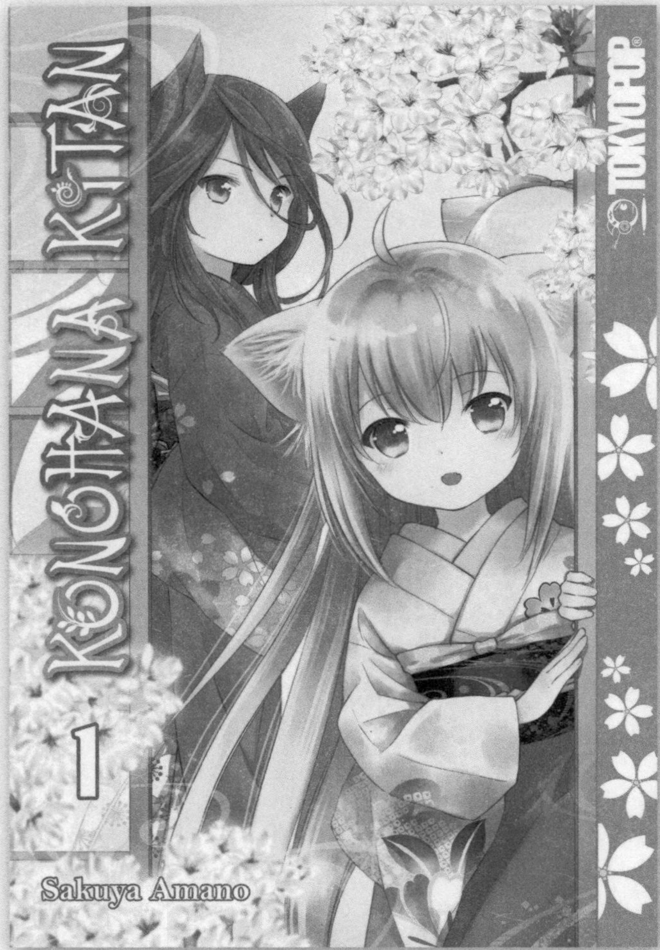
TOKYOPOP
KONOHANA KITAN
1
Sakuya Amano

FANTASY

Yuzu is a brand new employee at Konohanatei, the hot-springs inn that sits on the crossroads between worlds. A simple, clumsy but charmingly earnest girl, Yuzu must now figure out her new life working alongside all the other fox-spirits who run the inn under one cardinal rule - at Konohanatei, every guest is a god! Konohana Kitan follows Yuzu's day to day life working at the inn, meeting the other employees and ever-eclectic guests, and learning to appreciate the beauty of the world around her.